THE WEI

THE WELL-PROTECTED DOMAINS

Ideology and the Legitimation of Power in the
Ottoman Empire 1876–1909

Selim Deringil

New edition published in 2011 by I.B.Tauris & Co Ltd
First published in 1999 by I.B.Tauris & Co Ltd
6 Salem Road, London W2 4BU
175 Fifth Avenue, New York NY 10010
www.ibtauris.com

Distributed in the United States and Canada Exclusively by Palgrave Macmillan
175 Fifth Avenue, New York NY 10010

Copyright © 1998, 2011 Selim Deringil

The right of Selim Deringil to be identified as the author of this work has been asserted by him in accordance with the Copyright, Designs and Patent Act 1988.

All rights reserved. Except for brief quotations in a review, this book, or any part thereof, may not be reproduced, stored in or introduced into a retrieval system, or transmitted, in any form or by any means, electronic, mechanical, photocopying, recording or otherwise, without the prior written permission of the publisher.

ISBN: 978 1 84885 786 5

A full CIP record for this book is available from the British Library
A full CIP record is available from the Library of Congress

Library of Congress Catalog Card Number: available

Printed and bound in Great Britain by CPI Antony Rowe, Chippenham

Dedicated to my father

Efdal Deringil

For God's sake, let us sit on the ground,
And tell sad stories of the death of Kings:
How some have been depos'd; some slain in war;
Some haunted by the ghosts that have depos'd;
Some poison'd by their wives; some sleeping kill'd ...

King Richard II, Act III, Scene II

You may attack your enemy, you need not think whether you are right or wrong, sooner or later your judicial staff will find the best pretexts to prove you right.

Nicolo Machiavelli, *The Prince*

The Sublime State finds itself stuck among Christian states ... Even if our material and diplomatic resources were unlimited, we would still be obliged to seek the aid of some of the Great Powers ... However, all aid among states is based upon mutual suspicion and calculated interest ...

Said Paşa, Memorandum prepared for the Sultan

Contents

Acknowledgements		x
Map		xii
Introduction		1
1	'Long Live the Sultan!': Symbolism and Power in the Hamidian Regime	16
2	The Ottomanization of the Şeriat	44
3	'To Enjoin the Good and to Forbid Evil': Conversion and Ideological Reinforcement	68
4	Education: the Answer to all Evil?	93
5	'They Confuse and Excite Minds': The Missionary Problem.	112
6	Ottoman Image Management and Damage Control	135
7	The Ottoman 'Self Portrait'	150
8	Conclusion	166
Notes		177
Bibliography		237
Index		250

Acknowledgements

I owe thanks to a great many people for the help, advice, criticism, encouragement, and above all, the patience, that they were good enough to send my way. First and foremost thanks go to my colleague Selçuk Esenbel, who served as my 'inspiring muse', taskmaster, and first reader without whose help this book would simply not have been written. Similarly, my heartfelt thanks go to Daniel Goffman for his willingness to read drafts and provide incisive criticism, and to Edhem Eldem for making sure that I did not take myself too seriously. Ariel Salzmann also provided much appreciated criticism and made sure that I got my nose out of the archives and took at least an occasional look at the real world of writing. Caroline Finkel whose companionship in the Ottoman archives was invaluable, was also kind enough to provide logistical support on several visits to London, together with Andrew Finkel. Feroze Yasamee kindly read the manuscript and gave me an extremely thorough appraisal. Faruk Birtek was another friend and colleague who provided me with key insights, particularly in relation to the idea of 'fine tuning' in imperial structures. I also owe a great deal to Dru Gladney for providing me with an anthropological view of historical and other matters. Discussions with Professor Şerif Mardin, and his constant encouragement of my work, have been invaluable and for them my sincerest gratitude is in order. Another colleague who has had a formative influence on me is Engin Akarlı who encouraged me to learn Ottoman, and through whose work my interest in the Hamidian era began. I must also thank Professors Carl Brown, Norman Itzkowitz, and Avram Udovich for their support during my stay at Princeton University. In the same context owe thanks to Fikret Adanır for his efforts as co-organizer of a workshop on the Hamidian era, and for hosting me at Bochum. I have also profited greatly from discussions with the following: Mehmet Genç, İlber Ortaylı, Şevket Pamuk, Nükhet Sirman, Nilüfer Göle, Kemal Beydilli, Yaşar Ocak, Ekmeleddin Ihsanoğlu, Zafer Toprak, Butrus Abu Manneh, Hakan Erdem, Cem Behar, Philip Mansel, Gülru

Necipoğlu, Nevra Necipoğlu, Cemal Kafadar, Alan Duben and Gültekin Yıldız. Also, I am greatly in debt to my late father Efdal Deringil, to whom this book is dedicated, for his patient tutoring in my early days of learning the Ottoman script. Mehmet Genç, İdris Bostan, Nejat Göyünç and Hayri Mutluçağ, were more than generous with their time in helping me decipher documents in the archives. I thank them all for their patience.

As someone who is almost computer-illiterate I must express my thanks to Gülen Aktaş and Aydin Akkaya for the many hours of time they kindly gave, as well as Nadir Özbek and Emre Yalçin. Gülen Aktaş also drew the map. To Hatice Aynur I owe thanks for her help in correcting the transcription of Ottoman material in this paperback edition. For the cover photograph I am indebted to Roni Margulies who gave me the run of his exquisite collection of photographs from the Ottoman era. Also thanks are due to Anna Enayat, my editor, and all those in I.B.Tauris who spent time and effort on the manuscript.

On the material side I owe gratitude to the Fulbright Commission of Turkey for providing me with support during my sabbatical year at Princeton, to the Near Eastern Studies Department of Princeton University for hosting me, and to the staff of Firestone and Gest Libraries. I also owe thanks to François Georgeon and Paul Dumont as well as the Ecole des Hautes Etudes en Sciences Sociales for inviting me to give a series of lectures as visiting professor which enabled me to make use of the Biblioteque Nationale. Also the staff of the Başbakanık Archives were very helpful. All that said, it only remains to state clearly that all mistakes, omissions, oversights or exaggerations are entirely my own.

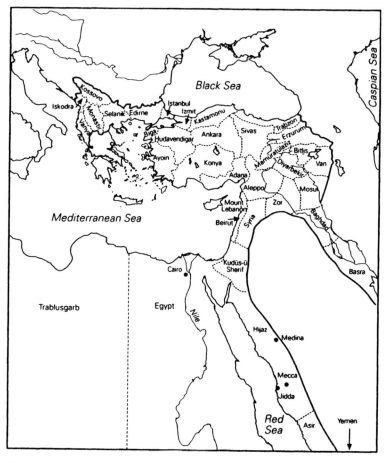

The Provinces of the Ottoman Empire in the late Nineteenth Century

Introduction

This is a book about a world that is no more. It looks at the last years of the Ottoman Empire and the reign of Sultan Abdülhamid II (1876–1909), a period which also saw the dawn of the modern Balkans and the Middle East. The Ottoman state was unique in many ways. It was the only Muslim great power. It was the only European Muslim power. It had emerged as the single most serious threat to European Christendom during the period when Europe was expanding as a result of the voyages of discovery and colonization in the late fifteenth and sixteenth centuries. Just as the 'new monarchies' in the emerging European state system were beginning to flex their muscles worldwide, they found themselves mortally threatened by an aggressive and successful power in their very own 'back garden'. Moreover it was a power that vaunted its superiority and seemed poised to conquer the First Rome, just as it had conquered the Second Rome in 1453. The Ottoman armies established a foothold in Otranto in 1479 causing the Pope to flee Rome.[1] Some historians have actually argued that the whole concept of 'Europe' was fashioned around the decline of the Ottoman threat.[2] Even after the days of its greatness were long over, the Sublime State continued to exist as a thorn in the side of a Europe which expected its demise at any moment, and stubbornly refused to die.

In the heyday of great power imperialism, at the turn of the nineteenth century, the Ottoman Empire had long been crumbling though, unlike all other ancient empires, it remained a military force strong enough to give the armies of the great powers a distinctly hard time.[3] Even in defeat, it was 'able to compete at a technical level with its European neighbours: Plevna was not a Tel el-Kebir or Omdurman.'[4]

This state of affairs has always been treated as something of an anomaly in European culture. It was not, quite simply, supposed to happen. Had not the Great Mughal ultimately succumbed to the technical and financial power of the gentlemen with the powdered wigs? Had not a handful of *conquistadores* completely overawed and overcome a native American population which had been terrified by cannon and called the horses and their riders, 'Gods with six legs and two heads'? Had not the mighty Zulus, the Chinese Son of Heaven, and the peoples of Micronesia suffered the same fate? It was, after all, 'natural' that by the nineteenth century the peoples of the world should be divided into 'ruling' and 'subject' peoples. In Europe, the former were all Christian, all except one. Only the Sublime Porte ruled millions of Christians as a Muslim empire. As the centuries wore on, this situation became more and more galling:

> Unfortunately for the peace of mankind, it has happened that the Turk is placed in a position where it is impossible to ignore him, and almost equally impossible to endure him; while by his origin, habits, and religion, he is an Asiatic of Asiatics, he is by irony of fate established in a position where his presence is a ceaseless cause of misery ... to millions of Christian people.[5]

In striking contrast, Said Paşa, who served nine times as Abdülhamid's grand vizier, wrote: 'We find ourselves stuck among Christian princedoms and states ... The Sublime State has been a member of the European family of states for some fifty years ...'[6]

This study is an attempt to put the late Ottoman state in the context of world changes and, as such, is a deliberate attempt to look at the world from Istanbul. I am interested in how the late Ottoman elite reacted to the world around them.[7] I think it is about time that these men be rescued both from their Kemalist denigrators and their 'fans' on the lunatic fringe of the Turkish Right, as well as from Western perpetrators of the image of the 'Terrible Turk'. Yet, I also hope to 'abandon wishful thinking, assimilate bad news, discard pleasing interpretations that cannot pass elementary tests of evidence and logic ...'[8] It is not my least intention, for example, to whitewash the Armenian massacres of the 1890s, although the book touches on this issue only tangentially.[9] Nor is this a book on legal history; it does not intend to ask whether Weberian concepts of legitimation can be fitted to the Ottoman case.[10] It is a book about *applied* legitimation policies. The emphasis will therefore be on giving a 'voice' to the late Ottoman elite. What was the world view of the Ottoman elite? How did they see the problems of their state and society, and what solutions did they propose? The first thing to be noted is that, like elites everywhere, the Ottoman service elite was not monolithic. Those who served were very differentiated internally when it came to cliques, coteries, cabals, and corruption. Some were more conservative, others more progressive, although hard and fast categories and facile labelling have led to much historically inaccurate stereotyping.[11] In this context, Engin Akarlı's words could not be more apt: '[We must] make a conscious effort to engage the voices preserved in the historical data in a genuine conversation, remaining critical of what we hear but also critical of our own position.'[12]

It may seem strange to the reader to find a discussion in the same book of, say, the Ottoman protest at the Egyptian delegation being given precedence over the Ottomans in the protocol governing Queen Victoria's jubilee celebrations, and an expeditionary force sent into the mountains of northern Iraq to convert the Yezidi Kurds to Hanefi Islam. Yet both incidents and the Ottoman reaction to them stemmed from the same root cause: the Ottoman elite understood only too well that their world was exposed to mortal danger from within as from without, from the corridors of Windsor Castle to the mountains of Iraq. This obliged them to devise policies which would legitimate their position in the eyes of both their own people, and the outside world.

This book is a study of what Carol Gluck has called 'the grammar of ideology by which hegemony was expressed' in a late Ottoman context.[13] It is my contention that the Hamidian period represents a critical point in time when, contrary to the standard view that the Ottoman Empire closed in on itself during this period, the only Muslim world empire did in fact succeed in joining the modern community of nations, albeit as a grudgingly accepted poor relation. The period also represents Turkey's response to the challenge to its existence from within and without, a challenge that was also met by other imperial systems, Russian, Austrian, German, and Japanese.

In more ways than one, the Ottoman Empire falls between the cracks of the fault lines that determined world politics in the nineteenth century, and this continues to determine the way the history of imperialism is written today. On the one hand, even at the turn of the century, it was still a force to be reckoned with and, unlike the Indian princely states or African colonized peoples, it was one which could not be pushed aside. On the other hand, it was the 'Sick man of Europe' whose demise was expected at any moment. It was heavily penetrated by Western economic interests, and suffered from chronic financial crises. It continued to lose territory in Europe, yet by the mid-nineteenth century it had the third largest navy in the world, and in the last quarter of the century, much to the alarm of the British, it actually succeeded in extending its influence along the Arabian Gulf.[14] The central point about this was that the sultan and his staff at the

4   *The Well-Protected Domains*

Sublime Porte controlled their own fate. Operating under severe constraints, to be sure, they were nonetheless able to carve out a critical space for manoeuvre in an increasingly hostile environment. This produced the basic dynamic which determined the relationship between the Ottoman statesman and his Western colleague.[15]

In pursuit of the exotic bird, or looking beyond the turban

The 'anomaly' of the Ottoman position has been reflected in the historiography pertaining to the Ottoman state which has been characterized by a tendency to 'exoticize' this uncomfortable phenomenon. The singularity of the Ottoman polity in terms of world power balances has led Western historians to term the state a 'slave synarchy'.[16] Caroline Finkel's warning against the seduction and 'resilience' of this simplistic model, which focuses on the 'static facade' and ignores comparable dynamics, is well taken.[17] Approaches which find it opportune to dwell on the 'peculiar' features of Ottoman society overlook the civil dimension, ignoring profit motives or any of the other impulses that drove people in the 'normal' (that is Christian) world.[18] Where the 'Turks' dwell is described as, at worst, a bastion of bloodthirsty tyrants or, at best, a decadent fleshpot of Oriental vice. The Ottoman polity is the alter ego, the ultimate 'other'.

Yet it is fascinating to read that no less an observer than Voltaire had a much more realistic assessment of Ottoman state and society:

> This government which has been depicted as so despotic, so arbitrary, seems never to have been such since the reigns of Mahomet II, Soliman I or Selim II, who made all bend to their will ... You see in 1703 that the padishah Mustafa II is legally deposed by the militia and by the citizens of Constantinople. Nor is one of his children chosen to succeed him, but his brother Achmet III. This emperor in turn is condemned in 1730 by the janissaries and the people ... So much for these monarchs who are so absolute ! One imagines that a man may legally be the arbitrary master of a large part of the world, because he may with impunity commit a few crimes in his household, or order the murder of a few slaves; but he cannot persecute his nation, and is often the oppressed rather than the oppressor.[19]

Interestingly the obsession with the exotic is not unique to Western historians. Turkish historians of remarkably recent vintage have also seized upon it to explain away the Ottoman past. Among the Left, who blame the ancien regime for Turkey's underdevelopment, it is fashionable to depict the past as a period when '*paşas* ate magnificent banquets while the people languished on olives'. Taner Timur is actually on record as having said: 'The sad thing is that these politicians did not themselves believe in the "reforms" they had to carry out.' Timur's central argument was that Ottoman statesmen like Ali, Fuad or Reşid Paşa acted solely to protect their class interests and then only under severe Western pressure. Their reforms were not 'true' reforms because they were not inspired by European 'Enlightenment thinking'. 'The Ottoman Empire was a different civilization with its unique characteristics.' Not even Oriental but, 'stagnated', it 'became "Orientalized"' under the unyielding influence of 'the scholastic world view'.[20]

The Turkish Right, in contrast to the positions held by the Kemalists and the Left, basks in self-adulation and cherishes the illusion that the Ottoman state was somehow *sui generis* and cannot be compared to any other polity. Faith in Islam and the organizational genius of the 'Turk' are self-completing and self-evident. These find a particular focus around the personality of Sultan Abdülhamid II, who has become a political symbol of the Islamic Right. As a writer of one of the 'classics' of this genre describes it:

> It is high time to declare that Abdülhamid II is a great saviour whose true nature as the essence and foundation of the Turk has been blackened by certain usurpers ... [He is] the last stand against the unthinking aping of the West, [a ruler] who remained loyal to the root sources of the Turk's spirit.[21]

Other writers of the same school focus on various aspects of Abdülhamid's reign to claim that he was 'courageous', 'a great diplomat', a 'committed patron of the arts', even 'liked sports' and 'was an accomplished carpenter'. Personal and political issues are seriously confounded in this sentimental discourse.[22] The deeply divergent perspectives on Abdülhamid held by Turkish 'Islamists' and 'Secularists' is but one instance of the 'deep emotional divide [that] exists between these two perspectives. Each camp tends to conceive the other as a representative of a hostile world view, as if they live in separate worlds.'[23]

Among modern Western historians of the Ottoman Empire the spectrum of views is somewhat more varied while still reflecting broadly the same tendencies. The Ottoman Empire is generally seen as a supine entity which 'constantly had things done to it'. Such a perspective, of course, grows out of the approach that could be termed the 'Eastern Question' paradigm which is itself a legacy of the nineteenth century.[24]

As Hobsbawm points out '... By the standards of nineteenth century liberalism, [the Ottoman state was] anomalous, obsolete, and doomed by history and progress. The Ottoman Empire was the most obvious evolutionary fossil ...'[25]

The tendency among the modern heirs of the 'Eastern Question school' has been to see the Ottoman state as an entity which only figured in European calculations as a factor in the 'balance of power'. Indeed the cast of its work is perhaps best exemplified by the fact that entire articles or books continue to be written on 'The Turks' with minimal references to works or to sources in Turkish.[26]

But the 'Eastern Question school' is at least the result of a *bona fide* scholarly tradition, if a somewhat outmoded one. At the lower end of the scale Western literature on the Ottoman state abounds with statements such as: 'Muslims do not care too much for the sea'; 'Moslems were virtually incapable of acquiring European languages'; 'the Janissaries were sheep dogs who had to be fed regularly on Christian meat.'[27] Or gems such as: 'Until 1918 the Arabian peninsula was ruled by the Ottoman Empire, so called because it had the same amount of intelligence and energy as a footstool.'[28] Or, in a more toned down vein we are told that, 'Attempts to attract Moslem students to the new Western-model schools such as Galatasaray proved a failure throughout the 19th century.' In actual fact Galatasaray produced generations of Muslims who became leading figures. In the same source, we read: '[In Islamic polities] capitals have frequently shifted. Even when a single city has remained the capital for a long time, its segmented nature and frequent additions of new palace and garrison quarters dilute its potential for communicating symbols of identity.' It remains unclear why more than one magnificent city should not be a factor reinforcing rather than diluting identity. Where previously writers of general history books used simply to ignore the Ottoman Empire, the recent 'non Eurocentric version' of history aims to redress the balance and in the process lets in gross errors and oversimplifications.[29] The harem becomes a major factor in Ottoman history and the Turks are once again portrayed as the 'uncivilized' threat to Europe. Clearly, the earlier versions of Western historiography were infinitely preferable.

But even at the upper end of the spectrum, in works written by scholars who have used Ottoman primary sources, the 'exotic' yet again becomes the focus. Even Carter Findley's pioneering work on reform in the late Ottoman bureaucracy has as a central figure a dervish-official who inhabits an (unexplained) 'tangled magic garden'.³⁰ The dervish-official Aşçı Dede is understood to be in some sense oriental because although he takes an interest in the Russo-Japanese War and lives dangerously, taking steamers and riding trams, he believes in oracles and has complete faith in the guidance of his spiritual mentor Sheikh Fehmi. Also, we are told, an Ottoman official in the late nineteenth century inhabited a 'culturally schizoid society', presumably because he had been exposed to a Western education that he really did not (could not?) understand. Abdülhamid's obsession with his personal security automatically labels him as 'paranoid' and the state in his reign as a 'police state'.³¹ In Findley, the quest for the exotic bird seems to have actually achieved its object. Ottoman diplomats, although they have come a long way, are still a crowd of buffoons because they have to comply with the ruler's whim to procure an 'all-white talking parrot' for the palace menagerie.³² This observation completely ignores the fact that royal menageries were at the time a fashion indulged in by most of Europe's royalty, from Prince Albert to the lowliest princeling in Germany. The London embassy also indulges in suspiciously oriental activities such as keeping track of Ottoman subjects who are known to be opponents of the regime.³³

In a journal article Masami Arai makes the statement: 'From the beginning of the nineteenth century ... most of the Ottoman reformers seem to have intended, consciously or unconsciously, to construct a nation state from the various subjects of their empire.' How one sets about constructing a nation state unconsciously remains a mystery.³⁴ Arai then contradicts his own point: 'The desire to construct a progressive nation-state in the Orient was so keen that no Ottoman intellectuals, whatever ideal they cherished – Westernist, nationalist, and even Islamist, could repress it.'³⁵ Why anyone would want to repress something they wanted so badly is explicable only in Freudian terms.

It is interesting to note that some contemporary Western writers who actually lived in the Ottoman lands were aware of the futility of seeking the exotic. In this context, it is worth quoting at length from Leon Cahun:

> Ask any random would be traveller in the Orient what he would like to see: he will tell you that he would want to see Jerusalem, Damascus, the cedars of the Lebanon, and if he is ambitious, Baghdad, the City of the Thousand and One Nights. He would also desire to see a *serail*, some *odalisques*, a caravan,

palm trees, and whirling dervishes.³⁶

Cahun then proceeds deliberately to disabuse the potential traveller of illusions. Jerusalem, he points out, is simply the equivalent of Lourdes. The *serail* these days amounts to nothing more romantic than 'un batiment de prefecture', *odalek'* and not *odalisque* are the equivalent of 'femmes de chambre'. There are no more palm trees in northern Anatolia than there are olive groves in Brittany and Normandy, and 'the whirling dervishes of the Orient are neither more numerous nor more interesting than the white pilgrims of France.' As for more stereotypes: 'My good potential traveller will not fail to believe that the Christians in the Orient are called *rayas* and are driven by *courbashe* wielding *pashas*.' Cahun points out that the term *reaya* simply means taxpayer and has been adapted by the British in India as *ryot*. As for the 'Turkish' character of the empire:

> The first time I encountered an Osmanlı officer ... I told him he looked typically Turkish. He flushed a deep red and heatedly told me that he was from Damascus as were his father and his grandfather before him, and that he had nothing in common with the *pouchts* from Istanbul. This Arab particularism did not prevent him from being very dedicated to the flag, or drinking the health of the sultan.³⁷

If one attempts to look beyond the turban, as Cahun does, and examine what actually drove Ottoman decision makers in the nineteenth century, it becomes evident that these people were not necessarily unique or 'exotic'. In fact, the broad sweep of change that was taking place in European societies as a whole at the same period was to find it paralleled in Ottoman society.³⁸

'Fine tuning' and the legitimacy crisis of the Ottoman state

In the history of states there occur periods of crisis during which the established relationship between monarch and people collapses. In Petrine Russia this occured when Peter the Great adopted the role of 'Imperator'.³⁹ In the Ottoman Empire, this crisis began with Mahmud II (r. 1808–39) continued under his successors and culminated in the Hamidian era.⁴⁰

The standard wisdom about the decline of the Ottoman state has been that it was a unilinear process which began sometime after the second siege of Vienna in 1683 and lasted until the collapse of the empire in 1918. Yet this teleological approach is outmoded. There now seems little doubt that the empire was actually much more a part of world trends in the seventeenth and eighteenth centuries than has been hitherto acknowledged.[41] I would, however, take issue with Salzmann's view that the 'Ottoman state became a victim of its own policies of centralization'[42] I would likewise entirely disagree with Todorova's rather startling statement: 'That the Ottoman Empire did not create an integrated society is beyond doubt; what some Balkan historians seem unable to understand is that this empire did not strive to achieve such integration.'[43] The Ottoman state was better administered and more powerful after the reforms of the mid-nineteenth century than in the late eighteenth century, and 'the nineteenth-century Ottoman reformer was more conscious [of his mission] than the eighteenth century reformer, at least he was in more of a rush.'[44]

Nor would it be an exaggeration to say that the modern state as it is understood today – meaning mass schooling, a postal service, railways, lighthouses, clock towers, lifeboats, museums, censuses and birth certificates, passports, as well as parliaments, bureaucracies and armies – was only constituted in the Ottoman Empire after the Tanzimat reforms of 1839.[45] Although Abou El Haj is quite correct to point out that the Tanzimat era is in many ways the outcome of a much longer prehistory than is commonly assumed, I believe he leans too far the other way in minimizing the qualitative changes that took place during this period.[46] Concepts such as the legal equality of Muslim and non-Muslim, the rule of law, the state's guarantee to safeguard the lives, property and honour of its subjects, and above all the very fact that the state was publicly undertaking to honour these promises, were a new departure. Yet even while setting out the reasons for the new laws, the Imperial Rescript of the Rose Chamber (*Hatt-ı Şerif-i Gülhane*, November 3 1839) was quite deliberately based on religious dogma, stating as its first principle that, 'it is evident that countries not governed by the Şeriat cannot prevail', even though much of what it decreed was indeed in contravention of the Şeriat.[47]

However, just as the state was permeating levels of society it had never reached before, making unprecedented demands on its people, it created new strains on society, leading to what Jürgen Habermas has called a 'legitimacy crisis' or 'legitimation deficit'.[48] Nor was this legitimacy crisis confined to the relationship of the Ottoman centre with its own society. In the international arena also, the Ottomans found themselves increasingly obliged to assert and reassert their legitimate right to existence as a recognized member of the Concert of Europe, as recognized after the Treaty of Paris which ended the Crimean War in 1856.[49] In a context of military weakness, diplomacy acquired vital importance, as did the process I shall call 'fine tuning' as regards the population of the empire.[50] Fine tuning involved the meticulous inculcation, indoctrination, enticing, frightening, flattering, forbidding, permitting, punishing or rewarding – all in precise doses – which had been the stuff of empire since Caeser crossed the *limes*. In empires such as the late Ottoman, when the state exists in an almost constant state of crisis or emergency, fine tuning acquires additional importance but also becomes more difficult. I would even venture to say that fine tuning is more the characteristic of a state which is constantly on the defensive.[51] Not necessarily humane and anodine, it can involve brute force and bloodshed, but only as a last resort. The most important aspect of fine tuning is that it is a process through which the legitimation ideology of the state is promoted and state policy is imposed on society. Legitimation involves the process of making state policy and resembles, 'That which is inscribed into the nature of things and is perennial,' as Ernest Gellner puts it.[52] This clearly is the ideal state of things. The spectrum between the ideal and the actual is the reality as reflected in the historical record. The creation of the 'perennial' and 'natural' state of things which fine tuning sought to accomplish was to be achieved through a reiteration of certain basic formulae, and their incarnation as the official mythology, or *mythomoteur*, of the late Ottoman state.[53]

Fine tuning was concerned in the first degree with the power elite, the men who formulated and applied policy. Even as autocratic a sultan as Abdülhamid II, who was in effect the last real sultan of the empire, had to rely on a staff who fed him information, advised him, indeed influenced him. So the so-called 'Red Sultan' or 'Oriental Despot' of legend, who rarely left his palace, and never left his capital, depended on these men, perhaps more than some of the previous sultans who had actually delegated authority to powerful grand viziers.[54]

In all societies the legitimating ideology of the state is in many respects the 'no mans land' where a tacit process of bargaining takes place between the state and its people. As Abou El-Haj puts it: 'The credibility if not the very effectiveness of ideology is based in part on the opening up of a meaningful discourse in whose initiation and validation the rulers and at a minimum some if not the majority of the ruled participate.'[55] In periods of legitimation crisis this process of bargaining is intensified. The Ottoman Empire was no exception, and the thirty-three years during which

Abdülhamid II reigned (1876–1909) are critical because they are years which are both formative and disruptive, both creative and destructive. They are formative because of the long-term implications of the various policies ranging from education, to railroads and military reform, to irrigation works, to the first modest beginnings of an industrial infrastructure.[56] Yet the same years are disruptive of much of the traditional fabric of society, as the state now came to demand not passive obedience but conformity to a unilaterally proclaimed normative order.[57] In fact the Ottoman Empire hedged towards a 'nationally imagined community', as Ottoman identity assumed an increasingly Turkish character, even if this identity was packaged in universalist Islamic terms.[58] Also the redefinition of the basic credos of the state as primarily Islamic implicitly excluded the still sizeable Christian elements who were seen as potentially seditious and subversive. The policies of these years were, therefore, destructive of much of the stability which had allowed the delicate symbiosis of various creeds in less turbulent times. It must be emphasized here, however, that in the application of various policies the Ottoman centre operated under crippling restraints. The most important of these were lack of financial resources and interference on the part of foreign powers, two increasingly overlapping phenomena.[59]

Sources

The bulk of this study is based on archival materials found in the Prime Ministry Archives in Istanbul. It has been my aim to understand the mindset of the late Ottoman power elite rather than chronologically study specific events. Therefore the material used is drawn from various collections according to specific themes, such as conversion, control of religious activity in the provinces, surveillance of missionary activity, and so on. I do not pretend in any way to have exhausted the materials on these topics and no doubt there is still a mine of information in the Başbakanlık that I have not touched. I have focused mostly, but not exclusively, on the Yıldız collection. The Hamidian regime was obsessed with information, and as a result the Yıldız Palace Archives occupy a disproportionately large volume among the archival collections of the late empire.[60] Many of these have only recently been opened to researchers.[61] Some of the major collections that I have drawn on are as follows.

12   The Well-Protected Domains

Yıldız Esas Evrakı (YEE) [62]

This is the main collection of the Yıldız Palace documents. A noteworthy feature of this collection is that it harbours the papers of most of the high officials who served in the period. These may range from a one-page commentary to extensive reports on specific and general topics.

Yıldız Sadaret Hususi Maruzat (Y.A HUS)

Correspondence between the palace and the grand vizier's chancery at the Sublime Porte. This collection consists of correspondence on a variety of topics ranging from the status of the yacht of the British consul in Basra (warship or not) to measures to be taken against Armenian partisans in eastern Anatolia.

Yıldız Sadaret Resmi Maruzat (Y.A RES)

The collection is of documents presented by the grand vizier to the palace which provide the background for imperial decrees (*irade*).

Yıldız Mütenevvi Maruzat (Y.MTV)

Although originally this collection was intended to deal with military matters, it is probably one of the richest collections of the Yıldız archive and includes a wealth of information on a great variety of topics. These include court cases involving religious disputes, tribal uprisings, decorations for foreign dignitaries, police reports on movements of Muslim subjects of foreign powers, etc.

Yıldız Perakende Gazeteler

Miscellaneous newspaper clippings from foreign and Turkish newspapers. This catalogue comprises thousands of newspaper clippings from the world press dealing with the Ottoman Empire.

Administrative divisions in the Ottoman Empire

At this point it would be useful to give some background information on administrative divisions and titles which occur in this book.[63] In the post-Tanzimat period, the administrative divisions of the Ottoman Empire were fundamentally reorganized along the French model of the Code Napoleon.[64] The first Regulation for the Provinces (*Vilayet Nizamnamesi*) was declared on 7 October 1864. This determined that the old division of the provinces according to *eyalet* would be replaced by the unit of *vilayet*, clearly modelled on the French departement. This was followed by the General Provincial Regulation (*Vilayet-i Umumiye Nizamnamesi*) of 1867, and the General Regulation for Provincial Administration (*Idare-i Umumiye-i Vilayet Nizamnamesi*) of 1871. The administrative divisions would be: *vilayet* (province), *sancak* or *liva* (sub-province), *kaza* (local district or township), *nahiye* (commune) and *kur'a* or *karye* (village).[65] The vilayet would be governed by a governor (*vali*). It would also have a provincial administrative council (*vilayet idare meclisi*) made up of the vali, leading officials, and representatives of the Muslim and non-Muslim population who assisted the vali in an advisory capacity only. The highest civil authority in the sancak was the *mutasarrıf* who would also be assisted by an administrative council (*liva idare meclisi*) reflecting much the same composition as the vilayet. The kaza or liva would be administered by a *kaymakam*, who would also preside over an advisory council. As centralization increased, authority in the villages went from the imam to the centrally appointed headman (*muhtar*).[66] This structure was to remain largely unaltered during the Hamidian period except for the important fact that the control of the palace over the Ministry of the Interior greatly increased.[67]

The book

This book is made up of two parts. The first deals with the recharged legitimation policies inside the empire, the second with efforts to project the desired image abroad.

The first chapter is an attempt to provide an overview of the symbolism of power in the Hamidian period. It focuses on state ceremonies, changes in mosque architecture to suite modern protocol, and the various emblematic manifestations of state power such as coats of arms, decorations, etc. It also deals with the repeated use of encapsulating phrases and clichés in Ottoman chancery language, which, I argue, are valuable clues helping to understand the world view of Ottoman decision makers.

The second chapter will deal with the application of policies which arose as the Hamidian state intensified pressure on its population, thus triggering new tensions which in turn created 'a universal pressure for legitimation in a sphere that was once distinguished precisely for its power of self-legitimation'.[68] This brought to the fore a new interpretation of religion as the official ideology, in the shape of the 'official faith',(*mezheb-i resmiye*), that of the Hanefi school of Islamic jurisprudence. Also the position of the sultan as the Caliph of all Muslims (the claim to worldwide Islamic leadership) and as protector of the holy cities of the Hijaz acquired new content. As will be shown, all these amounted to nothing less than the institution of a secular foundation for state ideology, but through the use of Islamic vocabulary and ideological tools. In previous centuries the sultan's position as caliph had been taken more or less for granted (although there were clearly periods like that of the Ottoman–Safavid wars of the sixteenth century when it was emphasized). Yet by the reign of Abdülhamid the desire of the state to administer and control with hitherto unprecedented intensity led to a situation where the role of the centre had to be constantly re-defined.[69]

Chapter three deals with what is perhaps the most striking new departure: the effort made to spread Hanefi orthodoxy through official proselytization. In a self-conscious effort to emulate the activity of the Christian missionaries, the Ottoman centre set out to defend itself by taking the initiative in actively seeking conversions to the Hanefi *mezheb*. Chapter four deals with the educational policies of the Hamidian state. Unlike the Tanzimat period, when the emphasis had been on elite middle to higher schools, the Hamidian period emphasized primary schooling. Another feature of the times was the increasing emphasis on the 'Islamic' content of the schools curriculum. The documents show us that the Hamidian regime tried to weed out of the educational system what it saw as harmful Western influences.

Chapter five focuses on the enemy who was also the example: the missionary. As the nineteenth century neared its end, missionary activity became a major feature of the West's claim to moral as well as physical superiority. Abdülhamid's Ottoman Empire found itself in the forefront of the anti-missionary struggle. Yet, members of the state elite were very aware that the only way to defend themselves against the missionary threat was to adopt similar tactics.

Chapter six begins the second part of the book which is devoted to the efforts the Ottomans made to project the desired image abroad: the increasing loneliness of the Empire as the only Muslim great power, and the Ottoman elite's obsessive attempts to defend their image against all slights, insults and slurs. With this aim in mind, the Hamidian regime mobilized what resources it could to counter what it saw as injurious to its prestige in the world press, on the theatre stage or at other public forums.

Introduction   15

Chapter seven deals with the active effort to present the desired image. It was a vital concern of the Sublime Porte to be represented in all congresses and conferences attended by the 'club of civilized powers'. The Porte made a point of being present at all the major world fairs. Reciprocity was acknowledgement of legitimacy. In the Hamidian era, Ottoman statesmen therefore became obsessed with reciprocity which could be procured through *representation*.[70] Abdülhamid would almost certainly have agreed with Edward Said 'that struggle [for empire] is ... not only about soldiers and cannons but also about ideas, about forms, about images and imaginings.'[71] The Hamidian regime sought to project the image in Europe that 'we are like you'. Just as the kaiser, the Austrian emperor, and the tsar were legitimate autocrats, so was Abdülhamid. After the defeat of Russia by Japan in 1905, 'when the Sultan's officers congratulated him on the defeat of his old enemy Russia, he replied that he did not by any means consider the result a matter of congratulation, because he and the Czar were the only autocratic monarchs in Europe, and the defeat of the Czar meant a blow to the principle of autocracy.'[72]

Chapter One
Long Live the Sultan! Symbolism and Power in the Hamidian Regime

Yamada Torajiro always made a point of bringing his guests to the ceremony of the Friday prayer, the *selamlık*. Japanese visitors to Istanbul were a rarity in the 1890s, and he was the city's only long term Japanese resident. On a bright May morning, Yamada and his guests stood spellbound as the Albanian Horseguards trotted up to the palace and took up their stations. The sun glinted on their spears as the band struck up the Hamidiye march. Next came the officers of the Imperial Guard, mounted on splendid Arab horses in their impeccable uniforms, and they too took up their positions inside the Yıldız Palace. Finally the sultan, accompanied by the empress dowager and the reigning empress emerged from the palace in his landau and proceeded to the mosque. As the clear cry of the muezzin sounded the call to prayer, the sultan alighted and all his troops in one voice shouted a loud acclaim. When his guest asked Yamada what they were shouting he replied: 'They shout, "Long Live the Sultan!", just as we shout "Tenno Heika Banzai!" in the presence of our emperor.'[1]

Ceremony as codified competition between states

It was no accident that Yamada and his guests were able to 'read' the ceremony of Friday prayer correctly. The nineteenth century was a period of standardized ceremony, from the Court of St James to the Meiji Palace.[2] What the Japanese visitors had witnessed was nothing other than the reinvigoration of the symbolic language of the sultanate and caliphate in a world context where pomp and circumstance had become a form of competition between states. This was particularly important for states like the Ottoman and the Japanese, which were not first-rung powers. As humorously put by John Elliot in his discussion of Spain under Philip IV: 'It is

Symbolism and Power in the Hamidian Regime   17

as if a form of "Avis Principle" operates in the world of political imagery and propaganda: those who are only second try harder.'[3]

There are indeed many common themes linking the cult of emperor shared by Ottomans, Austrians, Russians and Japanese. The Russian tsars from Nicholas I (r. 1825–1855) onwards tried to forge a direct link with their people by using a 'synthesis of Russian myths' in which 'official Orthodoxy serv[ed] purely a state function'.[4] This was precisely the way official Islam was seen by Abdülhamid II. As Nicholas I and Alexander III played up the image of the 'blessed tsar' Abdülhamid actually pushed the same title, 'the holy personage', (*zat-ı akdes-i hümayun*), further than any of his predecessors. The terms 'holy Russian land' or the 'the holy land Tyrol' found their obvious equivalent in 'the sacred name of the Sublime State', (*ism-i kaddes-i devlet-i aliyye*).[5]

It was hoped in both the Russian and Ottoman cases that by forging a link of sacrality directly with the people, inconvenient intermediaries like political parties and parliaments could be avoided. The same goal is seen in the Japan of the Meiji years, particularly in the 1880s and 1890s when there occurred what Carol Gluck has called 'a denaturing of politics', as Meiji statesmen, all the while preparing for the inevitable emergence of political parties, worked to somehow stigmatize political activity as 'disloyal' to the emperor.[6] The major difference between the Japanese, Russian and Ottoman cases, was that religion played a relatively minor role in the Japanese experience. Yet, in the 'constant repetition' of elements in the 'emperor ideology' (*tennosei* ideology), the attempt to focus almost reflexive loyalty on the person of the emperor was very similar to the Russian and Ottoman cases.[7]

In the Austrian example the mythology surrounding the House of Habsburg was the core of the official symbolism of the state, yet it coexisted with a constitutional polity after 1867.[8] One of the ways of meeting the challenge of nationalism was by trying to inculcate a sense of belonging to the 'Imperial Fatherland', particularly by creating an official 'history of the Fatherland' (*vaterlandische geschichte*) to teach the non-Austrian subjects who came to study at the University of Vienna.[9]

This is not to deny the differences between the Ottoman polity and its imperial legitimist contemporaries. Russia, Austria, Japan and Prussia/Germany all had at least a semblance of representational politics by the turn of the century. The Ottoman parliament, though a fairly lively body in its first days of 1876, had to await the end of Hamidian autocracy before it was revived in 1909. A ruler like Abdülhamid II, who laboured under the stigma of the 'Terrible Turk' or the 'Red Sultan', while trying to pose as a modern monarch, suffered the self-imposed handicap of his virtually complete isolation from his own people and the outside world. The following is the story of a desperate rearguard action fought in an effort to overcome this isolation in the international arena.

Levels of meaning in Hamidian ideology

As Sultan Abdülhamid II retreated further and further behind the high walls of the Yıldız Palace he became more and more of a myth. Yet this process of distancing himself from the people created a contradiction at the very core of his conception of state power. On the one hand, the Hamidian regime sought to penetrate ever further into the daily life of Ottoman society, and the Ottoman system had always stressed the personal visibility of the ruler. On the other hand, the sultan's obsession with his security determined that he was very rarely seen outside the palace walls. This left him open to the criticism, often levelled at him, that he was a 'passive caliph'. The sultan's myth had, as a result, to be 'managed' through a system of symbols which constantly reminded the people of his power and omnipresence.

In this context Abdülhamid II seems to have reverted to the ways of his ancestors before Mahmud II. Rulers like Mahmud, Abdülmecid and Abdülaziz, played the role of the modern public ruler who went out among his people to give a personal manifestation of state legitimacy. Unlike his immediate predecessors, but somewhat like his ancestors, Abdülhamid's aim was to create 'vibrations of power' without being seen.[10] In stark contrast to Abdülaziz, who made the first and only state visit by an Ottoman sultan to Europe in 1867 to see the World Exposition in Paris, Abdülhamid crushed all rumours that he was about to visit Europe.[11]

Communication with his people and the outside world had therefore to be made through a world of symbols. These were based almost entirely on Islamic motifs: 'It was from Islam that the Muslim Ottomans could draw the emotional resonance that could mobilize both the upper and lower classes. It was Islam that would provide the store of symbols which could compete with the national symbols of the Greeks and the Serbs.'[12]

In this process of competition through symbols, it was critical that the 'middle of the message' should get through to the population at large. In this context, Carol Gluck's study of a very similar effort in Meiji Japan is worth quoting at length:

> Three kinds of interactions can be identified in the process that produced a universe of shared significance from diverse ideological formulations. The first emerged from the stressed parts of ideological speech, what is called the 'middle of the message'; the second from the unstressed elements that often appeared as 'dependent clauses' of ideological utterance; and the third from the unarticulated element, identified as the 'deep social meanings' that made ideological discourse comprehensible to those who participated in it.[13]

This description can be usefully applied to the late Ottoman case. The first category, or 'middle of the message', was continuous reference to Islam, the sultan as caliph and the protector of the sacred places, etc. The second category, which Gluck also defines as a 'naturalization of meaning', occurred in the 'dependent clauses' of Ottoman civilization which found body in utterances related to nomads and other unorthodox or heretical elements such as the Shi'a or the Kurds: 'the settling and civilizing of nomads (*ürbanın tavattın ve temeddünleri*)' or 'the elimination of the state of savagery and ignorance of the nomads (*ürbanın izale-i cehalet ve vahşetleri*)', or 'they live in a state of heresy and ignorance (*bir hal-i dalalet ve cehalet içinde yaşarlar*)'.[14]

The category of 'deep social meanings', which remain unarticulated but come to be related to the 'givens' in Ottoman/Turkish society, present in the everyday life of the ordinary person, can be seen in the usage of terms such as 'civilization': 'that toothless monster called civilization' (*medeniyet denen tek dişi kalmış canavar*) in the actual words of the Turkish national anthem. Similarly, the reflexive uses of science (*funun*) or scholarship (*ilim*) as central to notions of 'progress' (*terakki*) inform the thinking of the reform-oriented Ottoman intellectual.[15]

Intellectual conditioning of the elite

Who were the people instilled with this mentality and expected to translate it into workable policies? What informed the decision making of the typical late-Ottoman bureaucrat-statesman as he sat in his office overlooking the Golden Horn? First, he was a man who had been imbued with the ideology of Islam from a very young age. Yet, a very close second, he was a man who had been exposed to the ideas of the Enlightenment, if in a most diffused form.¹⁶ The main preoccupation, not to say obsession, of the late Ottoman statesman was the *saving of the state*. This central cause is addressed by various statesmen in different ways and with emphasis placed on a variety of solutions. A major influence on their thought was Ibn Khaldun, who figures as a sort of touchstone in Ottoman-Islamic statecraft.¹⁷ A very good case in point is the late Ottoman statesman-historian Ahmed Cevdet Paşa who, although usually thought of as conservative, was the first major historian to be influenced by nineteenth-century 'scientific history'.¹⁸

Ahmed Cevdet Paşa translated a section of the *Mukaddimah* in which he paid homage to Ibn Khaldun as a historian who, 'knows only one measure that of verifying and revising what has been recounted.'¹⁹ Ibn Khaldun's cyclical conception of state power, by which states grew, achieved maturity and declined, impressed Ottomans like Cevdet Paşa who sought to place their civilization in this context. Ibn Khaldun's view of man as a predator who could only be kept in check by an overarching coercive authority, and his view that there existed only certain peoples who possessed the requisite nature (*asabiyya*) to constitute this authority, served in particular to legitimate the rule of the Ottoman house.²⁰ Cevdet Paşa is also responsible for the codification of Şeriat rulings which took the shape of the *Mecelle*, which still forms the basis of some aspects of civil law in successor states of the Ottoman empire.²¹

Yet, ever since the French revolution, the Ottomans had been aware of the new winds blowing in Europe. Particularly after the Tanzimat reform, Europe became a source of emulation to the point of embarrassment. Sadık Rıfat Paşa, one of the leading men of the Tanzimat, looked to Metternichean Austria and the 'great bureaucrats who had created modern Europe' for examples of the sort of enlightened autocracy he hoped to transplant into an Ottoman context.²² The aims of the Ottoman reformers were very akin to those of the French physiocrats: a contented people engaged in peaceful pursuits which would allow them, and the state, prosperity.²

The unification of Germany and the Risorgimento greatly impressed Ottoman statesmen, although Ahmed Cevdet Paşa had a somewhat jaundiced view of the 'nationalism question':

> When Napoleon III was fighting Austria over the matter of Italy, he came up with this 'nationality' business ... and this did damage to the system of government which had been practiced for all these years ... It always used to be the case that a legitimate government had the right to punish with force any

rebellious subjects ... However, Napoleon invented this new rule which stated that 'any government which is not wanted by any of its subjects must give up its rule over them ... This has caused great surprise among some states who firmly rejected it.[24]

The paşa went on to comment that Britain had supported this principle whereas Russia had categorically rejected it. This had led to the unification of Italy. Yet Italy was avenged by a unified Germany, and the evil-doer Napoleon got his just deserts.[25] Süleyman Hüsnü Paşa, a contemporary of Ahmed Cevdet, was also inspired by what he called, 'The European policy ... of integrating all nationalities, languages and religions.' He did, however, admit that 'Even if this were admissible by the Şeriat, the present conditions (of the empire) do not allow it ....'[26]

All manifestations of power and social interaction leave a trace to their origin. Translating Clifford Geertz to a late Ottoman context, to *read* the enlargement of the sultan's private pavilion in a mosque, or the playing of a certain piece of music on certain occasions, or the procession of decorated camels bearing the sultan's gifts to Mecca, or the formulae of power in the everyday language of the policy makers: all this is the stuff of historical texture.[27]

Broadly speaking, the symbols of power in the Hamidian Ottoman empire fall into four categories. Three relate to the sultan and his palace. There were, first of all, the symbols relating to the sacrality of the person of the sultan/caliph, such as coats of arms on public buildings, official music, ceremonies, and public works which reflected directly the glory and power of the Ottoman state. Secondly, there were the more specific and personal manifestations of imperial munificence such as decorations, specially donated copies of the Qur'an, imperial standards and other ceremonial trappings. Third were the religiously symbolic items acquired by the palace such as calligraphy purported to belong to Islamic great men and other artifacts of similar significance.

The fourth falls into a somewhat different category. It concerns the symbolism of language in Ottoman official documentation. Although not always directly related to the person of the ruler, certain key phrases and words which frequently recur in official documentation provide us with valuable clues as to how the Hamidian bureaucracy conceptualized such matters as the relationship of the ruler and the ruled, their attitude to the nomadic populations, and relationships between members of the state elite themselves.

Public symbolism and its manifestations

The immediate predecessors of Abdülhamid II had always taken great pains to appear as 'modern' monarchs by adopting the European practice of displaying portraits of the monarch in public places. Mahmud II had begun this practice. Various religious sheikhs blessed his portraits before they were placed in government offices and other public places, and a twenty-one gun salute was fired as a guard of honour marched past them. This became a tradition which was continued under Abdülmecid (r. 1839–1861) and Abdülaziz (r. 1861–1876).[28] Also in 1850, 'three large portraits of Sultan Abdulmecit arrived in Egypt ... and were paraded through the city [Cairo] in a great procession.' The portraits were then exhibited at the citadel among great pomp and celebration.[29]

Abdülhamid deliberately forbade the display of his likeness in public spaces. It is unclear whether this was out of considerations of Islamic orthodoxy which forbids the depiction of the human image, or an obsession with security. On 15 May 1902, the vilayet of Ankara reported that, 'a portrait of our August Master the Caliph has been seen in a coffee shop in Ankara'. The communication went on to say, 'because the nature of the location was not in keeping with the sacred character of the Imperial Image, [the portrait] has been bought and sent to the palace.'[30]

Abdülhamid, apparently in an iconoclastic show of Islamic orthodoxy, replaced the image of the ruler with uniformly embroidered banners bearing the legend 'Long Live the Sultan!' (*Padişahım çok yaşa!*) which served the same purpose.[31] This acclaim, which was shouted by soldiers and civilians, had long been the customary way of expressing loyalty to the ruler. Nevertheless, it also became much more standardized as part of the process of increased international competition in ceremonial displays, very similar to the acclaims of 'Long Live the Queen!' in the British Empire or 'Tenno heika banzai!' in Japan.[32] Verbal acclaims could also become a symbol of opposition. The Young Turk opposition to the sultan focused on the acclaim in a negative fashion: cadets at the Military Academy and the Imperial Medical School would refuse to perform it on public occasions, or mumble a rude version of it.[33]

Despite his fear of assassination (which turned out to be well founded, as there was an attempt in 1905), Abdülhamid maintained the tradition of public Friday prayers as a ceremony in which the ruler showed himself to the people. In the nineteenth century, Friday prayers acquired additional ceremonial trappings inspired by European examples.

A physical manifestation of this shift towards a modern public persona of the monarch was nineteenth-century mosque architecture. The classical Ottoman mosque was altered to suit the ceremonial protocol of European usage with the addition of a two-storey structure to the main building to serve as ceremonial public space to give a more secular character to the buildings. Aptullah Kuran has pointed out that the space in the imperial mosques designated as the personal prayer chamber of the sultan greatly increased in size from the late eighteenth century: '[The] appearance and evolution of the sultan's prayer platform, or loge, went beyond the prerequisites of architecture ... It emerged as a vehicle of pomp and circumstance.'[34] Abdülhamid's own mosque, the Yıldız, is said to, '[have broken] with the Ottoman architectural tradition altogether,' as there was an unprecedented increase in ceremonial space which actually outstripped the prayer space.[35]

The Friday prayer ceremony (*cuma selamlığı* or simply *selamlık*) would begin as the royal procession left the Yıldız Palace with great pomp, the Imperial landau escorted by Albanian House Guards in livery, and make its way to the Yıldız mosque. There, after prayers, special officials would collect petitions from the people.[36] It also appears that the occasion became something of a tourist attraction, as one contemporary account describes the groups of British, American or Germans whose carriages formed, 'a long line on their way to Yıldız to watch the *selamlık* ceremony.'[37] A sort of dais was built to accommodate foreign visitors, where they were permitted to watch the ceremonies and salute the sultan. They were also told not to make any brusque movements with their hands, as this could be misconstrued as an attempted assassination by the guards, who would react accordingly.[38]

A frequent spectator was Yamada Torajiro, whose account of the *selamlık* is particularly interesting because of his extremely detailed rendition. Yamada noted that the sultan would be driven to the mosque in his landau, but on the return journey he would mount a simpler *caleche*, and take the reins himself. Male members of the dynasty, his palace retinue, leading bureaucrats, and high ranking military, in that order, would then line up behind him. This could well have been a symbolic representation of the ruler taking in hand the reins of the state. He also noted that the 'empress dowager' and the 'empress' would take part in the ceremonial procession and accompany the sultan to the mosque, but in keeping with Islamic custom, where women do not go to Friday prayers, they would remain in their carriages. However, their very presence in the courtyard was a departure from Islamic practice. Yamada wrote in his diary that the ceremony was very moving as it 'reflected the former glory of a great empire that has now stumbled.'[39]

On one occasion the *selamlık* provided the setting for a show of personal courage on the part of the sultan. When a bomb exploded at the ceremony in 1905 and the sultan escaped unscathed as the result of an unexpected change in procedure:

> There ensued a general panic as debris and blood was strewn about. The sultan held up his hands and shouted in his deep voice: 'Don't panic!' He then mounted his carriage, took the reins, and as he passed the foreign dignitaries they all shouted 'Hooray!' in one voice.[40]

Another of the rare occasions when the sultan showed himself in public was the ceremonial visit to the Holy Relics at the Topkapı Palace and the shrine of Eyüp on the Golden Horn during Ramadan. Yamada again provides a detailed account. The sultan would set off for the old palace accompanied by 300 carriages bearing his *harem* and entourage. On this occasion the roads were prepared by 'covering them with a thick white sand'.[41]

How did these ceremonies appear to the wider population? Hagop Mintzuri, an Armenian baker's apprentice, later wrote in his memoirs that he remembered the sultan's arrival at the Sinan Paşa mosque in Beşiktaş for ceremonial prayers at the end of the fast of Ramadan:

> First the Albanian guards, dressed in violet knee-breeches, who were not soldiers or police and did not speak Turkish, would fill the upper part of our market square. Then would come the Arab guards of the sultan, dressed in red *şalvar* and adorned with green turbans. These too, did not speak Turkish and they would fill the road. Finally the Palace Guard of the sultan, chosen exclusively from Turks who were tall, sporting their decorations on their chests, would take up their positions as an inner ring in front of the Albanians and Arabs.

It is instructive that even an observer such as Mintzuri should have paid attention to the personnel forming concentric circles of security around the sultan. It is fairly clear from his 'reading' of their ceremonial placing, and the fact that he specifically pointed out that the Albanians and Arabs did not speak Turkish, while the innermost circle were 'exclusively Turks', that he was sensitized to the gradations of ethnic loyalty projected by the ceremonial guard.[42]

It is also possible that, as an Armenian, Mintzuri may have been more sensitive to this gradation, as the ceremony described must have been taking place in the late 1890s, not long after the Armenian massacres in the district of Kumkapı in Istanbul in 1895.[43] The Turks he was describing were almost certainly the elite Ertuğrul regiment, named after the legendary father of Osman, founder of the empire. They were chosen exclusively from the region of Söğüd, the mythical heartland of the Ottoman Turks, where the empire had its origins.[44]

Mintzuri also records how, as a young boy, he was deeply impressed by the ceremony of the departure of the sultan's gifts to Mecca and Medina, the *sürre alayı*. These gifts to the Holy Cities were a symbolic statement of the caliph's protection for the most sacred stronghold of Islam. Camels heavily caparisoned in gilded livery would parade though the streets of Istanbul bearing the ceremonial offerings. This too was an occasion for great pomp, and Mintzuri relates how a procession of bands would march through the streets playing the Hamidiye march.[45]

One of the rare occasions when Abdülhamid actually allowed the dignitaries of state to approach his person was at the Ramadan holiday (*bayram*) during the yearly ceremony of the kissing of the hem of his robe (*etek öpmek*). In a memoir written by a close aide we get some very interesting details of the actual conduct of the ceremony:

> The sultan's aids hold up gold embroidered handkerchiefs standing at either side of the royal personage. Rather than the actual hem of the robe, as each dignitary files past he kisses one of these and holds it up to his forehead in a gesture of submission (*biat*). Only to accept the greetings of the *ulema* does the sultan rise.[46]

In this adaptation of a very old custom, there was a significant departure from tradition to allow for the change in dress. At these ceremonies the sultan no longer wore a caftan, instead he appeared in dress uniform or a morning coat; thus the embroidered handkerchiefs replaced the hem of his robe. It is also significant that the caliph rose as a gesture of humility and respect towards religious functionaries.

In most of these public ceremonies there was a significant blending of old and new, Islamic and Western traditions. The *selamlık* became an occasion where Islamic tradition and Western-style protocol were combined, with foreign dignitaries and palace ladies present in the same ceremonial space. The *sürre* procession was accompanied by a military band playing Western marches, and the *biat* accommodated changing dress styles.

Official iconography

These events, however, remained very much the exception that proved the rule. It was to be from well within the sanctum of the Yıldız Palace that Abdülhamid made his declarations in symbols and official iconography. One of the most notable symbols of the renewed emphasis on power and ceremonial in the late nineteenth century was heraldry.

The Sublime State (*devlet-i aliyye*) was symbolized by the coat of arms of the House of Osman (*arma-i osmani*). The design had been commissioned from an Italian artist by Mahmud II. By the time Abdülhamid II came to sit on the Ottoman throne, it was such a well established part of Ottoman official symbolism that when the sultan asked for a detailed description of its contents in 1905, as he was apparently upset about the lack of uniformity in its depiction, the bureaucracy was momentarily embarrassed because no official authorized version seemed to be readily available. It was finally dug up and the contents described.[47]

In a detailed memorandum the sultan was informed that the Ottoman coat of arms consisted of both old and new, Turkish and Islamic, motifs, such as armaments and other symbolic objects. The central motif in the shield was 'the exalted crown of the Sultans', topped by the seal or *tuğra* of the regnant ruler. This was flanked by two heavy tomes, one symbolizing Islamic law, *Şeriat*, and the other modern law codes (*ahkam-ı şeriyye ve nizamiye'yi cami kitab*). Under these appeared a set of scales representing justice. The central motif was surrounded and flanked by symbolic armaments, the old balancing the new: arrow and quiver-infantry rifle and bayonet, old style muzzle-loading cannon a modern field artillery piece, a traditional scimitar, a modern cavalry sabre etc. The coat of arms also included traditional Islamic–Ottoman symbols such as a vase full of blossoming roses and incense, standing for the magnanimity of the state. The total design was flanked on the right side by a cluster of red banners and on the left by a cluster of green banners symbolizing the sultanic–Ottoman as well as the universal Islamic nature of the caliphate. Set under the entire design were the whole array of Ottoman decorations. Thus the central themes of the Ottoman coat of arms revolved around the continuity of the old and the new, the traditional and the modern.⁴⁸

Another feature of nineteenth-century commemorative iconography was the commemorative medallion. Perhaps the most interesting among the Ottoman examples of this genre, as a bid for modernity combined with time-honoured historical legitimation, is the medallion struck in 1850, during the reign of Abdülmecid (r. 1831–1861). An admirable document on the late Ottoman state of mind, it is emblazoned with the slogan 'Cet Etat subsistera. Dieu le veut'. On one side it features a fortress battered by heavy seas over which flies the Ottoman banner. On the rim are to be found slogans such as 'Justice égale pour tous', 'Protection des faibles', 'L'Etat relevé', and so on. On the reverse the motifs include the Central Asian Turkish cap, and engraved in various places the names Mahomet II (Mehmed II, the Conqueror of Istanbul in 1453) Solyman I (Sultan Süleyman the Magnificent r. 1494–1566), Reshid (Mustafa Reşid Paşa, grand vizier at the time and the major figure behind the Tanzimat reforms), Aali (Mehmed Emin Ali Paşa, together with Reşid, a major figure in the reform movement), and Coprulu (Mehmed Köprülü and his son Ahmed Köprülü, the architects of revived Ottoman power in the second half of the sixteenth century).⁴⁹

A similar effort to derive legitimation for the present by using symbols of the past can be observed in the prominent place given to the Ottoman genealogical lineage in the state almanacs (*salname*). In an almanac prepared for the vilayet of Bursa in 1885, the roots of the Ottoman family are taken back to the legendary Oğuz tribe and from there to Adam and Eve via Noah. The official dynastic myth of how the Selçuk Sultan Alaeddin Keykübad protected Osman, the founder of the dynasty, is duly recounted, claiming that the House of Osman is 'according to the research of experts one of the oldest in the world, and will last forever.'⁵⁰ Such manifest official fiction was an ancient tradition in Islamic court panegyrics, but what is interesting here is that it should be featured in a state almanac which is a creation of bureaucratic modernization and features such mundane data as the names of the various ministers, agricultural produce, and main geographical features of the area. The inclusion of this mythical lineage is all the more interesting as Woodhead tells us that the descent from the Oğuz tribe, 'and the speculative genealogy particularly popular during the fifteenth century', was, 'largely discredited' by the late sixteenth century.⁵¹ The fact that apocryphal genealogies should have been brought back in during the nineteenth century, when the Ottoman state was beginning to look distinctly shaky, is significant. The aim in this case was to stress that the rule of the Ottoman family was a permanent and inevitable feature of the landscape.

The *salname* are in themselves a manifestation of the 'pumping up' of the Ottoman foundation myth. The genealogy of the Ottoman sultans does not appear in the state almanacs (*devlet salnameleri*) until 1853 (1270 AH) although they begin in 1846.[52] It then disappears, to emerge again in 1868 (1285 AH). In the reign of Abdülhamid, the genealogy moves up from fifth place in the table of contents to third place. Individual entries under each sultan are also considerably expanded so that where earlier volumes gave only basic data such as dates of birth and death, those in the Hamidian period are much more detailed.[53]

Just as the Ottomans tried to emphasize preexisting traditions by including them in the symbols of state, they also attempted to curtail the circulation of what were considered 'rival symbols'. A correspondence between the chancery of the grand vizier and the palace, dated 8 June 1892, dealt with the issue of the importation of goods whose packaging bore the coat of arms of a rival power. The matter had come up over a crate of mirrors which were being sent from Greece to Crete. It must be remembered that these were turbulent years leading up to the autonomy of Crete and the Ottoman–Greek war of 1897. The sultan wanted to forbid the entry of such packages, but the grand vizier had to point out that there was no legal means by which the Ottoman customs could keep them out.[54]

On 2 July 1889, the Ministry of the Interior reported that certain 'illustrated plates' (*levha*), published in Moscow, had been seized in the Pera quarter of Istanbul, 'bearing the images of Byzantine emperors and Russian tsars'. It had come to the minister's attention that these plates had been distributed to the Greek Orthodox Patriarchate in Istanbul, and were accompanied by 'a history book bearing certain harmful information'.[55]

This episode stands as a striking illustration of the fact that the Ottoman authorities understood only too well the implications of the Russian tsars' claims to the status of protecter of all Greek Orthodox subjects in the Ottoman realm, and of their pretension to being 'descendants of the Byzantine emperors,' with Moscow as the 'Third Rome'. This event occurred in the reign of Alexander III who ascended the throne in 1883. It would have been entirely in keeping with the Moscow (rather than Petersburg) centred state symbolism of Alexander, who also stressed the mystic nature of tsardom.[56]

The Byzantine past was a sensitive issue as the Ottoman official mythology stressed the position of the Ottoman sultans as the successors of

Rome and Byzantium.⁵⁷ After the conquest in 1453, the Ottoman imperial tradition came into its own. Necipoğlu has confirmed that the Topkapı Palace was deliberately built on the site of the Byzantine acropolis.⁵⁸ Fletcher has also emphasised that, 'The city itself was symbolic of legitimacy in the Roman imperial tradition so that the Ottoman ruler ... now adorned himself with the symbols of Caesar.'⁵⁹ The cathedral of Hagia Sophia, converted to a mosque after the conquest, and purportedly the scene of the Ottoman Sultan Selim I's assuming the mantle of the caliphate in 1519, was especially significant. Abdülhamid was to accord particular importance to this mosque as the seat of the caliphate.⁶⁰

Thus, the news that, 'certain Greek and other visitors had been drawing and writing on the walls and galleries' of the mosque seemed particularly untoward. To prevent this sort of behaviour strict new instructions ordered that visitors should be escorted at all times.⁶¹

Indeed Istanbul had always occupied a central position in the symbolism aimed at reinforcing the legitimacy of the Ottoman sultans. Gülru Necipoğlu has shown that the ceremonial progress by a newly enthroned sultan to the mausoleums of his ancestors in Istanbul was itself a means of declaring his legitimacy: 'These tombs built posthumously by the successors of deceased sultans proclaimed Ottoman dynastic legitimacy architecturally by highlighting the uninterrupted continuity of a proud lineage.'⁶²

The presence of the mausoleums, Hagia Sophia and the Holy Relics of the Prophet in Istanbul all contributed to the city's symbolism. Reşid Paşa, possibly the greatest Turkish statesman of the nineteenth century, listed his 'three pillars of the state' (*üç rükn-ü devlet*) as Islam, the sultanate and the caliphate all of which were sustained by the House of Osman which protected Mecca and Medina and the continuity of Istanbul as the capital of the empire.⁶³

The visual confirmation of the sultan's sovereignty took the form of his monogram (*tuğra*) which appeared on all public works completed in his time. Clock towers erected all over Anatolia bearing the imperial coat of arms and other reminders of sultanic power became ubiquitous. Some of the clock towers were inaugurated in small Anatolian towns such as Niğde, Adana and Yozgad to commemorate the sultan's silver jubilee in 1901. Finkel has pointed out that 'specifically secular monumental architecture' represented by a clock tower highlighted the confrontation between Qur'anic time punctuated by the call to prayer from the minarets, and conversion to a new economic order 'founded on the conjoining of time to labour'.⁶⁴ Thus, particularly in Anatolia and the Arab provinces, these buildings were intended as physical manifestations of the 'middle of the message' and served as markers of a new concept of time and power.

Although clock towers and the like were secular bids for legitimacy, the small village mosques were also made into *lieux de mémoire*. One aspect of the sultan's symbolic representation in the provinces was the building of small uniform mosques bearing commemorative plaques that linked his name with distant Ottoman ancestors. One such order dated 8 September 1892 provided for the composition of chronograms (*ebced hesabı*) for commemorative plaques to be erected over nine mosques in villages in the Çorlu area in Thrace. The sultans chosen, one for each mosque, were: Osman II, Mustafa I, Ahmed I, Mehmed IV, Murad III, Selim II, Beyazıd II, Süleyman I (the Magnificent), and Selim I.⁶⁵

The records also show that the sultan built three mosques in the villages on the island of Rhodes, dedicated respectively to himself, his mother Tir-i Müjgan Hanım, and the legendary Ertuğrul Gazi.⁶⁶ Orders were also issued that the mosque built by Sultan Yıldırım Beyazıd, one of the earlier heroic sultans, in the small town of İnegöl, not far from Söğüd, was to be rebuilt as it was in ruins. This was duly done and sanctification ceremonies took place on the sultan's nineteenth accession anniversary.⁶⁷ Another symbolic connection between the days of early glory and the Hamidian regime, was the deliberate effort to echo the architecture of the Great Mosque (Ulu Cami) in Bursa in the architecture of the Yıldız mosque. It was specified that 'the pulpit (*minber*) of the mosque should resemble the pulpit of the Great Mosque in Bursa.'⁶⁸

Although religious/dynastic legitimation themes were being employed here, the function of these mosques was, if anything, closer to the secular message of the clock towers. It is also significant that both the clock towers and the mosques were built in small places, thus manifesting power at the local level.

One example of this 'grass roots' message is the commemorative plaque reported on by the Vali of Baghdad, which was to be erected on an obelisk by the Hindiyye dam in the vilayet. A fairly typical example of the genre, it bore the legend: 'To commemorate the Holy Name of the Caliph and to furnish an ornament to His Eternal Power.' The vali specified that the text would be in Arabic, which indicates that the target audience was the local population, rather than a general statement of power, which would probably have been in Turkish.⁶⁹

Şerif Mardin has noted that, 'The wide adoption of an imperial name in Anatolia is a marked feature of [Abdülhamid II's] reign.[70] In this effort to communicate through symbols, Abdülhamid was in a position very similar to the Russian tsar where the 'synthesis of the Russian myths, in which Orthodoxy could serve as a bridge from the sovereign emperor to the people' was employed to bolster the image of the Russian autocracy.[71]

In all these efforts it is important to note that the symbolic statements on the buildings, bridges, dams and clock towers were made in a specific historical context: the effort made from the Tanzimat onwards to reform and modernize Ottoman cities. In what Dumont and Georgeon call the 'struggle between state power and the local communities', symbolic manifestations of power such as coats of arms or commemorative plaques played a very critical role in the dynamic tension between state and society.[72] Timothy Mitchell has noted the obsession with 'an appearance of order' in Egypt in the late nineteenth century where similar developments were taking place. Ottoman public space was similarly 'ordered', when possible, to suit the symbolic statements the centre wanted to make.[73]

In nineteenth-century Istanbul, Çelik has pointed out that 'the regularizing of the urban fabric' occurred as a result of the desire of Ottoman statesmen to present a 'modern' appearance to the outside world. The 'regularizing' of the urban space, as in the case of Egypt, was not only intended to *'épater les bourgeois'*, but also represented an exercise of power on the part of the centre. The monumental character of historic buildings such as the Hagia Sophia and the Süleymaniye mosque were emphasized by creating clearings around them.[74]

Similarly, no expense was spared to restore the tombs of the legendary first two sultans of the House of Osman, Osman and his son Orhan, who were buried in Bursa.[75] Bursa was also frequently accorded special honours as, 'the crucible of the Sublime State' (*mehd-i zuhur-u saltanat*).[76] Indeed, a veritable cult of Ottomania was created around the historical heritage of the Ottoman dynasty, as Abdülhamid focused in an unprecedented fashion on the 'creation myth' of the Ottoman State.[77] Part of this was the elaborate commemorative ceremony (*ihtifal*) staged every year at the tomb of the legendary founder of the Ottoman dynasty, Ertuğrul Gazi, the father of Osman Gazi. The shrine of Ertuğrul in Söğüd, a small town in west central Anatolia, was turned into a commemorative mausoleum complex honouring the misty origins of the empire.

The tomb of Ertuğrul was rebuilt in 1886, and a fountain bearing a chronogram celebrating Abdülhamid as benefactor was inaugurated. The sarcophagus bearing what were reputed to be the remains of Ertuğrul was refashioned in marble, and a grave reputedly belonging to his wife was also rebuilt and turned into shrine in 1887. Sultan Osman's first grave was also rebuilt next to that of his father.[78] Together with this, twenty-five graves belonging to 'comrades in arms of Ertuğrul Gazi' received new stones. This activity looks distinctly like the 'invention of tradition' given that the identity of these people is unclear and only a few of the graves actually bear names. Even the historian of the site who eulogized the 'great founder of the Ottoman state' felt obliged to point out that, 'It is difficult to tell how Abdülhamid II established that the grave belonged to Ertuğrul Gazi's wife. We can only surmise that he relied on reliable hearsay.'[79] The Ertuğrul Gazi shrine is mentioned frequently in despatches. In 1902 considerable money was spent on the creation of an open square around the Ertuğrul Gazi Mosque by the expropriation and demolition of buildings hemming it in.[80]

The complex became the site for annual celebrations when the 'original Ottoman tribe' the Karakeçili, would ride into Söğüd dressed as Central Asian nomadic horsemen and stage a parade where they would sing a 'national march' with the refrain: 'We are soldiers of the Ertuğrul Regiment ... 'We are ready to die for our Sultan Abdülhamid'. This would be followed by a display of horsemanship and a game of *cirid*, the traditional Central Asian sport.[81]

It became a custom for the leader of the tribe to telegram the palace every year to the effect that, 'We have fulfilled our annual sacred duty of paying our respects to the shrine of the revered ancestors of His Imperial Majesty.'[82] Even the so-called 'mother of Ertuğrul Gazi', a Hayme Ana, was to be honoured with a special mausoleum built by imperial order in the village where she was reputedly buried.[83] The Hayme Ana mausoleum was maintained and refurbished regularly at considerable expense from the privy purse of the sultan.[84]

The sultan's renewed emphasis on the 'Turkishness' of the early days of the Ottoman state can also be seen in his treatment of the 'original Turkish dynasties'. He greatly honoured the Ramazanoğulları clan, who had been a Turkish *beylik* in the Adana region, because they claimed to be 'of pure Turkish blood'. Abdülhamid invited Emetullah Hatun, the leading matriarch of the clan, to Istanbul where she and her entourage were lodged at the Yıldız Palace and treated as honoured guests.[85]

The renewed obsession with the early days of the Ottoman empire in Abdülhamid's reign can be likened to the same sort of obsession with dynastic legitimation in such times of extreme crisis as after the Timurid debacle of 1402. Mehmed I, the strongest figure in the interregnum, 'spent some of his precious resources to build a mosque in Söğüd'.[86] Like Abdülhamid much later, Mehmed felt the need to issue a statement to the 'grassroots'.

From obscure towns and villages of Thrace and Anatolia to the holy cities of Mecca and Medina, the sultan took great pains to ensure that his munificence was acknowledged. His symbolic gifts acquired particular importance in the holy cities. On 6 April 1889, an imperial gift of several candelabra was delivered to the Ka'ba and presented during a ceremony which was held during Ramadan, ensuring that 'thousands of the faithful intoned prayers for the long life and success of His Imperial Majesty.'[87] Also, two ceremonial tents were erected in Mecca every year during the haj on the two hills of Arafat and Mina. These were erected only during the pilgrimage, and were the symbols of the sultan's presence as his annual haj message was read from the tent on Mina. It is significant that the tents were pitched on the two hills that served as the focus of excitement during the performance of the haj rites.[88]

Further visibility was ensured through the traditional practice of the sultan/caliph providing the holy mantle which covered the sacred stone of the Ka'ba (*setre-i şerif*) . On 6 September 1892, the palace was informed that the new mantle, with the sultan's name embroidered in gold, was ready. It was to replace the old one which still bore the name of Abdülaziz.[89]

The visual confirmation of sovereignty was also extended to non-Muslim places of worship. On 23 October 1885, the grand vizier, Kamil Paşa, reported that the Armenian Catholic church in Büyükdere in Istanbul had erected a commemorative plaque stating that the church had been constructed 'during the just and glorious reign of Abdülhamid II'. What is interesting is that the initiative seems to have come from the Armenian archbishop, who declared that 'this was being done for the first time in a Christian temple'. In fact the sultan was rather unsure about how appropriate this whole business was, and ordered that 'it be secretly investigated as to what the exact wording on the plaque consists of,' as 'if it is too prominently displayed it might be offensive to Muslim opinion.' Kamil Paşa reported back that it was a harmless display of loyalty, and in any case the plaque was displayed in an inner courtyard where few Muslim eyes would see it.[90]

It would seem, however, that Abdülhamid soon overcame his shyness and the erecting of official iconography on non-Muslim official buildings became commonplace. An order dated 16 March 1894 declared that the request of the Catholic Archbishop of Üsküb (Scopje) to display a plaque bearing the imperial monogram (*tuğra*) on the archbishop's residence was to be granted. The decision was based on the precedent which declared that 'since various archbishoprics of other confessions have in the past been thus honoured with the August Symbol', it was appropriate in this case, too.[91]

The matter of just where official iconography could be displayed sometimes led to amusing incidents, one such being the case of Manolaki, a Greek tea house operator in Istanbul who set himself up as the self-styled 'tea maker in chief to the Imperial Palace' (*saray-ı hümayun çaycı başısı*). The hapless Manolaki was hauled off by the police for having taken the pains to stage an elaborate ceremony where he slaughtered a sacrificial sheep and solemnly erected the Imperial monogram (*tuğra*) over his shop. The municipal authorities found his behaviour particularly reprehensible as this had led 'to other tradesmen presenting petitions to embellish their shops with the Imperial Arms'.[92] Although the Ottoman equivalent for 'Purveyors of fine teas to Her Majesty the Queen' was to be found in the official commercial almanacs Manolaki evidently did not qualify.[93]

Indeed, the use or misuse of the Ottoman coat of arms could attain crisis dimensions. On 28 December 1905, the Ministry of the Interior was to report that the American Embassy had interceded in favour of a certain Mr Rosenstein, the distributor of Singer sewing machines for the Ottoman empire. Rosenstein was claiming the right to display the imperial coat of arms in provincial branch shops in towns like Edirne and İzmit. A certain Karabet Basmaciyan had applied for permission to display the arms in his shop in Çatalca.

The firm's view was that the imperial permission, which was given for the central office in Istanbul, automatically applied also to the provinces. The ministry had other ideas: 'It is to be noted that the employees of this firm are mostly foreigners of uncertain demeanour (*mechul el ahval bir takım ecanib*), and many of them are Armenians among whom are some who have been known to be involved in the recent murderous attack (on the sultan).' The matter was becoming all the more serious as, 'the embassies are beginning to take a close interest in the matter.'[94] The fact that something as ostensibly peripheral as permission to use the coat of arms as a sales promotion gimmick for sewing machines should overlap with a major crisis such as the Armenian issue illustrates just how enmeshed symbolism was with the chronic instability of the times.

The 'Imperial Photographers', the Gülmez Brothers, who had been commissioned to take photographs to be sent to the Chicago World Fair of 1893, also applied for permission to 'grace their shop with the royal coat of arms' and the *tuğra*. It is highly unlikely that they were granted permission.⁹⁵

Louis Rambert, the director of the Imperial Tobacco Regie, recorded a similar event in his diary. The Ottoman customs seized crates containing the products of the Regie, on the grounds that they bore the imperial coat of arms. The affair created something of a diplomatic crisis as the ambassadors of France, Austria and Germany became involved. Rambert only solved the problem by producing an official authorization specifying that the Regie's permission to use the arms as part of its logo ran for another five years. ⁹⁶

Personal manifestations of royal favour

The nineteenthcentury was the century of decorations, as royal favour became channelled into precise dosages.⁹⁷ The Hamidian regime habitually used decorations as a form of investment in the goodwill it hoped they would foster in the recipient. Thus, symbolic manifestation of sultanic munificence had a co-optive aim. Decorating or otherwise rewarding men it could not discipline or control had always been a policy of the Sublime Porte. As real coercive power declined in the nineteenth century this became all the more prevalent. Yet, the decorations policy of the Ottoman centre must not be seen purely as an alternative to coercion. In a very real sense decorations were a manifestation of the integrative symbolic code and it has been pointed out above that the coat of arms of the Ottoman House was prominently featured on decorations.⁹⁸ As in the matter of the coat of arms, uniformity of the design of various decorations was a consideration for the sultan, who ordered that precise drawings illustrating all the state decorations be made and presented to him.⁹⁹

On 19 June 1892, the vilayet of Konya reported that certain Greek notables in the town of Isparta had been wearing their official decorations and uniforms to church during the Easter service. The governor proudly reported that he had put a stop to 'this inappropriate practice'. He was (no doubt much to his surprise) promptly reprimanded and told that 'these people are wearing their decorations as a gesture of pride and loyalty and should not be interfered with.' Evidently the local official was offended by the Christians sporting Islamic symbols such as the star and crescent on their chests in the profane space which a church constituted. He was overridden by his superiors who rapped his knuckles for interfering in a practice which they chose to approve of.[100]

Nor were decorations treated lightly by the recipients or potential recipients. When the Ottoman ambassador to Paris, Münir Paşa, was sent on a tour of the Balkan capitals and distributed decorations, the event caused quite a furore. The Ottoman High Commission in Sofia reported that the decoration of the King of Serbia's daughter with a high ranking medal (nişan-ı ali) and his delivery of a Compassionate Order (şefkat nişanı) to the Queen of Rumania, had caused heated discussion in the Bulgarian press. It was seen as a move by the Porte to support Serbian and Rumanian interests in the Balkans against those of Bulgaria.[101]

The fact that decorations usually came with an award of money meant that they were often solicited by some rather dubious characters. Such was the case of one Professor Adolphe Strauss, who wrote to Yıldız claiming that his articles in the Hungarian press had created such positive feeling towards the sultan that when they were read aloud in the Hungarian parliament the deputies spontaneously leapt to their feet shouting: 'eljen a sultan!' (long live the sultan). The good professor actually went on to recommend that several of his colleagues be awarded specific decorations: 'For Prof. Sigismonde Vajda, the Order of the Osmanieh Third Class would be appropriate since he already holds the Osmanieh Second Class …' and so on.[102]

Together with decorations, the presentation of copies of the Qur'an or ceremonial banners was also part of the symbolic dialogue between the ruler and ruled. One element that the sultan tried to woo were the Kurdish chieftains of eastern Anatolia.[103] On 11 September 1891, the vilayet of Trabzon reported that the ceremonial banners and Qur'ans sent to the Kurdish tribes of the Erzurum region had been received, and the proper ceremony in the presence of a military band and a guard of honour had been carried out.[104] The banners were manufactured in Istanbul especially for the Kurdish Hamidiye regiments and paid for out of the privy purse.[105]

Even in the besieged garrison in Medina in 1918, the regimental standards were solemnly decorated. To maintain morale, the garrison commander organized an essay competition which was won by an tract on 'flag protocol'. The writer specified that the flags which bore the coat of arms of the Ottoman state be dipped to salute the sultan, whereas in the case of those bearing suras from the Qur'an the sultan was to offer the salute.[106]

Symbolism and Power in the Hamidian Regime   37

The crack Ertuğrul regiment which served as the personal bodyguard of the sultan also had its *sancak* renewed in 1892. The privy purse reported that special care had been taken to ensure that 'the prayers, dates and other legends are identical to the one that is kept as a sample in the Imperial Treasury.'[107] Robes of honour (*hil'at*) were another form of the symbolic exercise of sovereignty. In these matters strict protocol was applied and precedent was seen as 'accepted procedure'. When the question of the award of a robe of honour to Sheikh Ibn-Reşid came up in 1885, the grand vizier, Said Paşa, advised against it. The vizier's reasons are interesting, for they illustrate the considerations that were weighed in these matters. Said Paşa pointed out that although it was customary to pay Arab sheikhs money to 'provide for the protection of the Hijaz roads', the granting of *hil'at* was reserved only for the sharifs of Mecca. If any such honour was awarded to Ibn-Reşid, it would mean that 'he would be considered an equal of the sharifs and this will imply that the state is dependent on him, thereby increasing his prestige among the Arab sheikhs in a way that would be detrimental to the influence of the state.'[108]

Particularly in the Arab provinces, decorations and other symbols of imperial favour were employed to 'win the hearts of the local sheikhs and notables'. The long-time Vali of Hijaz and Yemen, Osman Nuri Paşa, was to write:

> The nomads and sheikhs are lovers of justice. The best way to deal with them is to be entirely honest and honour promises made to them. Their men and women should always be given a good reception at state offices, their complaints listened to and the necessary measures taken. The notables among them should be given decorations and a fuss should be made over them as these people are very fond of pomp and circumstance.[109]

Symbolic objects acquired by the state

One means of emphasizing sacrality was for the palace to buy up symbolic objects which it deemed it should have in its safe-keeping. There is also evidence of this practice in the last years of the previous reign. Butrus Abu Manneh has drawn attention to the ceremonial progress, in May 1872, of 'the Prophet's sandals' from Hakkari in eastern Anatolia to Istanbul, and the grand ceremony conducted upon their arrival. The press gave reports of the progress every step of the way and offered accounts of miraculous happenings en route.¹¹⁰ Another instance of this was the order to buy what was purportedly a copy of the Prophet's handwriting in the form of a letter written to the ruler of the Ghassanids. Acquired from a certain Monsieur 'Perpinyani' (presumably Perpigniani) in 1875, it was ordered that it should be placed in the Imperial Treasury.¹¹¹

Objects like this, often of dubious authenticity, bought from people of foreign nationality, continue to come up in dispatches. Another such case was an item of calligraphy, supposedly an example of the handwriting of the Caliph Ali, which the enterprising Perpinyani had presented to the palace in 1877. The grand vizier Said Paşa pointed out that the item had been handed over to the treasury some time ago, and Perpinyani, backed by the French embassy, was now demanding his original fee of 5,000 liras plus interest of 1,000 lira because of the delay in payment and if not the return of the item. Moreover, he was threatening to sell the piece to the British Museum if he was not paid promptly.¹¹²

Many years later the matter had still not been settled. On 13 March 1892, ministers were still discussing the 'appeasement' of Perpinyani who continued to make a thorough nuisance of himself by repeated pressure through the French ambassador. It was estimated that 5,000 lira was a fair price, as the accumulated interest would actually amount to more.¹¹³ By August 1893, when the palace was informed that the matter had still not been settled, the ministers were told with evident exasperation that 'even if the authenticity of the item is less than certain it should be bought and placed in the Imperial Treasury where all such sacred items belong.' What was being said here in plain language was: 'buy it even though it is probably a fake.' A failure to do so might have resulted in a grievous loss of prestige, particularly if the ubiquitous Perpinyani did suceed in selling it to the British Museum.¹¹⁴

The news that the palace was prepared to pay good money for such items attracted potential sellers of a similarly dubious nature. One such case was a woman named Fatma, a resident of Makrıköy (Bakırköy) in Istanbul, who telegraphed that she wanted to present to the sultan what she claimed was the stirrup of the Caliph Ali. This stirrup, she said, had magical qualities: when porters (*hamal*) had difficulties lifting their burden, she would wash the stirrup and make them drink the water. The porters, thus fortified, would happily swing their burden unto their backs.¹¹⁵ The Minister of Police, Nazım Bey, took a somewhat jaundiced view when he was instructed to summon the item to inspect it. He reported that the woman had no real evidence beyond what her late father-in-law had told her, and that the stirrup was somewhat garishly fashioned as a dragon's head: 'although the shape of stirrups at the time is unknown, it is unlikely that the Caliph Ali would have used such a stirrup thus adorned.' Nazım Bey added that the inscription which conveniently adorned the stirrup – 'the stirrup of the Caliph Ali' – was 'suspiciously like the writing of our present time'.[116]

It is highly unlikely that the palace would have bought the item. In cases where members of the wider population approached the palace on such matters, it is worth bearing in mind that what was going on was a decorous form of giving alms to the poor. It is unlikely that Abdülhamid II would have been tempted to invest in the occult properties of Ali's stirrup and much more likely that, with the tale of misfortune that went with it (dead husband, son in the army, having travelled all the way from Bursa to make the gift), the petitioner hoped for (and probably received) the sultan's charity.

Another such case was that of Tahir Efendi. Like Fatma, a person of modest means and a minor official in the Ministry of War, Tahir Efendi brought forward what he claimed was a letter of patent (*berat*) entitling him to certain revenues as the descendant of the chief standard bearer (*sersancakdar*) of the Prophet Mohammed. The palace ordered that the matter be looked into and that 'it be examined if there is indeed such a hereditary rank'.[117] The chances are that Tahir Efendi was sent away with 'a little something' (*bir mikdar şey*), as the saying always went in the event of such occurances.

The symbolism of language in the Hamidian era

When one combs through Ottoman archival documentation, one comes across certain words, phrases, or clichés which frequently recur. Usually overlooked as part of chancery officialese, these phrases can provide useful clues to the way the state regarded its subjects, the relationships among the ruling elite themselves, and the way they perceived the basis of their rule.[118] This was noticed by a contemporary British observer:

> For ruling native subjects, the guiding word is *'akilaneh* (skilfully), while the brutal and often sanguinary conflicts among the peasantry are described by no fiercer a term than *na-saz-lık* (impropriety); the correction of the same to be performed in a peaceful mode, is called *tarteeb* (setting to rights). *Voormak* (to strike), a word implying resort to force is a word but rarely pronounced,

and then only in a subdued voice. These are specimens of the *tatlu dil*, the 'sweet tongue' of the Turkish rulers.¹¹⁹

The first thing that emerges from a close reading of these 'codes' is that the state's view of its people was never negative. The people as a whole were always good, they were occasionally led astray by certain malicious and perfidious elements, but were potentially always capable of loyalty. This was not the result, as it has been argued *ad nauseum* of the fact that the state considered its people a 'herd' or a 'flock'. Bernard Lewis has pointed out that in the course of the nineteenth century the Ottoman term *reaya* was replaced by *teb'a* which was, 'becoming the Ottoman equivalent of the English word "subject"'.¹²⁰ Particularly in the nineteenth century, the state was in desperate need of a reliable population, it was simply not in a position to dismiss the population as rebellious and to crush insurgency, even if it had the material means to do so, which more than often it did not.

In the case of the Yezidis, Iraqi Kurds who were targeted for conversion to Hanefi Islam, the people themselves were seen as 'simple folk who cannot tell good from evil (*nik ve bed'i tefrik edemiyen sade-dilan ahali*).' They were being led astray by their leaders who were 'fooling and provoking them' (*iğfalat ve teşvikat*).¹²¹ In another, totally different, context the same words come up. When refugees from Greece who had been settled on the Ottoman side of the border, threatened to go back to Greece because they had not been given the land promised them by the state, they too were termed as 'those who cannot tell good from evil (*nik ve bed-i fark etmez kimseler*)' and who had been led astray by the Greeks.¹²²

Nor was this attitude confined only to Muslims. When Protestant missionaries became active among the Christian population of the vilayet of Syria, the people were again seen as 'simple people who cannot tell good from ill and are having their beliefs poisoned' by evil elements (*nik ve bed-i fark ve temyize muktedir olmayan sade-dilan ahali*).¹²³ Similarly the Alevi Kızılbaş population of Tokad were described as, 'simple village folk (*sade-dil kır'a halkı*)' who were to be 'shown the high path of enlightenment' by instructing them in the Hanefi *mezheb*.¹²⁴ When American missionaries attempted to open a school in Konya, the view was again that this was ' an effort to fool the Armenian simple folk into increasing the influence and number of Protestants in the area (*ermeni sade dilanını iğfal*).'¹²⁵ When the population itself seemed to be involved in untoward activity their leaders were usually to blame and were qualified as 'confused or silly elements (*sebükmağz takımı*)'.¹²⁶ Nor were Christian missionaries the only source of perfidy and subversion working on the population. The Shi'i missionaries active in the vilayets of Mosul and Basra were also known to be 'perturbing the minds (*tahdiş-i efkar*)' of the people and inviting them to become Shi'a.¹²⁷

This motif of confusing and otherwise troubling minds comes up time and again. Even in mainstream Islam, matters which could provoke controversy were to be treated carefully. When the newspaper *Malumat* published a rebuttal of some anti-Islamic article published in Egypt it was reprimanded for 'confusing the minds' of the common people (*teşviş-i ezhan*) by allowing such debates to appear in the newspaper columns.¹²⁸ Hasan Kayalı has pointed out that this tendency continued into the Young Turk period when, in 1912, 'discussion of political subjects was banned in view of reports from the provinces that religious functionaries who would not be expected to "distinguish good from bad" in political issues were preaching on matters of elections and politics.'¹²⁹

When Fahrettin Paşa, the defender of Medina in 1918, was betrayed by his subalterns who spread about the rumour that he was deranged, his biographer was to characterize these men as 'those who had water on the brain but nonetheless succeeded in tricking some innocents among us'.¹³⁰

Another stock phrase particularly when it came to nomadic populations such as the Bedouin Arabs, or the Kurdish tribes, was that they 'live in a state of nomadism and savagery (*hal-i vahşet ve bedeviyetde yaşarlar*).' The Yezidi Kurds who lived in this state were to be 'gradually brought into the fold of civilization (*pey der pey daire-i medeniyete idhal*)', which was to be done through schooling and the constitution of a municipal authority in their area, Sincar.¹³¹ This vocabulary then, was the expression of both the age-old contradiction between the desert and the town, and the 'mission civilizatrice' mentality of the new Ottoman bureaucracy. As Mardin puts it, the Bedouin had to be 'liberat[ed] from the shackles of community life.'¹³² The sultan himself once told a European ambassador that in eastern Anatolia there were tribes, 'whose comportment is similar to savage tribes in America'.¹³³

The ultimate aim, of course, was to transform them into reliable members of the 'fundamental elements (*unsur-u asli*)'. The obsession with 'bringing civilization and progress to the Arabs (*ürbanın temeddün ve terakkileri*) and 'transforming them into a settled population (*ürbanın tevattınları*), occupied Ottoman officials from the mountains of Iraq to the sands of the Sahara. The main reason why the Ottomans wooed the Senusi sheikhs in the latter area was that they, 'reformed the character (*tehzib-i ahlak*)' of the Bedouin and, 'abated their savagery (*izale-i vahşet*)'.¹³⁴ The nomads were usually considered as something akin to wild creatures, who had to be managed lest untoward developments 'provoke their wild nature and hatred (*tevahhuş ve nefretlerini mucib olmak*)'.¹³⁵

The effort to create reliable military operatives was the source of another recurring formula: that the people should be incorporated into the ranks 'without lamentation (*sızıldısızca*)'. This word comes up every time there is a question of incorporating otherwise unruly peoples into the armed forces. The Yezidis, the North African desert Bedouins, and the Alevis of Anatolia were all to be thus treated. The fact was of course that there was no end of 'lament' on the part of these people.¹³⁶ When it became a matter of open rebellion then it was necessary to 'punish them and frighten like-minded ones (*kendileri tedib ve emsali terhib*).'¹³⁷

When it was a question of a Christian minority who had a complaint, the form was usually 'the complaints mixed with gratitude (*şükran ile memzuc şikayetleri*)', as in the case of the Armenians of Tokad who complained that they were being deprived of schooling.¹³⁸

Also there was a constant effort to present a good, or at least a defendable image towards the outside world. This was usually expressed by the stock phrase that something 'would not look good towards friend or foe (*enzar-ı yar ve ağyara karşu hoş görünmemek*),' or that it would 'cause loose talk (*tervic-i kil-u kal*).'¹³⁹ At a time when the Ottoman state was under constant pressure from the outside world to implement this or that treaty obligation, or to fulfil promises of this or that reform, it was of manifest importance not to provide additional opportunities to exert leverage.

Very often these utterances have what Şerif Mardin has called 'an incantatory quality', and appear to voice the feelings of a ruling elite that is trying to convince itself of its own legitimate right to existence.¹⁴⁰ The very name of the Ottoman state, *memalik-i mahrusa-i şahane*, (the well protected domains of His Imperial Majesty')was a testimony to this state of mind, and a monumental irony, because they were anything but well protected. Every time the danger of the disintegration of the state had to be mentioned it was accompanied by *huda negerde* (may God forbid), almost as though to voice the very words was to tempt providence.¹⁴¹

Another name for the state was '*devlet-i ebed-i müddet-i osmaniye*' the eternal Ottoman state, very akin to *Roma aeterna* or 'la France eternelle' and with the same 'halo of perpetuity'.¹⁴

Conclusion

The most crucial task any project of social and political legitimation must face in an *ancien régime* state is the need to make itself out to be part of 'the natural order of things', 'things as they always have been'. When the population at large accepts the historical inertia of a particular order of things, half the battle has been won; it then becomes a question of maintaining the status quo. The problem arises when the political centre tries to make new and more intensive demands on its population, or the expectations of the people change. Thus, the Hamidian order tried to perpetuate the image that it was what Ernest Gellner called 'the very norm of truth', yet on the other hand it tried to inject new muscle into this image by squeezing society for material and spiritual resources which could only be mobilized at the cost of altering the basic balance.[143]

The symbols drawn from the familiar Islamic traditions had long since been accepted because, as elegantly put by Edward Shils, 'one of the main reasons why what is given by the past is so widely accepted is that it permits life to move along lines set and anticipated from past experience and thus subtly converts the anticipated into the inevitable and the inevitable into the acceptable.'[144]

The problem in the Hamidian Ottoman state was that increased Islamic symbolism and reliance on the caliphate as the 'exemplary centre linking the earthly and celestial hierarchies', was an inadequate substitute for real power.[145]

Chapter Two
The Ottomanization of the Şeriat

In the besieged Medina of late June 1918, the Ottoman commander of the garrison, Fahreddin Paşa, issued an order to his troops to eat locusts. Since April 1918 the Medina garrison had been cut off from the outside world by Arab forces who had captured the stations of the Hijaz Railway linking Medina and Damascus. The garrison, well equipped in terms of armaments, was soon faced with starvation.[1] Yet, even in siege conditions, Fahreddin Paşa set about building a symbolic avenue into the city as a manifestation of the continuity of Ottoman rule. The garrison of Medina, which held out for some three months after the Mondros Armistice of 30 October 1918 when the Ottoman empire surrendered, were fully aware that they were defending the very basis of Ottoman legitimacy, its foundation in bricks and mortar. When asked to surrender after a prolonged siege by Sharifian forces, which lasted until January 1919, ending a three-year last stand since the loss of Mecca in June 1916, the Commander of the Hijaz Expeditionary Force sent the following message to the British command: 'As I am now under the protection of the Prophet and the most High Commander, I am busying myself with strengthening of the defences and the building of the roads and squares in Medina. I beg you not to trouble me with useless requests.'[2] Naci Kıcıman, who took part in the defence of the Sacred Precincts (Haram-ı Şerif), was to express his indignation in his account of the siege, which is something of a crie de coeur of a cosmopolitan late Ottoman whose world was collapsing around him: 'Was this to be the end then? The end of all these centuries of sacred service which it had been our honour to perform since the time of Yavuz (Sultan Selim I)...'[3]

As the monarchies of the nineteenth century, the Ottoman Empire included, came to find themselves increasingly hard pressed to legitimate their existence towards both their own subjects and the outside world, they felt 'the need to provide a new, or at least a supplementary, "national" foundation for this institution.'[4] The Ottoman rulers faced the challenge of nationalism, not only from their Christian subjects and ex-subjects in the Balkans, but also from their own Islamic peoples. As it became objectively necessary to mobilize the Ottoman people along the lines of something coming more and more to resemble an 'Ottoman citizenry', the rules of the game had to be altered accordingly. To use Gellner's phrase, the 'field of tension' between ruler and ruled shifted onto a different plane.[5]

The Tanzimat Edict (*Gülhane Hatt-ı Şerifi*) of 1839 was a critical milestone in Ottoman legal history, for it was nothing less than a public declaration by the sultan that he would respect the rule of law. The term *tanzimat* itself is significant as it actually means reordering.[6] Yet, although the common wisdom is that the edict was more or less entirely the result of Western pressure and the work of grand vizier Reşid Paşa, recent research is turning up evidence that points to an inner dynamic within the Ottoman ruling circles: Butrus Abu Manneh has convincingly shown that the initial formulations which provided the background to the edict emanated from the young Sultan Abdülmecid, who was nowhere near as passive as has always been thought, and his close circle of tutors and advisors.[7] Subsequent legal reforms included the Penal Code (1858), the institution of secular (*nizami*) courts in 1869, the empowering of the Ministry of Justice to control these courts, as well as the introduction of the principle of advocacy (1879).[8] However, what concerns us here is not the creation of legal infastructure, although that process provided the background for what follows. The object of this study is to examine how Islam was used as a mobilising force in a specific context.

At some point after the turn of the nineteenth century Ottoman power holders began increasingly to feel the need to address an appeal to those elements in society who were hitherto only commanded to obey. At that point they found themselves obliged to formulate a common series of reference markers. Ottoman state legitimation became the grey area where these markers were formulated, accepted, or rejected. Their formulation took place in the space where state power and society confronted one another, leading to a process of implicit negotiation between power holders and subjects. Depending on their interests, relative strengths and weaknesses, and the historical conjecture, the outcome was the late nineteenth to early twentiethth-century Middle East. After the Tanzimat reform of 1839 the Ottoman elite increasingly felt that it needed more than passive compliance with orders, and very gradually shifted the basis of legitimacy accordingly. The outcome was something akin to what Hobsbawm has called 'proto-nationalism'.[9]

The emphasis on the sultan's position as caliph of all Muslims served increasingly as an integrative 'icon' in the new 'religio-ethnic identification': 'The most satisfactory icons from a proto-national point of view are obviously those specifically associated with a ... divinely imbued king or emperor whose realm happens to coincide with a future nation.'[10]

The Ottoman statesmen of the late nineteenth century thus came to envisage a sort of 'Imperial supranationalism' in the form of 'Ottomanism'.[11] From being ostensibly supra-religious during the heyday of the Tanzimat (1839–76), Ottomanism would undergo a shift in emphasis to become more Islamic in tone and nuance during the reign of Abdülhamid II.

The Hamidian Hanefi caliphate

Soon after the 1876 'Turkish atrocities in Bulgaria' became the stuff of everyday politics in Britain, the British ambassador to the Sublime Porte, Sir Henry Layard, had a foretaste of what was to come:

> Layard had never seen the sultan angry before ... 'We are accused in Europe of being savages and fanatics ... [Yet] unlike the Czar, I have abstained till now from stirring up a crusade and profiting from religious fanaticism, but the day may come when I can no longer curb the rights and indignation of my people at seeing their co-religionists butchered in Bulgaria and Armenia ...'[12]

One of the foundation stones of Ottoman legitimation ideology, since the conquest of the Hijaz in the sixteenth century, had been the position of the Ottoman sultan as the 'Caliph of all Muslims on Earth' (*Halife-i Muslimin* or *Halife-i Rui-zemin*.)[13] As pointed out by Halil İnalcık, the claim to being the universal Islamic ruler gained new content during the reign of Süleyman the Magnificent because 'what was unique in Süleyman's case was that he believed in making all these [claims] a reality through the tremendous power he held.'[14]

The official myth ran that Sultan Selim I, the conqueror of Egypt, had received the mantle of the caliphate from the last Abbasid caliph in 1517. The myth, however, was by no means uncontested. Arnold points out that the factual basis of the alleged transfer remains somewhat murky.[15] Bernard Lewis has stated categorically that the story of the transfer was ' [without the] slightest shadow of a doubt apocryphal'.[16] İnalcık also refers to the episode as, 'a legend apparently fabricated in the eighteenth century'.[17]

The Ottomanization of the Şeriat 47

Fleischer states that '... Ottoman legitimacy was very weak from the standpoint of both Islamic and nomadic political tradition ... Their success, in fact, owed far more to efficiency than ideology.'[18]

What was to happen, then, when 'efficiency' radically declined from the eighteenth century onwards? How were the Ottoman sultans to sustain legitimacy in a world context where their position was under threat not only from the outside, but also from their own Muslim population?[19] The answer was the following: during the reign of Abdülhamid II (1876–1909) the Ottoman caliphate launched a major initiative aimed at commanding a new basis of solidarity among its Islamic subjects. This effort was very akin to policies attempted by the other legitimist monarchies of the time such as the Habsburgs and the Romanovs. The policy that Seton-Watson has called 'official nationalism' was an application of 'national' motifs by the ideologically besieged dynasties ruling multi-ethnic empires.[20] In its own context, and using its own historical colouring, the Ottoman caliphate attempted to imbue itself with a new mystique, a new self image. Duguid puts this new emphasis of the Hamidian era on the key concepts of 'unity' and 'survival':

> What is distinctive to the Hamidian period as opposed to that of Selim III, Mahmud II, or the Tanzimat, is that (the policy of reforms and changes) were consistently subordinated to a higher felt need, that for unity among the Muslim population of the Empire. In terms of policies and priorities, 1878 represents a fundamental shift in the Ottoman self view.[21]

It is significant that Abdülhamid's most feared enemies, the British colonial authorities, also referred to '... The new-fangled pretension that the Sultan of Turkey is Khalifeh of Islam ...'[22]

Abdülhamid was able to capitalize on a general feeling of impending doom and despondency among the people as province after province was torn from the empire.[23] The situation led Albert Hourani to comment that: 'The loss of most of the European provinces changed the nature of the empire. Even more than before it appeared to its Muslim citizens, whether Turks or Arabs, as the last manifestation of the political independence of a Muslim world beleaguered by enemies.'[24]

Islamic legitimation therefore came to be seen as essentially a 'defensive' position. As Huri İslamoğlu İnan accurately notes:

> Legitimation now became a defensive ideology consciously defined around Islamic motifs ... Against the unjust order imposed by the West, Islam, as a particularistic national ideology, came to stand for justice and equity. It is important to place the institution of the caliphate, and Islamic nationalism as it was consciously fashioned in the Hamidian period, in this context.[25]

In addition, since the Tanzimat Edict of 1839 had declared that Muslims and Christians were equal before the law, serious resentment had been fostered among Muslims who increasingly felt their position of superiority under the Şeriat was being undermined.[26]

It was in this setting that the 'new orthodoxy' based on the Hanefi *mezheb* as the official ideology was to take shape. The Hanefi school of Islamic jurisprudence had always been the closest to the hearts of the Ottoman rulers as the 'official belief' (*mezheb-i resmiye*).[27] The reason for this preference was the Hanefi interpretation of the caliphate, whereby a strong and able ruler was to be recognized as the legitimate sovereign of all Muslims on the condition that he protected Islam and upheld the Şeriat even if he was not from the original sacred Arab clan of Qureish.[28] Fleischer has pointed out that the official title of the Ottoman sultan as the 'Shadow of God on Earth' (*zill allah fi'l arz*) was a late invention based on the need to reconcile the steppe tradition of the Turks with the reality of aspirations to high Islamic universality: 'Universal sovereignty ... is the highest form of kingship, the legitimacy of which cannot be denied because such striking success gives tangible evidence of God's will.'[29]

During the reign of Abdülhamid II there occurred a self-conscious attempt on the part of Ottoman bureaucrat/intellectuals to recharge and redefine basic Islamic institutions, namely the Şeriat and the caliphate, as the basis of the quest for a new Imperial/national identity. No less an observer than the famous Dutch Orientalist, Snouck Hurgronje was to comment:

> The concession made by the Turkish Government in the period of their victories ... recognized in the conquered provinces that, along with the Hanafite, a judge belonging to the native rite should be appointed, (this) has nowadays [1885–86] come to be considered unnecessary ... The Turkish Government has suppressed them all ... except the Hanafite who became the sole judge in the Law of Religion.[30]

Süleyman Hüsnü Paşa, to whom we have already referred, had very interesting views on the subject. From political exile in Iraq he was to pen an extremely detailed memoranduwm, dated 7 April 1892, relating to measures to be undertaken by the state to ensure the integration of heterodox and heretical elements into the official belief.[31] After offering a rather sophisticated breakdown of the complex ethnic mosaic of Iraq which included Turks, Kurds, Arabs, Chaldeans, Nestorians, Armenians and Jews distributed across various sects and sub-sects of Islam and Christianity he commented: 'As can be seen from the above the elements belonging to the official faith and language of the state are in a clear minority whereas the majority falls to the hordes of the opposition.'[32]

This situation was to be remedied by systematic propaganda and the 'correction of the beliefs (*tashih-i akaid*)' of the 'heretics' or 'deviants' (*fırak-ı dalle*). (The term 'correction of beliefs' would become something of a watchword in the Hamidian regime.) In order to accomplish this the Ottoman state should, he proposed, sponsor the writing of a *Book of Beliefs* (*Kitab-ul Akaid*), to consist of some fifteen chapters, each dealing with one unorthodox element. The paşa was rather generous in his wisdom and the projected chapters of the book he suggested ranged from obvious targets such as the Shi'a through Christianity, Judaism to 'the pagan practices of Indo-China'.[33] It is also significant that one of the heretical beliefs was positivism referred to as 'the new philosophy (*felsefe-i cedide*)'. For this reason it was recommended that the book also be translated into French.[34]

Those who took up their pens in defence of the 'official faith' did so with the knowledge that the written word held a power to reach a far broader public than ever before through the world-wide distribution of newspapers and books. As Mardin has pointed out, what can only be described as social mobilization literature of an officially approved kind, and 'pocket libraries', reached even hitherto inaccessible areas such as Van in eastern Anatolia in the 1890s.[35] Much of this literature was deliberately written in relatively simple language with a view to reaching a popular audience. The 'official faith' was also disseminated far and wide through the press.[36] Similarly,'The tone and trend of Turkish papers is to intensify the hold of the Sovereign and Khalif on the imagination of the 'true believers', especially in the lower classes, even in the outlying districts of his extensive dominions.'[37] This attitude was also reflected in social mobilization literature as exemplified by the work of an obscure religious functionary from a small Anatolian town which included the comment, '... Thanks to the newspapers the brilliant rays of the One True Faith have even reached into Europe where it is now recognized that Islam is a scientific great religion (*fenni bir din-i ali*) ...'³⁸

The Ottomanization of the Şeriat

Ottoman legitimation also came to rely on a process that can only be described as the 'Ottomanization of the *Şeriat*'. The very fact that the Ottoman ruling elite felt the need to standardize and regularize *şer'i* rulings is indicative of their desire to rationalize and 'naturalize' Islamic practice. This attitude is best seen in the works of Ahmed Cevdet Paşa, and particularly in his codification of *fıkh* rulings, the *Mecelle*.³⁹ In the introduction to this monumental work, Cevdet Paşa points out that 'civilized and advanced countries (*medeni ve müterakki milletler*)' have constitutions that deal with civil law. However, he contends, because of changing times and the institution of civil law and civil courts (*nizamiye mahkemeleri*), judges were no longer trained in religious law, and yet they still had to refer to it: 'As indeed it has become difficult these days to find those talented in the *şer'i* science, it is equally difficult to find judges of the civil courts who are versed in the Şeriat. Even more striking is the lack of properly qualified *kadıs*, to staff the religious courts'.⁴⁰ The paşa also bemoaned the fact that Hanefi rulings were not systematically codified and existed 'in a state of disarray' (*dağınık bir halde olup*), something that had now come to be deemed undesirable.⁴¹ Cevdet Paşa took pains to point out that his effort at codification was a response to the, 'need to bring the science of *fıkh* up to date, and render it applicable to the needs of modern times.' The collection of Hanefi *fıkh* rulings in one source would, therefore, 'be a source of reference to all officials who would thus be able to accord their practice with the *Şeriat*'.⁴² The Şeriat would, as Brinkley Messick has pointed out, thus lose its 'open ended' nature whereby it had put the emphasis on the individual jurist, who had been given considerable leeway in interpretation. The aim was a standardization of rulings which would also be disseminated to the far corners of the empire and as such 'the legal text also foreshadowed the Western notion of the responsibility to the law of the ordinary individual, the citizen.'⁴³

Although Cevdet Paşa and his collaborators sought to standardize legal practice, in outlying distant provinces such as Iraq and Yemen the attempt to forge closer ideological effective links with the centre often met with great difficulties, particularly in Yemen which was in an almost constant state of rebellion. A report from the Yemen's provincial capital, San'a, dated 6 April 1884, referred to a petition of complaint prepared by one Kadı Hüseyin Çağman, a leading jurist of the area. Among the *kadı's* many complaints was the striking appeal that Istanbul reduce the number of civil courts (*nizamiye mahkemeleri*) in the Yemen and leave the population to seek justice in the *şer'i* courts. The petition and the accompanying letter from San'a both stated that, '... Since the people of the Yemen became Muslim some thirteen hundred years ago they have been seeking justice in *şer'i* courts, it is therefore injurious to the interests of both the local people and the state to insist that they use civil courts ...' It was, moreover, advised that the state take pains to ensure that it appoint to the province, '... Only those officials whose religious probity is beyond reproach.'[44]

It would appear, however, that even late in the century, the Ottomans were experiencing difficulties staffing government posts in Yemen. A memorandum by the vali, dated 31 October 1898, complained bitterly that although he had tried to fill lower level posts with Yemenis, this had not proved workable, 'because those who speak the official language of the state are so few'.[45]

Yet in Yemen, while a *modus vivendi* was established between the Hanefi and Shafi'i *mezhebs* and the Ottoman administration received the active support of the Sha'afi regions, in upper Yemen they met with constant hostility from the Zaidi imams who considered them 'foreigners'. Messick has pointed out that the ideological fault lines between the Turks and the Yemeni population were determined by their respective interpretations of the *Şeriat*: 'Refusing to allow the imams the discursive high ground, the Ottomans stoutly defended the empire's long-standing commitment to uphold the *shari'a* and mobilized a locally tailored *shari'a* politics of their own to counter that of the imams.'[46]

In an extensive report written by Osman Nuri Paşa, one of the most famous of Ottoman provincial administrators of the late nineteenth century, the emphasis is clearly placed on the 'civilizing' influence of the religious courts under Ottoman administration.[47] In a conversation with an Arab sheikh of the Hijaz, Osman Nuri Paşa urges him to, 'abandon his tribal habits and laws and come into the civilizing fold of the Şeriat.' There ensues a very interesting exchange in which the men discuss the taking of the lives of two young lovers who have eloped without the blessing of their elders. Upon the insistence of the sheikh the exasperated paşa entreats him to see reason: 'O Sheikh! What manner of law is this Arab law of yours to take precedence over the sacred law of the Şeriat!'[48]

Osman Nuri Paşa was to write in 1888 that the secular courts were 'drawing the hatred and provoking the fear and timidity of the local population,' who had always sought justice in şer'i courts. It was therefore imperative that the secular courts be given up in Yemen, otherwise 'it will be impossible to fulfil the aim of the state which is to win the hearts of the people to the projects of reform.'[49] In another detailed memorandum Osman Nuri Paşa recounted how he had abrogated the secular courts in the Hijaz and instituted şer'i courts in their place.[50] He also gave a detailed account of his efforts to win the hearts of the local population: 'Because this (institution of the religious courts) made it possible to put a stop to the numerous blood feuds in the area they were very grateful.' The paşa also emphasized that it was advisable to use the local influence of the sheikhs and sharifs as this influence used to favour the interests of the state meant that the desired objectives could be achieved without spilling blood.'

The primacy of the 'Ottomanized Şeriat' occurs throughout the documentation of the period. On 27 June 1882 the grand vizier's office prepared a memorandum stating that all care should be taken to ensure that proper procedure and decorum be observed in the legal procedures in the Hijaz. It was determined that all cases be tried according to high Islam and very few be left over to tribal customs. A Council of Inquiry (Divan-ı Tedkik-i Ahkam) was to be established which was to be presided over by the *kadı*, and its members were to be chosen from among local experts in Islamic jurisprudence. Istanbul was to ensure that only the most qualified *kadıs* were to be sent to the Hijaz and it was specifically stated that, 'All matters should be judged according to the sacred precepts of the Şeriat.'[51]

The Şeriat as the embodiment of order contrasted with local custom: the irony was that the same attitude was to be reflected in the policy of colonial regimes which replaced the Ottomans in the region: 'From the point of view of the colonizers, custom had to be either standardized or abolished altogether in favour of a unified legal system. Although the *Shari'a* was considered disorderly relative to Western law, when compared to 'custom' it appeared orderly.'[52]

The effort to monopolize official sacrality

Another striking feature of late Ottoman legitimation is the effort to monopolize and control official sacrality. This is best illustrated by the effort to control the printing and importation of the Holy Qur'an. On 15 December 1897, the Minister of Education Zühdü Paşa sent a memorandum to the office of the şeyhülislam reporting that Muslim subjects of Iran and Russia had made official applications to for the printing and sale of the Qur'an.[53] The minister reiterated that the law of 1276 (1858–60) specifically forbade the importation and sale of Qur'ans coming from Iran: 'It is well known that the Iranians have been bringing in copies of the Holy Qur'an into Ottoman dominions, particularly to the Seat of the Holy Caliphate (*dar-ul hilafet-i aliyye*). Here they secretly print them and circulate them. It is quite unnecessary to remind you that this practice is strictly forbidden.' It was accordingly determined that all Qur'ans would henceforth be printed at the official press.[54]

Although it is understandable that the Sunni Ottoman caliphate should be wary of Qur'ans produced by Shi'i hands, the same interdict applied to Qur'ans emanating from Sunni Kazan, and even the seat of high Islam, the al-Azhar *medrese* in Egypt: 'The importation of Qur'ans ... coming from Egypt is likewise forbidden according to long established practice.'[55] The historically specific character of the Ottoman practice comes out further on in the memorandum:

> ... Although it seems inauspicious to forbid the printing of Qur'ans to one who is of the *sunna*, if we open this door it will mean that we will be opening it to any Muslim from Kazan or India or Algeria ... This will mean unforeseeable dangers for the Holy Word which has survived untarnished for some thirteen hundred years. Particularly since these are troubled times in which the foreigner's calumnious views regarding the Holy Text multiply ... The matter may go well beyond the printing of the Qur'an and, God forbid, create untold complications for the Sublime State.

It was therefore determined that a commission for the Inspection of Qur'ans (Tedkik-i Müshaf-ı Şerif Komisyonu) should be established, and all publication of the Qur'an be undertaken only with its approval.[56]

The repetition of the orders over the years to prevent the printing of Qur'ans by 'Iranians and Russians ' indicates that the matter was never resolved and continued to be a source of worry. On 18 October 1901, the

Ministry of Education pointed out in a memorandum that it had been 'preoccupied for some time with these Iranians and Russians, and if they are granted permission, this will cause a very unfortunate precedent, actually becoming a matter of state.' The Commission for Inspection of Qur'ans was charged in no uncertain terms to:

> ... pay close attention to this matter of extreme importance. If we open this door, the Iranian, Algerian, and Russian foreigners, even though they are Sunnis, will cause a very dangerous precedent, leading, God forbid! to the Holy Text suffering various falsifications (*envai tahrifat*) in these troubled times when conflicting opinions and the agitations of the foreigners are on the increase ... (*efkar-ı mütenevvia ve ecnebiyenin şu zaman-ı galeyanında*.)[57]

In referring to 'foreigners ' or 'non-Ottoman Muslims', the minister was clearly making a point which runs throughout the Ottoman documentation of this period: that the legitimacy of the Ottoman caliphate was under threat, and to a considerable extent the threat emanated from Muslims living under Christian rule who could be manipulated to challenge Ottoman legitimacy. One might recall at this juncture that this document was prepared at approximately the same time that talk of the 'Arab caliphate' was gaining currency in Western orientalist/colonial circles. The reference to 'troubled times' and loose talk about Islam almost certainly reflect the degree of anxiety caused by these stirrings of ominous portent with which the Ottomans were only too familiar.

The obsession with foreign intrigue surrounding the Qur'an could be quite naive. At one point the palace actually ordered the Ottoman embassy in Stockholm to buy up any copies of the Qur'an in Sweden and Norway that they could lay their hands on, as 'it is improper for the Holy Book to be in foreign hands'. The ambassador replied in a somewhat embarrassed tone that the only copies were rare collectors' items in public libraries which would not consider selling them, and that 'public opinion here is not very well disposed to the Sublime State, making this a very delicate matter.'[58]

A well known opponent of the Hamidian regime, the philosopher and Young Turk Rıza Tevfik, also drew attention to the special pains the government took to control the circulation and content of books dealing with Islamic jurisprudence, noting in a somewhat ironic tone that more obviously 'harmful' publications such as the works of Büchner, Darwin, Spencer and Mill were sold freely in the Istanbul bookshops. He claims in a particularly scathing way that even the *Mızraklı İlmihal*, the basic school text dealing with the caliphate and legitimate government in Islam, was 'altered by that sham of a government, for which the British severely criticized them.' It is significant here that Tevfik should refer to the British, indicating that the fears of the government were not unfounded.[59]

The campaign against the Ottoman caliphate, and the alternative based on the Arab caliphate, gained momentum after Abdülhamid ascended the throne. Sir James Redhouse, the famous lexicographer, was to speak out in support of the Ottoman claim:

> The title is generally known and adopted by the orthodox Muslim world, by the Sunni church universal ... Their general acceptance has probably resulted in part from a consideration of the power of the Ottoman empire, and in part from its possession of the two holy cities of Makka and Madina ... one of (the sultan's) most valued titles being Khadimu-l Haramayni-'sh-sharifayn - Servant of the two Sacred Precincts.[60]

Thus, like the *Şeriat*, the conception of the caliphate became much more political than religious. It was no longer enough to be a Muslim, or indeed a Sunni.

Nothing illustrates this better than the case of the Algerians seeking asylum in Ottoman dominions after the French invasion of Algeria. The issue which caused the Ottomans considerable headache was the legal status of Algerians who had immigrated to the province of Syria, ostensibly escaping from the *dar ul harb*. Some of these elements worked to live in Ottoman dominions while conserving their French passports, thus benefiting from special privileges as French subjects living in Ottoman lands. On 20 November 1889, the Sublime Porte issued a decree stating that they would be required to choose within two years of their arrival whether to remain French citizens and leave, or to be automatically considered Ottoman citizens and stay. The Algerians of French allegiance would be forbidden to marry Ottoman women, and any Algerian contravening this regulation 'would be treated according to the regulations pertaining to Iranians' and would be forced to leave Ottoman soil.[61]

A Frenchman from Algeria, Gervais Courtellemont, who went on the *haj* in 1890 posing as a convert, noted that everywhere he and his guide were followed and treated with suspicion. Upon landing in Jeddah, 'From the very first outing we were treated as suspects, and questioned as if by chance in the shops where we made our purchases ... Not a soul invited us in for a meal ... a bad sign in an Arab land! Yes, decidedly, I was a suspect!'[62]

Another critical issue in this context was the acquisition of land and property in the Hijaz by non-Ottoman Muslims. On 7 April 1882 the Council of State prepared a memorandum where it reiterated the ban on the acquisition of property by Indian, Algerian and Russian Muslims. The reason stated was fear of potential fifth column activities:

> If we remain indifferent to the accumulation of property by devious means in the hands of foreign Muslims, with the passage of time we may find that much of the Holy Lands have been acquired by the subjects of foreign powers. Then, the foreigners, as is their wont, after lying in waiting for some time, will suddenly be upon us at the slightest opportunity and excuse and will proceed to make the most preposterous of claims.[63]

The long-time governor of the Hijaz, Osman Nuri Paşa, who served in the Yemen and Hijaz vilayets in the 1880s, was also obsessed with what he considered to be slack behaviour on the part of the government on the question of the accumulation of property in the hands of foreign Muslims. The paşa lamented the fact that 'most of the productive resources in this province (the Hijaz) are passing into foreign hands and this is having the shameful consequence of our own people working for foreigners.'[64] He also complained that Javanese and British Indian subjects were staying far beyond the time necessary for the pilgrimage, and benefiting from exemption from taxation while they studied in state schools, thus using scarce resources while not paying for them. 'It is therefore obvious that all those living in these lands should abide by the laws of the state and fulfil their tax obligations.'[65]

Courtellemont also noted that, 'Presently all the trades (sale of cloth, tools, manufactured objects) are in the hands of Indians and Javanese established in Jeddah and in Mecca. These people trade with the Dutch Indies and British India and no doubt, turn a considerable profit.'[66] Another factor noted by Courtellemont was 'the numerous printing presses owned by Indians who are serious competition for the local presses.'[67]

Ottoman versus non-Ottoman Muslims in the Hijaz

The confrontation between Ottoman and 'foreign' Muslims can also be traced through the archives of the Government of India. It is ironic that Queen Victoria's title as Empress of India, and Abdülhamid's title as *Hadem ül-Haremeyn* for the Hijaz used similar symbolic imagery. In the Ottoman context, this found symbolic emphasis in the official formula, 'the jewel in the crown of the exalted caliphate' (*gevher-i iklil-i hilafet-i seniyye*), which was the official title of the Vilayet of Hijaz.[68] The interesting aspect of this title used in conjunction with the Hijaz, is that it is almost an echo of the 'jewel in the crown' title referring to Queen Victoria's crown in her capacity as Empress of India.[69]

The British consul in Jeddah wrote on 7 May 1882 that the Ottoman ban on foreign Muslims' acquisition of property in the Hijaz was causing considerable discomfort among British Indian subjects. The consul noted that this new state of affairs might well cause poorer Indians to take up Ottoman nationality, although 'the better to do will probably be unwilling to sacrifice British protection, and considerable annoyance is caused among them.'[70]

Even in the matter of charitable gifts to the holy places the sultan showed the same jealousy. The British consul at Jeddah reported in a somewhat grieved tone that a silver ladder for the door of the Ka'ba 'worth 45,000 rupees' sent by the Nawab of Rampur had been turned down because ' the Sultan ... objected to a foreign subject [making such gifts] and sent orders that no such a one should have the privilege.'[71] The reflection of the issue in Ottoman documentation leaves no doubt about the basis for the sultan's exclusivism: 'All such gifts can only be made by the Exalted Personage of the Caliph who alone holds the august title of Protector of the Holy Places. No foreign ruler has the right to partake of this glory.'[72]

A major concern was that many of the *hajis* overstayed their welcome, becoming a drain on already scarce resources and, in the case of rich Indians who attempted to settle, a disturbing alternative focus for loyalty. At the end of the *haj* rites, town criers would announce the departure dates of caravans, encouraging people to leave. In the case of a prominent Indian nawab: 'He had brought with him great treasures with the intention of settling permanently in the Holy City. One evening after prayers in the Haram, he was approached by Abd El Montaleb [sic] who asked in very severe language why he was thus acting against practice by prolonging his stay.'[73]

The same jealousy and suspicion was in evidence towards Russian Muslims. The initial debate over the printing of Qur'ans became confused with a debate about who was qualified to do so when a Muslim Russian subject had applied to print Qur'ans.[74] Like the British, the Russian government also sought to protect what it saw as the interests of its subjects. In May 1894, a Hacı Mirza Mehmed arrived in Istanbul accompanying a crate which had been sent by the Emir of Bukhara to the Hijaz. The Russian embassy intervened with the Ottoman customs authorities to allow the crate transit without opening it for inspection, as ' ... This would break the hearts of the Muslims of Bukhara.'[75] The Ottoman government had to content itself with a rather lame face-saving solution: Mr Maksimoff, the dragoman of the Russian embassy, swore on his honour that the crate only contained fine cloths and 'that the crate did not contain any harmful goods (*eşyayı muzırra*)'.[76]

Rulers of independent Muslim states were also a problem. On 21 March 1891 it was reported that the Crown Prince of Morocco intended to go on the *haj* with a large entourage and that he '... would be bearing many gifts for the notables of the Hijaz,' Although it was admitted that it was his religious right to go on the pilgrimage, the fact that he would be bearing so many gifts 'gives rise to the suspicion that he has political intentions.' It was also stated that this suspicion arose because the ruler of Morocco had 'previously sent an envoy to Istanbul asking that he be permitted to buy property in the Hijaz and establish a pious foundation (*vakf*) there.' It is also significant that on this issue the Ottoman government did not hesitate to ask the assistance of a Christian power, Spain, which had designs on Morocco. The Ottoman ambassador in Madrid was instructed to ' ... make discreet inquiries of the Spanish Foreign Ministry to determine the truth of the matter.'[77] The unstated reason for this hesitancy bordering on fear was the fact that the sultans of Morocco had always claimed the caliphate as their own.[78]

Egypt was another problem. Although it was still officially a part of the Ottoman Empire ruled by a special governor, since the midle of the century Egypt had become a *de facto* independent state.[79] Furthermore, the Porte had never formally recognized the British occupation of Egypt in 1882, which put an end to its autonomy, and it was increasingly worried by British claims to defend the interests of Khedive Abbas Hilmi Paşa, who began to parade himself as an alternative caliph and protector of the holy cities. Using the young khedive as a stalking horse, the British consul, the domineering Lord Cromer, began to harass Ottoman interests in the

Hijaz and on the Ottoman–Egyptian border in Ottoman Cyraneica (Libya). This was precisely the sort of fifth-column activity that had caused Abdülhamid's nightmares.[80]

From time to time, the palace would receive intelligence to the effect that, 'The Khedive of Egypt is sending agents into the provinces of Syria and Yemen in order to cause uprisings leading to the annexation of these provinces by Egypt.' Repeated orders would be isssued to take the necessary measures to 'stop this intrigue'.[81]

In this context, any development emanating from Egypt which could even in the most remote sense be injurious to the sultan's prestige in the Hijaz, was to be nipped in the bud if at all possible. In the winter of 1886 a bad harvest in Egypt created the possibility that the country would not be able to send the Hijaz the traditional yearly stock of provisions, and the suggestion was made that the Holy Lands should be supplied from India as an alternative. The sultan himself took a hand in insisting that, 'The provisioning of the Hijaz from Bombay smacks of British intrigues as it will inevitably mean the increase of British prestige in the area.'[82]

The response to threats from colonial powers also subsumed a reappraisal of the Ottoman centre's relationship to this hitherto privileged province. A long memorandum written by Osman Nuri Paşa is worth looking into in some detail at this point.[83] Dated 18 July 1885, the memorandum dwells at length on reform measures to be taken in the Hijaz and other Arab provinces. The paşa states that the majority of the armies stationed in the Hijaz, Bingazi and Yemen were made up of 'the fundamental elements' (unsur-i asli) of the empire who were, 'the Turks and Anatolian peoples', who paid 'the blood tax', that is to say, fought in the armies. It was therefore imperative that the Hijaz be brought into line as a regular province of the empire and its population be made to contribute to its defence.[84] Osman Nuri Paşa was very evidently imbued with the mobilizing ethic of the nineteenth century which informed so much of late Ottoman statecraft:

> Although it is possible to transform all of the Muslim population into a fundamental element, events have shown that the time is not yet ripe. Even if it were possible today to blend all the Muslim tribes and nations together by causing them to lose their special characteristics through the application of rigorous policies, they would still be no more than the boughs and branches of the tree whose trunk would still be constituted by the Turks.[85]

Indeed, the over-representation of the Turks in the armies stationed in the Arab provinces meant that they were being withdrawn from the productive labour force in their own regions: 'those who are conversant in the science of economics (*ilm-i tedbir-i servet*) will know that this causes grievous loss to state revenues.' Osman Nuri Paşa also emphasized the danger of property accumulation in the hands of Javanese, Indian and Russian Muslims.[86] This 'Physiocratic' emphasis on productivity is thus combined with 'Ibn-Khaldunian' imagery and a proto-nationalistic appreciation of the nature of the late Ottoman state.[87]

If the Ottoman sultan were to have credibility in the eyes of Muslims as the 'Protector of the Faithful' he had to be seen to be providing for their well being. This meant above all guaranteeing the security of the pilgrimage to the holy cities.[88] It also meant that he had to ensure a just and fair basis for economic interchange during the *haj* season. The Hijazi natives, from the Bedouin who raided and pillaged caravans, to the local *mutawwaf* or guides, were notorious for overcharging pilgrims.[89] Every year Istanbul would issue orders and injunctions forbidding the charging of exorbitant rates for camel hire and 'guidance fees'.[90] The very fact of their repetition indicates, however, that the abuses continued.

An additional embarrassment was the fact that non-Ottoman Muslims would appeal to the protection of Christian governments, a move that was regarded as damaging to Ottoman prestige as the protector of pilgrims.[91] The state had to be seen to be performing its duty and due care was taken to publicize the construction of official buildings such as hostels in the local press.[92] It would appear that the symbolic communication worked both ways; sometimes the Hijazis themselves would build and consecrate a kiosk, 'In the honour of the descendent of the Protector of the *Shari'a*, our Benefactor unto whom obedience and loyalty are due.' Such an occasion was reported on 14 September 1892, on the occasion of the sixteenth accession anniversary of the sultan.[93]

Efforts to defend the Hijaz

As talk of the 'Arab caliphate' spread from the early 1880s onwards, the Sublime Porte felt the need to give special emphasis to the defence of the seat of its legitimating ideology. The most concrete symbol of this preoccupation was the Hijaz Railway.[94] Begun in the 1890s, it became something of a pet scheme for Abdülhamid, who hoped to combine symbolic achievement with logistical advantage. He took great pains to ensure that the project not be dependent on foreign capital and technology, and that each stage of its completion be well publicized in the Turkish and world press.[95]

Another measure considered was the creation of a special 'Hijaz Fleet' to defend the coasts of the vilayet. An order was to be placed with European shipyards for specially constructed coast-guard vessels which would be cheap to run (using both sail and steam), and would be used for policing the Red Sea and Persian Gulf coasts.[96] Although Abdülhamid deliberately set aside the large and costly fleet his uncle Abdülaziz had built up, he did invest in coastal defence and cheap but efficient coastal defence craft: 'Even otherwise critical observers of the sultan's naval policy conceded that the torpedo-boat flotilla was kept up to scratch.'[97]

By the 1880s the primary external threat to the unity of the empire was seen to emanate from that ever-present *bête noire* of late Ottoman politics – 'British intrigue'. Sometimes imaginary, sometimes all too real, this factor was to plague Abdülhamid for all his reign. The Hijaz, distant and vulnerable, was the object of the sultan's worst fears, the most recurring theme in them being the spectre of an 'Arab caliphate'.

Indeed, the Ottoman press mounted a pre-emptive propaganda campaign against any designs the British may have had in the area. In the early 1880s there were frequent references in papers like the Arabic semi-official *al-Cawaib* to the position of the sultan as Caliph of Islam receiving recognition in Zanzibar and Oman. This caused something of a stir in British circles. The British consul in Zanzibar reported on several occasions that he had received the personal assurance of the Sultan of Zanzibar that he had no special regard for the Ottoman sultan: 'Neither Zanzibar nor the mother province of Oman ever rendered allegiance to the Ottoman sultans ... The surreptitious attempts now being made by some of the papers (in Istanbul) are evidently designed to serve a political purpose – namely that of representing the whole of the Moslem world as subject to the nominal Khalifate of Islam.'[98]

The British consul in Muscat reported that he had confronted the Emir of Muscat with the *al-Cawaib* article and that the latter had denied any correspondence with the sultan.[99] The political resident in the Persian Gulf also reported that the people of Oman were mostly of the Ibadi sect, and that some even inclined to Wahhabism, and that they therefore totally rejected Turkish claims.[100]

The Anglo–Turkish struggle was also joined at the other extremity of the Arabian Peninsula, in the borderlands between British-held Aden and

Ottoman Yemen.¹⁰¹ On 4 October 1880, the Residency at Aden reported that the Ottoman commander of San'a had 'appropriated' several villages belonging to the Emir of Zhali, Sheikh Ali Mokhbil, a British client ruler. The resident suggested that 'the yearly subsidy' of L.50 paid to the emir should be slightly increased as his territory formed the border between British and Turkish possessions.¹⁰² A few months later the matter flared up again, and on 14 February 1881 the Aden Residency reported that 'the border issue' was reaching critical proportions as the Turks had been 'taking possession of different villages as (the) occasion offers'. This brought with it the danger that if they were not stopped, 'There is no saying to what lengths their rule might extend.'¹⁰³ Of course, as far as the 'Turks' were concerned, they were doing no more than taking back what was theirs. The resident enclosed a letter from the Ottoman governor general of Yemen and *müşir* of the Seventh Army Corps, Ismail Hakkı Paşa. The letter was a petition from the local people: 'On our oath we say that even if we are ruined ... and none of us remain alive, still we do not agree to be disobedient to the Porte Government, who serves the two Harams ... We will never bend our course to the English ... No one of us shall alter the Mussulman's way and will enter the English way.' The Viceroy of India, acting on this information, decided to ratify the agreement with Ali Mokhbil and increased his subsidy from 50 to 100 pounds sterling per annum.¹⁰⁴

The Government of India were particularly worried about what they called, 'The long cherished plan for the extension of Turkish authority along the Arabian coast and the Persian Gulf ...' This would lead to a situation where, 'Very important British interests in the Persian Gulf ... would at once become affected.'¹⁰⁵

The somewhat 'cloak and dagger' undertakings of the British in the area tended to justify the sultan's suspicions. On 21 December 1887, the grand vizier Kamil Paşa was ordered to look into the truth of the rumour that the 'Sudanese rebel army under Osman Dikna is preparing to invest Suakin and thence to attack the Hijaz ...' The sultan had received information that this was '... a British plot to use the Sudanese rebels to ... transfer the caliphate to an Arab government.'¹⁰⁶ Kamil Paşa responded that the rumour was somewhat off the mark as the British and Sudanese had just been bitter enemies and there was no indication that this enmity had abated. The sultan does not seem to have been satisfied, because on the same day Kamil Paşa again wrote that the rumour lacked substance as the Sudanese rebels had no means of sea transport. Even if they commandeered fishing vessels, the Ottoman gunship stationed in Jeddah was more than capable of dealing with them. Moreover, there was no indication that the rebels had any support among the Hijazi population.[107]

Some six months later the sultan's fears had still not abated. Kamil Paşa again pointed out that the rebels were not united and were not capable of mounting an amphibious operation. The paşa stated that the real danger to the Hijaz was not from the Red Sea but from the east, from Muscat. The grand vizier was very firm in pointing out that, ' ... For some time now the British have been fostering good relations with the Emir of Muscat whom we have neglected. There is every indication that the government of India had been supplying him with arms.'[108] Set against the information available from British sources it emerges that Kamil Paşa was certainly justified in his warnings against British activity in Muscat.

Militant mysticism

Towards the end of the nineteenth century the 'legitimacy crisis' of the Ottoman empire seems to be compounded by a split in the ranks of the legitimizers, the *ulema*. Mardin has noted that Abdülhamid, wary of the de-legitimizing power of the high *ulema*, as shown in their sanction for the deposition of his uncle Abdülaziz, let them 'sink into a morass'.[109] This meant that the lower *ulema* found a new avenue of mobility through the *tekkes* and the officially sanctioned media.[110]

While there was a primary emphasis on Sunni orthodoxy in the reign of Abdülhamid, one of the sultan's major propaganda weapons were the Sufi sheikhs. During the 1877–78 Russo-Turkish war, the Nakşibendi sheikh Hacı Fehim Efendi from Erzincan had personally fought in the Caucasus campaign.[111] Another Nakşibendi, Ubeydullah Efendi, had organized the local Kurds as an irregular force, some 2, 000 strong. Also Sheikh Ahmed Ziyauddin Gümüşhanevi had fought at the Batum front. These men were also active in 'promoting unity among the population ...' through the establishment of schools.[112]

Yet, as the absolute rule of the sultan became established, firebrand sheikhs wandering about uncontrolled came to be looked upon with disfavour. On 21 June 1887, it was reported from the vilayet of Ankara that a certain Dağıstani, Ahmed Efendi, had established himself near Ankara and had gathered about him some 2,000 followers. The report remarked: 'This number being likely to increase ... it is quite clear that this is not desirable.'It was therefore determined that the sheikh be given a stipend and removed to Damascus.¹¹³

Religious fervour and zeal were acceptable as long as they did not involve a sheikh establishing himself as an independent focus of allegiance. On 1 December 1890, it was reported that the famous Nakşibendi sheikh, Gümüşhanevi Ahmed Efendi had been investigated at the order of the sultan. It had been established that the worthy sheikh had something of a murky past. In the 1860s and 1870s Ahmed Gümüşhanevi had established himself at the Fatma Sultan Mosque in the vicinity of the Sublime Porte, where he had formed a circle of followers. This group had become exclusively devoted to Sheikh Ahmed, to the extent of beating up other religious figures who disagreed with him. What is more, they had established themselves in the Fatma Sultan mosque to the point of: 'dwelling permanently therein and treating the Caliph's chamber in the said mosque as a sort of bachelors' lair (*bekar odası*)'.¹¹⁴

There had been repeated efforts in the past to remove Gümüşhanevi from the capital, but he had been saved by the intervention of various highly placed ladies to whom he had been a source of 'spiritual solace'. Gümüşhanevi had collected one thousand *lira* from a prominent lady who had been told he was going to build a *tekke*, yet he had proceeded to construct a sixteen-room *konak* opposite the Sublime Porte and filled it with his followers. Even after the building was taken away from him because he had constructed it under false pretences, his followers had gradually moved back in and re-established themselves. The report deemed it very undesirable that this sort of thing should go on.¹¹⁵ Yet, despite this report, Gümüşhanevi remained close to palace circles and continued to preach in his *tekke* where he died in 1894. As a sign of special favour he was buried in the courtyard of the Süleymaniye Mosque. This special favour may well have been the result of the fact that the events discussed in the report occurred in the previous reign, and Gümüşhanevi was known for his opposition to the Tanzimat reformers, Ali Paşa and Fuad Paşa. Abu Manneh points out that Gümüşhanevi's teaching put a special emphasis on particular *hadith* which enjoined 'absolute obedience to the authority and total pacifism'.¹¹⁶ However, the more activist Khalidi Nakşibendi order, which was immensely powerful, was seen by the palace as volatile and dangerous. Sheikh Irbili Mehmed Es'ad was exiled by the sultan from İstanbul in 1897 and could not return as long as Abdülhamid was in power.¹¹⁷

The sultan's effort to ensure that the public be exposed only to the 'approved' religion is illustrated by the instructions sent to the şeyhulislam on 6 July 1883 warning him that the palace had been informed that 'impostors' were teaching in the mosques of the capital: 'These men, posing as Muslim preachers, simply don a turban and venture beyond religious subjects, some even talk about political matters.'[118] It was also reported as an extremely undesirable development that 'women of good family had been frequenting Bektaşi *tekkes* and imbibing alcoholic beverages.'[119]

Sufism, although not orthodox or mainstream, was a useful way of galvanizing grass-root support and reinforcing legitimacy, provided it was controlled from the centre.[120] As Abu Manneh pointed out in his seminal article on the subject: 'Sultan Abdülhamid seems to have been of the belief that his two predecessors ... the sultans of the Tanzimat period, neglected to create links with the common people especially in his Arab provinces.'[121] Abdülhamid's 'official faith' was propagated through such ideologues as Abulhuda al-Sayyadi, Sheikh Hamza Zafir, and Ahmad As'ad. A native of Aleppo, Abulhuda was of the Rifai order and had been close to the sultan since 1876, receiving the office of head of the Sufi Sheikhs (*Şeyh ül-meşaih*). Hamza Zafir, a member of the Shadhili-Madani order from North Africa, had become acquainted with the sultan before his accession to the throne. Ahmad As'ad was Anatolian by origin, but had become established as a dignitary of the Hijaz. He had been instrumental as the sultan's unofficial envoy to the Urabists during the events in Egypt in 1881–82.[122]

Abulhuda's main message was aimed at Syria, and there were 'some 212 titles of books and booklets attributed (to him)'. The continuous message in his major work, *Da'i al-rashad li sabbil al-ittihad wa'l-inkiyad*, was the legitimacy of the rule of Abdülhamid as caliph of Islam. He deliberately focused on the issue of the legitimacy of absolute rule, denying allegations to the effect that it was a Turco–Mongol import.[123] In this capacity Abulhuda was a weapon aimed directly against the notion of the Arab caliphate. As such he earned himself few friends in British-occupied Egypt. Kamil Paşa was to state in 1899 that, 'All the perfidious statements in the Egyptian press are a reaction to the recent anti-British policy of the Sublime State, and are a result of the vengeful sentiments of the Egyptian and Arab population towards Ebulhuda Efendi.'[124]

Sheikh Hamza Zafir's main target seems to have been Africa. Trimingham has pointed out that his work, *al-Nur al-sati* (the brilliant light), published in Istanbul in 1884, provided the basis for much of the pan-Islamic movement: 'From the Madani *tekkes* went out propaganda seeking to influence sheikhs of various orders. Emissaries, protected through the imperial power, won recruits among Algerians employed by the French ...'[125] What is interesting to note here is that Abdülhamid was attempting to do precisely what he feared the British and French would do to him that is to use Muslims of French or British allegiance as a potential fifth column.

In the eyes of foreigners, the Sufi mystics had quasi-occult functions and their influence on the sultan was seen as very sinister. One of the principal biographers of Abdülhamid has referred to, 'the sultan's superstitious belief in his [Ebulhuda's] prophetic powers ... .'[126] In a contemporary report the 'religious advisors' of the sultan are described as 'unscrupulous adventurers', who 'do their utmost to terrorize him into sanctioning the present maladministration ... .'[127] Even an established authority such as Trimingham notes that Ebulhuda maintained his influence on Abdülhamid through 'astrological' or 'divinatory' powers.[128]

Conclusion

In sum, the Ottoman ruling elite was trying to foster a sense of Ottoman identity both among its own members and among the wider population. Anthony Smith remarks that, 'Aristocratic ethnic cultures persist exactly because their identities form part of their status situation; culture and superiority fuse to create a sense of distinct mission.'[129] Although the elite circle itself was small, its message reached a far broader stratum. Mardin has noted that Said Nursi, a Kurdish mystic of humble origin from rural eastern Anatolia, was able to present the sultan with a petition in which he argued for the institution of secular Ottoman schools in the eastern provinces, as this would 'eliminate internal factional strife among the tribes and make them into good Ottoman citizens.'[130] This is very comparable to the ideas of Süleyman Hüsnü Paşa, a figure much higher in the social scale who had similar plans for the vilayets of Baghdad, Mosul and Basra.[131] Even in an obscure and poor vilayet such as Bitlis in 1889 the 'civilizational motif' was present in spite of the fact that the place was actually seething with unrest.[132]

At the level of 'official belief' the Ottomans made an attempt to fuse pre-existing values such as the Hanefi *mezheb* with new energy, and project it as the social cement for their increasingly intense relations with their subjects/citizens. In this sense Ahmet Yaşar Ocak's observation sums up the matter in a nutshell:

> The Islamism of the Hamidian period ... was entirely a reaction against classical Ottoman Islam. As such, essentially it was a *modernist* movement. Despite all its anti-Western posturing, because it favoured of modernization, it must be considered together with other modernist movements in Turkish history.[133]

In this sense too the Ottoman experience is very similar to the experiences of other nineteenth-century powers who tried to 'reinvo[ke] the values and customs of the past to serve an ever more complicated present.'[134]

The Ottoman state was in tune with world trends where, one after the other, empires borrowed the weapons of the enemy, the nationalists. What held true for Paris in the 1870s, also held true for Istanbul: the transformation of 'peasants into Frenchmen' paralleled the 'civilizing' or 'Ottomanizing' of the nomad.[135]

Chapter Three
'To Enjoin the Good and to Forbid Evil': Conversion and Ideological Reinforcement [1]

As the Ottoman 'punitive expedition' of October 1892 reached the first Yezidi villages on the lower terraces of Mount Sincar in the mountain fastness of northern Iraq, some Yezidi chiefs came forward with the promise that they would embrace Islam and guide the soldiers to the lairs of other Yezidis further up the mountain, if their villages were spared. The commander Asım Bey agreed. Soon after they set out, the Ottoman column passed through a narrow gorge, where they found themselves in a hellish crossfire from Yezidi tribesmen stationed on either side. Their 'guides' who had led them into the ambush quickly changed sides. A hundred Ottoman soldiers were killed and many more wounded. The news was heard in Mosul on 4 November and the military music in the government compound stopped.[2]

The Yezidi Kurds were one of the many groups that the Hamidian state attempted to integrate into the mainstream population and expose to the Ottomanized Şeriat. Thus imbued, these elements would also be more reliable as soldiers. Yet it was not enough to simply press people into service. In the short term this might prove effective, but the new ideological requirements of the state meant that, in the long term, the population had to be convinced as well as coerced.[3] In other words, the people had to be made to believe in, or at least acquiesce to, the legitimation ideology of the ruling power. This was done through a systematic policy of conversion to the 'official faith', the Sunni Hanefi *mezheb*. This policy was nothing less than a long-term bid to integrate elements which had been 'nominal Muslims' like the Bedouin, or 'heretical sects' such as the Yezidi Kurds, into mainstream ideology. Although officially Christians were not forced to convert, documentation indicates that Christian conversions increased in the period. Just as post-revolutionary France had worked to make 'peasants into Frenchmen', the Ottoman elite would attempt to transform 'nomads into Ottomans' while not neglecting to buttress the orthodoxy of the sedentary population.⁴

As the Ottoman Empire found itself increasingly short of usable manpower, the urgent requirements of defence meant that the sultan had to squeeze the population for the last reserves of fighting men. This chapter will examine how the state attempted to instill the new orthodoxy in various strata of its population.

The Yezidis: a case study of Ottoman conversion policy

The campaign carried out in 1891–92 to convert the Yezidis to the Hanefi *mezheb* is in many ways a microcosm of Ottoman policy towards elements which had hitherto been considered marginal and left more or less to their own devices. Standard practice usually followed a set pattern. First, an 'advisory commission' (*heyet-i nasiha*, or *heyet-i tefhimiye*) would be sent, usually including local notables or respected religious leaders. These were expected to get results through what would today be called the 'carrot method', a system of persuasion helped by decorations, bribes, sometimes invitations to leaders to come to Istanbul where, if they were lucky, they would be kept under comfortable house arrest. This method of employing 'lenient and moderate means' (*vesait-i leyyine ve mutedile*) was preferred because it was cheaper and far less destabilizing than the military option. If this did not achieve the desired result, only then would the Ottoman centre resort to sending a 'punitive expedition' (*heyet-i tedibiye*).⁵ The obvious problem with this second method was that the centre often had very little control over the amount of violence used, and this often resulted in massacre and wanton destruction.

The Yezidi Kurds had inhabited the mountainous regions of eastern Anatolia and upper Mesopotamia from time immemorial. Their religion, attracting some attention in the late nineteenth and early twentieth centuries as 'devil worship', with its obvious exoticism, held great appeal for travellers to the Orient.⁶

As far as the Ottomans were concerned, Yezidis were a 'heretical sect' (*fırak-ı dalle*) who could be called to account through Hanefization: 'The Yezidis, Kurds but not Muslims ... represented an anomaly in the mind of the pious Sultan.'⁷ Accordingly plans were made to assimilate them in the Cossack-inspired 'Hamidiye' regiments of light auxiliary cavalry then being formed in eastern Anatolia.⁸ In 1885 their exemption from military service was lifted and they were put on the conscription registers. Yet their attempted full integration into the Ottoman scheme of things seems to have awaited the fateful spring and summer of 1891.

On 18 May 1891, the 'advisory commission' (*heyet-i nasiha*), headed by a Major Abdelkadir, which had been sent to the Şeyhan region to 'convince' the Yezidis to perform military service, reported that they had gathered together all the Yezidi chiefs and imparted to them the decision of Istanbul, 'in a language that they would understand'.[9] But, these worthies wrote, although the attitude of the local population was favourable, little could be accomplished with their leaders, 'who have always led their people astray and have manipulated them to serve their selfish ends'. It was therefore recommended that, if these people, who numbered some 150,000, were to be called to account, their leaders had to be banished as soon as possible to areas of the empire where there were no Yezidis.[10] When the Yezidi leaders telegrammed Istanbul complaining that Major Abdelkadir was using brutal methods, the major wrote that this was proof of their 'perfidious nature'. He stated that the Yezidi leaders had given him a written guarantee that they would fulfil military obligations, but were now attempting to renege on it. It was reiterated that 'the correction of the beliefs of these people can only be successful if their leaders are exiled.'[11]

One month after this the palace was informed that a particular trouble maker was the *mir* (chief) of Şeyhan, Mir Mirza, 'without whose removal the aim of correcting their beliefs (*tashih-i akaid*) is a hopeless task'.[12]

On 25 June, the sultan's ADC, Şakir Paşa, evaluated the situation for Abdülhamid, stating that military service was a sacred duty incumbent on all Muslim subjects, and that it was unheard of that any group of people should be ' extended a special invitation and be asked to give written reassurances'.[13] The paşa also stated that military service should be given first priority, the 'correction of the beliefs' of the Yezidis could be undertaken once they had been included in the ranks.[14]

Yet it seems that, in the eyes of the sultan, religious orthodoxy was indeed more important than military service: the Yezidis must convert. The Muslim Yezidis in the area of Hakkari did indeed volunteer for service in the Hamidiye regiments. The view of the palace, however, was that as 'these regiments are made up of elements who are of the Sha'afi sect and whose religious resolve and loyalty is known, it is out of the question that the [heretical] Yezidi should be considered on equal footing with them.'[15]

In July 1891, an ambitious Ottoman general, Ömer Vehbi Paşa, was posted to the vilayet of Mosul as the 'commander of the reformatory force' (*fırka-i islahiye kumandanı*). Yet still the 'soft option' was favoured. On 13 October 1891 a Yıldız Palace memorandum stated that 13,000 *kuruş* had been spent on the construction of a mosque and a school in a Yezidi village called Patrak where the majority had converted to Islam.[16]

However, by the summer of 1892 Ömer Vehbi Paşa had already decided on more direct methods. In July–August he began a programme of intimidation which involved terrorizing Yezidi villages in the Şeyhan area, some of which had resisted the call to Islam. These were raided and severed heads were brought back to Mosul.[17] This intimidation brought a delegation of some forty Yezidi chiefs to the town. On 19 August, the paşa reported that he had gathered the local administrative council (*meclis-i idare*) and in a public ceremony called on the chiefs to embrace Islam. Some refused and were beaten, at least one died of his wounds.[18] The remainder, headed by the Mir Ali Bey, converted in a ceremony that was duly reported to Istanbul by the paşa as a great success:

> After repeated unsuccessful attempts through the centuries to bring them back to the true path, eighty villages of the Yezidi and thirty villages of the Shi'a have acceded to the honour of the True Faith. Yesterday, their leaders, with total freedom of conscience, accepted my invitation to come to Mosul and become Muslim. This morning, as the military band played the Hamidiye march, and rank upon rank of ulema intoned the holiest of prayers proclaiming the One True God, a great crowd of notables and military personnel gathered around the municipality offices. As a guard of honour stood to military salute, the müftü asked each one in turn if he accepted Islam of his own free will. Upon each confirmation the crowd shouted, 'Long Live the Sultan! (*padişahım çok yaşa*).[19]

Despite his brutal measures, Ömer Vehbi Paşa also intended to pursue education as a means of securing the long-term loyalty of the Yezidis. The day after he reported the conversion ceremony (*merasim-i telkiniye*) he wrote to Istanbul that he intended to build six mosques and seven schools in Yezidi villages and five schools and five mosques in the villages of the Şebekli, all of whom had converted to Islam.[20]

The paşa also wrote that the Yezidi Sanctuary at Lâliş should be converted to a Muslim *medrese* and twenty pupils should be given scholarships to study there under a worthy Sunni scholar who would also be funded by the state. It was important that local ulema should be employed in the schools of the area because they would be familiar with the language and customs of the people.[21] The vilayet council, probably at the paşa's prompting, telegraphed Istanbul in much the same vein, pointing out that it was advisable to use local ulema as they would be 'familiar with the character and language of the local people, well versed in political subtleties as well as religious dogma ' It is worth pointing out that this formula, or close versions of it *'emzice ve elsine-i mahalliyeye aşina ve dekayık-ı siyasiyeye dana ve hakayık-ı diniyeye vakıf ...'* is often repeated in Ottoman documentation dealing with measures against heterodoxy.[22]

It was deemed at this point appropriate not to disregard the soft option, and on 26 August the Ottoman Council of Ministers (Meclis-i Vükela) discussed a telegram received from Ömer Vehbi Paşa, in which the latter suggested that leading Yezidis be decorated for their praiseworthy conduct in accepting Islam. The paşa had claimed that if these chiefs were decorated and given a pension, 'they would promise to bring the Yezidis of the entire empire as well as those of Iran and Russia into the sacred fold of Islam.'[23]

In mid-September Ömer Vehbi Paşa reported that the teachers and prayer leaders assigned to the Yezidi villages had taken up their posts.[24] Yet things were not progressing to the satisfaction of the ambitious general. On 24 September, he reported that Mir Ali Bey and a few other 'troublemakers and traitors' had gone back to their 'hateful state of ignorance' and had reneged on their vows to Islam. These 'evil men who had been used to milking the villagers for years by parading bronze peacocks and other such craven idols among the villages and thus collecting large sums for their own use' had to be put down.[25]

At this point the Yezidi leaders further complicated matters by contacting the French consul in Mosul and telling him that the community was prepared to embrace Christianity if France could protect them against Ömer Vehbi Paşa.[26] This caused an outraged paşa to cable Istanbul to report that some of the Yezidi leaders who had been 'confounded and frustrated' by the state's efforts to bring civilization and education, 'thus preventing them from swindling and fooling the local population', had now appealed to the French consulate for protection. 'The effort being made to bring them back to the true path from which they have strayed through ignorance and heresy, is being presented to the foreigners in a different light, thus enabling them to continue their evil ways.'[27]

Acting on this information, in Istanbul the Council of Ministers recommended on 7 October that the Yezidi chief, Ali Bey, and others who had 'misled' their people should be exiled to Ottoman Tripoli.²⁸ By now the alternating 'carrot-and-stick' policy applied by Ömer Vehbi Paşa was having some effect. At the end of September it was reported that eight villages of 'heretics' from a sect called the 'Harlı' in the *sancak* of Zor, and the Mosul area had presented themselves in Mosul 'of their own free will', and announced 'that they had become Muslim'.²⁹ The Council of Ministers decided to approve the vilayet's suggestion that the leaders of these villages, together with the leaders of the Şebekli who had already converted, should be given low level decorations and be paid a pension of 1,000 *kuruş*. It was clearly stated that all of these 'achievements' were the result of 'auspicious developments of the era of our caliph' (*muhassenat-ı asriyye-i hilafetpenahi*)'.³⁰

On 11 October, the Vali of Mosul, Osman Paşa, asked for: '300 copies of the Qur'an (*kelam-ı kadim*), 700 primary school readers and 700 pamphlets teaching Islamic beliefs, for the instruction of the children of the Yezidi and Şebekli who had converted to the Hanefi belief.' It was said that this was the 'fruits of the exalted pious path (*asar celile-i takva şiarileri*)' taken by the sultan.³¹

At around the same time, in mid-October, Ömer Vehbi Paşa ordered a punitive expedition into Yezidi territory. The commander of the force was the son of the paşa, Asım Bey, a hotheaded young officer. The force cut its way through Yezidi villages in the Şeyhan leaving death and destruction in its wake.³² The sanctuary at Lališ was sacked and the ritual artefacts were removed. It was to be transformed into a *medrese*. This was followed by the expedition to the Sincar mountain where the Ottoman force was ambushed and suffered heavy casualties at the hands of the Yezidi hillsmen.³³

By the end of October 1893, the new Vali of Mosul, Aziz Paşa, telegraphed that he had carried out his orders to inform Istanbul of the circumstances of the 1892 defeat. He reported to his superiors that the tactical error which had been committed by Ömer Vehbi Paşa was the use of violence against the Yezidi who had in fact been peaceful. This had caused them to combine forces with their more militant tribesmen on Mt Sincar. The new governor also suggested the application of the old methods of first sending in an advisory commission 'made up of locally influential men'. Only if this did not yield results would it be necessary to 'punish [them] in an exemplary manner'.³⁴

The importance of the 'advisory commission' was particularly stressed and its participants told that the sultan would reward them generously if they were successful in bringing about the surrender of the rebellious chiefs without bloodshed.³⁵ On 1 December the governor confirmed that most of the leaders of the seventeen Yezidi villages in rebellion in the Sincar area could be made to repent through advisory commissions.³⁶

Although an uneasy truce was restored to the Yezidi areas, it was fairly obvious that the Ottoman centre did not envisage anything like a return to the *status quo ante*. The long term hope was to keep the region quiet, while inculcating Hanefi orthodoxy through a network of schools. In the last days of 1893, the Yezidi leader, Mir Mirza Bey, applied to the vilayet of Mosul for the return of the sacred relics which had been removed from the Sheikh Adi sanctuary during the raids of 1892. He was told in no uncertain terms that it was out of the question that these should be given back to him, or to any other Yezidi chief, and that the sanctuary had now definitively become a *medrese*.³⁷

Meanwhile, complaints regarding the excessive brutality of Ömer Vehbi Paşa, and his bullying of the local notables, had been reaching the sultan throughout 1892 and 1893. A commission of inquiry was duly established and it reported from Mosul on 24 November 1892 that Ömer Vehbi Paşa had 'undertaken actions totally contrary to imperial interest and ran the risk of plunging an area as important and sensitive as Iraq into a state of chaos.' He had exceeded his orders and had 'indulged in excesses beyond his authority (*ifrat ve tefrite kaçtığı*).'³⁸

On 28 November, the chiefs of staff commented that 'Imperial instructions were to attempt to disperse the rebels without spilling blood, and only to resort to force if the [Ottoman troops] were fired upon … .'³⁹ A few weeks later, the commission had a remarkable report to submit: some twenty Yezidis had presented themselves before it with the grisly evidence of seven severed heads, which they claimed had belonged to men slaughtered by Asım Bey's forces. The commission felt that this was scandalous behaviour and 'that such acts present an ugly spectacle to friend and foe.'⁴⁰

Extremely damning evidence was brought to light by the commission in Mosul who reported on 6 February that the so-called 'conversion ceremony' reported by Ömer Vehbi Paşa was a total sham: 'not one of the Yezidi leaders in fact converted sincerely, and those who did, did so to avoid the public beating and insult which was meted out to their peers … Therefore the paşa's report that these people had, one by one, converted by word and heart is totally without foundation.' The commission also reported that the commander's forces had 'undertaken such actions totally contrary to the imperial wishes as beatings and torture of villagers in

Şeyhan and Sincar in order to secure their conversion.'[41] On 19 August, the palace ordered that the commission of inquiry dismiss Ömer Vehbi Paşa from his post and that he be ordered back to Istanbul to face a court martial.[42]

It seems that the Yezidis had still not been included in the ranks of the Hamidiye regiments by December 1893. At this time the vilayets of Mosul and Van were ordered to carry out a census of Yezidi villages and to continue the efforts to educate their children.[43]

The ideological seesaw between the Ottoman centre and the Yezidis was to continue. As late as January 1914 they had still not been subjugated. On 25 January 1914, the vilayet of Mosul was to report that the Yezidi chiefs had accepted that they would be issued with Ottoman identity cards, but on the condition that the section declaring religion should read 'Yezidi'.[44]

The Yezidi story remains a curious one. In many ways it is a microcosm of the Ottoman attitude to marginal sects whom they wanted to convert ideologically so that they could be utilized as reliable members of the population. The 'carrot and stick' policy was obviously subject to abuse by the men on the spot who received mixed signals from the centre. On the one hand, they would be told 'not to spill blood' and to settle the matter at hand through the good offices of 'advisory commissions'. On the other, a strong willed general or officer would be ordered in no uncertain terms to procure the submission and conversion of unruly elements. Added to this there were the logistical problems of communications and deployment of troops in hostile and inaccessible terrain. In such circumstances considerable initiative fell to the commanding officer, yet he was told that he must ask for instructions before undertaking any decisive action. This confusion lies behind much of the massacre and counter-massacre that went on in the eastern provinces of the Ottoman state during these years.

The 'correction of the beliefs' of Muslims and marginals

It became the practice in Abdülhamid's reign for the corps of religious teachers to be used as a sort of religious secret police-cum-missionary organization whose religious training and credentials would be determined by the centre. 'Freelance' preaching was decidedly frowned upon and seen as dangerous.

By 1892 it was established that preachers and 'missionaries' (*da'iyan*) would only be allowed to preach after they had graduated from four years of study and received a diploma (*rüus*) from the şeyhülislam. The preachers in question were to include the sons of prominent religious functionaries (*zadegan*) who, upon the successful completion of their studies, would be given the highest diploma, the *Istanbul rüusu*.⁴⁶ It would appear that this policy was implemented throughout the Hamidian era. As late in the reign as 1902, the şeyhülislam's office was to write to the palace, reporting that the latest crop of *daiyan* had graduated from their special *medreses*, and were now 'ready to take up teaching posts in the provinces'. The letter expressed special thanks to the sultan for his award of one thousand lira out of his privy purse to be apportioned among the teachers.⁴⁷

The enforcement of orthodoxy went together with conversion of heresy. Even elements who were nominally Muslim were not beyond the searching gaze of Istanbul. On 2 December 1884, the Council of Ministers, acting on the sultan's orders, arranged to send twenty religious teachers to the vilayet of Syria, to inculcate the 'true' Islam into the local population. This was deemed necessary as 'the Islam of the local population, sedentary and nomad alike, consists of nothing more than something they inherited from their ancestors, indeed, their Islam does not go much beyond their having Islamic names.'⁴⁸ It was necessary that such unthinking practice be replaced by 'a consciousness of the honour of being Muslim'. This would prevent them being 'duped by missionaries and Jesuits who set out to deceive them.' It had been determined by a special commission in Damascus that special teachers, familiar with the local vernaculars and customs should be sent out to travel with the nomads and bring them back to the true path. In settled areas schools and mosques would be established. The Council of Ministers declared: 'This practice should also be extended to Yemen and Baghdad, thus teaching the people the rules and practices of Islam and ensuring their obedience to the caliphate'.⁴⁹

Yemen in particular continued to be a problem area where Hanefi 'official belief' was besieged by what Istanbul perceived as the heretical beliefs of the Zaidi, a Shi'i sect.⁵⁰ This made it all the more remarkable that the *Vali* of Yemen should write on 2 November 1898, that some of the leading Zaidi *alims* had asked for a Hanefi *medrese* to be built in San'a. The vali pointed out that this request was somewhat 'unexpected' (*hilaf-ı memul*) coming from these people, 'who have not been renowned for their loyalty'. Yet the vali recommended that the *medrese* be opened as the Zaidi of the towns were 'relatively more moderate' and susceptible to reason than were the 'savage tribes'. Education, he pointed out, achieved 'gradual but lasting results'.⁵¹

A report from the same province dated a year later left little doubt as to the aims of Ottoman primary education in Yemen: 'The people of Yemen are ignorant of Islamic history, particularly of the great works and deeds of our August Master, the Caliph. The programme of primary schools in the region should be of a nature to reinforce the Hanefi *mezheb*, and instill the feeling of obedience towards the sultan ... .' The same report stated, however, that where the Sha'afi *mezheb* was predominant, school religious textbooks should accommodate Sha'afi doctrine.[52]

This practice was to continue to the end of the century and well into the 1900s. On 20 July 1899, the Yıldız Palace recorded that an imperial order had been issued for the sending of twelve qualified teachers to the Ma'an valley in the southern part of the vilayet of Syria, to work among the Bedouin. It was declared that this was necessary because 'these people are entirely bereft of the light of Islam, and have to be taught the religious sciences and the rules of Islam.'[53] It is particularly interesting, in the light of this order, that when the Bedouin of the Karak region in the Ma'an valley revolted against the Ottomans in 1911, they selectively targeted the Hanefi schools and mosques for destruction, leaving such obvious targets as the Christian and Jewish quarters relatively undamaged.[54]

Nor was the orthodoxy of the Turkish heartland in Anatolia taken for granted. In May 1899, the şeyhülislam's office in Istanbul ordered preachers (*va'iz*) to be sent to the district of Mihalıçık near Ankara because 'It has come to his Imperial Majesty's attention that the people of this place are completely ignorant of the *Şeriat* and the *Sunna*.' In the same vein it was decided to send preachers to Trabzon, as 'the people of Trabzon and its environs have strayed from the true Islam and have ventured down the path of ignorance.' In both Ankara and Trabzon the assignment of the preachers was the same: 'to teach religion and to correct beliefs' (*ta'alim-i diyanetle tashih-i akaidleri*).'[55]

It would appear that something of a religious crisis occurred in Anatolia at this time. In the late 1890s there was a very real fear that in many areas the population might convert to Christianity as a result of missionary activity. As it turned out this was a totally unfounded panic. But the question greatly worried Ottoman officials at the time because in many of these areas the people had converted from Christianity in the late eighteenth to early nineteenth century. The crisis also intermeshed with the Armenian massacres which brought intense pressure from the West for the Ottoman government to fulfil its pledges of reform.[56] The position of 'General Inspector for Anatolia' (*vilayat-ı şahane müfettiş-i umumisi*) was created in some measure as a safety valve against Western pressure. The first general inspector was none other than the most trusted of the sultan's ADCs, Ahmed Şakir Paşa.[57]

On 16 January 1898, the vilayet of Trabzon reported to Şakir Paşa that, '[it] had heard that some people in the region had the intention of converting back to Christianity (*irtidad*) as a result of 'the deception of the priest.' An investigation had been launched in the districts concerned but 'because of the great size of the monasteries in the area and the numerous priests' it was advisable that this investigation keep a somewhat low profile as 'the priests might otherwise show things in a different light, and they are not above complaining to foreign officials.'[58] A year and a half later the vilayet of Trabzon was to report that the rumours had come to nothing. Yet, considerable furore had been caused.[59]

Nor was this furore unfounded. After the Ottomans officially admitted freedom of religion with the *ferman* of 1856, there were indeed cases among recent coverts where attempts were made to return to Christianity. A striking example is that of the İstavri or the Stavriotae. The İstavri were Greeks of the Black Sea regions of Trabzon and Gümüşhane who had converted to Islam at various periods of persecution since the end of the seventeenth century, but had remained crypto-Christians, openly declaring their faith only after the guarantee of religious freedom granted by the Hat-ı Hümayun Reform Edict of 1856.[60] Some had resettled in the *kaza* of Akdağ Madeni near the central Anatolian town of Yozgad in the 1830s. A contemporary Western account referred to them as:

> Crypto-Christians proper, belonging to the Greek rite and Greek by speech, [who] also existed till recent years in the neighbourhood of Trebizond: they were known as the 'Stavriotae' from a village Stavra in the ecclesiastical district of Gumushane. They are said at one time to have numbered 20,000 in the *vilayets* of Sivas, Angora, and Trebizond: now all have returned to the open profession of their faith.[61]

When Şakir Paşa personally inspected the situation in the summer of 1897 he referred to the İstavri as 'a people of two sets of religious practices (*iki ayin icra eder ahali*)'.[62] As such they represented the height of anomaly in the Ottoman system.[63] In earlier periods, they had simply been bypassed; but now, when the empire had to squeeze every last resource in order to survive, like the Yezidis and other hitherto marginal groups, they found themselves the focus of the unwelcome attentions of the state. They amounted to a considerable population numbering some 'eighty four households' in Akdağ Madeni itself and were also to be found in the surrounding villages amounting to a total of 'some one hundred and forty households'. They had taken Muslim names and done military service, thus 'appearing to be Muslims while secretly remaining Christian'. Their community leaders had maintained contact with the Greek Patriarchate in Trabzon, to the point where one of them, a Mahmud Efendi, was clandestinely referred to as 'the representative of the patriarch'. In 1879 they had openly applied to return to Christianity, thus becoming exempt from military service; but permission had been denied, causing Şakir Paşa to remark: 'this then led them into devilish machinations' (*bir mecrayı şeytaniye süluk ile*)'.[64] These 'machinations' consisted of refusing to register their births, deaths and marriages in the population registers, and burying their dead in the Greek cemetery. They had also taken to openly giving their children Christian names, and marrying into the Greek community. Şakir Paşa felt that all this was very dangerous as 'such an example can cause confusion in the minds (*tağşiş-i ezhan*) of other simple Muslims'. Yet the inspector general of Anatolia recommended nothing worse than the temporary exile of the community leaders and the reprimanding of the Patriarch of Trabzon. He added that 'reliable imams should be sent to their villages, they should be severely adjoined to send their children to school and give them Muslim names.'[65]

However, it appears that the İstavri continued their errant ways. Some months after Şakir Paşa left the area, the *mutasarrıf* of Yozgad was to report that the İstavri continued to marry among themselves and bring up their children in the İstavri tradition.[66]

The İstavri became something of a personal obsession for Ahmed Şakir Paşa. More than a year after his visit to Akdağ Madeni, he still wrote lengthy reports on 'this heretical people (*erbab-ı dalalet halk*)'. He pointed out that although they were relatively few in the region of Yozgad, in the area from which they originally came, the *kaza* of Turul in Gümüşhane, they were equal in number to the population of an entire township (*nahiye*). Their hope was to avoid military service and 'procure the friendship and protection of Europe'.[67]

Instructions had been given to the authorities in the area that 'they be told that the only result of their changing religion would be that they would be cursed by their neighbours', and would still not be exempted from military service. The paşa noted that it was a waste of time to try to preach to those 'whose minds were already poisoned', but the target should be their children, 'whose beliefs should be corrected (*tashih-i akaid*)'. The paşa's methods for forcing the parents to send their children to school were somewhat insidious and smacked of blackmail:

> On the face of it the ostensible reason is that their children should be educated. If the [parents] persist in returning to Christianity, they should be told in an unoffical manner that their children liable for military service will be compelled to serve in the military units of Yemen, Trablus (Libya), and Hijaz. This method is sure to do away with any such inclination and they will become as zealous in their beliefs as the Pomaks of Bulgaria.[68]

The paşa was also conscious of Western pressure. He pointed out that it was necessary to build and operate schools not only in the İstavri villages but also in the whole region so that 'the complaints of the foreigners can be met with the answer that the compulsion to send their children to school applies equally to all.'[69]

The İstavri continue to come up in despatches well towards the end of the Hamidian period. The vilayet of Ankara reported on 10 May that an Orthodox priest by the name of Kirilus had been active in fomenting sedition among the İstavri. The report claimed that the said Kirilus posed as an Ottoman subject was but actually a Greek from the island of Corfu. He had been actively collecting money for the Greek nationalist organization, the Philiki Etheria, from among the İstavri community and had, it was claimed, actually caused the conversion to Christianity of some Muslims.[70] One of these, a certain Sofracıoğlu Ömer, had married a Greek girl after his conversion. On hearing this, the authorities had conscripted him and sent him off to serve in the army. Yet unredeemed, upon return he moved in with his wife's family and began attending church. All this was enough to cause the Vali of Ankara considerable grief: 'It is absolutely without doubt that the continuation of this state of affairs will engender countless dangers for the Sublime State and the Holy Şeriat.' The despicable acts of these people are like a wound oozing pus into the healthy flesh of the Muslim population.'[71]

The year 1905 saw a concerted effort to solve the İstavri problem. The vilayet of Ankara was ordered in no uncertain terms to register the İstavri as Muslims. The minister of the interior, Mahmud Memduh Paşa, together with Şakir Paşa made this into something of a pet project. The protestations of the patriarchate and the foreign embassies proved to be of no avail. In several instances, the vilayet of Ankara and the mutasarrıf of Yozgad actually declared that they had granted freedom of religion. This proved, however, to be a subterfuge, designed to force more İstavri into the open. The priest Kyrillos Caratzas and several İstavri leaders were marched to Ankara where many died in prison. Freedom of worship only finally came to the İstavri after the revolution of 1908 and the deposition of Abdülhamid.⁷²

The Balkan Muslim population, greatly reduced since the empire was shorn of most of its Balkan provinces, was also a focus for 'correction'. Towards the end of 1889 it was reported that 1,600 people in the district (*nahiye*) of Elbasan, in Ottoman Albania, had declared that they were Christian, and therefore not eligible for military service. Istanbul ordered that a local prefect (*müdür*) be appointed to the area and that these people 'be brought into the circle of salvation of Islam' through the appointment of teachers and the construction of schools. The state would thus 'establish contact with the population', who were to be expected to supply soldiers as they had in the past.⁷³ A group which had always been suspect in the Balkans were the *dönme*, the Jewish converts to Islam. On the 24 April 1892, the Ottoman Council of Ministers discussed the case of a *dönme* girl, Rabia, who had fallen in love with her tutor, a Hacı Feyzullah Efendi. It was stated in the minutes of the council that, 'Rabia, a girl of some eighteen or twenty years, having developed a relationship with Hacı Feyzullah has run away to his dwelling and there declared that she has converted to Islam and abandoned the *avdeti* faith.⁷⁴ What is immediately striking here is that the Ottoman official documentation refers to the matter as conversion (*ihtida*), although the *dönme* were officially Muslims. The girl took refuge with the municipality mayor and her family demanded her return. The assessment of the council was that 'although the Avdeti are called Muslims, and should therefore not object [to the marriage] they have always abstained from intermarriage with Muslims.' In the end it was recommended that the couple be brought to Istanbul by the first boat, where Feyzullah would be provided with some form of employment in a government office.⁷⁵

Şerif Mardin has also drawn attention to the 'quite novel proselytizing in the Balkans' by the Melami and Nakşibendi Sufi orders as the borders of the Ottoman Empire shrank rapidly in the nineteenth century.⁷⁶

The Kurds who served as auxiliary forces in the eastern Anatolian provinces, the Hamidiye regiments, were also to be instructed in the 'correct' religion by the institution of schools and mosques at the expense of the sultan's privy purse.⁷⁷ The Kurds who were deemed to 'have strayed from the true path' were to be put back on the straight and narrow by the printing and distribution of 'religious guides' (*ilm-i hal*), which would be printed in Turkish and Kurdish and would be distributed among them.[78]

A group of unorthodox people who had always drawn the ire of the Ottoman ruling class were the Kızılbaş, or the 'Red Heads', so described for their traditional head covering.[79] Known as a problematic branch of the Shi'i faith, these elements could not fail to attract the attention of the Hamidian centre at a time when emphasis on orthodoxy was so pronounced. On 4 January 1890, the Ministry of Education was instructed to send preachers and *ilm-i hal* to the Kızılbaş of the vilayet of Sivas. This was necessary because 'the number of Kızılbaş in the area, while once quite small, has recently increased day by day as a result of their ignorance.'[80]

The mutasarrıf of Tokad in east-central Anatolia was ordered in 1891 to undertake a census of the Kızılbaş population in his area. He duly reported that 33,865 Kızılbaş lived there. His instructions were that these people were to be 'rescued from their ignorance and shown the high path of enlightenment' through the appointment of preachers and the distribution of religious tracts. In the meantime, the imams in these villages were to be summoned to the provincial capital where they were to be 'trained' in the local *rüşdiye* secondary school. Also, 'advisors' (*nasih*) were to be sent to the villages for extended stays, as 'if they are left in the villages for some time they can be more effective in saving these poor pagans who have not had their share of salvation.'[81]

On 2 August 1891, the Governor of Sivas wrote a long memorandum dealing with the Kızılbaş. He stated that owing to the neglect of the previous reign and its officers (an opening that was sure to get Abdülhamid's attention), 'the numbers of the ignorant and deviant have increased greatly'. He then went into detail on their 'pagan' religious practices such as 'worshipping dry twigs which they esteem greatly as a branch of the tree of paradise.'[82] The paşa had a much more serious lament, however: the Kızılbaş also believed that to die in battle did not automatically open the door to paradise, as was the credo in the orthodox Muslim faith. This made it obvious that 'as together with everyone else, they serve in the regular forces, this superstition, which has possessed them from an early age, will make them highly unreliable in war.' Therefore all effort was being made, in keeping with official instructions, to establish the 'new style' schools in their villages and to train village *imams* as instructors as 'it is more likely that we will be able to rescue the young from the pit of sin and educate them into abandoning their fathers' beliefs than those who have reached the age of thirty or forty whose eyes have been darkened by heresy.'[83] This dichotomy between 'darkness' and 'illumination' is indeed a Qur'anic motif,

Conversion and Ideological Reinforcement 83

as was noted by Hasluck who devoted considerable attention to the problem of conversion to Islam: 'A convert to Islam is not unnaturally regarded as a person specially illuminated by God, being thus enabled to see the true faith in spite of the errors of his upbringing.'[84]

Another people who had been victims of 'errors in their upbringing', and became a target of the conversion policy were the Nuseyri. A sect found in northern Syria, the Nuseyri in the region of Latakia attracted the attention of Istanbul in 1889. A payments register for the Ministry of Education records that, 'because the efforts of the Christian missionaries have not been lacking among them, it is established that seven primary schools should be established in the area in order to invite them into the fold of Islam.[85] Indeed, Abdülhamid II appointed an *imam* for the Nusayris in order to lead them in orthodox prayer.[86]

By March of the next year, school construction had advanced and Ali Reşid Efendi from Trablus (Tripoli) 'renowned for his learning and loyalty' was appointed as inspector of the schools in the area.[87] Throughout these years the Nuseyri continue to come up in dispatches. In June of 1891 the *mutasarrıf* of Lazkiye reported that the Nuseyri notables of the Sahyun district had called on him and presented him with a petition declaring that they had voluntarily accepted Hanefi Islam, and now wanted schools and mosques, 'to confirm them in their faith and to instruct them'.[88]

Inspector Sheikh Ali Efendi had been present and had recommended that fifteen schools and as many mosques were needed in the area otherwise, 'if these people are left in their forlorn state of ignorance, this will butter the bread of the missionaries who will then be able to tell them, "you see, your government cannot help you".'[89] Although the Ottoman Government considered the Nuseyri as heretical or deviant Muslims, the missionaries considered them a 'pagan sect' and protested against the closure of missionary schools in their area.[90]

The Nuseyri were also to attract the attention of the indefatigable Ahmed Şakir Paşa. During a tour of inspection of the vilayet of Aleppo in mid-1898, the Nuseyri of the *kaza* of Antakya (Antioch) had approached him with petitions complaining that their conversion to Hanefi Islam had not been accepted by the notables of the area, who would not allow them in the mosques.[91] Şakir Paşa had looked into the matter and had come to the conclusion that the attitude of the notables was due to the fact 'they use [the Nuseyri] as a slave-like labour force and if they become Muslim they will no longer be able to do so.' He deemed it absolutely necessary that the notables be compelled to accept the conversion of the Nuseyri:

'[If this is not done] a tremendous opportunity will be wasted. I have recently seen mention in the European press that thirty thousand Nuseyri have miraculously converted to the True Faith at the merest gesture of His Sacred Majesty. The political value of this development cannot be squandered in the narrow interest of a few landowners.'[92] It is interesting that the Paşa put the onus on the international propaganda value of the sultan's position as Caliph of all Muslims.

Syria continued to be the focus of Ottoman missionary zeal. Another obscure sect in the Lazkiye district who were deemed 'in need of having their religious practice and belief reinforced' were the Hıdaiye. On 19 July 1896, the Sublime Porte recorded that schools had been built in their area and able teachers had been appointed. It was also decided that the primary schools in the districts of Markab and Cebele were to be upgraded to secondary school (*rüşdiye*) status, and a total of some forty schools in the area were to be regularly supervised by an inspector.[93]

Conversion of Christians

The process of conversion from Christianity to Islam is one of the most vexed issues in Ottoman studies. It seems from the evidence that forced and arbitrary conversion was officially scorned, while it probably went on informally. Even according to an unsympathetic Western account: 'Under the Ottoman Turks at least there is very little historical evidence of conversion on a large scale in Asia Minor. So long as the *rayahs* were not dangerous, they could be 'milked' better than true believers, and conversion *en masse* was to no one's interest.'[94]

During the earlier part of Sultan Abdülhamid's reign, the possibility of Christian subjects serving in the ranks was seriously considered. A memorandum prepared by Grand Vizier Said Paşa, on 26 February 1880, pointed out that the Greek Metropolitan in Istanbul had suggested that Christian and Muslims serve in separate units. This was dismissed as dangerous by the Council of Ministers who pointed out that 'in the Cossack and Dragoon units [of Russia] Christian and Muslim serve together in brotherly fashion.'[95] It was also pointed out that in the anti-Austrian resistance during 1875-76 'Latins and Muslims fought side by side'. The sultan, however, became increasingly suspicious of arming his Christian subjects, on the grounds of security and also because the inclusion of Christians in the ranks would mean the loss of the considerable revenue gained from the military exemption tax (*bedel-i askeri*) levied on them.[96]

Conversion and Ideological Reinforcement 85

However, the evidence from the Ottoman archives indicates that Christian conversion did become more frequent during the last quarter of the nineteenth century. Indeed it is possible to speak of a late Ottoman conversion policy regarding Christians, the basis of which was that conversion was only admissible if carried out through 'proper channels' and followed 'proper procedure'. As in the cases of the *Şeriat* and the Hanefi *mezheb*, what we have here is a 'bureaucratization' of the conversion procedure. This procedure is spelled out clearly in the Ministry of Interior's frequent circulars to the provinces dealing with complaints about conversions (*ihtida*) which had taken place 'against accepted practice' (*usul-ü cariye hilafında*). The central idea informing decision-making on this issue was to show that the conversions had been voluntary. This point did not escape the attention of a British traveller who noted:

> The whole procedure that is prescribed in cases of conversion to Mohammedanism from any form of religion is judicious, moderate, and calculated to distinguish between real and forced conversion, and to give the former co-religionists of the convert every opportunity of satisfying themselves that the conversion is voluntary.[97]

The accepted practices had some striking features. One of these was that, 'during the act of conversion the highest ranking local priest belonging to the confession of the convert [has] to be present'.[98] It would appear that what was happening here was a 'bureaucratization' of an earlier practice. Cypriot sources from the seventeenth century testify to the fact that in Cyprus when a Greek converted to Islam, the practice was that a priest should be present to ascertain that there was no coercion, and to 'strike the convert off his list'.[99]

According to the nineteenth century-regulation, together with the priest, the convert's parents or next of kin should be in attendance. The documents testifying to the act of legitimate conversion were to be signed and sealed by Muslim and Christian officials alike. The procedure should not be hurried, and if a few days delay was required for the priest or the next of kin to arrive, the conversion ceremony was to be put off. Only those children who had reached the age of puberty were allowed to convert. Also, in the case of girls who came to the ceremony veiled, 'the veil should be lifted to ascertain identity'. If the convert was above the age of puberty, they should not be forced to go back to the home of their parents, and should be settled in 'suitable Christian or Muslim homes'.[100] The careful legalese of the circular report can, however, be read in another way. This and many other circulars repeat the same thing: frequent cases of illegal conversion were being reported in the Greek and Armenian communities. The Greek Patriarchate frequently complained that members of its congregation had approached it with tales of woe involving underage children converting as a result of being abducted.[101]

The abduction of young girls seems to have been particularly rife. The legal advisors of the Porte were to note that, 'often these children are kept in the imam's house where they are made promises that if they encourage others like them [to convert] this will be in their interest.' What seems to have been happening was that convert children were being used as decoys for others to follow in their footsteps (*emsalinin celbi için kendilerine icrayı mevaid ve iraiye-i fevaid*).[102] This was seen as truly reprehensible behaviour and the legal advisors bemoaned the fact that provincial administrators were lax in the punishment of those who abducted young girls. It was also seen as reprehensible that in the case of children who were under age, 'these children are hurried off to Istanbul and this causes loose talk and complaints.'

Another problem was the case of separated parents. If one of the parents accepted Islam the children would be free to choose which religion they were to belong to after the age of fifteen, 'according to the usage of the past forty years'.[103]

In the matter of deciding the age of young converts a clash occurred between the Greek Patriarchate and the Ottoman authorities. The Patriarchate demanded that the baptism certificates should be the basis of determining whether the convert was of age, whereas the Ottoman authorities maintained that the legal basis for such procedure were the Ottoman birth certificates.[104] By 1913 the minimum age for conversion was increased from fifteen to twenty.[105]

The Armenian crisis in Anatolia provided the background for many of the incidences of conversion. On 3 March 1895, it was reported that a sizeable population (some 200 households) of Armenians had converted to Islam in Birecik, in central Anatolia. As this was at the heart of the 'Armenian question', the British and Russian embassies had taken a close interest in the matter. The Ottoman government had therefore consented to send a mixed commission to the area consisting of two officials from the vilayet of Aleppo, and the dragoman of the British Embassy, Fitzmaurice. The commission had interviewed leaders of the convert community who were named as, 'ex-Gregorians Haçik Efendi, now called

Mehmed Şakir Efendi, and Abos Efendi, now called Şeyh Müslim Efendi, ex-Catholic Hacıkebuzan Efendi now called Mehmed Nevri Efendi, a Protestant notable Abraham Ağa, now called İbrahim Efendi.'[106] The leaders of the community openly stated that 'the recent events had caused them to fear for their lives and that was why they became Muslim.' They also promised that they would not convert back to Christianity once the danger was over: 'also the conversion of the church which they had made into a mosque was done entirely at their own expense ... and they had no intention whatever of converting it back into a church.' Indeed, if any of their number wanted to return to Christianity, they declared, those people would be refunded the sum they had spent on the church/mosque and told to go on their way. The Armenians interviewed were then asked to sign the report written by the commission. There was apparently some disagreement between the Turkish members and Fitzmaurice as to the wording; the Turkish side wanted the wording: 'and no matter what happens even when they are completely safe or have gone to a safe place they (promise) not to abandon Islam.' Fitzmaurice objected stating that this was against the freedom to change religion guaranteed by the law and was mortgaging these peoples' future. The Turkish side consented and the final report read: 'for the present time they do not intend to abandon Islam.' The community representatives, the report recorded, also stated that 'they had not been subjected to any pressure or force in accepting Islam but had only acted out of fear of recent events, being obviously in a state of great distress and poverty after the recent calamities and the sacking of their property.' The report ends here and is marked 'conforms to original'. Yet there is something remarkable in this document. At the bottom of the page, under the seals of the signatories, a scrawled sentence reads: '18 Şubat 1311. Judging from the demeanour of some of them it seems that they intend to return to their old religion.' One can only surmise that once Fitzmaurice's back was turned after he had signed it, a Turkish member of the commission hurriedly penned the addition.[107]

On 14 May, the sultan was presented the report of the commission with an accompanying note from the grand vizier stating that Fitzmaurice had 'been given permission to join the commission'.[108] On 28 May the Vali of Aleppo was asked for his opinion on the matter. The Ottoman official reiterated that the Armenian converts had converted 'only because they feared for their lives' (*sırf muhafaza-i hayat maksadına müsteniddir*).[109] He pointed out that the state had to choose one of two options. If it wanted to allow the Armenians to remain where they were, and revert to Christianity, it was necessary to 'execute some among those of the Muslims who had taken part in the killing and looting, in order to frighten the [rest of the population]' and to counter popular outrage at re-conversion. This would only work, however, for the urban areas. Those who lived in the countryside would still not be able to circulate among the Kurdish tribes who were their neighbours, 'which is in fact the very reason for their insistence on the sincerity of their conversion'.[110] The other option was for the state 'not to officially acknowledge their conversion but to leave things to time, as in their present state they can go about their business in peace'. Eventually, those among the converts who 'wanted to return to their original religion can, with the state's permission, be moved somewhere far away from Birecik where they can live as members of their original faith'.[111] This document is remarkable on two counts. Firstly, the Ottoman official is quite prepared to consider the exemplary punishment of Muslims. Secondly, the state's official position towards the converts is very far removed from the classical Islamic position where it is permissible to kill someone who abandons Islam. The vali clearly stated that the Armenian converts insisted on the sincerity of their conversion in order to be able to live among their Muslim neighbours, 'which they would not be able to do if they reverted back to their old faith,' presumably meaning that they would be killed according to the classic precepts of the şeriat. The vali was quite prepared to admit that the Armenians could be allowed to return to Christianity simply if they removed themselves bodily to some place where they would not be known.[112]

By early July it seems that the situation had once again become tense. The vali reported on 16 July that, 'The Birecik Christians, including members of the administrative and civil courts, have taken off their turbans and reverted to their old faith.' They had also taken back the key to their former church. Tension was mounting in the *kaza*: 'Those among the people who are zealous Muslims are already grumbling that the conversion of these people was not acceptable, as there is also evidence of foreign intrigue it is to be feared that the smallest incident might spark off very untoward events.' The vali's tone was worried and he called for regular troops to be sent up from Adana, 'with the shortest possible delay'.[113]

The vali was right to point to foreign interest in the matter. On 12 May 1896, the Russian embassy expressed close concern for the fate of the Birecik converts, and declared that if they were allowed to return to their original religion the news would be well received in Europe.[114] About a year later the matter still evoked enough interest in London for Lord Salisbury to be asked a question in the British parliament on the issue of 'forced conversion'. Salisbury answered that the British, in consultation with all the other embassies in Istanbul, had urged the Ottoman government to allow the Armenians to return to their original faith.[115]

A similar case was reported from the vilayet of Ankara on 30 May 1891. An Armenian woman convert, having gone back to her native Yozgad in central Anatolia to see her child 'whom she had left there before her conversion', was waylaid by the local priest 'who tricked her into going to his dwelling'. There, members of the local Armenian community put pressure on her to convert back, and threatened to kidnap and remove her to the town of Sis. A police official was sent from Ankara, but he abstained from marching in to the priest's quarters, 'in order to avoid giving the impression of a forcible removal.' He had instead arranged for the local headman (*muhtar*) to intervene and had the woman brought to the residence of the local müftü. It was decided in Istanbul that 'it is in no way permissible to hand over someone who insists on her loyalty to Islam.' As in the case of the *dönme* girl, it was recommended that the woman and her husband, who was a policeman, be brought to Istanbul.[116]

Naturally, conversion was taken quite seriously by the Armenian authorities, who kept close watch over such cases. On 3 July 1872, it was reported from Muş, that a woman, Peroz, had two husbands, one in Bitlis and one in Muş. Having run into difficulties with her first husband, who announced that she might no longer consider herself his wife, she decided to become Muslim. 'We tried to change her mind at the government palace for two hours but could not convince her and now the Dajigs want to marry her off to a third person, but we forbade them, saying she already had two husbands. Now we hear that she wants to return to Christianity. We ask you (the Patriarchate in Istanbul) to petition the Sublime Porte ... so that the woman may escape the claws of the Muslims.'[117]

The Ottoman records also mention cases such as that of a certain Mehmed, an Armenian convert from Gümüşhane. The remarkable thing about Mehmed, was the fact that the sultan personally paid for his circumcision, and arranged for him to be employed as a cleaner at the hospital where he was circumcised and to receive a salary of 300 *kuruş*.[118] A legendary case of abduction and forced conversion is the story of Arménouhie Kévonian, a young Armenian girl from the Muş region who was abducted by a Kurdish Sheikh, Musa Bey, in 1889. Forced to convert by the Kurds, young Arménouhie secretly retained her faith, and international pressure forced the Ottoman government to bring Musa Bey to court in Istanbul.

Although Musa was actually acquitted, causing considerable outrage in Armenian and European public opinion, the girl was restored to the Armenian community.[119]

As the tensions between Muslims and Armenians mounted in the 1890s, the Ottoman centre became more attentive to the smallest detail that could influence inter-community relations. On 3 September 1890, the Vali of Sivas reported that the Armenians of Sivas had applied to build a church and a school on property belonging to them. He recommended that they be allowed to do so on the following grounds: 'Because Muslim and non-Muslim live in mixed neighbourhoods in Sivas, there has been no opposition to the building among the Muslims. Because the Armenians generally tend to live in separate neighbourhoods, the fact that they are mixed in with Muslims here, makes for good relations (*hüsnü hıltat*) and the maintenance of law and order is thereby facilitated.'[120] Presumably the paşa was aware of the fact that inter-communal violence occurred more readily when communities were segregated, making it easy to stigmatize the 'other'.

The matter of conversion 'by due process' continues to be the dominant theme throughout the period. On 4 February 1903, it was reported that a number of Christians from Alkuş, in the vilayet of Mosul, had been rounded up by a Sheikh Muhammed Nur, marched into Mosul, and there converted to Islam. It was stated that 'although they publicly signed a petition asking to convert, some of them secretly made it known that they were not sincere in their conversion and had only undertaken such an act out of fear of Sheikh Muhammed.' The sheikh had also 'pressured some of the local *ulema* to expedite the regular process, and a priest who should have been present, was not sent by the Patriarchate.'[121]

A few days later, it was to be reported that the local Islamic population of Mosul were in a great state of excitement because 'the due process of law had not been carried out during the conversions, and the local Patriarchate did not send a priest.'[122] On 14 February, the Vali of Mosul reported that the local Muslim population had attacked the government building. It was said that this was because: 'the vali had accepted the conversion of the Alkuş Christians who had converted against their will, without the official procedure being observed (*muamelat-ı resmiye ifa olunmaksızın*).' There is a very distinct air of foreboding in the document, and the Ministry of Interior declared that it feared for the vali's life.[123]

On 3 November 1891, a group of Christians from Antioch complained that 'they had been denied the honour of Islam' by the officials of the town. Istanbul ordered that the matter be investigated, particularly in relation to what denomination the petitioners belonged to, as ' there is freedom of religion'. Strict instructions were given that, 'they be treated according to accepted practice and regulations were also given.'[124]

Conclusion

In examining Ottoman conversion policy and ideological control in the Hamidian era, the interesting aspect of this rather murky story lies in the different ways in which the Ottoman elite perceived the various minorities and specific cases. Their reaction to the recalcitrant Yezidi was very different from their reaction to the *dönme* girl who could have complicated matters if she was to remain in her native Salonika. The Armenian converts and potential 're-converts' were a much more serious problem and one which achieved international proportions. The Kızılbaş had always been a thorn in the side of the Ottomans, but the response of Selim I in the sixteenth century had been very different to that of Abdülhamid II. The former could afford to contemplate the massacre of large numbers of Kızılbaş, whereas the latter's main concern was the question of their reliability in the army. It is particularly significant that even sections of the population who were ostensibly 'mainstream', such as the people of Ankara and Trabzon, were seen as being in need of 'ideological rectification' in a way that was not wholly dissimilar from that imposed on the Bedouin of the Ma'an valley.

Another fact which emerges from the evidence is that the *şeriat* ruling making it admissible to execute Muslims leaving the faith (*mürted*), was no longer officially practised. After the *ferman* of 1856 officially allowed everyone the freedom of religion, the Ottomans had to officially admit Christian missionary activity. This led to a fear among the Ottoman ruling classes that the religious base of state legitimation ideology was slipping from under them. Ahmed Şakir Paşa was to state unequivocally that 'As the basis of power (*üs-ü saltanat*) is the Muslim population, the power of the state will increase in proportion to the number of its Muslim subjects ... Therefore we must do our utmost to prevent the defection of those such as the İstavri and to accept the conversion of those such as the Nuseyri.'[125]

The evident desire of the Ottoman centre was to stabilize the religious-ethnic status quo. There was nothing new in this policy. What was particular to the times was the constant affirmation and re-affirmation of what should have been the norm anyway. In this context the impression derived from the documentary evidence is one of worry-cum-panic among the administrators. In the immediate aftermath of the Armenian massacres and general upheaval in Anatolia in the late 1890s, the large number of orphans was a great cause of concern to the Porte. It was feared that both Muslim and Armenian orphans would be the target of Protestant missionary activity. An imperial order, dated 1 August 1897, reflects this attitude quite clearly as it provides for the constitution of a mixed commission whose specific brief was 'to prevent the spread of the influence of foreigners and to ensure that each remains in his own confession, and to prevent the conversion of His Imperial Majesty's subjects to Protestantism as well as other foreign creeds.' The commission was to be made up of three Muslim officials, (one each from the şeyhülislam's office, the Ministry of Education, and the Ministry of the Interior), two Armenians, and one Greek Orthodox.[126]

In the event, Muslim conversion or re-conversion to Christianity remained minimal, but this was not something that could have been taken for granted at the time. A memorandum prepared by the sultan for Ahmed Şakir Paşa reflected this state of mind: 'Although the Sublime State cannot force anyone to accept Islam, we can never tolerate the conversion of Muslims to Christianity.'[127] It is now time to turn to the issue of how the desired legitimating principles were to be instilled in the subject/citizen population through education.

Chapter Four
Education: The Answer to all Evil?

The wiry little man looked distinctly out of place in the imperial audience chamber of the Yıldız Palace, like a small bird of prey that had accidentally flown in through the window. His Imperial Majesty warily eyed the slight figure clad in Kurdish hillsman's garb. He had been told that the young man before him, already a sheikh with a considerable following, was a potential asset for Islamic mobilization in Anatolia, a matter close to his heart. Yet, something bothered him in the fellow's manner, particularly his way of looking the Commander of the Faithful straight in the eye. The sultan's disturbance was to turn to shock as the man, introduced as Sheikh Said-i Nursi from Bitlis, addressed him in the familiar form (*sen*) and went on: 'You have been a passive caliph. Anatolia cries out for schools. Van is overrun with missionaries who have provided excellent schooling for the Armenians. Why is there not a Kurdish university on the shores of Lake Van?' Clearly the man had taken leave of his senses. He was immediately set upon by the chamberlains and bustled out of the imperial presence. The dignitary who had introduced him hastened to make profuse apologies and point out that the young Kurd must be deranged. Yet that evening, when the excitement of the day had died down, the sultan reflected on the event, and in his heart he knew the Kurd was right.

In the second half of the nineteenth century the Ottoman Empire came into its own as an 'educator state' with a systematic programme of education/indoctrination for subjects it intended to mould into citizens.[1] Together with the Russian, Austrian, French, British, German and Japanese empires, the Ottoman Empire set about creating what Hobsbawm has called 'a captive audience available for indoctrination in the education system', in a 'citizen mobilizing and citizen influencing state'.[2] Education had always been an integral part of the Ottoman statesman's 'mission civilisatrice' since the Tanzimat reforms early in the century; but in the Hamidian era mass education was extended to the primary school level.[3]

As in other imperial states, the main aim was to produce a population which was obedient, but also trained into espousing the values of the centre as its own. In this sense legitimist monarchies were definitely adopting the road taken by their ideological enemy, the French Revolution. As Eugene Weber pointed out in his pathbreaking book 'teaching the people French was an important way of "civilizing" them'.[4] Count Uvarov, the Russian minister for education responsible for the policy of 'Russification' of non-Russian peoples in the empire, could not have agreed more when he told Nicholas I (1825–55) that the whole basis of his rule was 'Orthodoxy, autocracy, and nationality'[5]

Indeed, the Russian example was very much on the minds of Ottoman statesmen like Ahmet Şakir Paşa, who advocated mixed schooling in primary schools for Muslim and non-Muslim, using as a precedent Russian educational policy in Poland, Tataristan and the Caucasus. Şakir Paşa also advocated the exclusive use of Turkish as the language of instruction, as 'linguistic unity was basic to national unity'.[6] In an Ottoman context this translated itself into the administration of ever increasing doses of the approved religion through the school system in an effort to induce conformity. It also meant combating rival educational systems such as that of the Christian minorities and the missionary schools.

Ottoman education policy in application

On 2 March 1887, the şeyhülislam's office presented a memorandum to the Yıldız Palace dealing with an imperial order to revise the curricula of secondary and higher schools. The memo stated that, 'for a nation to securely establish the basis for its religion the matter should be tackled at its source.'[7] The şeyhülislam's view was that religious education was sorely lacking in primary (*ibtidaiye*) and secondary (*rüşdiye*) schools, as was knowledge of Arabic, 'the pillar of the Ottoman language'.[8]

Higher secondary/middle schools (*idadi*) and the Imperial Civil Service School (*Mekteb-i Mülkiye-i Şahane*) were also to have their curricula revised and additional hours of religious instruction inserted. The same was true for the Imperial Military Academy (*Harbiye*), the School of Medicine (*Tıbbiye*), and the School of Engineering (*Mühendishane*). In these at least the şeyhülislam was prepared to admit, 'although we are not qualified to judge their scientific teaching matter it should be sufficient to fortify religious belief by the addition of reading materials of a religious nature.'⁹ The Galatasaray Lycée, an elite high school on the French model, and with a heavy emphasis on French language, was singled out by the şeyhülislam because of 'its special nature'. The students of this school he stated, 'had to be kept away from Western books harmful to the interests of the Sublime State.' Also the fact that some Muslim schools were teaching in foreign languages was a decidedly bad thing and, 'should be avoided altogether'. Only approved books would be translated into Ottoman.¹⁰ The director of the Galatasaray Lycée added that, 'Latin and Philosophy lessons should be removed, nothing should be taught relating to the lives of European philosophers.' Religious instruction should be increased and entrusted to teachers whose loyalty was beyond question and who would instruct the students on the life and deeds of the Prophet Muhammed and his followers.¹¹

The memorandum also included a detailed breakdown of the lessons to be taught in the five-year *rüşdiye*. In the first year, religion and Arabic accounted for eight out of twelve hours of teaching per week. The Turkish grammar lesson was also to be based on a 'book of Islamic morals'. Geography and 'the globe showing European countries' was only to be introduced in the third year and that for only one hour out of twelve. The whole of the five years' instruction was to be very heavily weighted in favour of classical Islamic learning. Geography was to be taught only in the third and fourth years for one and two hours respectively. At each Ramadan the students were to memorize by rote the works of Abu Hanifa, and before each recess prayers would be said for the long life and health of the sultan.¹²

Maps of the world were also carefully inspected to ensure that no official claims to territory on the part of the Ottoman State were omitted. On 7 April 1898, it came to the palace's attention that, 'maps of the Asian continent which were being used in primary schools included certain errors as to the Asiatic frontiers of the Sublime State.'¹³ It was duly ordered that the maps be confiscated, and new maps drawn. These latter were only to be distributed to schools after they had been submitted to the palace for inspection.¹⁴

This parochialism was reflected in a denunciation of the history master of Galatasaray, a certain Midhat Bey, who was roundly criticized for 'going beyond the set book and talking about ancient Egypt, Greece and Rome'. It was stressed that his behaviour was particularly offensive as 'the first duty of every instructor should be the correction of the beliefs (*tashih-i akaid*) of his students.' The instructor was also accused of having what would today be called an 'attitude problem': 'he has been known to make light of the four sacred schools of Islamic jurisprudence by mentioning them in the same breath as the idolatrous gods of ancient Greece. He also makes fun of the other instructors as well as the Christian religion.'[15] The man was probably very popular with his students.

The emphasis on training a loyal and competent state elite, which would be thoroughly imbued with the values of the centre, was a basic consideration of the Ottoman higher educational establishment. As stated in a circular directive from the Ministry of Education to all the higher schools, students graduating from these institutions were expected to be 'of good character and breeding, ready to serve their state and country unwaveringly'.[16] At the Civil Service School (the Mülkiye) in particular, all instructors were ordered to 'take every opportunity to instill the sacredness of duty to the state, which must be the first thing in the consciousness of every civil servant.' All instructors were ordered to stress religious lessons and Islamic jurisprudence (*fıkh*). As in the case of the Galatasaray teacher mentioned above, all were specifically and sternly enjoined, 'not to venture into topics beyond the curriculum'.[17] Even topics which were not religious were submitted to strict censorship. The Ministry for Education was ordered to inspect the international law textbooks used at the Mülkiye, and 'to delete any harmful materials'. A commission was duly established to inspect the course textbooks used in the school, and to report on those which were found objectionable.[18]

In another elite institution, the Imperial Naval Academy (*Mekteb-i Bahriye*), the religious probity of the student body became a matter of close concern for the sultan. The school authorities were asked to provide the names of the books used in religious instruction classes, and both the names and the titles of the instructors of religion. The palace also wanted to know whether or not prayers were being said regularly and where the students attended Friday prayers. The school authorities assured the palace that the utmost attention was devoted to religious probity and that signs which outlined daily religious obligations were posted everywhere in the school under the title 'General Behaviour' (*harekat-ı umumiye*).[19]

A general circular was sent out from the palace to all military secondary schools demanding to be informed about the nature of religious instruction enforced. The Minister for Military Schools, Mustafa Zeki Paşa, replied on 23 January 1898 that students who missed one prayer were punished by being confined to grounds on their days of home leave. Students who missed their fasts during Ramadan were also punished by being imprisoned in the school.[20]

Another way of attempting to prevent the spread of 'harmful' ideologies among the young was to prevent them from studying abroad. In the last years of the Hamidian regime this inclination became more acute. Particularly in Salonika, where the crypto-Jewish *dönme* elite had accumulated considerable capital, and could afford to send their sons to Europe, this was seen as a problem. The inspectorate for the vilayets of Rumelia was to note that: '[These young people] go to Switzerland and France to study and acquire experience in commerce. Failing that they attend the schools of commerce in Salonica belonging to the French, Italians, Greeks or Rumanians. Either way this is detrimental to their Islamic and Ottoman upbringing.' The inspector suggested that additional classes in commerce and finance be added to the curriculum of the elite Terakki and Fevziye schools in Salonika, which most of sons of the local leading families attended, in this way 'preventing the pollution of their Islamic morals by study abroad'.[21]

The intensification of religious instruction was to spread to all the elite educational establishments by the turn of the century. The Ministry for Military Schools was to attribute to this policy, '[The fact that] the survival of the Sublime State depends on the preservation of the Islamic faith.'[22] The most immediate instrument for the 'survival of the Sublime State', namely, the army, also became a focus for religious education. It was confirmed on several occasions that 'the rank and file are having the approved religious texts read to them at regular intervals', to instill in them the 'sacredness of their duty'.[23]

As far as the 'sacredness of duty' was concerned, Abdülhamid's efforts do not seem to have been in vain. As Carter Findley has expressed it: 'To the extent that an effort to train a new type of civil official had occurred under Abdül-Hamid, however, the effort was his, made chiefly through the School of Civil Administration.'[24] Findley points to the beginnings of 'a new professionalism' in the Ottoman administrative cadres.[25]

Another extensive memorandum prepared some eight years later was even more explicit about instilling a sense of its own mission in the Ottoman ruling class: 'It is His Imperial Majesty's wish that men of great firmness of religious faith and national zeal be trained to believe that their happiness is one with the eternal Sublime State.'[26] The memorandum declared that 'everyone should be required to have an education while preserving his religion and traditions .... Also all forms of progress in a state are contingent upon the training of students and in the preservation of their religion and national honour.'[27] Therefore utmost attention had to be paid to teachers, so that the wrong kind of teacher did not poison the minds of the future generations.

Despite the conservative tenor of these instructions and directives, it would appear that the actual programmes that were formulated were more realistic. Although a table specifying the curricula for schools from primary to Mülkiye, was heavily weighted in favour of religious studies, Qur'an reading (*tecvid*) always having a preponderant place from primary school to the highest level, more practical considerations were also at work. In the provincial *idadi* middle schools the programme was also to include courses like cosmography, general and Ottoman geography, Economics, geometry and agricultural science. Moreover, in some areas provision was made that some of these could be taught in Arabic, Armenian, Bulgarian or Greek. In the Arab provinces, particularly in intellectual centres like Damascus, the government schools continued to be centres of learning, and were greatly influential in the formation of the Arab elites who would later go on to become the first leaders of independent Arab successor states.[28] French language and translation also seems to have continued to figure in the curricula of Galatasaray (despite the best efforts of Recai Bey) and in the Mülkiye curriculum, in addition to training in Arabic, Greek, Bulgarian and Armenian. Another aspect of the instructions was the strict supervision of students 'lest they show signs of wayward and unreliable behaviour.'[29]

The extensive reports and memoranda written by Ottoman officials stationed at various outposts of the empire shed very useful light on how these men perceived 'national' education. Osman Nuri Paşa, the longtime governor of the Hijaz and Yemen vilayets, left several such memoranda.[30] The paşa's view of education was in general directly influenced by Enlightenment thinking: 'The people of a country without education are like so many lifeless corpses, not benefiting humanity in any way (*maarifsiz memleket ahalisi cemiyet-i beşeriyye'ye nefiyyi olmayan ecsad-ı mefluce gibidir*).' The paşa maintained that although religious schooling was 'the only basis for the protection and reinforcement of Islamic zeal (*asabiyyet-i Islamiye*)', rational and political learning acquired through 'modern education' was also essential for the continuing strength of Islam. The *medreses* of the Holy Lands were sorely lacking on this score, and were in any case 'full of

Indians, Javanese and Turks, which means that the learning dispensed here only benefits foreigners.'[31]

The Dutch Javanese Muslims, British Indian Muslims, or Turkish subjects of the Russian empire, who filled these medreses in the holy land, like those non-Ottomans in the Hijaz, are perceived very clearly as foreigners, interloping on scanty Ottoman educational resources.[32] In matters of taxation Osman Nuri Paşa bemoaned the fact that the foreigners in the Hijaz paid no taxes, complaining: 'It is a source of great sorrow that the foreigners, who already control much of the land and real estate of the Holy Lands, benefit from exemption [from taxes] even more than the local inhabitants.' He advocated the taxation of the foreigners and recommended that the proceeds be used to lighten the load of Ottoman taxpayers elsewhere.[33] The local Arab tribes should be 'gradually civilized' through education and 'thus by their own hands brought to destroy their [savage] customs.' Also, the sons of local Arab notables such as sheikhs, *sharifs* and other highly placed religious functionaries should not be allowed to inherit their fathers' positions without first passing through the Ottoman schooling system and acquiring the appropriate diplomas. The teaching of Turkish was of extreme importance as, 'one of the primary means of blending in the various tribes and peoples of a state is the unification of language (*tevhid-i lisan*).'[34] Bismarck and Mazzini would have fully agreed.

A more cynical view of educational policy was put forward by Ahmet Şakir Paşa during one of his tours of inspection in Anatolia. The paşa strongly advocated giving priority to the establishment of primary schools in regions whose loyalty was doubtful.[35]

Another target of Ottoman 'special schooling' was the Shi'i population of largely Shi'i vilayets such as Mosul, Basra and Baghdad. The attempt to indoctrinate Shi'is involved children of modest backgrounds. A letter from the governor of Baghdad, dated 30 December 1891, stated that in keeping with the sultan's instructions, ten Shi'i children were being sent to Istanbul from Baghdad and Kerbela. Yet the governor had seen fit to include two Sunni boys, 'to set the minds of the Shi'a at rest and show that these children were going to Istanbul to study as the result of the Sultan's generosity.' As the families who volunteered were poor, six of the boys were to have clothes made at the state's expense and the sultan paid their travel expenses and the fees of their travel chaperones. It is worth quoting from the document at length as it openly declares that the aim of the exercise was to train future propagandists/missionaries:

Since so much money has been spent [on these children] it is important that the necessary benefits be derived from their education. The training of those among them who are Shi'i should ensure that they abandon this sect and become Hanefi, in order to enable them to convert their countrymen to the Hanefi sect upon their return.[36]

The Iraqi provinces of Baghdad, Basra and Mosul come up very frequently in dispatches relating to education. Geographically remote, and religiously suspect because of the heavy Shi'i presence and the proximity of Iran, the Ottoman valis in these provinces adopted something of a siege mentality when it came to educational policies. In this vein, the Vali of Mosul, İsmail Nuri Paşa, reported to Istanbul on 11 November 1892 that 'Mosul constitutes a strategic barrier between the Shi'is in Baghdad and Iran.' Its population was mostly Hanefi or Shaæafi and was therefore deemed reliable. The effort to convert the Yezidis and the Şebekli had been a success. The Yezidi shrine of Sheikh Adi in Şeyhan had been converted into a teacher training school for Hanefi scholars. Education in Turkish should be emphasized even more as this was a vital matter. The most revealing aspect of the dispatch lies in the vali's use of military imagery in educational matters:

> If the light of education is made to shine in these provinces, this will provide a line of defence and a screen of resistance for our frontiers against the covetous glances of the foreigner ... This will block the roads against the illegitimate sect of Shi'ism by erecting educational defence works in its path.[37]

Clearly, the *ibtidaiye* and *rüşdiye* schools that the imperial centre was encouraged to institute in the region were envisioned as so many fortresses against foreign penetration. The military imagery went hand in hand with the *mission civilizatrice*, as the vali did not neglect to stress that the tribes, 'who live in a state of nomadism, savagery and ignorance', had to be 'brought into the community of civilized peoples'.[38]

When it was a matter of this or that element of the Muslim population misbehaving, education was always seen as the first cure, as an alternative to the military option. When the vilayet of Mosul reported that a Kurdish tribe, the Peşderli, had been ransacking the countryside, and asked permission to send in troops, the instructions from Istanbul were quite explicit: 'Before troops are sent against them, in order to avoid spilling Muslim blood ... their leaders should be advised and admonished ... moderate methods (*vesait-i leyyine*) aimed at winning them over ... like schools ... should be made use of.'³⁹

That education was the alternative to 'the stick' if only by a hair's breadth, is brought out in the following statement by an Ottoman local official addressing the population of a village who were resisting the establishment of a gendarme post: 'With people like you only two things are possible. One, schools in which to educate you to see the necessity of law and order ... the other is the stick. Now, schools take fifteen years to produce a man such as I want; the stick is a matter of five minutes ...'⁴⁰

The Tribal School

Much of what officials like Şakir Paşa or Osman Nuri Paşa advocated was taken up by Abdülhamid II. One such initiative was the establishment of the Tribal School or Mekteb-i Aşiret. As a vehicle of inculcating Ottoman patriotism in Arab and Kurdish boys, a special school was established by imperial order (*irade*) and opened its doors on 3 October 1892.⁴¹ The school was initially founded for the purpose of training the children of leading Arab sheikhs and notables to be good Ottomans and to counter increasing British influence around the Arabian peninsula. The idea was then extended to include the sons of Kurdish sheikhs and some Albanians.

Starting as a two-year boarding school, eventually building up to five, it was stated that a major aim was 'to bring civilization' to the Arab tribes and to ensure their loyalty to the Ottoman state. The curriculum stressed intensive Turkish, although at its earliest stage, given that the boys would speak no Turkish, Arabic and Turkish would be used together.⁴² To start with four students between the ages of twelve and sixteen would be sent from each of the vilayets of Aleppo, Syria, Baghdad, Basra, Mosul, Diyarbekir, and Tripoli; and four from the *sancaks* of Bingazi, Jerusalem and Zor. That they sent five students each was evidence of the special importance accorded to the Yemen and the Hijaz vilayets.⁴³ Although originally intended for the sons of leading Arabs, demands from the Kurdish sheikhs, particularly those who were in command positions in the irregular Hamidiye cavalry, soon meant that their sons, too, were (somewhat grudgingly) accepted into the fold. They in turn were joined by sons of Albanian notables who likewise put pressure on Istanbul to have their sons admitted.⁴⁴

There was indeed enthusiasm among the Arab and Kurdish sheikhs for their sons to be admitted. The Ministry of the Interior reported on 20 September that Arab sheikhs, 'who normally do not even let their children venture far out of their tents, have been happily bringing their children with their own hands, because they know that their ignorance and rudeness (*cehl ve nadaniyet*) will thus be replaced by the light of civilization.'⁴⁵ The minister also reported that sheikhs were even competing with each other: a Sheikh Ali al-Necri from the *sancak* of Zor, when told that the year's quota was full, bitterly protested that if his son was not taken he would lose face, and that he was even ready to pay for his travel expenses.⁴⁶

On 3 October 1892, the Vali of Mamuretülaziz (modern Elazığ) reported that the orders to send three boys from his area had been made known to the local 'notables and respected leaders' of the Kurdish tribes.⁴⁷ This had caused great enthusiasm among them and six boys rather than the stipulated three were 'extremely eager to make the journey'. The vali pointed out that given the 'sensitive nature of the Dersim area' it would be inadvisable to turn back the extra three, and recommended that all six be admitted to the Tribal School.⁴⁸

The prestige of the school increased to the point where powerful families were using their influence with local authorities to pass their children off as members of tribes to have them admitted too. The provincial authorities were instructed to 'ascertain whether or not the prospective student was of the tribal element,' and turn back those who were not.⁴⁹

The demand for education on the part of the Kurdish population is brought out in Şerif Mardin's study of the legendary Sheikh Said-i Nursi. When actually granted an audience by Abdülhamid, Nursi, then an impetuous young sheikh, spoke out very plainly in favour of a Kurdish university which he demanded be established in Van. Nursi told the sultan, in no uncertain terms, that if he hoped to compete with the Protestant missionaries, modern Islamic education was his only hope.⁵⁰

The Tribal School was established in an old palace in Beşiktaş which had once belonged to the Ottoman family. The first principal was the ubiquitous Recai Efendi who also remained assistant principal of the Mülkiye. Life at the school could not have been easy for these bewildered boys, a long way from home and not speaking the language. The regime was very strict and they were kept under virtual house arrest, only being allowed out occasionally and then under strict supervision.

The discussion of the issue of confinement to the school grounds is very interesting as it sheds light on the mentality of the Ottoman educators. The students had first been permitted to spend weekly holidays with relatives and friends in the city. Soon it became evident that in the early days of the school this was not a very good idea; those who had relatives and could go out were viewed with envy by those who had no such contacts. The minister of education, Zühdü Paşa pointed out that, 'because many of the students are still in their state of nomadism and savagery, they have yet to understand the blessings of civilization.'[51] Part of this 'savage' behaviour consisted of 'jumping over the school wall in an attempt to escape.' It was therefore much more preferable for the students to be strictly supervised and confined to the grounds, 'until they appreciate their surroundings.' On Fridays they were to be taken around the great mosques of the city 'to give them a chance to see the splendour of the spectacle,' which they would doubtless appreciate as 'they are people of the desert and have not had much contact with civilized folk.'[52]

The list of 'directives for the administration' stipulated that all the boys' letters to their families were first to be censored by their teachers, and anything untoward be 'corrected'.[53] A weekly register of events at the school was to be kept and 'no erasings were to be permitted: any change in wording can only be done by drawing a line through the mistake, still leaving it clearly legible.' At the end of each day the boys were to be assembled and instructed on the glory of the Islamic faith and the duty incumbent on each Muslim to obey the sultan who was caliph of all Muslims.'[54]

It would appear that Abdülhamid assumed something of the role of a *pater familias* with his young Arab and Kurdish charges. The sultan was regularly presented with a table showing the yearly marks each student had achieved in each subject. On one particular occasion the Palace made it known to the school administration that, '[It has] come to HIM's attention that some of the students have been behaving badly, it is most undesirable that these students should be sent back to their homes with evil in their characters (*mesavi-i ahlak sahibi*).' The school administration was strictly enjoined to ensure the proper behaviour of the boys,'lest they be held responsible'.[55]

About one year later 'proper behaviour' seemed fairly thin on the ground as it was reported that 'Arab and Kurdish students have been involved in a fight using stones, shoes and fists, resulting in light injuries to four Kurds and six Arabs.' No less a personage than the minister of education, Zühdü Paşa, immediately descended on the school with a military escort. The minister took pains to report that 'the matter appears to have been the result of a small argument, and does not involve any internal or external provocation.' The comment clearly implied fear of possible ethnic strife between the Kurds and the Arabs, who were supposedly learning to be brothers.[56]

After four (later five) years at the school the students would be expected to attend the Mekteb-i Sultani and then the Mülkiye, eventually returning to their home provinces as teachers and officials.[57] A memorandum from the Imperial Arsenal (Tophane-i Amire) dated 22 September 1897, drew attention to the fact that the first fifty graduates of the Tribal School had completed their studies, and had been sent on to the Military Academy (Harbiye) and the Mülkiye. There the Kurdish boys had been given one year's training in cavalry tactics, and the Arabs trained as civil servants. The commander of all military schools, Zeki Paşa, pointed out that a certain delay had occurred in their being sent back to their home provinces, and that this was causing gossip. As fledgling Ottoman military and civilian officials the graduates were to be given third, fourth and fifth rank position (*salise, rabia, hamse*) in the Ottoman bureaucratic system and sent back forthwith.[58]

After a period of further training in their home region, the graduate of the Mekteb-i Aşiret who had completed his studies in the Military Academy or the Civil Service School would be expected to serve in hardship posts such as Yemen, Bingazi, or Mosul. This caused considerable problems because the young graduates of these elite institutions looked down on appointments to areas which they regarded as backwaters, and wanted to stay on in Istanbul or, at worst, to be sent back to the provincial capital of their own regions.[59]

The Tribal School lasted until 1907 when it was suddenly closed down, ostensibly because of a food riot among the students. One can only surmise that the student population was stirred up by something more serious than flies in their soup: nascent Arab nationalism perhaps, or the spread of Young Turk propaganda since the Young Turk 'Revolution' was to follow one year later.[60]

The Ottoman attitude to non-Muslim education

Contemporary discussions about the education of both the general population and the elite are pervaded by a sense of impending danger. In them, the empire is envisioned as a besieged fortress where the utmost care must be taken to counter the subversive activities of a potential fifth column.

For that reason non-Muslim educational establishments were kept under the closest supervision and were always regarded with extreme suspicion. A circular from the sultan to his ministers clearly drew the following parallel: 'While the Sublime State's Greek and Armenian subjects are fewer in number compared to Islamic subjects, even in villages of five or ten houses we see the construction of big churches and schools ... while many mosques languish in a state of disrepair and many *medreses* have become almost vacant.'[61] There was a distinct shift of emphasis in the Hamidian era as the relatively tolerant atmosphere of the Tanzimat period evaporated.[62] As early as 1858, under the Law on Education, all non-Muslim schools were made subject to license and their activities allowed only if they conformed to the regulations of the Ministry of Education.[63] It must be said, however, that although these laws were passed and stringent regulations made, the fact that they were incessantly reconfirmed in subsequent years indicates that the Ottoman authorities had very real difficulties applying them.

The 1869 Law on Education authorized the inspection of the curricula of non-Muslim schools. In 1880 this was reinforced, and local educational commissions were assigned the duty of supervising the schoolbooks and syllabuses of such establishments.[64] Turkish language teaching was made obligatory in non-Muslim schools in 1894.[65] Turkish teachers were assigned to non-Muslim schools and their salaries paid by the Ottoman government.[66] In 1887 the inspectorate of non-Muslim and foreign schools' was established for the first time.[67]

Interestingly enough, one of the most stringent memoranda on the need to curtail non-Muslim education, came from a Christian teacher, an Armenian by the name of Mihran Boyacıyan Efendi, teacher in the Beirut *idadi*. In 1891 he was to warn of the danger of Christian schools in Beirut, and particularly the danger of Muslim children attending them. He also stressed the importance of Turkish language and Ottoman history teaching in non-Muslim schools.[68]

The Ottoman archives are full of orders to close down this or that school ostensibly for lacking a license. On 20 March 1890, the Ministry of Education pointed out that the Wallachian (*Ulah*) and Greek schools in the vilayet of Manastır (present-day Bitóla in Macedonia) were all without licenses and should be closed down.[69]

Teaching the Armenian language in government schools in the provinces was also a problematic issue. The Ministry of Education was firmly instructed not to appoint a teacher of Armenian to the *idadi* of Erzurum as 'it is sufficient to confine the teaching of Armenian to the schools in Istanbul where officials are trained.'[70] The teaching of Armenian in provincial government schools was deemed 'not unlikely to have a bad effect on the population of Erzurum, the majority of whom speak Armenian.'[71] This information is paralleled by H. B. Lynch's account, a travelogue, where he recorded that an Armenian private secondary college in Erzurum, the famous Sanasarean College was being harassed in 1894 by the local authorities. School textbooks on Armenian church history and Armenian culture had been confiscated.[72]

This indicates very clearly that the Ottoman authorities understood only too well the connection between language and nationalist ferment. The issue becomes all the more significant when we learn from Andreas Tietze that 'significant portions of the Greek as well as of the Armenian communities in Constantinople were Turkophone and had little or no knowledge of the language of their own ancestors.'[73] The extent of this is shown by the case of the Jesuits of Galata who, in 1702, obtained the Armenian patriarch's agreement to preach in Turkish in Armenian schools.[74] Given that Turkish was so widely spoken among Armenian and Greek communities, the emphasis placed by Armenian and Greek nationalists on the use of their own language represented a very direct challenge to the Ottoman system.

So deeply was this challenge felt that the state considered suspect even such seemingly innocent facets of school life as schoolchildren's songs in Armenian. On 6 May 1890, the vilayet of Bursa was instructed to 'punish in an exemplary fashion' the teachers and director of an Armenian school in the Ayna Göl district, as the examination of the song books used in the school had revealed 'their subversive nature (bazı efkar-ı faside)'.[75] Similarly, on 26 August 1890, the Armenian Patriarchate complained to the Ottoman authorities that 'some of their prayer books which were a thousand years old have been banned as subversive.' The Ottoman authorities recommended that the genuine old prayer books should be permitted but the interdict should apply to 'the newly written [books] which include symbols and abbreviations (rumuzlu) which are potentially harmful.'[76]

In the same year, the Ministry of Education was informed that correspondence which had been intercepted between the Greek embassy in Istanbul and the Greek foreign ministry had revealed that Greek schools in the Ottoman Empire were being actively encouraged by the Greek government to teach 'in accordance with Greek educational practices'.[77] A novel by Kozmas Politis, which has recently been translated into Turkish, gives some indication that on this score the Ottoman authorities were right to suspect the worst. It gives a charming description of schoolmasters of a Greek school in Izmir (Smyrna) in the late 1890s taking their boys on a field trip to the countryside around the city. The boys visit some Greek ruins on a mountain top where they are made to stand in silence for one minute 'in honour of the ancient Hellenic past'. They are then quizzed on the Greek names of mountains and rivers they see before them, at which point the schoolmaster in charge tearfully declares, 'all this was Hellenic once – it will always be Hellenic!'[78]

Conclusion

The project of Ottoman education policy was to reinforce the ideological legitimacy of a social order which felt increasingly threatened by changing world conditions. This could only be done through the education and indoctrination of the people, 'which ... raised unprecedented problems [for the state] of how to maintain or even establish the obedience, loyalty and cooperation of its subjects and members, or its own legitimacy in their eyes.'[79]

There were very real constraints on the establishment of an empire-wide educational system. The most basic was money. Although all local administrations were expected to contribute a share of their revenues as the 'education budget' (*maarif hissesi*), very often this money was not forthcoming, and schools were not built and teachers left unpaid.

A representative complaint on these lines came from Yemen in 1890 when the teachers of the primary school in San'a protested that they had not been paid for some time.[80] Similarly, the vilayet of Baghdad complained in 1890 that it had attempted to raise funds for the local *rüşdiye* secondary school by seeking donations from 'charitable persons', but had been unsuccessful.[81] In 1899, the vilayet of Kastamonu was to propose the payment of village primary school teachers in kind, the parents of the pupils providing a certain proportion of their agricultural yield at each harvest.[82]

The other major problem was the low level of literacy. Carter Findley has estimated that literacy went from 'perhaps 1 percent in 1800 to 5–10 percent for the empire in 1900.' Although the educational reforms started from a very low base, by the Young Turk era *rüşdiye* middle schools were to be found throughout the empire. By the end of the empire, the areas that are now Syria and Iraq had '570 Ottoman government schools with 28,400 pupils in elementary and 2,100 in secondary grades,' from which many went to higher schools in Istanbul.[83] Modest village primary schools made a favourable impression on foreign travellers who noted the presence of girls: 'In the village of Topaklı-Keui, in the school we noted with great surprise that many girls were seated next to the boys. This is a symptom of the great moral progress recorded in Turkey, and is a definite indicator of the coming salvation of women in that country.'[84] Official propagandists were also directed to write about the progress in education as an indicator of successful reform. Princess Annie de Lusignan visited the 'Sani, Turkish school for girls' and came away suitably moved by its clean and orderly appearance: 'I should have to write several books in order to do justice to the efforts of the Sultan on behalf of national education, or to give any adequate idea of his ceaseless activity in that great cause.'[85] Abdülhamid also made a point of showing foreign visitors around his 'showcase schools' designed to impress them. A major feature in the photograph albums sent to leading foreign libraries as the 'Imperial Self Portrait' were picture after picture of grave little girls clutching their diplomas.[86]

As the monarchies of the late nineteenth century 'sidle[d] towards a beckoning national identification', the Ottoman Empire found itself in the same boat as the Russian, Japanese, Austrian, German, and even Chinese empires.[87] Almost at the same time as Count Uvarov advocated 'autocracy (*samoderzhanie*), Orthodoxy (*Pravoslavie*) and nationality (*narodnost*)' as the foundation of the Russian state, Reşid Paşa, the moving force behind the Tanzimat reforms, envisaged the 'basic pillars of the Ottoman State' as 'Islam, the House of Osman, the protectorate of Mecca and Medina, and Istanbul as the capital of empire.'[88]

To foster the feeling of 'belonging' among their people was the basic dilemma of all imperial education systems and nowhere more so than in the cases of Russia and the Ottoman Empire, where the sheer scale of the country and the variety of their peoples meant that 'the emerging popular conception of national identity included only a rudimentary concept of citizenship ...'[89] Nor was there any 'supra-ethnic concept of nation or empire to which diverse peoples could be attracted with a modicum of voluntarism.'[90] In this context the gap was filled by a recharged conceptualization of religion and/or direct attachment to the quasi-sacred person of the emperor/sultan. This attachment was to be inculcated through mass schooling. It is interesting to note that efforts to standardize education were made in the Russian and Ottoman empires at very similar times. The Russian statute on primary schools is dated 1864, whereas the Ottoman Ministry for Education was established in 1857, and the general Law on Education was passed in 1869. In both educational systems religious instruction had a central role.[91]

In 1897 religion and church Slavonic accounted for 9 out of 24 hours of instruction per week in Russia, and in Ottoman schools we have already noted the renewed emphasis on Qur'anic study (*tecvid*) from primary to higher schooling.[92] In both the Ottoman and Russian cases heroic figures from history and an image of a glorious past was used to instill a sense of common identity in schoolchildren.[93] For instance, the romantic poet/author Namık Kemal, and in particular his early work, became standard reading for schoolchildren.[94]

Another similarity between the Russian and Ottoman cases was the attempt to assimilate non-Turkish and non-Russian elements in the value system of the centre. Just as the Ottomans tried to instill Ottomanism in Arab notables' children in the Tribal School, the Russians attempted 'Russification' of non-Russian peoples.[95] Sheikh Cemaleddin, the son of the legendary leader of the Dağıstani people of the Caucasus, Sheikh Şamil, was taken hostage during the twenty-seven-year (1834–61) campaign to subdue the area, brought up as a member of the Russian elite and made a member of the crack imperial guard.[96] In similar fashion, the sons of leading notables would be appointed to the personal guard of Abdülhamid.[97] Another similarity in the Russian and Ottoman cases is the low level of literacy and available schooling.[98]

Like Thomas Babington Macauley, the president of the Committee of Public Instruction in India in 1834, whose aim was to create an indigenous elite who would be 'Indian in blood and colour, but English in taste, in opinion, in morals and intellect,' and like the Russians who educated Cemaleddin in Petersburg with the aim of making him 'Russian',[99] the aim of the Tribal School was to create Arabs, Kurds and Albanians who would be Ottoman.

The main thrust of Japanese education policies in the late Meiji period was the effort to build a 'civil morality' fostering loyalty to the 'national polity' (*kokumin*).[100] Although religion *per se* in the Japanese context of Confucianism and Buddhism clearly meant something very different from Islam or Orthodoxy, the attempt to build an emperor cult as the focus of loyalty for a citizenry, and the role of education in the process, bears certain striking similarities. In the first place, the dialectic between Western and native themes in the struggle between progressive and conservative elements is observable in all three of the Russian, Ottoman and Japanese cases. Just as there was a see-saw effect between Tanzimat liberalism and Hamidian conservatism there was a similar tension between Japanese liberal reformers and palace circles who felt that Westernization was detrimental to Japanese native values.[101] The Japanese Education Ordinance of 1879 was revised in 1880, and the Ministry of Education compiled a list of unacceptable texts, while moving ethics instruction to the top of the list of subjects to be taught in elementary schools.[102] All this rings a bell when we recall that instructors were reprimanded for teaching Greek and Roman civilization in Ottoman schools in precisely the same years that Western philosophy was removed from the curriculum, and that religious instruction was moved to centre stage.[103]

The basis of Ottoman education policy was therefore in keeping with contemporary world trends, an effort to gradually 'civilize' subject populations into espousing the value system of the centre. The words of Osman Nuri Paşa serve as an eloquent testimony to this aim: 'It would be against reason to construct a mechanism of government which would be totally in contradiction to the customs and beliefs of the nomadic population ... The spread and progress of modern education in a country is best served by the [reconciliation] of the needs of the country and the customs and habits of the population.'[104]

It is clear that in the documents cited above religion and nationality are being used interchangeably. In 'religious tradition' and 'national morals' (*adab-ı diniye ve ahlak-ı milliye*) the order could just as easily be reversed as 'national traditions' (*adab-ı milliye*), and 'religious morals' (*ahlak-ı diniye*). The word *hamiyet* meaning 'zeal' was often used as 'religious zeal' (*hamiyet-i diniye*) or national zeal/patriotism (*hamiyet-i milliye*).

That the 'national zeal' which the power holders were seeking to instil emerged with a vengeance in the opposition was the ultimate irony. There is no escaping the fact that the increasing dosage of 'correct' ideological conditioning in the elite schools was in direct proportion to the spread of the influence of the Committee of Union and Progress in these institutions. The organization that was to seal the fate of the Ottoman Empire was founded in 1889 as a student organization in the Imperial School of Medicine.[105]

This was soon followed by the establishment of CUP branches in the Imperial Military Academy, the Imperial Civil Service School, and the School of Law. There was a general purge of suspected CUP sympathizers from the Military Academy in May 1895. In the same year, CUP members clandestinely made contact with the British embassy.¹⁰⁶ CUP membership rapidly increased in the elite schools. This caused a great deal of concern, a government report was to comment, in 18 December 1895: 'It is particularly distressing that these elements should be found among the students of the imperial schools whose aim is to train men of solid character and morals, loyal to the Sublime State ... This would indicate that stricter control should be exercised over the teachers and students of these schools.'¹⁰⁷

But the Ottoman ruling elite would not have the field to themselves in attempting to instill their values. Together with the opposition of the CUP they would have to contend with the opposition of foreign missionaries. It is to this challenge that we now turn.

Chapter Five
'They Confuse and Excite the Mind':
The Missionary Problem

Reverend Blakeney Davis peered out into the gloom of the Anatolian plain. Dusk was falling and the huge sheep dogs had begun their nightly uproar. Soon it would not be safe to go out in the dark; the brutes did not yet know him and somehow particularly objected to his presence. So this was Sivas, he sighed, where he had come to do the Lord's good work, a long way from Freeport Maine. The local Armenian population were suspicious and indifferent at first, but now a few of the poorest boys had begun to attend the mud hut he grandly called his 'Academy for Central Anatolia'. The local kaymakam had called yesterday, a sullen-faced man who kept poking his riding crop into their personal effects and asking if they had brought explosives with them from America.

None of the challenges to the legitimacy of the Ottoman state, and all that it stood for, was more dangerous in the long term than that posed by missionary activity. The threat posed by the soldier, the diplomat, the merchant, all had to do with the here and now; the missionaries, through their schools, constituted a danger for the future. To a large extent, the measures discussed in the previous chapters, to convert or reinforce the orthodoxy of marginal elements, were designed as a reaction to the missionary presence.

Throughout the world the missionary appeared as the representative of a superior culture, the 'white man's burden' personified. The Ottoman-missionary struggle thus also serves to put events in the Ottoman empire into a world perspective. Missionary activity was proving to be the thorniest of questions from Latin America to Africa to China. Ottoman diplomats, who would closely monitor missionary activity in an obscure corner of the globe such as Hawaii, were well aware of the implications of this global reach.¹

Missionary activity in Japan had been the reason for the anti-Christian stance of some Meiji bureaucrats in their fight to stigmatize Christianity as 'incompatible with loyalty'.² Although the Japanese and Ottoman attitude to religion was very different, and the Meiji Restoration became much more secular in the 1870s, Christians were stigmatized as disloyal to the state.³ In reaction, the Buddhists 'emulated the practice of their Christian rivals, expanding charitable institutions in Japan and undertaking missionary work in Taiwan and Korea.'⁴ At around the same time the turn of the century, the Ottomans began implementing their policy of Hanefi missionary activity.

The situation in China was more comparable to the Ottoman experience. Even weaker than the Ottomans in their capacity to resist Western encroachment, the Chinese focused much of their resentment and anger on the missionaries and their Chinese converts. The Empress Dowager Tzu Hsi, a contemporary of Abdülhamid, declared that: 'These Christians are the worst people in China ... They rob the poor country people of their land and property, and the missionaries, of course, always protect them, in order to get a share for themselves.'⁵ No doubt Abdülhamid would have fully agreed.

Edward Said comments that: 'Even the legendary American missionaries to the Near East during the nineteenth and twentieth centuries took their role as set not so much by God as their God, their culture, and their destiny.'⁶ Not only did the missionaries undermine the efforts the Ottomans were making to legitimize the basis of their rule at home, they also proved influential in creating adverse conditions abroad by feeding the Western press with anti-Turkish sentiment: 'Many missionaries and Western journalists proceeded upon the confident assumption that the Terrible Turk belonged to a retrograde race of Devil-worshippers.'⁷

Particularly after the British occupation of Egypt in 1882, the Protestant missions felt that the way was open for the conversion of Muslims to Christianity. Together with the Cyprus Convention of 1879, which established a British protectorate over the island, these developments were seen as the thin end of the wedge, making possible the triumphant advance of Christianity in the Middle East. In Tibawi's words:

> ... by 1882 Protestant missionaries ... had made clear their attitude towards the legitimate Government and territorial integrity of a state in which they resided and worked. Not only did they publicly declare their intention of sub-

verting its established religion, not only did they openly pray for the extinction of the state and the absorption of its territories by their own Governments, but pending the achievement of these ambitions they claimed special privileges and exemptions, and with these very claims they accused the Ottoman authorities of intolerance, fanaticism and bigotry.[8]

The last ditch ideological defences erected during the Hamidian era, the increasing emphasis on schooling and the attempt to enforce Hanefi orthodoxy were perhaps best understood for what they were by the missionaries. The secretary to the American Mission in Syria, Henry Jessup, had to confess surprise that 'the Turks are not after all on their last legs.'[9] In the 1880s Jessup admitted that they faced a situation which, 'discount[ed] previous predictions of Islamic decay, and cite[d] as evidence of revival throughout the Ottoman Empire the opening of schools for boys and girls ... and the building of new mosques.'[10]

Missionary activity gathered momentum during the 1880s and 1890s with British, American, Russian, and French missionaries parcelling out spheres of their 'work'. This led to a situation in which, according to Jeremy Salt, 'the relationship that developed between the missionaries and the Ottoman government was one of mutual suspicion and mutual dislike.'[11] Indeed, by the 1890s the missionaries had come to be regarded by the sultan as 'the most dangerous enemies to social order', among all the foreigners living in his domains.[12] Before we go any further into this tense relationship, it is worth looking at how Abdülhamid II himself saw the situation. On 25 May 1892, he dictated the following to his private secretary:

> In England, Russia, and France, there exist Bible Societies which become exceedingly rich through the donations of rich and fanatical Christians who bequeath all their wealth to them in their wills ... Although the English, Russian and French governments seem not to be involved in their activities, they secretly aid and abet them in sending missionaries into darkest Africa. In this way they spread their beliefs among the local population. By increasing the numbers of their followers this religious influence is then transformed into political leverage ... Although it is obviously desirable to take firm measures against them, if open opposition is brought to play, the Sublime Porte will suffer the vexing interventions of the three powers' ambassadors. Thus the only way to fight against them is to increase the Islamic population and spread the belief in the Holiest of Faiths.[13]

It is interesting to note how close the sultan's description of the ambivalent relationship of the missionaries with their governments comes to the assessment of an eminent modern historian: 'Missionary effort was by no means an agency of imperialist policies. Often it was opposed to the colonial authorities ... Yet the success of the Lord was a function of imperialist advance.'[14]

We are, therefore, when we speak of the struggle between the missionaries and the Ottoman government, dealing with nothing less than ideological war, a war that challenged the very basis of Ottoman legitimacy among Christian and Muslim.

Ottoman defence against missionary incursion

The legal basis for proselytizing in Ottoman domains, the missionaries claimed, stemmed from the Tanzimat rescript of 1839 and the Reform rescript (*Islahat Fermanı*) of 1856, which together guaranteed the freedom of all Ottoman subjects, Muslim and Christian alike, to choose whatever religion they wanted to belong to.[15] Although the principle of these two documents was never called into question, the Ottomans interpreted 'freedom of religion' as 'the freedom to defend their religion'. The Foreign Minister Ali Paşa was to instruct his ambassador in London to ask Earl Russell the following questions:

> Can it be supposed that whilst condemning religious persecutions, the Sublime Porte has consented to permit offence and insult to any creed whatever? That at the same time as she was proclaiming liberty to all non-Mussulman creeds, she had given them arms against Islamism? That she had, in fine, destroyed at the same stroke the guarantees with which she surrounded the liberty of religious convictions?[16]

This defensive attitude was actually written into Article 62 of the Treaty of Berlin in 1878, an interpretation which actually amounted to 'an official recognition by Europe of the Turkish definition of religious liberty. It is so worded as to allow the Turkish Government to take any measures which it may deem proper to prevent Mohammedans from changing their faith.'[17] The fact was that this measure had very little to do with religion, and everything to do with the Hamidian regime's new political definition of religious loyalty: '[The] Turkish Government was never more determined than it is now to prevent all defection from Islam ... It is now a political rather than a religious principle, designed to maintain the strictly Mohammedan character of the Turkish Government, and to retain all political power in the hands of the Turks.'[18]

Although the precept in the şeriat allowing the killing of any convert from Islam was formally disallowed, the spirit of its draconian ethic still lived in the popular psyche.[19] Sultan Abdülhamid himself was to tell Layard that although in principle any Muslim was free to embrace Christianity, 'be he the Sheikh ul Islam himself', the reality on the ground was something else: 'there were parts of the empire where the population was not only very fanatical, but frequently almost beyond the control of the local functionaries when their fanaticism was aroused.'[20]

The Ottoman definition of religious freedom is clearly expressed in a communication from the grand vizier's chancery, dated 22 March 1896. In this document the grand vizier of the time, Rifat Paşa, reported that the Council of Ministers had discussed the issue of the expulsion of missionaries who had been 'involved in activities injurious to public order'. He pointed out that, 'the activities of these missionaries such as the effort to cause people to change their religion, is totally contrary to the present laws guaranteeing freedom of religion (serbesti-i idyan).'[21] The Ottoman government had already taken measures to ensure the control of Istanbul over missionary teaching and other activities by measures such as the Law of Education (1869) which stipulated that all foreign schools had to submit their curricula and teachers to public inspection.[22] Yet, the evidence shows that these restrictions were never effectively enforced and missionary schools filled the vacuum left by the insufficiency of Ottoman education. The Ottoman sources indicate that the local officials were briefed to do their utmost to curtail the spread of missionary schools. On 21 January 1892, the governor of the vilayet of Syria reported that he had compiled a list of foreign schools 'constituted by devious means' such as converting dwellings to schoolhouses. He had established that there were 159 such establishments in his area. The vali noted that although the state had been making great effort to increase state primary schools, these were still insufficient and this meant that 'Jesuit and Protestant schools therefore accept non-Muslim children free of charge, clothe and feed them and even pay subsidies to their parents.'[23] The presence of these schools was also seen as the thin end of the wedge as far as the Muslim population was concerned. The vali continued: 'It is therefore necessary that in the approaching holy month of Ramadan special ulema should be sent to preach secretly to the Muslim population about the ills that will accrue to them if they send their children to Christian schools.'[24] The emphasis on secrecy is significant, as any overt activity against the foreign schools was likely to draw the wrath of the foreign consuls.

Throughout the 1880s and 1890s Istanbul constantly renewed orders to the provinces to prevent the proliferation of unlicensed foreign educational and religious establishments. The fact that the matter came up so frequently suggests that the problem was never solved. On 12 January 1898, the vilayet of Aydın received very strict instructions to prevent the admission of Muslim children into foreign schools. The reason was very clearly the political implications of such schooling, 'the attendance of foreign schools by Muslim children will lead to such evil results as the damaging of their national and religious training (*diyanet ve terbiyeyi milliye*) and, God forbid, may even result in their abandoning their religion.'[25] The Vali of Aydın was to report on several occasions on the matter of conversion, stating that he 'had no knowledge of any Muslim who had converted'.[26] On 28 February 1892, the vilayet of Syria was told that a team of local ulema was to be charged with the task of 'imparting to the local population the ills that will result from their children attending Christian schools'. It was determined that Rıza, Muhsin, Cemal, Reşid, Mustafa, Ahmed and Mehmed Efendis should be sent on a tour of the vilayet with a total salary of 14,000 *kuruş*.[27]

By 25 June these 'official ulema' had reported back to Istanbul on the measures needed to protect Muslim children from missionary schools. The measures suggested, however, did not go beyond the education of Muslim children by village imams. For this each village should be equipped with adequate reading primers.[28] Yet the effort to enforce the licensing of foreign schools continued to be plagued by foreign intervention. On 28 March 1892, the Sublime Porte issued a circular stating that the deadline given to foreign schools and churches for them to procure licences or be closed down had expired. The circular lamely concluded that the deadline was to be extended yet again for a further three months.[29] This is not to say that the Ottoman officials did not realize what had to be done to control what they called the 'spreading of foreign influence behind the shield of education'. On 28 October 1898, a Special Commission on Education reported that more teeth had to be put into the current laws regulating foreign religious establishments.[30] The commission had no illusions about the fact that 'these schools established by foreign priests and missionaries ... seek to convert the population into the Protestant and Catholic faiths and to confuse and excite their minds.'³¹ The 'confusion of minds' was a recurrent theme in the official documentation. This confusion even went to the extent of causing 'some youths to end up marrying foreign women (*yabancı karılarıyla istihsal-i rabıta-i izdivac*)' and thus 'daring to act against the teachings of Islam'. On 26 June 1906, a memorandum prepared by the Council of Ministers declared that this was caused by the fact that Muslim schools were lacking in 'proper training in religious morals ... which would fortify youth [against such waywardness].'³²

The Ottoman government made every effort to prevent the spread and circulation of missionary literature. On 29 March 1892, the decision was taken to apply the regulations concerning the circulation of religious literature to 'travelling booksellers', usually a euphemism for people distributing Bibles under the auspices of the Bible Society.³³ But this was often counterproductive. On 9 March 1896, the translation bureau of the Porte translated an article from the *London Daily News* claiming that the Ottoman authorities were infringing on the provisions of the reform edicts, and were confiscating Bibles and religious books found on foreign travellers. It was alleged by the Bible Society in Istanbul that this had been done on several occasions, followed by a public burning of the confiscated materials. The Porte made haste to deny this allegation by arranging for the publication of articles in the Western press.³⁴

Ottoman officials were well aware that rules and regulations were losing their clout each time the state backed down before foreign protest. The Military Reform Commission prepared a memorandum, on 27 December 1891, dealing with the matter of unlicensed schools and churches. These, it said, should be closed down forthwith and the clamour of protest not be listened to. In response to any protest, the foreigners were to be told: 'Yes, there is freedom of religion, but this freedom must be exercised within the laws and regulations.'³⁵

Nor did the officials of the Porte nourish any illusions about the stiffness of the competition they were up against. On 2 March 1892, the Porte sent instructions to the Ministry of Education, to appoint a teacher of French to the Ottoman *rüşdiye* in Nablus in Palestine. The local population were sending their children to 'Latin schools' so that they might learn French 'even before they had learned their religious beliefs'. The French teacher appointed had to be good enough to compete with the French tutors in the foreign schools, as 'only then will the population send their children'.³⁶ The other interesting aspect of this document is that it illustrates that the officials understood that it was not enough simply to forbid people to send their children to the schools; an alternative service of more or less equal quality had to be provided.

Another case of a similar nature found its way into the records from the other end of the empire. On 1 October 1889, the vilayet of Işkodra in Albania reported that the local *idadi* lycée had been closed for lack of funds. This was playing into the hands of the Italian consul, who was promoting the local Catholic schools as alternatives, and it was inevitable that the local population would indeed send their children to those schools if Istanbul failed to make adequate provision.[37]

The missionaries who were most prominent in the Ottoman Empire in the last quarter of the nineteenth century were the French, British and Americans. It is proposed here to treat them under their national categories, although in the case of the British and Americans, in particular, there was considerable overlap in their activities.

French missionary activity

The French missionaries were the group who were active in Ottoman dominions for the longest time. In 1622 Pope Gregory XV had established the institution of Propaganda Fide whose object was to convert the heathen and bring back into the Catholic fold the ancient Christian communities of the Orient. Catholic missionary work in the Near East had been assigned by Propaganda Fide to the French Capucin, Carmelite, and Jesuit orders.[38]

In the early 1890s French diplomatic–missionary activity picked up in the eastern provinces of the empire. The French missions were particularly active among the Nestorian population of Mosul. On 23 May 1892, the Vali of Mosul reported that several 'special missions' had been sent by the French in the last four years, 'which leaves no doubt as to the existence of a French master spy (*ser-hafiye*).' The vali reported further that the Nestorian religious leader, the Maresh-Maun, had complained bitterly about Catholic poaching among his flock. The Chaldean patriarch, supported by the French, was bringing constant pressure to bear on the Nestorian leader. The Maresh-Maun bemoaned this fact which, he feared, would mean that very soon the entire Nestorian community would become Catholic.[39] Indeed, the sultan himself felt strongly enough about missionary poaching among his Christian subjects to send them a circular warning them to be on their guard.[40]

The French presence also comes up in dispatches during the Yezidi conversion campaign of 1892–93. At the height of the campaign, Yezidi leaders approached the French consul in Mosul with the offer that the whole community would become Christian (and presumably Catholic) if the French supported them against the Ottomans.[41] This was seen as the height of treason by the Ottoman authorities whose worst fears of missionary meddling seemed to be realized.[42]

Lebanon was another area where French missionary influence seemed to be undermining the legitimacy of the state.[43] In an unsigned letter in Arabic, this danger was clearly noted. The letter stated that 'since Napoleon [Bonaparte's] invasion of Egypt and Syria ... France has not renounced her aims in the region.' Through the efforts of the Jesuits, France had established very real presence in the region among the Maronite Christians, 'through the education of thousands of their children.'[44] This reached such an extent that 'ten years ago during the war between France and Prussia some fifteen thousand Maronites volunteered to fight in the French ranks. Let it be noted that in the late war with Russia [1877–78] it did not occur to them to form even one company of volunteers to fight for their country.'[45]

A report written by one of Abdülhamid's major grand vizier's, Kamil Paşa, also pointed to the continuing interest of France in the Lebanon, 'since the time of Napoleon Bonaparte'.[46] He did not fail to mention that 'the high quality schools that the French have established in Beirut have produced thousands of Ottoman subjects who feel indebted to France.'[47]

Kamil Paşa's report seems to have been provoked by a very interesting letter written by an Arab Catholic, Yusuf Zeki Efendi, which sheds further light on the activities of the French-inspired religious functionaries. Yusuf Zeki took part in an Easter service in Damascus where the bishop's sermon amounted to nothing less than a propaganda speech. He reported that the bishop harangued his flock in the following terms: 'O Syrians! See how you are progressing thanks to France! Thanks to the French you are being educated in the sciences! You are protected by this most learned and enlightened of nations! Your children are protected by such a just and compassionate state which is above all other nations!'[48] Yusuf Zeki wrote that the Syrians had been favourably inclined to France until the British invasion of Egypt, but when they had witnessed what the British did in Egypt they had become wary of France. Now France was trying to re-establish her ascendancy through members of the clergy such as the bishop whose sermon he had heard.[49]

What was the extent of Ottoman control over the construction and maintenance of Christian places of worship and schools? What were the criteria for the granting or denial of permission for such establishments? It is fairly clear that in places like Beirut or Damascus where French and other influence was already well established, Istanbul ran into serious difficulties. But in the Ottoman heartland of Anatolia their control was more effective. One such case was reported from the vilayet of Mamuret-ül-aziz (present day Elazığ), where the Capucin priests had applied to establish a church which would also serve as a school by converting a dwelling.[50] The local authorities reported that the projected construction was a modest affair capable of accommodating some thirty students. It was pointed out that the location was surrounded by high walls and was some distance from the barracks and the military training ground. The priests had erected a bell tower 'but ha[d] not yet rung their bell'. The Catholic Armenian population of the area amounted to no more than 'some eight or ten households including the priests' own servants.' The only disadvantage was that it was situated in the Muslim quarter. But this was compensated for by the high wall. In this case, the local authorities recommended that permission for this church be granted, 'so that they will not have recourse to the intermediary of the French embassy.'[51]

The ringing of church bells, in particular, appears to have had a symbolic significance for the Ottoman authorities. On 22 June 1897, it was reported that a Jesuit from Izmir, Father Dominique, had erected a belfry over his dwelling which served as a school. The bell was particularly objectionable: 'the ringing of this bell under the pretext of calling children to school and other such mistakes must be prevented and not allowed to recur in future.'[52]

French official support for these institutions was never lacking, and as much as the Ottomans tried to impress upon the French that this was their domestic affair, they were unable to prevent such interference entirely. On 15 June 1896, the vilayets of Trabzon and Erzurum were instructed to provide all the necessary support for a Jesuit inspector of schools from France who was to tour the schools in the area. This 'was the special request of the French embassy.'[53]

The inspection of schools was indeed a matter of great delicacy; it revealed in microcosm the clash of two sovereignties. The Ottomans claimed that they had the right to inspect all Christian schools in their domains, whereas the French and other authorities tended to view their schools as ex-territorial. On 11 March, Grand Vizier Kamil Paşa wrote to the Ministry of Education reiterating that, by imperial order (*irade*), no Muslim children should attend Christian schools and that this should be checked through the inspection of various French schools. The schools in question, however, replied that they would only allow inspection through the intermediary of the French consuls. This provoked Kamil Paşa's ire: 'It is also necessary to know what is being taught to the Christian children of the fatherland.'[54]

When some Jesuits were expelled from France in 1902, the Ottoman Ministry for Foreign Affairs and the provincial authorities were instructed that, 'these people are not to be admitted into Ottoman domains. A country which is expelling certain elements has no right to prevail upon another to accept them.'[55]

Although Catholic missionary activity was a thorn in the side of the Ottomans, it was nonetheless a familiar 'evil'. Compared to the rigour and aggressiveness of the newly arrived Protestants, the Catholics appeared positively soft. Also, the Catholic presence had a much longer history. Indeed part of the effort to appear as a member of the club of Great Powers centred around the Porte's diplomatic recognition of the Papacy. Relations with the Holy See had been improving steadily since the 1880s.[56]

In 1894 the Catholic Patriarch of Istanbul was to write to the palace that the pope had received in audience the Nestorian and Malachite patriarchs, together with 'other well wishers of the Sublime State'. The outcome of the meeting had been, 'a document in Latin and French', wherein it was stated that, 'from now on the Roman clergy (*efrenc rahipleri*) will be strictly forbidden from interfering in the affairs of the Ottoman Catholics who will be responsible solely to their local Patriarchates.' This would mean that all mission schools would be run only by Ottoman Catholics and the papacy would defer to the local patriarchates in all matters. The Pope had also stressed the importance of the Eastern patriarchates in matters of state security: 'They are to take every opportunity to enjoin their flocks not to associate with subversive and corrupting elements, and to remain loyal to their legitimate sovereign'.[57]

In 1898, when it was decided to send an Ottoman ambassador to the Vatican, the Caliph finally recognized the Pope, who was seen by the West as his opposite number. It was also thought that improved relations with the Vatican would enable the Porte to counter Protestant missionary pressure, and keep better control of its Catholic population.[58]

The effort to move closer to the Catholic world was reflected in the Porte's continued protection for the Armenian Catholic monastery in

Venice. This was part of the policy of attempting to separate the Catholic Armenians from the Gregorians, the latter being the target of most major massacres. The Armenian Catholic Patriarchate in Istanbul noted that the monastery, whose students bore Ottoman passports had, 'remained loyal subjects and benefited from Ottoman protection for the last two hundred years.'[59]

British missionary activity

Although British and American missionary activity overlapped in many instances, for the sake of clarity it is proposed to treat them separately here. The relationship between the British and American missionaries and the Porte was often much more acrimonious than that of their more established French counterparts. Indeed, the implication in the documents is that the Catholics, on the principle of 'the evil you know', were preferred.

The British occupation of Cyprus in 1878, and the supposedly 'temporary' British administration of the island, was to provide the first clue as to the nature of British religious politics.[60] Kamil Paşa wrote, on 30 August 1884, that 'under the guise of rationalization of the education system' the British authorities were discontinuing the salaries of some Muslim primary school teachers and combining several village schools. They had also established a school in the Muslim quarter of Nicosia which was administered by 'a Protestant priest' who was charged with teaching the children English. The Orthodox schools were in good shape and were not being interfered with, but the British measures were causing a radical decrease in the number of Muslim village primary schools.[61] Kamil Paşa feared that this was the first step to their being replaced by Protestant schools.[62]

On 23 June 1884, the British Embassy complained that the attempt to build a Protestant school in Aleppo was being hindered by the local authorities. The British consul in Aleppo had reported that this was all the more objectionable as the Catholic schools and churches in the city were not being interfered with in any way. This 'preferential behaviour [runs counter to] official Ottoman guarantees that all foreign schools in the empire were being dealt with on a basis of equality.'[63]

Even matters of extreme detail came to be dealt with at the highest reaches of state. Such a case was the affair of the Protestant cemetery in

Basra. On 16 August 1907, the Vali of Basra reported that there had been continuous correspondence with the local British consul over this cemetery which had become unusable due to frequent flooding. The consul had demanded that the Protestant community be given an alternative location. The matter was discussed at length and the affair was closed when the Ottoman authorities agreed to make the necessary payment for the construction of a protective dike.[64]

On 26 January 1892, it was reported that 'English priests' had been seen in the vicinity of Kevar, a district on the Ottoman–Iranian border. These priests, it was reported, had been distributing books and pamphlets among the Nestorian population. One of them had been apprehended and an investigation launched. The sultan decreed that they be 'chased away in the firmest possible manner (*suret-i hakimanede oralardan def'leri*).'[65]

The fear of 'English priests' seems to have been voiced from far-flung corners of the empire. The vilayet of Yemen reported, on 3 April 1891, that 'missionaries from Aden' had appeared on the Yemeni coast and had been seen distributing literature in Arabic to the locals. Istanbul sent firm instructions that this be stopped and 'it be established just what sort of book they are circulating and if it is the Bible, which Muslims do not need, they should be confiscated.'[66]

Yet it appears that not all the contact between the Ottoman authorities and British missionaries was of an antagonistic nature. The Alliance Evangélique, 'a very influential and respected religious group' according to Grand Vizier Cevad Paşa, was thanked by the sultan for 'its recent statements indicating that the excitement of British public opinion regarding the Armenian affair was quieting down.' The London embassy was instructed to thank Mr Arnold, the secretary of the organization, in the name of the sultan for what was regarded as an intercession favourable to the Porte.[67]

Another worrying development for the Ottoman authorities was the tendency for the American and British diplomats in the empire to work together on the missionary issue and support one another's nationals. This was reported by the Ottoman embassy in Washington, which gave details on how the British consul in Trabzon had informed the American minister in Istanbul about the details of the burning of the American mission school in Merzifon by the local Ottoman police.[68]

American missionaries

Perhaps the biggest headache for the Ottomans were the American missionaries.[69] The latest arrivals on the Ottoman scene, this particular brand of New England zealot was to constitute an enigma for Istanbul which only saw their efforts to educate minorities as an attempt to undermine state legitimacy.[70] The problem lay in the fact that the two sides could not possibly speak the same language. The missionaries, very often at odds with their own diplomatic representatives, somewhat naively thought that what was good for the Armenian or Bulgarian Ottomans would somehow end up being good for the Muslim majority. The Ottomans authorities, from the sultan down, felt that they were establishing nests of sedition and training revolutionaries.

Most disturbing was the fact that the Protestant subjects of the Ottoman empire unlike other Christian minorities, were not a collectively recognized member of the *millet* system. A palace memorandum stressed this fact, pointing out that 'this makes it possible for the Protestant governments to pose as the spiritual champions of the protestant Ottomans.'[71] It was therefore necessary to bring their status into line with that of other Christian communities 'according to the precepts of the Reform Edict [1856]' by establishing a body which would be responsible to the Ottoman government.[72]

The relationship between Istanbul and the missionaries became increasingly characterized by mutual accusations and bad blood. Things were made all the more complicated by the Armenian massacres of the 1890s.

Ottoman representatives in the United States closely monitored missionary publications such as the *Missionary Herald*, and translations from this paper often turn up in Ottoman records. One example among many was the despatch sent by the Ottoman minister in Washington which included an article from the *Herald* reassuring the missionaries' backers at home that, despite the troubled state of the Ottoman interior, their work was going on. The article waxed particularly poetic on the achievements of evangelical missionary schools in Kayseri, Kara Hisar, Ödemiş, and Trabzon.[73] The legation was to report, on 4 March 1894, that the American missionary societies had reconfirmed their commitment not to support 'Armenian intrigues' and as a gesture they had stopped funding an Armenian church in Worcester Massachussetts.[74]

Any anti-missionary views which appeared in the American press were avidly clipped and sent back to Istanbul. On 26 September 1893, the Ottoman legation in Washington reported on a congress of world religions which had been held in Chicago. At this meeting of religious dignitaries from all over the world, the Buddhist delegate had taken the American audience to task telling them, 'How dare you judge us? How many in this audience have read anything to do with the Buddha's life?'. When only five people raised their hands, the Buddhist delegate told them, 'So only five of you know about the belief of four hundred and seventy five million people. You complain that you have not been able to convert people of other faiths ... this is the height of selfishness.'[75] The Japanese delegate then took his turn to tell the audience that the aim of the missionaries that came to Japan was to prepare that country for foreign annexation. He went on to say,' I am proud to say that I was the first to start a society to work against Christianity in Japan.' The delegates also roundly condemned missionary activity in China which was causing suffering and bloodshed.[76]

On 26 October, the legation reported that no less a paper than the *Washington Post* had spoken out strongly against missionary meddling in other countries, and the paper's view was that they might be more useful at home. It was suggested that the Ottoman press publish a translation of the article.[77]

An altogether remarkable document illustrating just how wary the Ottomans were of the American missionaries, is a report from the Ottoman-consul general in New York, Munci Bey, dealing with the history of missionary penetration of the Hawaiian islands.[78] The consul began his report by saying:

> As is well known, these missionaries are an infamous band who use religion to achieve political power and advance their material interest ... When they first arrived on these islands whose mild climate is very suitable for the growth of rare and beautiful plants, and whose people are of a soft and accommodating disposition, it was as if they had fallen upon a free banquet the likes of which they had never seen before.

He went into great detail on how money was collected in public meetings describing a mass hysteria verging on that of the televized evangelists of modern times: 'In a state of mind that approaches a trance, they strip off their rings, necklaces, gold watches and chains, and throw them into the collection box.'[79] Evidently having made a detailed study of the matter, Munci Bey went on to describe in detail the establishment of the Dole Fruit Company, the leper colony on Molokai, and the agitation on the part of the missionaries for the protectorate status of the islands. He concluded on an ominous note: 'As these missionaries are also active in our August Master's well protected domains, and their malicious work is observable daily, I judged it advisable to give an example of what manner of evil they are capable of.'[80]

The Ottoman diplomatic representatives continued throughout the 1890s to give their government up-to-the-minute information on Ottoman matters as reflected in the American press. On 14 April 1896, the Ottoman minister in Washington gave detailed translations relating to the matter of the arrest and deportation of George Perkins Knapp from the Bitlis Boys Academy, for alleged incitement of Armenians to revolt. He reported that the American press had compared conditions for missionary work in the Ottoman empire favourably with the conditions obtaining in Russia. But the arrest of Dr Knapp had provoked a hail of protest.[81] The general gist of the reporting was that the Ottoman government was upset that the missionaries were informing the world about the massacres of Armenians.[82] The legation was instructed to inform the American authorities that there was no general plan to expel all American missionaries as had been reported in the American press.[83]

It would indeed have been impossible for the Ottoman authorities to expel all missionaries given the degree of international pressure, although no doubt they would have wanted to. But they did make every effort to keep track of their activities. On 6 December 1899, the Foreign Ministry reported that several American and English women had arrived in Erzurum intending to go to Van on a 'humanitarian mission'. The American Legation had intervened on their behalf, pointing out that if the Ottoman authorities gave these women all the help they could (such as providing them with an armed escort) this would have a very good effect on European and American public opinion. If they were hindered in their movements quite the opposite effect would be achieved.[84] The vilayet was instructed to speed them on their way and make sure they did not dally in Erzurum.[85]

The various vilayets were constantly warned to be on their guard for missionaries in their areas. On 23 September 1897, the vilayet of Aleppo warned that a Dr Michael Westerly was seen 'going here and there' in the region, and was being kept under surveillance. The vilayet was instructed that '[this person] be given his passport and sent on his way forthwith'.[86] Surveillance seemed to be the key word from one end of the empire to the other. On 24 May 1895, the matter of travelling American Bible Society representatives was brought up at the Council of State. The vilayet of Manastır (in present-day northern Greece) had been approached by these representatives who had complained that the obligation placed on them by the law regulating the permits of travelling booksellers was too onerous because it included such 'unreasonable' requirements as the yearly renewal of such permits, together with a fee 'which was causing much expense and hardship'.[87] They were demanding a flat rate and a permit without a time limit which would be valid throughout the empire. The Council reiterated that it was required that 'such travelling salesmen be regulated by law' and refused to make any changes.[88]

The preoccupation with bad press abroad is evident throughout the Ottoman documents. On 2 August 1891, the vilayet of Sivas complained that the Armenian community was itself responsible for unfair practices in tax collection. Various taxes were levied on the community as a whole and it was their responsibility to apportion shares to individual households. But because the self-serving rich apportioned equal shares on rich and poor alike, this meant the destitution of the poor as the local authorities were then obliged by law to foreclose on their property. In the foreign press this became another instance of Turkish oppression. The missionaries then stepped in and told the Christians, 'you see, we who have come all this way are here to help you when your own government is unable to do so.'[89] There was also considerable exaggeration of grievances on the part of Christian minorities.[90]

Although the missionary record denies any help to Armenian revolutionary organizations, the Ottomans thought otherwise. On 29 December 1896, the Ottoman consulate in Hoy (northern Iran) reported that a Mr Howard and a Mr Elliot had been in the town for some two months. They had been followed by members of Ottoman intelligence services who had established that they had been in touch with Armenians who had been active in the recent events across the border in Van. They had also been promising Armenians money if they emigrated to the United States via Russia. Some of the money they were distributing came from the Armenian revolutionary organization, the Dashnaktsutiun. Elliot had then moved on to Van and Howard had made his way to England via Russia.[91]

There was deep-seated mistrust bordering on hatred on both sides. An American clergyman, George H. Hepworth, who was sent to eastern Turkey as part of an official inspection team sent there by the sultan to investigate the attacks on the Armenian population, painted a very bleak picture: 'To educate an Armenian is regarded by a Turk, who obstinately refuses to be educated, as very close to a crime; and both the educator and the educated are denounced.'[92] Even if one leaves aside the proto-racist comments about Turks who 'refused to be educated', it is clear that the missionaries were either hopelessly naive about what result their education was going to have, or worse, deeply cynical. As the educational facilities provided by the American Board were often far better than those provided by the Ottoman state, this could only have the effect of further intensifying the racial hatred that was brewing in the region, and undermining the legitimacy of the government, which was not helped by its own weakness. The naive aspect of their aims is brought out very clearly by the most up-to-date apologist for the missionary cause: '[The] American Board sponsors never intended to educate only the youth of one *millet*, but rather hoped that it would have an impact on all of the ethnic communities in south-eastern Turkey.'[93] This was exactly what Istanbul feared. The analogy drawn by Grabill is perhaps exaggerated, but it does make the point: 'The American Protestants did not imagine how they might have behaved if for several decades in their homeland a foreign educational system directed by Muslims had devoted itself to, say, Afro-Americans, with the result that the black Islamic minority became more proficient than the majority of white Americans'.[94]

The fact was that the massacres that occured throughout the 1890s were a severe embarrassment for Istanbul, all the more so as local officials were evidently involved in events such as the burning of the American school in Merzifon in 1893, for which the sultan paid $2,200 damages.[95] The constant pressure and bad press, which culminated in Abdülhamid II being termed as 'the Red Sultan' was exactly what they did not need.

This is best born out by the effort made to establish the exact number and location of Armenian orphans, in order to ensure that the state was seen to be taking care of its own. The Ministry of the Interior was ordered, on 4 April 1899, to ascertain just how many Armenian orphans were being taken care of by foreign missionaries and provide an alternative. The directive given to the ministry stated: 'Because the places set aside for the care and education of Armenian orphans ... have been closed down, and this is a humanitarian matter, if the Sublime State takes care of these children without leaving this important duty to the foreigners nothing can be said ...'[96] The key phrase here is 'nothing can be said' which alludes to the constant foreign pressure on the government.

Another important aspect of the Ottoman–Missionary struggle was the element of anti-Catholicism in the Protestant missions. Cyrus Hamlin, the founder of Robert College, the American college which began life in 1863 as the Bebek Seminary on the banks of the Bosphorous, saw this struggle as the 'survival of the fittest' and referred to the Jesuit schools as the 'Roman peril'.[97] This intense sectarian competition between missionary organizations sometimes reached the stage where it caused 'the transformation of religion into a sport and trade'.[98] The Ottomans were able to tap into the rivalry quite successfully. Yet it meant that sometimes they came across some fairly dubious characters. A remarkable example of this was their relationship with Revd Edward Randall Knowles, a Catholic clergyman from West Sussex, Massachusetts. On July 1897, the Ottoman legation in Washington filed an interesting despatch. It had been contacted by Knowles who had demanded that he be decorated with the Mecidiye Medal third class for his services to the Ottoman State.[99] These consisted of various articles favourable to Ottoman interests, published in fairly obscure New England missionary papers. Knowles sent the Ottoman legation in Washington a sample of cuttings from these papers. He wrote that Armenian revolutionaries were earning publicity at the cost of thousands of innocent lives, and he spoke of them as '[revolutionaries] whose unprincipled agitations at a safe distance have made victims of thousands of innocent souls.'[100] Knowles also held forth on the commendable qualities of Islam, such as abstinence and inheritance rights of women.[101] In appallingly bad French, Knowles offered his services: 'Je désire vous offrir mes services gratis et sans prix comme un agent de presse ... à ma propre dépense et charge absolument! Je vous ai envoyé plusieurs livres se regardant moi [sic]. En recompense ne pouvez vous moi donner [sic] l'Ordre de Mecidieh 3ème classe ...' The good reverend also appears to have been something of a quack telepathist, who was involved in, 'transmission of thought, without electricity or wire ... in a sympathetic unity of consciousness between the persons communicating ...' [102] No doubt Abdülhamid took a rather jaundiced view of this last item.

At a more serious level, there can be little doubt that the thorniest question in the Ottoman–missionary confrontation was the issue of schooling. Through these institutions the missionaries undermined Ottoman legitimacy in their own country. The evidence indicates that this confrontation became more severe at the dawn of the twentieth century, and became more and more embroiled with the Armenian crisis. On 16 January 1906, the vilayet of Konya was ordered to prevent the establishment of a Protestant school for girls by a certain Mademoiselle Maria Garber who 'by using the [foreign] press and by preaching has worked towards the confusion of the minds of Armenian simple folk, aiming by this to increase Protestant influence in the region.' It was also pointed out that this was a pattern whereby the school would be established without a license, thus confronting the state with a *fait accompli*.[103]

It is also clear from the evidence that the Ottoman authorities realized that as they could not close down all of these schools, the only way to counter them was by competing with them on their own ground, that is to say, by improving the quality of Muslim schools. On 6 June 1905, the vilayet of Beirut wrote that the only way to, 'ensure that Muslim children are saved from the harmful clutches of the Jesuits and Protestants [in this city] is for there to be established a network of modern schools capable of competing with them.'[104]

The general feeling was that, as it was impossible to close these schools down, it was at least desirable that they be brought under license. A Council of Ministers report dated 18 October 1903 established that there were nearly 200 American educational establishments in the empire. Of these only four American schools who had received imperial fermans from the beginning. Seventy-five were accorded this permission after the fact, and the remainder did not hold valid licenses. The record of the council meeting made it clear that as of late the American minister had increased his pressure on the Porte to grant the additional licenses. It was also made clear that a list of teachers would be required to make sure that 'men of ill will working against the interests of the Sublime State were not employed'.[105] The American Legation kept up the pressure demanding that American establishments enjoy the same rights accorded to French schools, such as freedom from taxation. This demand was seen as particularly dangerous as '[it] would have the undesirable result of increasing the number and influence of Protestant establishments.'[106]

Although the American Legation disclaimed official endorsement of missionary establishments, in the last years of Abdülhamid's reign it actually stepped up the pressure to have the Porte grant official licenses to their schools. As American self-confidence increased after the Spanish American war and the conquest of the Philippines, this was reflected in their relationship with the Porte. Early in 1906, the Porte attempted to negotiate with the American Legation by telling them that they would grant licenses to American missionary establishments if they formally undertook not to admit Muslim children. The US representative told Foreign Minister Tevfik Paşa that, 'the American Government cannot accept that its nationals be treated any differently than the French, Russians, or the British.' It was even more troubling to hear the American add: 'The United States also has millions of Muslim subjects like the British, the French and the Russians.' The implication was very clear, Tevfik Paşa had to conclude that 'because America has become a Great Power like the others, we are forced to accept their views.'[107]

Conclusion

The fact was that the missionaries were the best placed Westerners at the time to correctly assess the Hamidian regime's efforts at ideological regeneration. The missionary problem must be seen as one in a whole series of threats to the state's efforts to mould what it had increasingly come to regard as an Ottoman proto-citizenry.

The conversion of Muslims to Christianity was something the American missionaries always strenuously denied. This official line was repeated throughout the period by the missionaries themselves and by their sympathizers: 'In imparting education they did not proselytize. The converts were not made in their colleges and schools. They sought, first and foremost, to organize an improved system of education for a people already Christian, but deplorably ill-educated and debarred by the Turkish policy for many centuries from receiving any proper education.'[108] The Muslim majority may not have been an immediate target but it definitely 'stood on the broader horizon'.[109]

The Armenians, particularly in Anatolia, had been ill-educated. But then again so had the Muslims. Yet, it is true that the educational efforts of the state were directed particularly at Muslims in their efforts to create a politically reliable citizenry. The irony of the situation lies in the fact that the Ottoman aims were exactly the same as those of the missionaries, to the point where the words of a contemporary observer could apply equally well to both camps: 'The work of the American missionaries has been to produce an educated middle class in Turkish lands.'[110] The 'educated middle class' that the Hamidian regime was aiming to create was to be predominantly, but not exclusively, Muslim. The fact was that the missionaries achieved precious little success among the Muslim middle classes, as Karl Barbir has succinctly put it: 'The role of the Christian missionaries and the schools they created, while important in stimulating Westernization, pale in comparison to the Ottoman empire's much more

The Missionary Problem   133

pervasive modernizing educational efforts during the period of the Tanzimat.'[111]

The other irony was that in the matter of schooling as in the matter of conversion, the Ottomans and the missionaries competed with each other. Just as Süleyman Hüsnü Paşa advocated the creation of a Muslim missionary society, and Hoca Tahsin Efendi formed a 'Society for the Study of the Geography of Muslim Lands' whose purpose was to be a 'duplication of the efforts of Christian missionaries', the Hamidian governors of the 'well protected domains' understood only too well that the only way to compete against high-quality education was to create a viable mirror image.[112] The tragedy was that it was a question of too little too late.

Not only in their relationship with the missionaries, but also vis-à-vis the Ottoman non-Muslims, the Ottoman efforts to evangelize and their attempts at creating a new ideology of Ottoman nationalism must be seen against the background of the 'nationalizing' of the Greek Orthodox churches.[113] In the case of the Armenian and Greek schools, Ottoman intellectuals and officials clearly appreciated that modern schooling could achieve much in terms of national identity formation, and were inevitably influenced.[114] The Islamic intellectual militant, Sheikh Said-i Nursi, would in fact draw specific parallels between his 'Kurdish academy', the medrese that he sought to establish on the shores of Lake Van, 'to educate tribesmen into becoming fully-fledged Ottoman citizens, and the missionary establishments in the same region.[115] The fact was that some Muslims were only too willing to send their children to missionary schools, and a few even helped their foundation. The land for the campus of Central Turkey College in Antep was donated by a Turk and a haji at that 'a large tract of land for the campus had been donated by an Aintab Turk, Kethüdazade Hacı Göğüş Efendi.'[116]

Yet, for those involved in the struggle between Islam and Christianity, there was never any doubt as to what the stakes were: the survival of one or the other in an ideological war reminiscent of the late Cold War. A pamphlet by Hafiz Mehmed Sadık, printed in Istanbul, made this very clear. After bemoaning the fact that 365 million Muslims were living under the Christian yoke, he put the blame squarely on the missionaries:

[The defence of these millions of Muslim brethren] must be primarily carried out by the intellectuals of the Islamic world. There should be no doubt that the main aim of the missionary movement today is the destruction of our religion and social morals. For this reason it is imperative that the intellectuals of Islam should persevere in their religious struggle (*mücahede*) against the united forces of the missionary high command (*misyoner erkan-ı harbiyesi*).

The military imagery is significant here, all the more so as the writer appealed to Muslim intellectuals to wage a 'spiritual Holy War' (*manevi cihad*) against the perfidious foe.[117]

The same sentiments are clearly reflected in a pamphlet by Dr Muhleisen Arnold, a figure well known in nineteenth-century missionary circles,: 'Not only does the creed of Mohammed spread over nearly a fifth portion of the globe, but Moslem delusion and despotism extend their baneful sway over Palestine, Syria, Arabia, Egypt, and Asia Minor ... this abomination of desolation has been left standing where it ought not ...'[118] Arnold also spoke of 'reclaim[ing] the souls of Muslims from the power of Satan.'[119] The two gentlemen would have understood each other.

When all was said and done, however, the undeniable truth was that missionaries made very little headway among Muslims and Jews. Although their later claims that they did not try are highly suspect, and smack of *ex post facto* justification, the fact remains that, relatively speaking, very few Muslims converted to Christianity. At the turn of the twentieth century a missionary who had worked in Turkey was to deplore the fact that: 'All our work is practically destroyed; not a single church of Moslem converts in existence in all the Turkish area after a hundred years of foreign missions.'[120] Even the most radical zealot like Henry Jessup in Syria, who continued to the end to entertain hopes of converting Muslims, had to keep secret the number of converts he made and smuggle them out of the country.[121]

The greatest irony of all had to wait over a century to materialize. The Arab Protestants, most of whom had been converted from Greek Orthodoxy, were told by the American and European synods in the mid-1980s that it had all been a huge mistake, and that 'now they should go back' to Greek Orthodoxy. The American Principals of the missions had decided that Eastern Christianity had always been in effect 'really constituted by the Greek Orthodox Church'.[122] No doubt His Imperial Majesty would have permitted himself a smile.

Chapter Six
Ottoman Image Management and Damage Control

Colonel Selaheddin Bey looked up at the grey English sky. A steady drizzle was falling and it dripped off his epauletted dress uniform. What a change after the burning sands of Yemen! The mourners had begun to gather around the graveside where General Christopher Teasdale OBE, VC was to be laid to rest. General Teasdale had once been Miralay Teasdale of the Ottoman Fourth Army charged with the defence of Kars during the Crimean War. Knight of the Garter and Master of the Horse to the Prince of Wales, Teasdale had fought heroically in the service of the sultan. Now it was time for the Ottoman state to show its appreciation by sending the younger military attaché of the London embassy to his funeral. As the vicar intoned 'ashes to ashes, dust to dust', the reporter from the obituaries column of the *Pall Mall Gazette* noted that the handsome young Turk cut a fine figure in his gold braid, even if he did look distinctly uncomfortable.

As their world shrank around them, the Ottomans realized that a vital aspect of survival was the projection of a positive image abroad. In a world where there was increasingly less space for the 'unspeakable Turk', in Gladstonian parlance, this was more often that not a question of damage control as Ottoman statesmen tried desperately to make the case that they were a Great Power recognized by the Treaty of Paris of 1856, with a legitimate right to exist. Their effort centred around two major areas. First was the attempt to contain the damage done by incessant pejorative publications in the international media, and in other forums such as the theatre, which sought to project the Ottoman state as a degenerate nest of bloodthirsty tyrants at worst, or a decaying fleshpot of 'Oriental' vice at best. Second came the presentation of a positive image, in the course of which any opportunity to appear in the mainstream of world events was seized upon. Such opportunities ranged from financial aid for medical purposes to both the Russian and Japanese sides in the Russo–Japanese war, to the presentation of 300 liras to the victims of forest fire in the United States.

The aim in all of this was to buttress the Ottoman state's shaky claim to be a member of the civilized world and the Concert of Europe. Just how shaky this position was is brought out very clearly in the assessment of a contemporary British writer:

> They are Mahometans on Christian ground ... They are exceptional Mahometans in a Christian system. The difficulties created by their position are great; but for four hundred years they have not been great enough to prevent the Christians doing political business with them ... As Mahometans they are ... impracticable members of the European system.[1]

Ahmed Cevdet Paşa was to note the irony of the Ottoman position in similar terms: 'While Rumelia, the most precious of European lands was under Ottoman control, the Europeans refused to consider the Sublime State as European. After the Crimean War, the Sublime State was included in the European state system.'[2] The implication here is very clear – once much of Rumelia, the richest of the Ottoman lands, was lost, the Europeans would be only too happy to consider the Ottoman state as 'European'.

The Ottomans' deep concern with their image predated the Hamidian reign. Thus, a leading statesman/poet of the Tanzimat era, Ziya Paşa, had pointed out that Catherine II of Russia conducted a much more effective public relations campaign by winning over men like Voltaire and Diderot. Ziya Paşa had also reacted to the neo-Hellenism of the fledgling Greek state, and protested that the Ottomans did not do enough to refute Greek claims that, while Greece was the land of Socrates, the Ottomans were habitual tyrants.[3]

It appears very clearly from a close reading of the Ottoman archival records that the Ottoman decision makers would have well understood Edward Said: 'That struggle [of imperialism] is complex and interesting because it is not only about soldiers and cannons but also about ideas, about forms, about images and imaginings.'[4]

General damage control and image management

It is no accident that one of the major collections in the Yıldız archives consists of newspaper cuttings from over 100 newspapers ranging from *The Times* and the *Debats* to obscure Serbian or Bulgarian publications.[5]

These were combed daily by the Foreign Ministry Foreign Press Service (*Hariciye Nezareti Dış Matbuat Müdürlügü*) for material injurious or complimentary to the Ottoman state. It was a thankless and Sisyphean task, as at the time of the Armenian massacres and the general liberal wave in Europe, the 'Grand old Turk' of Crimean War fame was long forgotten. The best the Ottoman diplomats and other officials could do was, therefore, indeed damage control, or at the very best 'image management'. The Porte was only too aware of the importance of European public opinion and attempted to influence it by sponsoring officially inspired Ottoman and foreign writers, or resorting to downright bribery. This often put them in a weak position as European and other journalists were very often not above blackmail.

The difficult nature of the task is well reflected in a telegram dated 7 April 1885 from Musurus Paşa, the Ottoman ambassador in London, who was given instructions to work on *The Times* with a view to making it less anti-Ottoman. The ambassador reported back that he was not at all sanguine about the prospects of working such a transformation, as the editorship of *The Times* had recently changed. He somewhat lamely concluded, 'nonetheless I will do my best to make *The Times* change its language.'[6]

It is not surprising to see that a newspaper as influential as *The Times* should feature quite prominently in the nightmares of Ottoman Foreign Ministry officials. Again it was *The Times* that published a letter forwarded by its Paris correspondent on 25 July 1885, claiming that Europe would know no peace until the power of the sultan as caliph was reduced to that of the pope, with responsibility to spiritual matters only, and Istanbul put under the protection of a mixed commission representing all the Great Powers. The London Embassy was again instructed to write an official riposte.[7]

A relative of Musurus Paşa, Musurus Ghikis Bey, was also to present a favourable impression of the Ottoman state as the 'bulwark of civilization on the shores of the Aegean Sea'. In 1901 he published an article in the influential French journal *Questions Diplomatiques et Coloniales*, claiming that the Ottoman Empire 'could become something else rather than a mass of peasants labouring for the fisc ... and can indeed become the committed advocate of reform in the Orient'.[8]

Publications could even cause diplomatic incidents. One such event occurred over the publication of an article in the exclusive opinion-making journal, *The Nineteenth Century*, by the famous ex-ambassador to the

Porte, Sir Henry Elliot.[9] In this article the ambassador argued, in sum, that the Turkish reform movement, not being given the support it deserved by the Liberal government, was vanquished by Abdülhamid II, who then proceeded to do away with its principal author, Midhad Paşa: 'Abdul Hamid was enabled to recover despotic power, unchecked by Parliamentary or other control ... the hopes of an improved government vanished into thin air, and now the prospects of Turkey are more gloomy than at any previous time in her history.'[10] There ensued a rather muddled exchange of telegrams between Istanbul and London, the gist of which was that the sultan was assured that the *Nineteenth Century* article had caused only limited excitement, having been picked up only by the *Pall Mall Gazette* and there 'only inserted as a small item among the advertisements'.[11] The Ottoman ambassador reported a few days later that Sir Henry Elliot had approached him at a reception in an effort to explain himself, but Musurus told him 'that I cut off all relations with him and made plain the anger and hurt caused by [the article]'. He further claimed that Elliot had later written to the Foreign Office expressing his regrets.[12]

Elliot got his answer when a work was commissioned a year later from Anne Marie de Lusignan, a Cypriot living in Istanbul under the sultan's protection. She claimed that, 'under the reign of HM Abdul Hamid II the condition of the Ottoman Empire might be much better described as one of robust convalescence than of sickness and ruin.'[13] Lusignan entered into a direct polemic with Elliot's *Nineteenth Century* piece, stating openly that Abdülaziz had been murdered and 'this was the first time in the history of Turkey that men accused of a serious political crime were tried by ordinary law, and in the presence of the public, the representatives of the foreign powers and the foreign press.'[14]

Yet not all publications were anti-Ottoman, nor were all pro-Ottoman publications officially inspired. On 2 March 1889, the London embassy reported that an article written by a 'Hayd Clarck' had appeared in a journal called *Diplomatic Flashes*, extolling the fairness of the Ottoman administration towards Armenians who, he maintained, were much better off than the Armenians in the Russian empire. The writer, it was reported, had lived many years in the Ottoman Empire and had been a close friend of the late Ali Paşa.[15]

A good example of image building is the draft article written by Selim Melhame, an Arab and one of the sultan's closest aides, 'for publication in the most influential Paris newspapers'. In this article there is clear emphasis on the sultan's position as 'legitimate autocrat' similar to Russian or

German rulers. After giving extensive coverage to all the beneficial and constructive aspects of Sultan Abdülhamid's reign, Melhame's article continued:

> Before his Imperial Highness' reign the contacts between European rulers and the Ottoman empire were confined to the Sublime Porte; thus in the absence of direct communications relations became cold and distant. In previous practice the Porte was almost entirely under the influence of the Great Powers' ambassadors who easily imposed their wishes ... But now His Imperial Majesty can deal directly with European rulers and thus settle all the most difficult problems.

The bothersome intermediaries were thus being dispensed with. Melhame also went into great detail on the importance the sultan accorded to restoring the solvency and credit worthiness of the state. Nor was it accidental that he should dwell at some length on the sultan's legitimate right to remove any official failing in his duties. The late Midhad Paşa still cast a long shadow.[16]

Annie de Lusignan also spoke out against intermediary power holders, in this case parliamentary democracy: 'It was said long ago by a distinguished oriental that in a multitude of counsellors there is confusion. From such a confusion and its terrible results Abdul Hamid has saved his people ... .'[17]

Abdülhamid exerted considerable effort to appear as one of the club of European autocrats. Part of his early diplomacy had included an approach to Bismarck proposing a German, Austrian, Ottoman alliance similar to the Three Emperor's League. Although this was designed primarily against Russia, relations with Russia improved considerably after 1880.[18]

Blackmail was another problem that the image-obsessed Abdülhamid often found himself confronted with. A striking case was that concerning the famous Hungarian orientalist, Arminius Vambery. A well known figure in Hamidian Istanbul, he was allegedly many things, including confidant of the sultan, as well as double agent for the British and the Ottomans. The word got out in mid-October 1888 that Vambery was about to publish a booklet mocking the person of the sultan and his Yıldız Palace coterie.[19] Despite the intercession of the Ottoman Embassy in Vienna at the Austrian Foreign Ministry, and the efforts of an Ottoman diplomat who was sent to see him in Budapest, Vambery insisted that he would publish in Hungarian and in English. However, Vambery first denied that he had written such a booklet, but admitted that he had been insulted by the cold reception he had received in İstanbul during his last visit, which he blamed not on the 'Exalted Personage' himself, but on the palace clique.[20]

As the matter unfolded, it became apparent that Vambery had indeed admitted that he had written such a piece, but was willing to negotiate. His price for witholding publication was two hundred gold liras plus 'the gift of a catalogue in the Imperial Library listing three hundred and ninety four manuscripts'.[21] Foreign Minister Said Paşa recommended payment from a fund known as 'the fund for secret foreign press' (*matbuat-ı ecnebiyye-i hafiyye tertibi*). Evidently relations with Vambery improved after that. On 18 February 1889, the Vienna embassy reported that Vambery had called on them and expressed his thanks for the gracious welcome he, and several members of the Hungarian Academy, had received at Yıldız, including a visit to the Imperial Library. Apparently Vambery got rather carried away in his rendition, claiming that when the academy members reported to their fellows back in Budapest, every time the sultan's name was mentioned the room full of Hungarian academics cheered, 'Long Live Sultan Abdülhamid Khan!'[22]

The ubiquitous Vambery continued to come up in dispatches. The Ottoman embassy in St Petersburg reported on 14 May 1889 that a conference given by Vambery in London, where he had 'extolled the accomplishments of the Ottoman Empire in the last thirty years', had drawn the attention of the Russian newspaper, the *Noya Vremya*. The Russian paper, however, attacked the orientalist whom it referred to as a 'Hungarian vagabond' whose views were outdated. The paper claimed that the Russian empire had no designs on the Ottoman empire, and in fact preferred the sultan to rule the straits rather than a rival power like Britain.[23]

The presentation of the Ottoman Empire as a savage place, where travellers were not safe, was a theme frequently echoed in the foreign press. No doubt brigandage and highway robbery were realities in Ottoman dominions, nonetheless the cover of the *Petit Journal* published in Paris, depicting bandits attacking a train in the east of Anatolia, drew vigorous protests from the Porte. The pictures went against the civilized image they desired to project.[24]

Another incident that smacked of blackmail involved a Hungarian news service called the 'Informateur Hongrois', and concerned the news item published in several Hungarian newspapers to the effect that Abdülhamid was planning to visit Europe. The palace reacted most virulently to this event, calling it a 'malicious and agitating rumour'. The Ottoman ambassador in Vienna made contact with the owners of the news service who told him openly that 'the regular payments that were being made to their firm from the Ottoman Government had been discontinued; if such payments were resumed they would pay more attention in the future to news items regarding the Sublime State.'[25] Even seemingly innocuous publications could cause major diplomatic incidents: when a booklet concerning the 1877–78 Russo–Ottoman war appeared in Vienna, allegedly 'full of lies and enmity', the palace took a personal interest in attempting to ban its circulation.[26]

The foreign press was regularly scrutinized for articles on religious questions. When the French journal *Dix-Neuvième Siècle* ran a piece claiming that the şeyhülislam had pronounced that the haj was not compulsory, the Paris embassy was instructed to publish a rebuttal, stressing the absolute obligation of every Muslim with the material means to visit the Holy Precincts. The implication of the French article went directly counter to one of the most basic claims of legitimacy of the Ottoman state, and may well have been motivated by fears of pan-Islamism spreading among hajis who were French subjects.[27]

Indeed, the Ottomans seem to have had a rather cynical view of the freedom of the press. On 28 November 1895, the Ottoman minister to Washington wrote:

> Although it is undeniable that the United States of America has recorded great progress in science, technology and industry, the daily press is full of torrid nonsense, libel, and downright lies. Any group of rabble or scum (*baldırı çıplaklar*) can get together and publish any blasphemy or invective. There is no respect for religion or rulers, and they do not hesitate to attack even their own president in the most scandalous language, to the extent of calling President Cleveland a drunk. It is useless to bring libel suits against such people because the publicity only serves to increase their fame. Good families are ruined every day by such malicious attacks. Therefore it would be correct to say that this is a savage country.[28]

Presenting a positive image: the press and the theatre

Apart from newspapers and journals, another sphere where the Ottomans strove for image management was the theatre. In the heyday of popular orientalism, it was fashionable for European companies to put on productions that emphasized the exotic. What Said has called 'Orientalizing the Oriental' could take the form of a genuinely noteworthy academic treatise or, equally, that of a vulgar cabaret. Another of the tasks of Ottoman representatives abroad was to prevent the staging of such productions which they saw as demeaning and insulting.[29]

Ottoman diplomats usually worked through the good offices of European statesmen, sometimes at the highest level. The French president Sadi Carnot was awarded a decoration, the *Nişan-ı imtiyaz* (The Ottoman equivalent of the *Legion D'Honneur*), for 'his extraordinary goodwill and help' in securing the banning of a play on the Prophet Mohammed.[30]

Some nine years later it was reported that Mohammed would be the subject of another play in Paris, staged by no lesser a troupe than the Comédie Française. Again, the Ottoman embassy interceded to prevent the event.[31] The following year notices appeared in the London press that a play on Mohammed would grace the London stage. The Ottoman ambassador immediately saw Lord Roseberry who set his mind at rest, telling him he had heard of no such project, and in any case Britain would also be wary of giving offence to her millions of Muslim subjects.[32]

The Porte had less luck with an opera concerning Mehmed II, the conqueror of Istanbul, which was due to open in Milan in December 1893. The Ottoman embassy in Rome interceded but were told that the Italian Foreign Ministry could do nothing. The embassy then approached the author of the opera who assured them 'no disrespect or injury to national honour' would result from the performance. The production, he promised them, had nothing to do with two previous versions of the opera due to be staged in London and Paris, 'which were banned because of the intercession of the Porte'.[33]

The authors of offending plays or pamphlets were often anonymous, only surfacing to extort money from the Porte. On 19 July 1890, the Ottoman ambassador in London reported that he had managed to get his hands on the anonymous script of a play 'viciously lampooning the Sublime State and the August Person'.[34] Upon investigation it was discovered that the author was Osman Millingen, a colourful figure and the son of Dr Millingen, Lord Byron's doctor. An interesting discussion ensued between the ambassador and Sir Philip Currie who told him that in Britain the freedom of the press meant that British politicians had to put up with the most vulgar lampooning. The ambassador replied 'public morals are seen very differently in the Ottoman state and attacks on the August Person are very dangerous.'[35]

Some of the cases where the Ottomans felt their honour was being injured bordered on the ridiculous. One such was the little skit acted out in a minor *café chantant* in Amsterdam that caused a furore. The Ottoman resident at the Hague was ordered to look into the matter, as the action of the skit evidently centred around 'a harem' and a 'sultan'. The Ottoman representative, Karaca Paşa, assured the palace that 'these *cafés* are places of little consequence only frequented by the meanest sort of people.'[36] Karaca Paşa, did not omit to include a brief sketch of the 'play': Dutch peasant boy and girl as well as gentleman are shipwrecked off a strange Oriental shore. The boy is made a eunuch, the girl becomes the favourite of the sultan. Gentleman (who is sweet on the girl) attempts a rescue, but after pleading with the sultan, at which point 'on execute quelques danses', he ends up becoming the 'commissaire de police du Harem'.[37]

Even seemingly innocent items could be seized upon as harbouring negative symbolism. Louis Rambert, director of the Ottoman Tobacco Regie, was one day approached by the Ministry of the Interior over a poster the Regie was using to sell cigars: 'The poster depicted in vivid colours a tall Englishman and lady smoking cigars astride donkeys, posing in front of the Pyramids; next to them is a beturbanned Muslim smoking his water pipe. In the background are the mosques and skyline of Cairo.' Rambert, who was Swiss, found it most comical that the Ottoman government should object to the poster. He obviously did not realise that the admission of the poster would very clearly have amounted to an acknowledgment of the British occupation of Egypt, a *fait accompli* that the Ottomans never recognized.[38]

Protocol and the Ottoman Empire as a 'world power'

Actions that could enhance the image of the Ottoman state were purposefully sought. When the United States suffered from exceptionally heavy forest fires the sultan made a point of sending 300 gold lira as succour for the victims. The Foreign Ministry reported that this gesture had received very favourable publicity in the American press.[39]

During the Russo–Japanese war of 1905, the Council of Ministers first considered sending a Red Crescent field hospital to both sides, but the cost of a such a venture proved prohibitive. It was thus decided that the Ottoman government would send financial aid for medical purposes to both belligerents as 'this was in keeping with humanitarian practice undertaken by other states.' The decision was based on the fact that the Russian government had sent such a field hospital to Turkey during the Greco–Ottoman war of 1897.⁴⁰

Abdülhamid also made a special effort to be part of the inter-monarchical protocol of the crowned heads of Europe. On the occasion of Queen Victoria's jubilee celebrating the fiftieth anniversary of her accession to the throne, the Ottoman ambassador to London, Musurus Paşa, was most upset that Nubar Paşa, the 'foreign minister' of the khedive of Egypt, 'should pose as the envoy of an independent state' when Egypt was still nominally part of the Ottoman Empire. He interceded with Lord Salisbury to ensure that Nubar attended the service at Westminster as part of the Ottoman delegation. It must be recalled that, since 1882, when Britain had occupied Egypt, the country had in effect become a British protectorate. The Ottomans never recognized this and until the Great War the British went along with the polite fiction that Egypt was still part of the empire. What seems ironic now would have appeared quite normal in those days – that Musurus Paşa, a Greek, should defend the honour of his state against the transgressions of Nubar, an Armenian, representing another Muslim power.⁴¹ The Ottoman delegation had already survived a crisis when it became evident that the special envoy, Ali Nizami Paşa, sent to convey the sultan's congratulations, did not hold the proper diplomatic credentials. This would have meant that 'the Rumanian and Serbian ambassadors would be received in audience ahead of the sultan's representative.' It was hurriedly arranged that Nizami Paşa receive a telegram clearly endowing him with the necessary credentials.⁴²

The Ottoman Embassy in London continuously had trouble with those it considered 'Egyptians who did not know their proper station'. When the sons of Khedive Tevfik applied directly for an audience with the Prince of Wales, the ambassador was livid at 'the rudeness of these men' who only got their audience in the company of the Ottoman ambassador.⁴³ This was not just empty posturing, as it must be recalled that at precisely this period, the Khedive of Egypt, Abbas Hilmi Paşa, was involved in a show of independence from the Porte. The jubilee celebrations indeed coincided with the khedive's visit to London and he made a point of boycotting them. This was considered churlish behaviour by Istanbul.⁴⁴

On the occasion of Queen Victoria's sixtieth anniversary the Porte was more careful. It was determined that the Minister of Protocol (*Teşrifat Nazırı*), Münir Paşa, should be sent 'because of his considerable experience in such matters'. It was also determined that he would be accompanied by an Englishman in Ottoman service, Admiral Woods Paşa.⁴⁵

On 25th January 1892, Queen Victoria wrote to 'My Good Brother the Sultan of Turkey', advising him that, it has pleased The Almighty to call from this World my much beloved Grandson, His Royal Highness Prince Albert Victor.' The letter ended, 'With earnest good wishes that your Imperial Majesty may long be preserved from all similar causes of sorrow!'⁴⁶ The sultan replied, expressing his condolences,'naturally We are affected by all that affects You, and are much saddened by this tragic event. There is no other solace than to surrender to the will of God.'⁴⁷

Sultan Abdülhamid's twenty-fifth coronation anniversary demonstrated that to some extent the sultan had been successful in his efforts to be included in European royal protocol. The very fact that the celebrations were held is significant since twenty-five is not a particularly auspicious number in Islam. Here too, as in other matters, European protocol patterns were followed. Even Louis Rambert, the director of the Ottoman Bank, was to lament:

> The celebrations have taken place and the Red Sultan of a few years ago can now congratulate himself that the whole of Europe is at his feet ... All the powers have sent special emissaries, Russia and England their most vaunted admirals, the French Republic a general of cavalry, Italy yet another admiral, Germany an illustrious personality ... And as for the ex subjects, they are in gyrations of loyalty ... Bulgaria sent its entire cabinet ...⁴⁸

Even the most modest opportunity was seized upon to present a favourable image. The Ottoman Embassy made a point of sending a military attaché, in dress uniform, to the funeral of General Teasdale, the former *miralay* because '[the General] had been decorated by the sultan during the Crimean War for his bravery in the defence of Kars.' The incongruous sight of a young Ottoman officer, standing to attention as the rain dripped over his finery in an obscure English village was said to have had 'a very good effect on military and political circles here'. Although Teasdale had been in retirement he had maintained close relations with the Ottoman Embassy 'in his capacity as a former comrade in arms and the Master of Horse to the Prince of Wales'.[49]

Foreign newspaper reporters who actually began to understand the difficulties facing the Ottomans could end up being quite sympathetic in their reporting of what they saw. Charles Williams, a freelance correspondent attached to the staff of Gazi Ahmed Muhtar Paşa, the commander of the eastern front during the 1877–78 war with Russia, wrote: 'I have seen much which has endeared to me for ever the Ottoman nation ... But any stick is good enough. in the opinion of some Christians, to beat a Turk with and the rule which they make so elastic in the case of the Muscovite is very rigid indeed when it is brought to bear on the Osmanli ...'[50]

The Ottoman–Russian comparison was quite current among intellectuals who pontificated on the two 'barbaric' empires of late nineteenth century Europe. R. G. Latham, a Cambridge don, was to write:

> The creed of the Sultan is, at least, the equal to the Czar as the representative of a great section of a great creed ...That the Ottoman Empire is a mere encampment, that the Ottoman Turks are mere squatters, that the Ottomans hold Constantinople by sufferance, that they should be driven back to the deserts and steppes of their original Asia, are flowers of rhetoric which may be found in writings of influential authors ... As far as the question of time is concerned, the title of the Ottomans to Constantinople is what that of the English was to London in the reign of Edgar ...[51]

Of course much of this grudging acceptance and admiration centred around the fear of Russia, and the accepted wisdom that the Ottoman Empire and Britain had a special relationship against a common enemy. The rhetoric of the Liberals had still not entirely effaced this even during the Armenian massacres of the 1890s: 'O'Connor and Sykes shared an attachment to Abdul Hamid's regime ... as well as a belief that a special relationship existed between the British and Turkish Empires ... this had survived the attack of London Liberals who pictured the Ottoman Empire as a slaughter-house where the 'Terrible Turk' butchered helpless Bulgarians and Armenians.[52]

The sultan knew who to cultivate. When the influential dilettante Orientalist, Mark Sykes, and his wife visited Istanbul on their honeymoon, they were given the 'image tour' which included, 'a hospital for small children recently built by Abdul Hamid in memory of one of his daughters, and a new school the Sultan had founded for sons of Kurdish aghas and Arab sheikhs.'⁵³ Sykes' admiration of the Ottomans as a 'ruling people' was based on his youthful travels in Turkey. While travelling in eastern Anatolia in the company of a Turkish military detachment, they had a brush with bandits. The officer in charge, to whom Sykes had just offered a cigarette, 'calmly lit his cigarette [while bullets buzzed around his head] then ordered the infantry to divide into two detachments and chase the would-be robbers away.' Sykes marvelled at his coolness; like 'an English officer on field duty' he seemed to think no more of the affair 'than a farm boy would of crow scaring'.⁵⁴

The similarity of the Turks and the British as imperial powers also drew the attention of other writers. Karl Blind, in 1896, was to severely criticize Gladstone's comment that the Turks were 'the one great anti-human species of humanity' with the remark: 'How if he had been reminded by a member of the anti-human race that there are some Irish Home Rulers and Secessionists who, in *United Ireland*, speak of England, on account of her rule of the sister Isle and her many polyglot dominions, as the "Anglo–Saxon Grand Turk".'⁵⁵

Indeed the Ottomans gloated over Gladstone's troubles with the Irish Question. On 23 May 1883, the Ottoman embassy in London reported that 'the Irish issue has caused no end of troubles for Mr Gladstone.'⁵⁶ Three years later, the embassy wrote that the 'Queen has no affection whatever for Mr Gladstone' whose Irish policy was 'looked upon with great dislike by classes of good breeding.'⁵⁷ The Irish and Armenian questions were linked together by Annie de Lusignan: 'As a matter of fact there are more Christians in high office in Asia Minor than there are Catholic nationalist magistrates in Ireland, and religion is less of a bar for advancement under Sultan Abdul Hamid than under Queen Victoria.'⁵⁸

It would appear that 'people of good breeding' in England did indeed have some sympathy for Abdülhamid. As Constance Sutcliffe wrote in 1896: 'It is, for instance, as intolerable to Ali Baba that an Armenian should sit by the wayside and mix Rahat-Lakoum as it would be for the Duke of Allshire that a Hottentot should place himself on the crimson benches of the House of Lords and take part in debate.'⁵⁹ On the Ottoman side, it was felt that foreigners had no idea of what life in Turkey was like. Fatma Aliye, Cevdet Paşa's daughter and one of the first Ottoman women to have intellectual aspirations, wrote in 1891 that foreigners had no idea of what true Muslim Turks were like as they only came into contact with 'Westernized' Turks. She felt, therefore, that it was necessary to invite visiting dignitaries into 'true Muslim homes' and show them true Turkish life.⁶⁰

The Ottoman self-conceptualization as an imperial power like all the others was reflected in a work assessing the colonial penetration of Africa. Mehmed İzzed, a palace translator, spoke of a 'dark continent' where 'civilized' powers sent colonists. The Ottoman state was encouraged to do the same and spread 'the light of Islam' into 'savage' regions. The general tone of the book is very much in keeping with the 'white man's burden' approach of late nineteenth-century colonialism. İzzed's very definition of colonialism is worth quoting at length:

> The concept that we express in our language with the terms, *müstemlekat* or *müstemirât* is called a 'colony' in European languages. The practice of colonialism is the process whereby civilized countries send surplus populations to continents whose people are in a state of nomadism and savagery (*hal-i vahşet ve bedeviyette bulunan*), thereby rendering them prosperous. This also means that [the civilized] country thus acquires new markets and adds the colony to its territories.⁶¹

It is interesting that the terms the Ottomans usually used to refer to their own nomads and tribes – living in a 'state of nomadism and savagery' – should be used in a colonial context here. Clearly, the Ottoman notion of 'civilizing nomads' appears here as a migrant concept in a colonial setting.

Conclusion

Why was the *fin-de-siècle* Ottoman elite obsessed with its image abroad? How does this fit into the world context? The truth of the matter was that, in the late century, the whole world was discovering the power of the popular press, and the Ottomans were no exception. The Ottoman archives are full of newspaper cuttings referring to various aspects of the Dreyfus affair. The scope and implications of the matter were very well understood by the Porte and the palace, down to Zola's famous declaration, 'J'accuse'.⁶²

When Gladstone's pamphlet 'The Bulgarian Horrors' caused mass demonstrations in London, it became very evident that something had to be done to counter the negative propaganda. One of the answers was of course counter-propaganda, particularly counter-propaganda aimed at the

Muslim world. On 15 April 1880, the British ambassador in Istanbul, Henry Layard, wrote to Salisbury that the newspaper *Vakit* had announced the expected arrival of Mehmed Emir Ali Khan, an eminent Indian Muslim, 'to gather subscriptions for the Holy War'.[63] The Ottoman-financed *Paik-i Islam*, an Urdu and Arabic publication printed on the official presses in Istanbul, was aimed at the Muslims of India. This newspaper was seen as a serious threat by Sir Louis Malet, the undersecretary of state for India: 'If a printing press were found in the Vatican from which were issued by the Pope's connivance journals for circulation among the Irish Catholics, stirring them up against British rule it would hardly be treated so lightly.'[64] In another India Office memorandum it was openly stated that: 'There have been of late many proofs of the fact that Mahometans in general very are widely impressed with the belief that their interests as a religious community are closely dependent on the maintenance of Osmanli power.' This situation was largely the result of, 'the greatly improved facilities of correspondence, of travel, of the interchange of thoughts and ideas'.[65] The contrapuntal character of the Muslim international press was well understood by India Office officials. When the Ottoman papers published an appeal for public collection of subscriptions for the Muslims displaced by Russian armies, the India Office view was that, 'It is very much in tone the sort of appeal that would be made in England if it were prepared to collect subscriptions for distressed Christians in Syria for example.'[66]

The effort to present their views in the press was also to involve the Ottoman ruling elite in propaganda for internal consumption. A very interesting example of this is the magazine *Servet-i Fünun*, a Turkish equivalent of *L'Illustration* or the *London Chronicle*. The magazine featured extensive illustrations covering what would today be called 'human interest' stories. Some of the themes that frequently appear are 'cruelty to blacks in the United States', 'a tram robbery in the middle of Paris', 'appalling living conditions of Chinese coolies in San Francisco', or 'British captain throws his mistress overboard on the high seas'. All of these stories come with vivid illustrations depicting a hapless black person being burned at the stake, or a pretty young woman clinging to the boots of the cruel mariner as she dangles over the side. The connecting theme appears to be the degenerate and violent nature of the Western world.[67]

Chapter Seven
The Ottoman 'Self Portrait'

The dervish *zikr* on Fifth Avenue was coming to a close. The five 'dancing dervishes from Arabia' twisted and turned to the accompaniment of flutes and drums. As the tempo quickened in the late summer heat, and sweat beaded the brows of the dervishes under their tall *külahs*, several street urchins started to laugh and mimic the bizarre strangers. 'I remember seeing something rather similar among the Chipewwa,' remarked a tall well dressed lady to her companion in the Panama hat. 'Well blow me down, don't they ever get dizzy!' shouted a man rather the worse for drink. The crowd grew larger as the *ney* built up to its reedy falsetto climax and the drum beat louder. A few policemen on horses appeared to investigate the commotion. Suddenly, the music stopped and a man stepped forward wearing a smile and a *fez* and holding a collection box.

Attempts to minimize 'the exotic'

The Ottoman's obsession with their image was most certainly a reaction to what would today be called Orientalism. Edward Said's idea that 'Orientalism is fundamentally a political doctrine willed over the Orient because the Orient was weaker than the West,' would have struck a resonant chord among many Ottomans in the late nineteenth century.[1] This was the state of mind which informed the actions of the Ottoman minister to Washington DC when he intervened to stop the 'dancing dervishes of Egypt' from performing their *zikr* in the streets of New York.[2] The minister, Mavroyeni Bey, had had it brought to his attention that, 'some thirty men from Egypt had been brought to the United States by a Christian named Malluh from Syria who had promised them money and fame.' Although a handful of the 'performers' were bona fide dervishes, most were 'people of the meanest sort who had been bribed (*esafil-i nasdan ve cebeleden*).' Having become destitute, and being obliged to continue performing in order to eat, their presence in the streets of New York was 'causing insult and injury to Islam'. The minister had instructed the Ottoman consul in New York to arrange for their removal. He also wrote to the State Department urging that they put a stop to the insult. There ensued a very lively exchange of correspondence with the State Department telling the minister that 'they could not interfere in the internal business of the States,' and Mavroyeni retorting that 'he knew the American constitution as well as they did and how would they like it if the Shakers were to perform on the streets of Istanbul?'[3] The 'dervishes' were rapidly shipped off home.

The struggle against 'the exotic' could indeed take on the proportions of a diplomatic incident. As in the case of the dervishes, a 'Panorama of the delights of the Bosporous' was to provide further headache for the Porte. In December 1893, representatives of a British firm arrived in Istanbul declaring that they proposed to stage a 'live panorama depicting the delights of Istanbul' in London. The object of their visit was to procure the services of the various 'components' of the display, sleek rowing boats, brawny oarsmen and lissome dancing girls were to be rounded up and transported to London. When the Yıldız Palace got wind of this the reaction was instantaneous. The grand vizier was ordered to stop 'such mockery that will damage national honour and propriety ... (*ahlak ve adatı milliyeyi tezyif*).'[4]

The sultan personally objected that, 'certain gypsy and Jewish women should be displayed as the so-called specimens of Oriental peoples ... all such display is demeaning and uncalled for.' Although the firm actually pleaded that 'they were not depicting real people but were only creating an illusion', the palace remained unmoved. The British Embassy became involved, arguing that 'this was against freedom of commerce and the arrangements had already been made.' As a solution the firm was told that they could buy the rowing boats but that no 'live displays' were to be permitted.[5]

Attempting to escape the designation 'exotic', Ottoman statesmen sought to capitalize on aspects of their society and civilization which were attuned to the mainstream of world trends. By emphasizing symbols which had come to denote modernity, the Ottoman state was staking its claim to the right to exist. One very telling testament to this effort is the collection of photograph albums that the sultan arranged to be presented as gifts to the Library of Congress in 1893 and the British Museum in 1894.[6]

The themes of the albums provide very useful clues to the 'imperial self portrait'. The photographs cover four main categories. 'Category I' consists of 'Views, Buildings, Monuments and Antiquities'; fairly basic scenic photography such as views of the Bosphorous and the Golden Horn, the imperial mosques, and the various palaces.[7] 'Category II' features, 'Military, Naval, Rescue, Ancillary Services, Military and Industrial Establishments'.[8] This is a much more interesting selection which depicts scenes such as 'The launching ramps for rescue boats at Riva', featuring strapping coastguardsmen standing by well-found rescue craft, or 'Divers of the Imperial Naval Arsenal' gazing complacently at the camera wearing full paraphernalia. Also featured in this section are 'Cannon drill on the Imperial Frigate Mahmudiye', and ' Imperial firemen at drill', the latter a particular irony in a city notoriously plagued by disastrous fires.[9] 'Category III' is perhaps the most interesting and features 'Educational institutions'. Here it is plain that the Hamidian state considered not only its elite educational establishments but also relatively humble schools as showpieces of its claim to modernity. It is particularly significant that girls of 'The Üsküdar School of Trades and Crafts' or the 'Emirgan Primary School for Girls' are shown with their heads uncovered, sporting handsome diplomas. The 'Aşiret School' for the children of tribes and nomads is particularly well represented. On 4 November 1892, the Ministry of War reported that, according to decree, it had arranged for the photographs to be taken of 'those students in the Mekteb-i Aşiret who are well proportioned of body and limb (*mütenasib-ül aza*)'.

The pictures were to be taken in groups of two and were to be of uniform size. The famous photographers, Abdullah Frères, were to be commissioned.[10] The results of their labours feature in the albums as Arab and Kurdish boys staring at the camera wearing somewhat puzzled expressions and 'full local costume'.[11] 'Category IV' is entitled 'Horses, Imperial Stables, and Yachts'. This category is significant as it serves as a message to the outside world that the sultan understood the 'engine casings of power'.[12] Photographs in this series feature 'Asil, a white horse', 'Gazelle, a bay mare born at the Imperial Stud Farm', 'The Imperial Yacht Sultaniye', 'Sleeping quarters aboard the Sultaniye'.[13]

The emphasis on yachts and horses was part of Sultan Abdülhamid's effort to be part of what Benedict Anderson has called 'the semi-standardized style' of 'civilized' monarchy in the late nineteenth century.[14]

International congresses

Another way of 'minimizing the exotic' and appearing as a member of the civilized family of nations was through participation in international congresses. The nineteenth century was the century of the international congress with subjects ranging from the preservation of wild species in Africa, to improvements in the conditions of the blind, to world health problems. In relation to the various congresses of Orientalists in particular the Ottomans found themselves in a delicate position. On the one hand they wanted to be included in such prestigious world events, on the other they feared being the objects rather than subjects of 'study'.[15] Therefore, when Dr G. W. Leitner, the organizing secretary of the ninth congress to be held in London in September 1891, called on the Ottoman sultan to be the official protector of the congress this was to cause some serious soul searching. Leitner made a point of stressing that the previous congresses had been protected by various crowned heads of Europe and that the Maharajah of Jahore was to be on the organizing committee. As there was likely to be 'discussion of the various aspects of Islam', but 'these were not to be directed to any religious or political aim and were to be of a purely scholarly nature,' it was decided to send Ottoman observers to the conference. There is, however, no record that the sultan accepted the trusteeship.[16] The Ottomans were also represented at the Thirteenth World Congress of Orientalists in Hamburg, but rather than sending a specialist they settled on a diplomat of moderate rank from the Berlin embassy.[17]

An international congress on archeology provided another forum where science combined with national prestige. At the meeting of the World Archaeology Congress in Moscow in 1892, the organizing committee made it known to the Ottoman representative that they would like to hold the next congress in Istanbul. The ensuing debate in the Council of Ministers centred around the fact that 'all civilized nations take part in the congress,' and that if it were held in the capital of the Sublime State, 'this would serve as an opportunity for the whole world to witness the progress in education and science that has taken place [in the sultans' reign].' It was also pointed out by the ministers that since the discussions of these congresses had nothing to do with politics and were only concerned with science, they should not be objectionable.[18]

The desire to be included in even fairly ephemeral events in order to present a respectable profile is discernible throughout. One such event was the occasion of the meeting in London of representatives of those powers with African possessions. The topic was the preservation of the wild animals, birds and fish of the continent. The Council of Ministers decided that since the Ottoman state had such possessions in Africa, it should be represented.[19] In the same vein it was decided that the Ottoman state should be represented at the World Congress to Improve the Conditions of the Blind, to be held in Brussels in 1902. The discussion related to the topic stressed the point that 'many of His Imperial Majesty's subjects suffer from this condition.' [20]

The Hamidian state and world fairs: 'The whole world is watching!'[21]

The world fairs presented one of the most spectacular arenas for the display of pomp and power in the heyday of imperialism.[22] The Ottoman state had made a point of being present at nearly all these fairs since the first World Exposition in London, in 1850.[23] In the Hamidian period, with the increased emphasis on the presentation of a 'civilized profile', attendance at the fairs acquired a new importance. As Burton Benedict put it: 'A world's fair can be seen as one of a series of mammoth rituals in which all sorts of power relations, both existing and wished for are being expressed.'[24] In a world ruled by giants such as Britain, France, and Germany, the Ottoman Empire was inevitably relegated to the position of an 'also ran'. Yet, the very fact that it felt obliged to participate, and spent money it did not have on 'being there', shows that for the Ottoman Empire this was not just a matter of picayune posturing. Its 'fairs policy' consisted of two main elements. First, there was the aim of presenting the Ottoman Empire as the leader of the Islamic world yet a modern member of the civilized community of nations. Second, constant vigilance aimed to repell any slight or insult to the Sublime State's prestige.

This obsession with prestige was the principal motivation for Hasan Tarhan Paşa, the Ottoman ambassador in Spain, when he reported that in the Barcelona fair of 1888 a 'panorama of the Battle of Plevna' had been on display. The Battle of Plevna in Bulgaria was the critical turning point of the Ottoman–Russian war of 1877–78. The heroic defence of the position by Ottoman forces led by Gazi Osman Paşa had captured the world's imagination and sympathy at the time. The ambassador reported that, as far as he could see, there was nothing objectionable in the display, but he was sending a photograph of the panorama to Istanbul.[25]

The Ottoman 'Self Portrait'   155

The occasion of the opening of the 1889 Paris Exposition on the centenary of the French revolution was something of an embarassment for the powers still ruled by monarchies. The Ottoman ambassador in Paris, Esad Paşa, somewhat anxious as to the appropriate course of action, telegrammed that the British, Austrian, Russian and German ambassadors had made it clear to him that they would absent themselves from Paris on the occasion. This would mean that he would be the 'only ambassador of a Great Power to attend the ceremony'. He was instructed by the Porte to absent himself 'from so insalubrious an event so damaging to the idea of monarchic sovereignty.'[26]

The Chicago Columbian Exhibition of 1893 is most interesting from the Ottoman perspective, as the considerable material relating to it in the Ottoman archives invites the following questions: How did the Ottomans see their position as the only Muslim Great Power? What was the rationale informing them in their selection of what to display? What were the perceived threats to the image they wanted to project?

The usual arrangement when the Porte decided to take part in a fair was for it to contract out the whole affair to a commercial firm. The firm in question for the Chicago event was a certain Ilya Suhami Saadullah & Co. On 24 May 1892, the Ministry of Trade and Public Works forwarded to the Porte a copy of the contract it had concluded with Saadullah & Co. The contract provided for the building of an 'Ottoman Bazaar' in the shape of the Sultan Ahmed fountain at the entrance of the Topkapı Palace.[27] The building was to be quite a modest affair of 400 square meters. Yet, the feeling among the ministers was that a definite location should be settled as soon as possible with the fair administrative committee 'lest delay oblige us to accept a dishonourable location'. It is thus very clear that the Ottomans were very alive to the matter of prestigious location in an exhibition.[28]

Saadullah & Co. were also to make plaster casts of the Egyptian obelisks in Sultanahmet Square, as part of the Ottoman exhibit would consist of replicas of these monuments. The contract also provided for the construction of a mosque which would be open to prayer by all Muslims at the fair, with the critical proviso that 'proper Muslim etiquette (*adab*) should be observed at all times and visitors to the fair be admitted [into the mosque] only at the discretion of the [Ottoman] representatives.' Part of the exhibit was to be a theatre, and here, too, stringent conditions were laid down: 'no plays injurious to the honour and modesty of Muslim women or damaging to national honour and prestige (*haysiyet ve adab-ı memlekete mugayyir*) are to be performed'[29] in close proximity to a 'mosque', as seen in the Egyptian exhibit at the Paris Exhibition.[30]

When the Ottoman minister to Washington, Alexander Mavroyeni, reported on the opening of the Chicago fair he gave a realistic assessment of the 'Turkish village'. His view was that, 'although it cannot hope to compete with the exhibits of countries who spend thousands of francs, given our means it is a success.' He, too, reported on the mosque which was part of the Ottoman display and was being used by Muslims at the fair. Mavroyeni, however, had one disturbing development to add: some 'Nestorians' had built a mosque outside the perimeter of the fair and were charging money to display 'Muslim devotional practices'. He had intervened with the Chicago city authorities to have the 'mosque' closed down.[31]

The Ottoman's were objecting to what Edward Said has termed 'representations *as representations*, not as "natural" depictions of the Orient.'[32] The effort to depict themselves as 'modern' or even 'normal' clashed head on with the West's relentless quest for the 'unchanging Orient'. It was this contradiction that we encounter in the matter of the photographs to be sent to the Chicago fair. As the sultan himself dictated to his private secretary: 'Most of the photographs taken [by European photographers] for sale in Europe vilify and mock Our Well-Protected Domains. It is imperative that the photographs to be taken in this instance do not insult Islamic peoples by showing them in a vulgar and demeaning light.' Yıldız ordered that all photographs taken were to be vetted by the palace before they were sent to Chicago.[33]

Once the exhibit opened, the Ottomans made every effort to appear as second to none, even in matters of minor protocol. When the fair administration decided that each nation represented at Chicago would have a special day as a 'national day', the Ottomans were initially a bit resistant. However, they rapidly recovered and informed the fair administration that the anniversary of the sultan's accession to the throne was their 'national day'.[34] It was also determined that the band should play the Hamidiye March on the occassion, and that specially made gas lights be displayed reading 'Long Live the Sultan! (*Padişahım Çok Yaşa!*)' when lit. There was also to be a fireworks display.[35]

To coincide with the Ottoman exhibit at Chicago, the publication of a newspaper in Turkish, Arabic and English was planned. The editor was to be the Syrian intellectual Süleyman al-Bustani. It was specified that publication in Chicago could take place providing 'that nothing about politics is mentioned and only news relating to the Ottoman exhibit, and the progress seen in all things in The Well Protected Domains is featured.'[36]

The most fascinating aspect of Ottoman involvement in the world fairs phenomenon was the way decisions were reached as to what to display and how to display it. The process of selection of those facets of their society and civilization that the Ottomans wanted to show the world provides a kind of code matrix to the Ottoman self-image. When a certain Raci Bey from Acre proposed the creation of an 'Ottoman Hippodrome' (*Osmanlı At Meydanı*) for the Chicago fair, his view was that 'it is well known that among the most coveted and popular of Ottoman products are fine Arab horses and camels which are renowned throughout the world.' Raci Bey proposed to export some forty horses and riders as well as several camels. This, he stated, 'would serve to increase the glory of the Sublime State through the presentation of its natural resources and subjects, by drawing the admiring regards of foreigners'.[37]

In this letter Raci Bey enclosed a 'Programme for the Ottoman Hippodrome at the Chicago Fair'. In six articles he set out his ideas for the display. In article one, under 'Horses', it was stated that 'forty horses of fine breed will be picked and each shall be given a special name.' In article two, under 'Camels', Raci continued: 'Six of the most robust Arabian beasts shall be chosen, the spectacle of a whole train of these mighty animals being led by one small Arab boy will cause much amazement.' In article three under 'Riders', Raci really warmed to his subject: 'only handsome Arabs of impressive stature will be chosen by examination of their traditional skills of horsemanship and javelin throwing (*cirid*).' These men must also be 'of honourable character (*ehl-i irz gürühundan*)'.[38] Because the traditional Arab horsemanship games were 'irregular and chaotic', and in order to 'prevent any occurrence which might not look good to foreigners', Raci proposed that the riders in question be put through a 'period of training' before embarkation which would involve a sort of *dressage* with the riders sporting Ottoman and American flags.[39]

It seems that Raci Bey's proposal was accepted by Istanbul as an order was issued to send to the fair two Ottoman regular cavalry officers 'skilled in the arts of horsemanship' who would train the Arab riders.[40] A display along these lines was indeed taken to Chicago and appeared in the fair as 'Bedouins in their encampment'.[41]

From the above it would appear that the Ottomans had internalized much of the West's perception of the 'Orient', even as they were striving for equality. The horses had to have 'special names' because this was how things were done in polite society. The 'little Arab boy' leading away a whole string of fabulous beasts, any one of which could have trounced him, was also a suitably exotic motif. The proviso that the horses and their riders be 'handsome', that they refrain from coursing about in a babble of noise and dust (one can almost hear a paşa in Istanbul add 'in the Arab manner'), and ride around in an orderly fashion, shows the extent to which the Ottoman *mission civilizatrice* informed their thinking. The fact that the original suggestion came from an *Arab* subject who was seeking to please Istanbul (doubtless also to make some money), gives the story an additional twist.

The same intertwining of self perception and perception by the outside word can be traced in the debate over the sending of janissary models to the Chicago fair. The suggestion came from a certain Nuri Bey, a notable of Gemlik on the Aegean shore, who proposed that an 'Ottoman Museum' be set up at the fair, featuring models of janissary troops wearing their traditional garb. This proposal was opposed by the Sublime Porte who felt that 'this would evoke unpleasant memories among the Christians'. Nuri, however, appealed to the Ottoman commissioner at the Chicago fair, Hakkı Bey, pointing out that, 'today the Ottoman nation has reached the level of European civilization and the [present] appearance of the military and civilian personnel of the Sublime state is proof enough [of this].'[42] Hakkı Bey's view was that all this fuss was unneccessary as life-size models of janissaries were already on view in Istanbul, and he saw no reason why they should not be displayed at the fair given that 'in America and in Europe there exist such museums where the most bizarre of old military costumes are proudly put on display.' If a good impression was to be conveyed, said Hakkı Bey, 'the jannissaries should be displayed side by side with the modern Ottoman officer in full dress uniform, which will show the progress that has been recorded since the Tanzimat.'[43]

Hakkı Bey regularly reported on the progress of the Ottoman Pavilion at the Chicago fair. Evidently, he had a clear conception of the basics of showmanship and representational protocol. On 13 February, he was to telegram that, 'the German commissioner to the fair has given a lavish banquet at the Hotel Lexington at which all the flags of participating states were displayed and the Ottoman flag had pride of place.' As these banquets were likely to go on, it was 'only in keeping with the glory and splendour of the Sublime State' that the Ottoman commissioner be given funds, too, to enable him to reciprocate.[44] Hakkı Bey also requested that he be sent two guides who spoke English and were capable of giving information on the various displays in the Ottoman exhibit. He was duly granted both requests.[45]

By 15 May he was writing that the fair was getting off to a slow start, with the Russian and Belgian pavilions only just being completed. He noted that the fair would not get into full swing for another few weeks. The goods scheduled to arrive for the Ottoman pavilion had also been late and many needed repair. Most worryingly, the Navy display, consisting of the sultan's ceremonial state rowing boats, had gone missing. Hakkı Bey also gave news about the 'Ottoman Hippodrome' project. Raci Bey and his Bedouin riders, as well as the horses and camels, had indeed arrived safely but, he lamented, 'the field put aside for the hippodrome is at present a morass of mud'. The Bedouin, who were in severe danger of catching pneumonia, had been found suitable quarters. The two Ottoman cavalry officers, Tevfik Bey and Sabit Bey, had been accommodated in the building occupied by Hakkı Bey himself. But things did not augur well for the project: 'the affairs of this firm are distinctly lax.'[46]

Apparently everything was downhill from then on as things did not go well for the Ottoman cavalrymen. The original arrangement meant that Raci Bey's firm was to pay their expenses, but the firm rapidly went bankrupt, leaving Hakkı Bey responsible for the officers and the Bedouin. The exasperated commissioner was to write: 'as it is not quite suitable for the Imperial government to take legal measures against a firm which is not doing very well, and as it is not in keeping with the glory of the Sublime State for its officers to be destitute [arrangements should be made for them to be sent back].' The officers were duly shipped back at the earliest possible date.[47]

Financial considerations indeed placed a constraint on Hakkı Bey's efforts at a proper presentation of the Ottoman self portrait. He was to lament that, 'the Americans do not provide any service gratis, and we are presented with a bill for even the smallest service.' Although the Porte had budgeted 7,500 lira for the fair, a few weeks after the opening it was becoming clear that additional funds would be necessary. On 15 May, Hakkı Bey gave a detailed breakdown of the monies he had spent and asked for an additional 2,500 lira.[48] A major consideration was always the keeping up of appearances. Hakkı Bey stated that as all the countries' commissioners had office premises in addition to their pavilions, it was unthinkable that the Sublime State should not do the same. Accordingly an office building 'of most pleasing appearance' had been built and furnished with carpets and precious cloths from the state carpet factory at Hereke. It was also necessary to give banquets at the opening and on the occasion of the birthday of the sultan. To justify these expenses, Hakkı

Bey emphasized the importance of the Ottoman presence in the fair:

> As this [fair] is an event at which all the civilized nations of the world are represented, and even obscure states such as the Kingdom of Johore from the Malaca peninsula, and some small Central American republics whose very names are unknown, make great sacrifices to show themselves, it would be unthinkable for the Sublime State not to do the same ... [49]

These words from the Ottoman commissioner at the Chicago fair almost echo the statement made by a contemporary literary critic, J. Snider, who called the Chicago Midway Plaisance the 'sliding scale of humanity'. Nearest to the central point of the white city were the Teutonic and Celtic races as represented by the German and Irish villages the Islamic World was situated somewhere down the middle of the Midway.[50] According to this scale, the Ottomans were in a respectable neighbourhood, the 'Turkish village' was in the same block with the 'German village', 'Panorama of the Bernese Alps', and the 'Dutch village', and just down the road was 'the Murano Crystal exhibition'.[51]

Hakkı Bey got what he wanted as Ottoman goods continued to arrive in Chicago. In August the Ottoman exhibit was in full swing as large samples of Ottoman handicrafts and jewellery arrived and were placed in 'four large glass cases shaped as crescents around a case fashioned as a star'. These were 'exquisite examples of Ottoman porcelain called the Hamidian style worked with jewels and with some depicting historic scenes' which, when placed in the Womens' Building, 'found great favour with the ladies as they rushed to see them and marvel at the workmanship.' Also displayed was a scale model of the Sultan Ahmed fountain at the entrance of the Topkapı Palace. It was further reported that the Ottoman exhibit had 'eclipsed the displays of all other nations'.[52]

The evident desire to compete successfully as a modern civilized member of the club of Great Powers also expressed itself in the effort to prevent objectionable portrayals of things 'oriental'. The Ottomans particularly objected to the display of 'dancing girls and dervishes'. During the Anvers fair in 1894, the Sublime Porte instructed its embassy at Brussels to 'prevent the display of anything which can touch our national honour and religious beliefs'.

They specified that 'shameful displays of Islamic women or dervish life are to be prevented at all cost.'[53] It appears that their fears had some foundation. A certain Agob Balyan was reported to be acting as the agent of a

Belgian firm which intended to stage such a display, and was 'going about Beyoğlu and Sulukule contacting gypsy women and buying objects supposedly used during Mevlevi dervish ritual'.[54] The Ottoman embassy in Brussels duly appealed to the administration of the fair and was assured that any stand or display 'injurious to the modesty of Muslim women or damaging to national pride' would be immediately closed down.[55]

A few years later, the Ottomans were approached with an invitation to take part in a fair that was to be held in Brussels. The Ottoman honorary consul in Brussels, Monsieur C. H. Sudre, appealed to the Porte to take part, 'in order to show the world the progress accomplished by the Ottoman state in the glorious reign of His Imperial Majesty.' If the sultan were to provide the Ottoman stand with his patronage and protection, 'as had the king of the Belgians and other sovereigns of Europe', it would be properly represented.[56]

The sensitivity to becoming the 'object' of display was not exaggerated or misplaced. At the Budapest fair of 1896 the Ottoman representative discovered to his horror that paying visitors were being admitted to the mosque at their pavilion, 'to watch Muslims praying'. Measures were immediately taken to have the mosque closed down.[57] The fact that such a 'display' took place was all the more surprising as the Ottoman exhibit was run by the ubiquitous Arminius Vambery who would be expected to know better. The display included agricultural and artisanal produce as well as 'things of historic value which had been taken from Hungary.'[58]

It is interesting to note that in many instances the Porte's sensitivity focused on what would today be called orientalist depictions of Islamic women and dervishes.[59] This sensitivity comes out very clearly in the proposal of the famous publicist, Ebuzziya Tevfik, to supervise the creation of a 'Museum of Ottoman costume' for the Paris Exposition Universelle of 1900. Tevfik pointed out that as he was in partnership with a Frenchman, 'whose only concern is to make money', it was absolutely necessary that he be present to supervise the propriety of the exhibit:

> If this exhibit is not supervised by someone who has the greatest regard for his national honour, the Europeans, who always exaggerate, will no doubt render our costumes and civilization unrecognizable. They will depict our historical costume in the most garish fashion, making it virtually unrecognizable, and most of all, display our women in the most scandalous fashion, totally contrary to the precepts of the Şeriat and the values of Ottoman honour.[60]

Tevfik went on at some length about the total acceptability of the depiction of old Ottoman military costume yet, as in the case of the Chicago Fair of 1893, he too specified that the military costumes 'would not be janissaries'. If properly supervised, said Tevfik, the exhibit would 'act as a very good countermeasure for all the unfavourable publicity that is propagated against our nation in Europe...'[61]

The Paris Fair of 1900 was to be an event of considerable importance for the Ottomans. As early as the summer of 1896, measures were taken by the Ministry of Trade to begin a selection of the goods to be sent, and to arrange for the purchase of a suitable location on the fair premises. It was also determined to send an Ottoman representative to oversee construction. It was recommended that Yusuf Razi Bey from the ministry's railroad department be sent, as he 'had been educated in Europe'.[62]

Yet, it appears that the Sublime Porte was none too keen on its own subjects visiting the Paris fair. The Ministry of the Interior mentioned that 'since in the previous fair in Paris (1889) many Ottoman subjects who went became destitute, placing a great burden on the embassy in repatriation expenses ...', it was now deemed desirable to ask for a cash bond from those who wanted to go. It was also stated that a thorough inspection of the identities of those intending to travel to Paris was to be carried out.[63]

A few months later the Ministry of Trade reiterated that it was of the utmost urgency to send a representative as 'the other participating states have already done so.'[64] Yet, by 2 February 1897, no representative had been sent and the Paris Exposition committee was beginning to pressure the Ottoman embassy which recommended that a military attaché at the embassy, Leon Bey Karakyan, be appointed as temporary commissioner.[65] It appears that, by the end of 1897, the Porte had still not appointed its official representative, or purchased its lot. The Ottoman ambassador wrote that he had been approached by the chief commissioner for the fair, Monsieur Picard, who had told him that if the Porte did not reply soon it would not be admitted. The ambassador evinced some alarm that the best locations for the 'Grands Palais' had already been taken.[66] The French kept up the pressure, and on 21 June 1898 the head of the Istanbul Municipality reported that the French embassy was complaining that the plans put forward by their architect, Vallacery, for the Ottoman pavilion were not being considered with due speed.[67]

Some months later, by 8 September 1898, the Ministry of Trade had determined that some 50,000 lira were needed for the Paris fair. A commission had been established, headed by Hakkı Bey from the Sublime Porte Legal Councillors' Office, 'because of his experience during the Chicago fair', and including Saadullah Efendi, the contractor who had undertaken the official Ottoman exhibit in Chicago. It was also determined that the Ottoman exhibit would cover 'over 500 square meters'. Each vilayet was to be ordered to inform the Ministry of Trade as soon as possible as to what it proposed to exhibit.[68] Things seem to have speeded up by the end of the month. The Ottoman ambassador wrote to the Porte that the total projected expenditure for their exhibit was to be in the region of 300,000 francs, of which 10,000 was immediately needed for the building of a wall around the Ottoman lot, and as contribution to the fair's railway fees. The ambassador specified that 'special accommodations have to be provided for important guests to our exhibit in order to entertain them in a manner fit for the glory of His Imperial Majesty.' Specially woven Gördes and Uşak carpets were to be shipped forthwith as, 'we are behind the other countries in our preparations and this means we have to double our efforts.'[69]

It would appear that the Ottoman exhibit at Paris, when it actually materialized, was quite a success. Horses were again prominent, with the Imperial stud winning nine prizes. The prize-winning horses were to be photographed and an album presented to the sultan.[70] Also, the Ottoman pavilion ended up being built on the prestigious Rue des Nations, between the pavilions of the United States and Italy. It was the only Islamic power to get such treatment; Persia's much smaller pavilion was in the back row, between Peru and Luxembourg, and Egypt was treated as a British colony.[71]

Private entrepreneurs, who invested a great deal of money in displaying some aspect of the 'exotic Orient, also put pressure on the sultan. On 30 December 1903, a banker, Monsieur Konta, wrote to the Sublime Porte asking that it co-operate in the putting together of an exhibit at the St Louis fair. Jerusalem would be featured and an Ottoman pavilion included. Konta promised to undertake to deliver safely all the components of the Ottoman exhibit and to return them. The centrepiece of the exhibit would be an exact replica of the Mosque of the Caliph Omar: 'As His Imperial Majesty Abdülhamid Khan is the Caliph of all the Muslims who will visit the fair, from China to Sumatra to Java and Africa, it is only appropriate that he appoint the imam and the müezzin.' The organizers also promised to collect donations for the Hijaz Railroad. The Ottoman cruiser, Mecidiye, which was being built at an American shipyard, would be launched for the occasion, with the entire crew being shipped out at the firm's expense to man her. The proposal seemed too good to be true, and the bite came at the end: 'If for some reason which we are unable to fathom the Porte refuses our request, we will be obliged to apply to the good offices of the Egyptian, Tunisian, Algerian and Moroccan governments ... As our sole aim is to celebrate the glory of His Imperial Majesty, we would only resort to such a measure with the utmost reluctance.'[72]

Evidently Monsieur Konta had been well briefed about Abdülhamid's obsession with his claim to being the sole Defender of the Faith and Protector of the Holy Places.[73] The Foreign Ministry took pains to point out that the conditions offered were most advantageous, and that to bring in the governments of rival Muslim powers, some of whom were under Christian control, would be a grievous loss of prestige.[74] It would appear that some of the conditions at least were met as an order was issued absolving all goods destined to the St Louis fair and returning from it from customs duties.[75]

Another matter which was seen as a loss of prestige at the St Louis fair was the display staged at the Bulgarian pavilion of burned out villages in Ottoman Rumelia. At the height of the Balkan crisis, this was just the sort of publicity the Ottomans did not want.[76] The agricultural fair that the Bulgarians had organized in Plovdiv in 1892 had already been snubbed by Istanbul. It was felt that it would be inappropriate to participate in a prestige event in a country which had only recently been an Ottoman province, and was still technically under Ottoman suzerainty.[77]

Conclusion

It will be recalled that when the British firm which proposed to launch a 'panorama of the Bosphorous' was prevented from collecting the live components of its display, it retorted that it was 'not depicting real people but only creating an illusion'. Similarly, when the Ottomans planned their 'Ottoman Hippodrome' for the Chicago fair, they too created an illusion when they objected to 'unruly Arabs' and specified that the Bedouin horsemen be trained by regular army cavalry officers. However, the two illusions pulled in opposite directions. The frustrated 'panorama of the Bosphorous' pushed the exotica of the Orient, whereas the Ottoman efforts were precisely to play down the exotic and present a 'civilized' image of their Arab subjects. Yet, in a strange paradox, the Ottomans were viewing 'their' Arabs through the very same prism through which the Europeans viewed them. Inadvertently, the Ottoman self-image adopted much the same value system as that of the West: 'Yet, European paradigms were not simplistically appropriated; they were filtered through a corrective process, which reshaped them according to self visions and aspirations.'[78] In a sense, therefore, the Arabs in the Ottoman Hippodrome were to some extent 'people as trophies', with the 'corrective' elements of regular cavalry drill.[79]

As world fairs were 'mammoth rituals' involving 'blatant efforts to manufacture tradition and to impose legitimacy', it was imperative for the threatened Hamidian state to make a good showing.[80] In this process of 'communication, discussion, and mutual recognition among ... unequal partners [Islam and the West]' the Ottomans assigned themselves the thankless task aiming for a recognition as the only Islamic Great Power which wanted to participate in modern civilization.[81] In this sense, Zeynep Çelik is incorrect in her assertion that: 'The Turks who wrote about their visits to the international fairs ... did not analyse the differences between their culture and the representations of that culture abroad ... The Egyptians, in contrast, were deeply concerned about the image of their country.'[82] The cases discussed in this chapter show that the Turks were concerned to the point of obsession with their image. What was being undertaken by the Ottoman state was nothing less than a symbolic statement of its right to exist in a world which was constantly trying to relegate it to history.

Chapter Eight
Conclusion

The basic contention of this study has been that a 'legitimacy crisis' took place in the Ottoman empire in the second half of the nineteenth century. This was a crisis that had both external and internal dimensions. The external dimension was the uphill struggle to secure the acceptance of the Ottoman state as a legitimate polity in the international system. The internal dimension was the struggle to overcome the 'legitimation deficit' that accrued as the state permeated society physically and ideologically to an unprecedented extent.[1] A further contention has been that the Ottoman empire in the period 1876–1909 was undergoing an experience that was broadly similar to that which was being experienced in the world at large in the same period. In the Ottoman case a background of crisis lay behind it. I have argued that the Ottoman experience represents a case of imperial adjustment to the challenges of the times, comparable in varying degrees to that seen in other multi-ethnic legitimist systems. Finally, a major theme has been the effort made to create a modern secular state using traditional religious motifs and vocabulary.

The 'tacit knowledge' of a service elite

In a situation of constant crisis it was imperative that the staff of the empire, from grand vizier to the lowliest *kaymakam* in the provinces be imbued with the correct ideology. Ideally, for a member of the service elite, the sultan's authority should constitute the 'natural order of things'. Then and only then could he set about inculcating the same values in the population at large. The framework to support such a system was to be created through elite education, service in the field, shared experience, and the system of rewards and punishments intended to instill respect (or, failing that, fear) and loyalty.

Conclusion 167

The intention was to induce that phenomenon which Edward Shils has called the repository of 'tacit knowledge' in a service elite: 'Some of [scientific knowledge] remains inarticulated, but that too is presented and received. The transmission of the articulated part of the rational, scientific tradition is made effective by the reception and mastery of its inarticulated part. The mind of the recipient is formed by this reception of both the articulated and the unarticulated.'[2]

The way the universe of 'tacit knowledge' changed in the Ottoman Empire is observed by Şerif Mardin: 'The gradualness with which the Turkish world view changed may be seen in that by the end of the reign of Mahmud [II] (1839) the net increment of his rule, in this respect, had been purely and simply the establishment of the *respectability of change*.'[3] The fact that the new sultan, Abdülmecid I, should use migrant notions from the vocabulary of Young Ottoman progressives, like 'fatherland' and 'liberty', in his accession speech is further proof of 'genuine change in the political athmosphere'.[4]

Although the change was indeed slow and incremental, if one examines the century between the reigns of Mahmud II and Abdülhamid II (1808–1909) it becomes apparent that the political context changed a great deal. It was explicitly stated in the Tanzimat Edict of 1839 that people had rights and liberties which could not be arbitrarily taken away from them. To understand how this would become 'tacit knowledge' in Shils' sense, and figure in the calculation of fine tuning that informed the rule of Abdülhamid, let us take the case of Abdülhamid's highly unpopular measure of exiling and executing the great reformer Midhat Paşa. It was before then accepted as part of the normal order of things that grand viziers could be summarily executed. Mahmud II for example had executed the powerful Pertev Paşa. Carter Findley indicates that Pertev had indeed enjoyed such power as the favourite of the sultan that the populace knew him as the 'uncrowned king (*tuğsuz padişah*)'. When he fell from power on 12 September 1837, and was ignominiously executed by poisoning and strangling, his rival Akif Paşa secured a pithy announcement of his death in the official gazette, stating that he had 'died suddenly (*füc'eten*)'. It is striking, too, that Pertev's son-in-law, Vassaf Efendi, a secretary at the palace and also a favourite, and Pertev's brother, Emin Efendi, should both suffer judicial torture before their execution.[5]

However, by 1881, when Midhat was exiled to Taif in the vilayet of Yemen, and there strangled, the legal norms guaranteeing freedom and rights had also led to an accumulation of tacit knowledge that made this act reprehensible, even though the infamous 'exile clause' in the 1876 constitution was evoked as justification. Even if the Yıldız Tribunal, as it was grandly called, was little more than a kangaroo court, the very fact that Midhat Paşa was tried at all is indication enough of just how much things had changed.[6] Moreover, the palace never officially admitted that it had ordered the execution and claimed that he had died from 'natural causes'. In fact Uzunçarşılı, who wrote the major monograph on the issue, states that Abdülhamid deliberately put about the rumour that Midhat and some of his companions had escaped, in order to 'dispell suspicions that they had been killed'. The sorry tale of Midhat's exile and execution is veiled in furtiveness and the awareness that a shameful act was being committed pervades. The guardians of the prison where Midhat was kept attempted several times to poison him to give the impression that his death had indeed been natural. After the execution, Midhat Paşa's servant was imprisoned for three years to prevent him from telling the true story.[7] The odium surrounding Abdülhamid's name has been carried over to the present day in the historical literature which views him as an ogre and Midhat as a 'martyr'.[8] Mahmud II, on the other hand, is seen as a courageous reformer, despite the fact that it was he who ordered the ruthless massacre of thousands of janissaries, the so-called 'auspicious event' (*vak'ayi hayriye*)'.[9]

It was this shift in the tacit knowledge of the elite which enabled them to provide the impetus for secular reforms within the 'cocoon' of a religious vocabulary. Starting with the Tanzimat Edict of 1839 itself, which gave the Şeriat first priority, but went on to make critical breaks from it, the *mission civilisatrice* of the Tanzimat man was carried forward into the Hamidian era. Talking about the Tanzimat, Cevdet Paşa stated: 'During the reign of Abdulmecid Khan the auspicious Tanzimat was declared, and all subjects were declared equal before the law. This was what the Şeriat demanded (*icab-ı Şer'isi bu idi*).' On the matter of reform, the paşa was to state: 'Because changing times require that even some rulings of the *şeriat* change, it is no longer possible to continue the ways of a century ago.'[10] In a similar tone, Küçük Said Paşa, referring to the Şeriat as the 'basic law of the state' referred in the same breath to 'the need to suit measures to changing times as is ordained by the Şeriat'.[11] The Şeriat therefore became a fluid notion and was used in conjunction with, indeed as the ultimate justification for, change.

As Kantorowicz pointed out in the case of European jurists seeking to legitimate change: '… the jurists custom of borrowing from ecclesiastical

Conclusion   169

language for secular purposes had its own tradition of long standing, for it was a practice as legitimate as it was old to draw conclusions *de similibus ad similia*.'[12]

The standard historiography on the nineteenth-century Ottoman Empire proceeds on the spurious assumption of the split between the so-called 'Westernizing', and 'revolutionary' reforms of the Tanzimat and the 'conservative' Hamidian period. However, Ortaylı's character sketch of the 'Tanzimat man' is equally valid for the 'Hamidian':

> The Tanzimat administrators combined pragmatic reformism and conservatism in their personalities, and as such, their world views, modes of behaviour, policies, are all typically representative of the new man in nineteenth-century Ottoman society. Yet it is also evident that this new Ottoman would consciously continue the world view and life style of the old masters of society.[13]

A report prepared by Ahmed Cevdet Paşa, one of the most prominent statesmen of the nineteenth century, provides a striking insider's view of this world, and is therefore worth citing at some length.[14] In remarkably straightforward language, Cevdet talks about critical issues such as the foundation of the legitimation of the state, Islam as a unifying factor, Ottoman relations with the Western powers, and the position of Christians in the empire, and as such this document represents a valuable 'repository of tacit knowledge' of a leading Ottoman:

> Since the time of Yavuz Sultan Selim [Selim I] the Sublime State has held the caliphate and it is thus a great state founded on religion. However, because those who founded the state before that were Turks, in reality it is a Turkish state (*bir devlet-i Türkiye'dir*). And since it was the House of Osman that constituted the state this means that the Sublime State rests on four principles. That is to say, the ruler is Ottoman, the government is Turkish, the religion is Islam, and the capital is Istanbul. If any of these four principles were to be weakened, this would mean a weakening of one of the four pillars of the state structure.[15]

It is striking that one of the most competent and oft-quoted of Ottoman statesmen should explicitly say that the Ottoman state was, in the first instance, Turkish. Although other Muslims have their place, the Turks must always come first:

> The Sublime State is a great structure made up of various peoples (*akvam*) and strata (*sınıf*), all of these constituent elements are held together by the sacred power of the Caliphate. Because the only thing uniting Arab, Kurd, Albanian, and Bosnian is the unity of Islam. Yet, the real strength of the Sublime State lies with the Turks. It is an obligation of their national character (*kavmiyyet*) and religion to sacrifice their lives for the House of Osman until the last one is destroyed. Therefore it is natural that they be accorded more worth than other peoples of the Sublime State.[16]

Yet, the paşa took care to point out that the Arabs were 'those who spoke the language of our religion', and should therefore be respected. Unfortunately, he added, this fact seemed to escape the notice of, 'some state officials in Arabia who still insult the Arabs by calling them *fellah*. Naturally the Arabs therefore hate the Turks.' If these errors were corrected, and responsible officials appointed to the Arab provinces, 'The Arabs who have been under the rule of the House of Osman for all these centuries, will not seek to go their own way, or those who do will be so few as not to matter.'[17]

Nor were the Christians to be neglected:

> Some people of conservative bent argue that it is not advisable to employ Christians in important positions. This is the greatest of errors. Ever since the Abbasid Caliphate, in commercial and financial matters, Christians were employed. The very founder of the Ottoman state, Osman Gazi, was accompanied by his comrade in arms, Mihal Bey, and history is unclear about whether Mihal ever converted to Islam.[18]

Also, in his famous *Tarih*, Cevdet was to praise highly the efforts of Ferah Ali Paşa, 'the spiritual conqueror of the Circassians and the Abhaz'. The paşa receives honourable mention for 'spreading Islam (in the Caucasus) and teaching the Circassian and Abhaz tribes what state and nation is (*devlet ve millet ne olduğunu öğretmiş*) and binding them for ever to their rightful sovereign, the Caliph of Islam'. Although the events Cevdet recounts took place in the late eighteenth century (1195–99AH), his whole treatment of the subject is much more in keeping with the nineteenth-century mobilizational ethic that stirs in his other writings, such as the report mentioned above.[19]

The Ottoman Empire in world perspective

It is often forgotten that, at the turn of the century, the majority of the world's countries were still monarchies. The institution of monarchy had suffered a mortal blow as a result of the French Revolution, but it took the First World War to finally dispatch it. In the interim, not only did monarchies survive but, in cases such as the Japanese, actually revived themselves. The Ottoman sultan, the Meiji emperor, The Russian tsar, the Habsburg emperor were all drawn towards the twentieth century at different tempos, but down broadly similar paths. All invested in a recharged state mythology, which they sought to inculcate through mass education. All invested to varying degrees in the inevitable technical trappings of modernity: railways, the telegraph, factories, censuses, passports, steamships, world fairs, clock towers, and art-deco palaces. All looked to each other to see how their peers were playing the role of 'civilized monarchy'. This process of emulation among the crowned heads of the world had a definite competitive bent, but the model was inevitably the concept of modernity as seen in the core cultures of Western Europe, perhaps even more specifically, the France of the Second Empire.

The Ottoman Empire's story, as told in this book, has been largely the story of the participation of the only sovereign Muslim world power in this process of adaptation. The attempts of the Ottoman sultan to reinforce his ideological position at home overlapped with his efforts to resist the ever-increasing pressure of rival empires. The Hijaz and the *haj* became the arena of confrontation between the Ottoman centre and Muslims from India, the Dutch East Indies, Russian Central Asia, and Egypt, all of whom the Ottomans suspected of serving as stalking horses for the imperialist powers.

The use of the term 'non-Ottoman Muslim' or simply 'foreigner' for these elements was indicative of a fundamental recasting of Ottoman identity, and a corresponding shift in attitude to their own people. What was occuring was nothing less than a move towards conceiving a loyal population as a proto-citizenry. It was no longer enough to be any Sunni Muslim what mattered was the passport one held.

The Ottoman saw himself as an equal participant in the zero-sum games of world politics, and demanded to be treated as such. The European saw him as an anomaly, a master who should really be servant, a ruler who should really be a subject. It was this dichotomy which produced the Ottoman obsession with image and a determination to defend it against all slights, insults and slurs. Even worse, of course, was the possibility of being ignored. This was the rationale that informed the Ottoman statesmen who understood full well the importance of what Edward Said has termed 'representations'.[20] Thus a good part of the Ottoman legitimation effort was directed towards aiming the right 'representations' at the outside world.

Nor was this simply a question of decorum, of pretty posturing or the polite niceties of diplomatic move and counter move. The Ottomans were aware that it was *precisely* decorum and ability in diplomatic subtleties that determined who remained standing and who fell, whose summer palaces were burned by foreign troops on the rampage, and who maintained their dignity even when bloodied in war.[21] Ahmed Cevdet Paşa was to note the importance of reciprocation in matters of protocol:

> One of the new usages of the times is that on the occasion of the accession anniversary and birthdays of foreign rulers guns are fired in salute, their ships are decorated, and their ambassadors receive the congratulations of other missions. Although these ceremonies were carried out in Istanbul and the sultan also sent his congratulations, the foreign powers did not reciprocate. For the official days of celebration of the Ottoman empire were religious holidays. Now since the Ottoman state has joined the European family of nations, Fuad Paşa has set aside the birthday and accession day of the sultan and made them official holidays. This obliged the European states to reciprocate ...[22]

The humiliation of 1876, when the representatives of the foreign powers had met in Istanbul to discuss Turkish reforms, without a Turkish delegation, still rankled.[23] The Hamidian state made a point of participating in all major and many minor international conferences, ranging from the 1884 Berlin Africa conference which was to determine spheres of influence in the continent, to the conference on the protection of flora and fauna in the same continent. The claim of the Sublime Porte in both instances was the same: 'we have the right to be present because we also have posessions in Africa.'[24]

Another world arena where Istanbul made a point of being present, were the world fairs, or *expositions universelles*. Abdülaziz had actually been the first Ottoman sultan to travel outside his empire for peaceful purposes when he visited the Paris Expo of 1867. Although Abdülhamid stamped on all rumours that he was going to visit Europe, he made a special effort to see that the Ottoman state was represented at all major fairs.

'De-legitimation'

The Ottoman caliphate was abolished on 3 March 1924 by something as banal as an act of parliament. The crowds did not surge into the streets, and the cobbles did not run red with blood. An institution that had been recognized as the highest authority in Islam vanished overnight. How did this happen?

Kantorowicz refers to Richard II's ritual disrobing of the trappings of monarchy as 'a coronation in reverse'.[25] In this context, the scene depicting the Young Turk delegation delivering the *fetwa* of deposition to Abdülhamid also bears important clues as to the process of de-legitimation. The parliamentary delegation was to tell the sultan: 'We come representing the parliament. The nation has deposed you. But your life is secure.'[26] The phrasing here, with its reference to the 'nation' having deposed the monarch, is very evocative of the Jacobin attitude to 'Louis Capet' (Louis XVI). The delegation states that the 'nation' has deposed 'you' (using the familiar *sen*, or *tu.*, form of you).[27] But in the next breath, the speaker, Esat Toptani, goes on to speak as a man conditioned by the ancien regime: 'but your life is secure' and here the 'your' is the respectful form *siz* (like) *vous*.[28] The wording of the actual *fetwa* of deposition itself is also interesting because it provides vital clues as to what constituted valid grounds for de-legitimation. The very first reason given for the deposition is: 'If a person (*zeyd*) who is the Imam el Muslimin removes and deletes certain important matters relating to the *şeriat* from the holy books and causes the said books to be banned or burned ...'[29] Here reference was being made to the attempt to monopolize the printing of the Qur'an and its importation from non-Ottoman Muslim lands. It is ironic that a measure which Abdülhamid hoped would reinforce orthodoxy and bolster his position as caliph, was in fact used as the major accusation against him.[30] The second accusation brought against the sultan was, 'the killing, imprisoning, and exile of subjects without *şer'i* justification'. This was a clear reference to the exile and execution of Midhat Paşa, and as such it is very significant that a practice that had been a frequent occurence, the exile and execution of a grand vizier, now had to be justified. A clearer manifestation of the shift in the 'tacit knowledge' informing Ottoman state tradition could not be wished for. A further dimension of the same shift was the fact that the *fetwa* was accompanied by an act of the national parliament.[31]

In fact the Ottoman Hanefi Caliphate ended with the deposition of Sultan Abdülhamid II. The sultan/caliphs who followed him were more or less the puppets of the Young Turk junta. Whatever mystique remained in the office of the sultanate/caliphate was completely hollowed out by deposition, defeat in war, the attempt to militarily oppose the Kemalists in Anatolia, and the escape of the last sultan, Mehmed Vahdettin, on board a British warship. This latest episode shows how far things had moved. The news of Vahdettin's escape created something of a shock in the Grand National Assembly and actually caused one of the members, and a *haji* at that, to comment: 'I told his Excellency the Paşa [Mustafa Kemal] that [the British] were up to something... I actually said they will take the fellow and go ...' The use of the familiar term 'fellow' is striking here, all the more so as the word used in Turkish, *herif*, is in fact quite rude.[32]

The period from the abolition of the sultanate (1 November 1922) to the declaration of the Republic (23 April 1923) to the actual abolition of the caliphate on 3 March 1924, is in many ways the 'coronation in reverse' of the last Ottoman caliph/sultans, as the caliphate is first shorn off from the sultanate and then abolished altogether. During this period as a means of discrediting the House of Osman, Mustafa Kemal embarked on a systematic campaign of vilification.[33] Halil İnalcık has pointed out how the 'Caliphate question' became a symbolic issue between Kemal and his opponents, both sides using religious arguments.[34] Meanwhile, attention was given to how the affair was to be presented to the world Islamic community. In the course of 1923, when Kemal was preparing the ground in Turkey for his coming move, the Grand National Assembly in Ankara issued an official statement.[35] The official position was that the caliphate was not being abolished, but in being separated from the sultanate was reverting to its original form. In fact the whole institution of the caliphate was very deliberately played down and de-emphasized. The declaration stated that this was purely an administrative matter, and was not even a theological issue: 'il resort de ceci que la question du califat n'est pas, comme on le croit à la base de la religion.'[36] The sublime irony was that the selfsame Hanefi *fıkh* which had for centuries been used to legitimate the Ottoman caliphate was now used to de-legitimize it. In the document there are repeated references to the famous Hanefi *alims*, including Abu Hanifa himself who is cited as never having legitimated the rule of the Ommayad and Abbasid caliphs. The Ottoman sultans therefore, were only given the title, 'par suite d'une simple habitude'. In fact the whole issue of who should inherit the caliphate had been deliberately left vague by the

Prophet, and the office was actually a purely temporal authority, 'comme un Président de République'.[37] The document set the trend for future discussions of the 'caliphate question', as Hamid Enayat has noted: 'The document is also significant because of its pioneering value in modern discussions of the caliphate: nearly all critics and supporters of the caliphate after its abolition seem to have done no more than develop its broad propositions.'[38]

In the historiography of the Arab lands, the Ottoman period has consistently been seen as a period of decline and degeneration; yet a revisionist approach is developing. The writers in this school point out that the history of the region cannot be understood, as Youssef Choueiri points out 'unless the Ottoman option is restored to its centrality in the Arab World ...This restoration can no longer be the familiar drawn-out decline, but as a response to European penetration and domination.' Choueiri also draws attention to the need to 'grasp Ottomanism in its secular dimensions and implications'.[39] In the case of mid-nineteenth century Egypt, Ehud Toledano warns against 'the imminent loss of the Ottoman historical context' which has led to a distortion of terms and their relation to the past. Toledano echoes Albert Hourani's warning of losing the 'Ottoman background of the Middle East'.[40] In the Syrian context Philip Khoury points out that the French mandate system that replaced the Ottomans ran into serious difficulties because:

> There was a significant difference in the nature of the new imperial authority it was illegitimate and thus was unstable. France was not recognized to be a legitimate overlord as the Sultan-Caliph of the Ottoman Empire had been. The Ottoman Empire had behind it four centuries of rule and the very important component of a common religious tradition.[41]

It must also be recalled that the majority of the Arab subjects of the Ottoman Empire stayed loyal right to the bitter end. British expectations of massive desertions from the Ottoman army during the First World War proved futile, despite brutal measures undertaken by the Young Turk regime.[42]

So, was everything in vain? Did the last ditch defence of the Ottoman centre fail completely? Were the Kemalists a total break with the Hamidian past? The answer is no to all three questions. In fact a direct thread can be drawn from the gilded antechambers of the Sublime Porte to the ramshackle parliament building in Ankara. Cevdet Paşa and Mustafa Kemal, not to say Abdülhamid and Mustafa Kemal, would have found that they had much in common. The 'young officials' who 'were propelled into the realm of abstract possibilities', and who 'transcended the present and soared into the future', in soaring took much of their Ottoman intellectual baggage with them.[43] Ankara, in fact, took Cevdet Paşa's offering of a 'land of the Turks', but set aside the religious cocoon. In effect, Cevdet Paşa's vision was to become history. The generation which took Turkey into the twentieth century cut its ideological teeth on a certain corpus of intellectual raw material. This was the 'tacit knowledge' which the Kemalist cadres soaked up in Abdülhamid's schools and which was frequently quite distinct from the approved curriculum. The interpenetration of the two worlds, Western and Eastern, since the late eighteenth century, and with accelerated tempo since the Tanzimat reforms, had produced a society where the religious could express itself in secular terms, just as the secular could use religious motifs. The Kemalists were in many ways the personification of this cross-civilizational synthesis, a graft that took.

The countless memoranda in the Ottoman archives, the reports, telegrams, pleas for help, calls for money, troops, the anguish behind the cold officialese, the ruthlessness behind the clinical orders, the subtle equilibrium of weighed possibilities, all represent aspects of the 'fine tuning' process. Of course we now know that the empire collapsed despite all the efforts detailed above. But that should not blind us into thinking that the failure of all these policies was self evident or inevitable. The decision makers and the policy formulators of the time sincerely believed that they could 'save the state'. Ahmed Cevdet Paşa is a representative voice: 'All these dangers demand that the Sublime State carry out the neccessary reforms. If a serious and effective policy [of reform] is carried out, the Sublime State will, in a matter of ten or fifteen years, be strong enough to resist all danger.'[44] The true 'tragedy' in the Greek sense of seeing what is coming, of knowing what to do to avoid it and yet of being unable to resist the march of events, is largely the story of the preceding chapters. In more ways than one, as Ilber Ortaylı has eloquently expressed it, this was really 'the longest century of the empire', when everything hung in the balance and the Ottoman lengthened his stride.[45]

Notes

Introduction

1. Halil İnalcık, *The Ottoman Empire in the Classical Age: 1300–1600.* (London 1973) p. 30. The Ottoman garrison only surrendered in 1481 after the death of Mehmed the Conqueror. Albert Hourani noted the specificity of the Ottomans when he called them, 'the Romans of the Muslim world'. See Albert Hourani 'How Should we Write the History of the Middle East?' *International Journal of Middle East Studies* 23 (1991) pp. 125–36.
2. Hugh Seton Watson, 'On Trying to be a Historian of Eastern Europe' in Harry Hanak (ed.) *Historians as Nation Builders.* (London 1988) p. 7.
3. Eric Hobsbawm, *The Age of Empire* (London 1991) p. 283.
4. F. A. K. Yasamee, *Ottoman Diplomacy. Abdülhamid II and the Great Powers 1878–1888.* (Istanbul 1996) p. 4. The legendary siege of Plevna took place between July and December 1877 when an Ottoman army, much against Western expectations, held off the Russian forces in a heroic defence. The Ottoman commander, Osman Paşa, surrendered with full military honours. For an eye witness account of the battle see William von Herbert, The Defence of Plevna (1877). Tel el-Kebir was the battle in the Egyptian delta where the nationalist forces of Ahmed Urabi were cut to pieces by a British expeditionary force in September 1882. Ahmed Urabi was deliberately humiliated in a show trial and exiled to Ceylon. On this see, Alexander Schölch, *Egypt for the Egyptians. The Socio-Political Crisis in Egypt 1878–1882* (London 1981). At the battle of Omdurman in the Sudan, the Sudanese Mahdi's forces were routed by the British. On this see Mathew Anderson, *The Ascendancy of Europe 1815–1914* (London 1972). pp. 227–8.
5. Mr Owen Davis, 'Those Dear Turks. A Lecture at the Congregational Church, Lee, on 1st November 1876,' *Papers on the Eastern Question.* (London 1876) p. 15.
6. Prime Ministry Archives Istanbul (Başbakanlık Arşivi) hereafter BBA. Yıldız Esas Evrakı (hereafter YEE) 31/1950 Mükerrer/45/83. Said Paşa was referring to the Ottoman Empire's inclusion in the European Con-

cert with the Treaty of Paris of 1856. (*Düvel ve emaret-i Hiristiyane içine çakılub kalmışız*).
7. I refer here to the state power elite, the people involved in decision making in the establishment, not the opposition. Although the Young Turk opposition to Abdülhamid saw itself very much as part of the elite, their views will not be alluded to here. For an excellent recent source on the Young Turk opposition see, Şükrü Hanioğlu, *The Young Turks in Opposition*. (Oxford 1995).
8. Thomas L. Haskell, 'Objectivity is not Neutrality' *History and Theory* vol. 29, (1990) pp. 129-57.
9. This is by design and not by accident. The 'Armenian Question' as it has been somewhat insultingly called, is a major issue which merits scholarly study in its own right. For two excellent recent studies of Armenian nationalism see R. Grigor Suny, *Looking Towards Ararat. Armenia in Modern History* (Bloomington and Indianapolis 1993) and Claire Mouradian, *Armenie, Que sais je* (Paris 1995). Also the works of Anahide Ter Minassian and Ara Sarafian.
10. For a very competent example of legal history on the Ottoman Empire see, Huri Islamoğlu-Inan, 'Köylüler, Ticarileşme Hareketi ve Devlet Gücünün Meşrulaşması,' *Toplum ve Bilim* 43/44 (1988-1989) pp. 7-31.
11. Engin Deniz Akarlı, 'The Problems of External Pressures, Power Struggles, and Budgetary Deficits in Ottoman Politics under Abdülhamid II (1876-1909): Origins and Solutions,' Princeton University PhD Dissertation 1976. Particularly pp. 1-9, and pp. 77-98.
12. Engin Akarlı, 'Abdülhamid II Between East and West,' Paper presented at the colloquium: 'Education, Nation Building and Identity in the Period of Abdülhamid' Bad Homburg, Germany July 12-15 1993, p. 23.
13. Carol Gluck, *Japan's Modern Myths*. (Princeton 1985) p. 41.
14. L. Carl Brown, *International Politics and the Middle East. Old Rules Dangerous Game*. (Princeton 1984). Particularly p. 67: 'The overwhelming majority of the Ottoman Muslims did, however, identify with the Ottoman Empire. It was the last great Muslim state holding out against European encroachment'.
15. Some more recent work in the old British diplomatic history tradition does however indicate a refreshing revision of classic positions. See, David Gillard, 'Salisbury,' in Keith M. Wilson (ed.) *British Foreign Secretaries and Foreign Policy*. (London 1987) p. 133: 'Ironically the most intelligent of the rulers in this region [the Middle East] during the Salisbury era faced the same problems as he did, namely how to defend their interests in a dangerous world with inadequate resources, and were just as skilled as he was in the economical and realistic use of power in pursuit of strictly limited goals.' .

16. Perry Anderson, *Lineages of the Absolutist State* (London 1974). Particularly statements like that on p. 365: 'The economic bedrock of the Osmanli despotism was the virtually complete absence of private property in land.' When? Where?.
17. Caroline Finkel, *The Administration of Warfare: the Ottoman Military Campaigns in Hungary. 1593–1606*. (Vienna 1988) particularly pp. ix and 313. See also, Finkel, 'French Mercenaries in the Habsburg–Ottoman war of 1593–1606: the Desertion of the Papa Garrison to the Ottomans in 1600, *SOAS Bulletin*, vol. LV part 3 (1992) pp. 452–71.
18. Rifa'at 'Ali Abou-El-Haj sounds the clarion cry against such an approach. See, *Formation of the Modern State. The Ottoman Empire Sixteenth to Eighteenth Centuries*. (Albany 1991) p. 62: 'First of all, it is necessary to reaffirm a simple truism which has been consistently denied in the scholarly literature: Ottoman society, like all human societies throughout history, was fluid and dynamic.'.
19. François-Marie Voltaire, *Oeuvres completes de Voltaire. Essai sur les moeurs. et l'Esprit des nations*. (Paris 1858) vol. 3 bis. p. 271. My translation. Voltaire may have meant Selim I rather than Selim II.
20. Taner Timur, *Osmanlı çalışmaları* (Ankara 1989) pp. 85–6, also Timur, *Osmanlı Kimliği* (Istanbul 1986) p. 36. Also, Timur contends, on p. 71: 'Documents of 'reform' such as the Tanzimat Rescript (1839), the Reform Edict (1856), and the Constitution (1876) were not the product of serious liberal and secular thought, but were much more the result of the diplomatic crisis known as the 'Eastern Question,' Also in *Osmanlı Kimliği* p. 162 : 'Let us underline the fact that the Ottoman ruling classes were always in the course of history completely at one with the established system with which their interests always overlapped. Let us not forget that in the 19th century as the state continuously got poorer, the Ottoman ruling elite lived in a state of luxury seldom seen by their western counterparts.' The sad thing is that these ahistoric statements are made on the basis of considerable research in mainly Western sources. Timur uses no Ottoman archival material.
21. Necip Fazıl Kısakürek, *Ulu Hakan II. Abdülhamid Han.* (Istanbul 1981) p. 11.
22. See for example, Mustafa Müftüoğlu, *Abdülhamid. Kızıl Sultan mı?* (Istanbul 1985) pp. 6, 181, 151, 210. There is a veritable Abdülhamid library which keeps growing as more publications of the same genre continue to appear. Most are repetitive of each other, and contribute little if anything to furthering the debate. For a more recent example see, İhsan Süreyya Sırma, *Abdülhamid'in İslam Birliği Siyaseti* (Istanbul 1983).
23. Akarlı, 'Abdülhamid II Between East and West', p. 11.
24. The classic example of the genre is M. S. Anderson, *The Eastern Question. 1774–1923: A Study in International Relations* (London 1966). For a good

revision of the Eastern Question paradigm see Brown, *International Politics* p. 39: 'Giving due attention to Ottoman History as seen from within provides a corrective to the narrowly Eurocentric perspective of the classical Eastern Question.' .
25. Eric Hobsbawm, *Nations and Nationalism Since 1780* (Cambridge 1990) p. 38.
26. For example, Ulrich Trumpener in his 24-page bibliography of his *Germany and the Ottoman Empire 1914–1918*. (Princeton 1968) cites only six sources in Turkish. In an article he wrote sixteen years later on the same topic Trumpener actually reduces the number of his sources in Turkish to one. See, Ulrich Trumpener, 'Germany and the End of the Ottoman Empire' in Marian Kent (ed.) *The Great Powers and the End of The Ottoman Empire* (London 1984) pp. 111–40. For notable exceptions to this state of affairs see works by Feroze Ahmad, Caroline Finkle, Feroze Yasamee et al.
27. J. Armstrong, *Nations before Nationalism* (Charlottsville 1982) pp. 295, 249. On the culinary delights of the Janissaries see Joel Carmichael, *The Shaping of the Arabs* (New York 1967) pp. 261–2: 'The essence of the Ottoman slave system was the training of the sheep dogs that ran the human cattle of the Ottoman Empire'; and Bryan S. Turner *Weber and Islam* (London 1974) p. 128: 'Continuing the metaphor, the principle of ruling through trained slaves was successful until, in the sixteenth and seventeenth centuries, the Imperial Household ran out of adequate supplies of dog-meat.'
28. P. J. O'Rourke, 'Give War a Chance' (New York Atlantic Monthly 1992) as quoted in Karl K. Barbir, 'Memory, Heritage, History: Ottomans and Arabs' in L. Carl Brown (ed.) *Imperial Legacy. The Ottoman Imprint on the Balkans and Middle East* p. 100.
29. Armstrong, *Nations Before Nationalism*, pp. 64 and particularly p. 77: 'A Moslem historian notes that huge harems and entourages were more characteristic of Ottoman and Chinese monarchs than they had been of relatively modest Arab caliphs.' The source cited is Halil Ganem, *Les Sultans Ottomans*. (Paris 1901, 1902) who happens to be a well known anti-Ottoman polemicist and who also happens to be a Christian.
30. Carter Findley, *Ottoman Civil Officialdom. A Social History* (Princeton 1989) p. 184. See also *Bureaucratic Reform in the Ottoman Empire. The Sublime Porte 1789–1922* (Princeton 1980).
31. Ibid., pp. 135.
32. Ibid., p. 226.
33. Ibid., pp. 226–7.
34. Masami Arai, 'An Imagined Nation: The Idea of the Ottoman Nation as a Key to Modern Ottoman History,' *ORIENT* vol. 27 (1991) pp. 1–2.
35. Ibid., p. 4.
36. Leon Cahun, *Excursions sur les Bords de l'Euphrate*. (Paris 1885) pp. I–II.

37. Ibid. My translation. Cahun footnotes the term *poucht* and defines it rather coyly as: 'A term I deliberately refrain from translating. Let the readers who do not know Turkish substitute the worst insult that they know.' The term means catamite.
38. Şerif Mardin, *Religion and Social Change in Modern Turkey. The Case of Bediüzzman Said Nursi* (New York 1989) p. 202.
39. Michael Cherniavsky, *Tsar and People. Studies in Russian Myths* (New Haven and London 1961) p. 115–16.
40. Şerif Mardin, 'Centre Periphery Relations: A Key to Turkish Politics?,' *Daedalus* (1973) pp. 169–90.
41. Ariel Salzmann, 'An Ancien Regime Revisited: "Privatization" and Political Economy in the Eighteenth-Century Ottoman Empire,' *Politics & Society* vol. 21 (1993) pp. 393–423. See also Abou El Haj, *The Formation of the Modern State*.
42. Ibid p. 411.
43. Maria Todorova, 'The Ottoman Legacy in the Balkans' in Carl Brown (ed.), *Imperial Legacy, the Ottoman Imprint on the Balkans and the Middle East* (New York 1996) p. 48.
44. İlber Ortaylı *İmparatorluğun En Uzun Yüzyılı* (The Longest Century of the Empire) (Istanbul 1983) p. 11.
45. For a good sampling of some recent research on the Tanzimat see: *Tanzimat'tan Cumhuriyet'e Türkiye Ansiklopedisi*. (Encyclopaedia of Turkey from the Tanzimat to the Republic).
46. Abou El Haj, *Formation of the Modern State*. p. 62.
47. See *Düstur* (Register of Ottoman Laws) 1. Tertip Istanbul Matbaa-i Amire 1289. (Istanbul Imperial Press 1872) p. 4. See also, J. C. Hurewitz, *The Middle East and Africa in World Politics* (New Haven 1975) pp. 269–71 for an English translation of the Rescript.
48. Jurgen Habermas, *Legitimation Crisis* (Boston 1973) p. 71. Habermas defines the 'legitimacy crisis' as: 'The structural dissimilarity between areas of administrative action, and areas of cultural tradition, [which] constitutes, then a systematic limit to attempts to compensate for legitimation deficits, through conscious manipulation.'.
49. See, Selim Deringil, 'Legitimacy Structures in the Ottoman State: The Reign of Abdülhamid II (1876–1909)' *International Journal of Middle Eastern Studies*, vol. 23 (1991) pp. 345–59.
50. I owe this term to my colleague Professor Faruk Birtek of the Department of Sociology, Boğaziçi University. On the incorporation of the Ottoman Empire into the European diplomatic network see, J. C Hurewitz, 'Ottoman Diplomacy and the European State System' *Middle East Journal* 15 (1961) pp. 141–52.
51. For a masterful study of how fine tuning worked in a precise context see: Engin Deniz Akarlı, *The Long Peace: Ottoman Lebanon 1861–1920* (Berkeley,

Los Angeles, London 1993). This is a meticulous study of the Ottoman administration in Lebanon in the nineteenth century. In the same context see: Leila Fawaz, *Occasion for War: Civil Conflict in Lebanon and Damascus in 1860* (London 1994).
52. Ernest Gellner, *Nations and Nationalism* (Oxford 1983) p. 11.
53. Anthony Smith, *The Ethnic Origin of Nations* (Oxford 1986) p. 24.
54. Ali Fuad Türkgeldi, *Mesail-i Mühimme-i Siyasiye* (Ankara 1966).
55. Rifa'at Abou-El-Haj, 'Aspects of the Legitimation of Ottoman Rule as Reflected in the Preambles of the Two Early Liva Kanunnameler,' *Turcica* vol. 21–3 (1991) p. 371. Abou-El-Haj points out that although the legitimation of Ottoman rule in Syria, in Arabic, appears in the preamble of the first *kanunname* of 1519 when Syria was incorporated into the empire, in similar preambles in *kanunname* formulated sixty years later the legitimation tract does not appear, but is mentioned in passing in the body of the register itself. Moreover it is now in Turkish.
56. On educational reform in the Hamidian period see, Bayram Kodaman, *Abdülhamid Dönemi Eğitim Sistemi*.
57. See Deringil, 'Legitimacy Structures' p. 346.
58. Benedict Anderson, *Imagined Communities* (London 1991) the term 'official nationalism' belongs to Hugh Seton Watson. See also, Selim Deringil, 'The Invention of Tradition in the Ottoman Empire 1808–1908'. *Comparative Studies in Society and History*, vol. 35 (1993) pp. 3–29.
59. Şevket Pamuk, *The Ottoman Empire and World Capitalism* (Cambridge 1987); Roger Owen, *The Middle East in the World Economy 1800–1914*. (London 1987). Zafer Toprak, *Türkiye'de Milli İktisat* (Istanbul 1983). Feroze Yasamee 'The Ottoman Defence Problem'.
60. Other sources I have used but have not included here for reasons of space will be presented in the notes. For a discussion of the nature of late Ottoman archival documentation see also, Akarlı, *The Long Peace*, pp. 200–4.
61. The Prime Ministry Archives have recently published a guide to the archives. See: *Başbakanlık Osmanlı Arşivi Rehberi* (Ankara 1992).
62. The coding used here is the actual coding used in the catalogues.
63. The aim here is merely to provide information and terminology. The detailed study of administrative reform is beyond the scope of this study.
64. İlber Ortaylı, *Tanzimattan Sonra Mahalli İdareler (1840–1876)* (Ankara 1974). This is still the best book on local administration specifically, and is unique in that it ties in reform in local administration with the overall picture of foreign policy, legal reform etc. The other standard reference on this topic is Findley, *Bureaucratic Reform*.
65. Ibid., p. 43. Ortaylı points out that the status of the Nahiye was never very clear. Originally intended as a unit halfway between Kur'a and Kaza, often grouping several villages, its application proved problematic.
66. Ibid., pp. 54–69; 98–101.

67. Findley, *Bureaucratic Reform*, pp. 250-1.
68. Habermas, *Legitimation Crisis*, p. 71.
69. As noted by Suraiya Faroqhi in her recent work based on primary source research in the Ottoman archives: '[In the first two hundred years of their rule in the Hijaz] the Ottoman Sultan's activities and responsibilites in the Hejaz are discussed in official documents with some frequency, but practically no texts have come to my attention which link the Sultan's role in this matter to his responsibilities as caliph ...'. See Suraiya Faroqhi, *Pilgrims and Sultans. The Hajj under the Ottomans*. (London 1994) p. 8.
70. For a very similar treatment of the problem to mine see: Timothy Mitchell, *Colonising Egypt* (Berkeley 1991).
71. Edward Said, *Culture and Imperialism* (London 1994) p. 6.
72. Sir Charles Eliot, *Turkey in Europe* (London 1965 reprint of original published in 1907) p. 426.

Chapter One

1. The scene above is my fictional reconstruction based on Selçuk Esenbel's, 'İstanbul'da Bir Japon, Yamada Torajiro' *Istanbul* no. 9 April 1994, pp. 36-42. It is interesting that Yamada used terms like 'Dowager Empress' for the Sultan's mother, and 'Empress' for his first wife, drawing parallels with Chinese court ritual which he would have been familiar with. See also, Selçuk Esenbel, 'A fin de siècle Japanese Romantic in Istanbul: The Life of Yamado Torajiro and his *Toruko Gakan*.' *SOAS Bulletin*, LIX part 2 (1996) pp. 237-52.
2. See particularly, E. Hobsbawm and Terence Ranger (eds) *The Invention of Tradition* (Cambridge 1983); Sean Wilentz (ed.) *Rites of Power. Symbolism, Ritual and Politics Since the Middle Ages* (Philadelphia 1985) and David Cannadine and Simon Price (eds) *Rituals of Royalty. Power and Ceremonial in Traditional Societies* (Cambridge 1987). Also Gluck, *Japan's Modern Myths*.
3. See John Elliot, 'Power and Propaganda in the Spain of Phillip IV' in *Rites of Power*, p. 151.
4. Cherniavsky, *Tsar and People*, p. 151.
5. Ibid., p. 119. On the 'Holy Russian Land' see Hobsbawm, *Nations and Nationalism*, p. 49.
6. Gluck, *Japan's Modern Myths*, pp. 49-60, particularly p. 60: 'By adding something to the political to make it patriotically unpalatable, politics was denatured even as the constitutional system was first beginning to function'.
7. Ibid., p. 249.
8. Istvan Deak, 'The Habsburg Monarchy: The Strengths and Weaknesses of a Complex Patrimony,' Monarchies Symposium, Columbia University October 26-7 1990. Unpublished.

9. Walter Leitsch, 'East Europeans Studying History in Vienna' in Dennis Deletant and Harry Hanak (eds) *Historians as Nation Builders* (London 1988) pp. 139–56. In the event the young Poles, Czechs, Serbs etc. ended up writing their own 'National Histories'.
10. Gülru Necipoğlu, *Architecture Ceremonial and Power: The Topkapı Palace in the Fifteenth and Sixteenth Centuries* (Cambridge Mass. & London 1991) p. 59.
11. Zeynep Çelik, *Displaying the Orient, Architecture of Islam at Nineteenth Century World Fairs* (Berekley, Los Angeles 1992) p. 32–6; BBA Y.A HUS 303/87 5 July 1894, Sublime Porte Foreign Ministry, telegram from Vienna Embassy no. 307.
12. Mardin, *Religion and Social Change*, p. 129. On the Ottoman effort to keep pace with the world-wide augmentation and competition in ceremonial, see Selim Deringil, 'The Invention of Tradition as Public Image in the Late Ottoman Empire, 1808 to 1908' *Comparative Studies in Society and History*, 35 (1993) pp. 3–24.
13. Gluck, *Japan's Modern Myths*, p. 249.
14. On the conception of the average cultured Ottoman of nomadism as the antithesis of civilization see Mardin, 'Center–Periphery Relations'.
15. Mehmet Akif Ersoy, *Safahat* (Istanbul 1990). On the conceptualization of these terms by Ottoman intellectuals see, Şukrü Hanioğlu, 'Osmanlı Aydınında Değişme ve "Bilim"' *Toplum ve Bilim* vol. 27 (1984) pp. 183–92.
16. Mardin, *Religion and Social Change*, pp. 38, 119, 172.
17. There is, however, some debate on the actual extent of reading of the *Mukaddimah* undertaken by Ottoman/Turkish historians. See Cornell Fleischer, 'Royal Authority, Dynastic Cyclism, and 'Ibn-Khaldunism in Sixteenth-Century Ottoman Letters,' *Journal of Asian and African Studies* XVIII 3–4 (1983) pp. 198–219. Particularly footnote 2 where Fleischer points out that a few of the standard Turkish references on the subject are inaccurate.
18. Ahmed Cevdet Paşa, *Tarih-i Cevdet* (Istanbul 1309 [1891]) 12 vols.
19. Ümit Meriç, *Cevdet Paşa'nın Cemiyet ve Millet Görüşü*. (The Views of Cevdet Paşa on Society and the State) (Istanbul 1979) p. 13. This is someting of an 'engaged-partisan view' of Cevdet Paşa, who is said 'not to have needed Montesquieu or Taine' because he was 'Muslim and Ottoman'. p. 11. See also Cevdet Paşa, *Tezakir* (Ankara 1986) p. 79.
20. Ibn Haldun, *Mukaddime*, (Istanbul 1990) pp. 103, 331, 364. The intricacies of Ibn Khaldun's *asabiyya* are far too complex to be discussed here. My aim is merely to mention the adaptation of his work to the ideological core of late Ottoman statecraft.

21. Brinkley Messick, *The Calligraphic State: Textual Domination and History in a Muslim Society* (Berkeley 1993) pp. 54–8. Messick's work deals with the heritage of Ottoman law in Yemen.
22. Şerif Mardin, *The Genesis of Young Ottoman Thought* (Princeton 1962) p. 179.
23. Ibid. Şerif Mardin quotes Sadik Rifat Paşa as stating that his aim was to establish, 'une force legale de nature a contenir le peuple et en meme temps empecher tout acte d'injustice.' p. 187.
24. Ahmed Cevdet Paşa, *Ma'ruzat*. Transcribed and prepared for publication by Yusuf Hallaçoğlu (Istanbul 1980) p. 42. My translation.
25. Ibid.
26. BBA YEE 14/1188/126/9. Baghdad 9 Ramazan 1309/7, April 1892.
27. Clifford Geertz, *Negara. The Theatre St°ate in Nineteenth Century Bali* (Princeton 1980) p. 135: 'Ideas are not and have not been for some time, unobservable mental stuff. They are envehicled meanings, the vehicles being symbols ... a symbol being anything that denotes, describes, represents, exemplifies, labels, indicates, evokes, depicts, expresses-anything that somehow or other signifies ... Arguments, melodies, formulas, maps, and pictures are not idealities to be stared at but texts to be read, so are rituals, palaces, technologies, and social formations.' .
28. Irfan Gündüz, *Osmanlılarda Devlet-Tekke Münasebetleri* (Istanbul 1989) pp. 150–1.
29. Ehud Toledano, *State and Society in mid-Nineteenth Century Egypt* (Cambridge, England 1990) pp. 50–3. Toledano points out that the Khedive of Egypt, Abbas Paşa, derived his legitimacy from his status as vassal of the Ottoman sultan. This was to contrast greatly with the behaviour of the khedives of Egypt after the British invasion of 1882, when, with British encouragement, they posed as independent rulers and even laid claim to the Caliphate. See below, Chapter 2.
30. BBA Y. Mtv 230/24, 6 Safer 1320/15 May 1902, Vilayet of Ankara to Imperial Secretariat no. 136. It is interesting that the portrait should actually have been paid for. No doubt in a similar situation today, it would simply be confiscated.
31. Islam forbids the depiction of the human image but, if his priceless photograph collection is anything to go by, Abdülhamid seems to have been less concerned with this than is commonly thought. His hesitancy over displaying his personal likeness may also have been prompted by security considerations.
32. In Japan this form of vocal acclaim was used for the first time in the presence of the Emperor in 1889 after the promulgation of the constitution 'patterned as had been advocated, after the European 'hooray'.' See Gluck, *Japan's Modern Myths*, p. 45. On the augmentation of ceremonial in the British case see, David Cannadine, 'Splendour at Court: Royal

Spectacle and Pageantry in Modern Britain, c.1820–1977' in *Rites of Power*, pp. 206–43.
33. Şükrü Hanioğlu, *Osmanlı Ittihad ve Terakki Cemiyeti ve Jön Türklük 1889–1902* (Istanbul 1985) p. 63.
34. Aptullah Kuran, 'The Evolution of the Sultan's Pavillion in Ottoman Imperial Mosques,' *Islamic Art* IV (1990–1991) p. 284.
35. Ibid., p. 283.
36. Mehmet İpşirli, 'Osmanlılarda Cuma Selamlığı: Halk Hükümdar Münasebetleri Açısından Önemi' in *Prof. Bekir Kütükoğlu'na Armağan* (Istanbul 1991) pp. 459–71.
37. Louis Rambert, *Notes et impressions de Turquie. L'Empire Ottoman sous Abdul-Hamid.* (Geneva and Paris n.d.) p. 76.
38. Celal Esad Arseven, *Sanat ve Siyaset Hatıralarım* (Istanbul 1993) pp. 81–2.
39. Selçuk Esenbel, 'Istanbul'da bir Japon: Yamada Torajiro', p. 40. I am grateful to Selçuk Esenbel for the observation concerning the sultan's change of carriages. Another contemporary noted that in 1879, the sultan actually rode to ceremonial prayers. See Ali Said, *Saray Hatıraları* (Istanbul 1992) p. 72.
40. Arseven, *Sanat ve Siyaset Hatıralarım*, pp. 82–4. The author was a member of the Palace Guards and was present at the scene.
41. Ibid., p. 40. There is an interesting similarity here with the practice in China, where the empress dowager, a contemporary of Abdülhamid, would travel to her summer palace only after the roads were strewn with 'yellow powder', yellow being the imperial colour. See, Sterling Seagrave, *Dragon Lady: The Life and Legend of the Last Empress of China* (London 1992). See also Rambert, *Notes et impressions*, p. 132: '[The] roads would be covered by a fine yellow sand.' On the historic origins of the visit to the shrine of Ebu Eyyub el Ansari see, Nicolas Vatin, 'Aux origines du Pelerinage à Eyüp des Sultans Ottomans' TURCICA vol. 27 (1995) pp. 91–9.
42. Hagop Mintzuri, *Istanbul Anıları 1897–1940* (Istanbul 1993) pp. 14–16. By 'Arab soldiers who did not speak Turkish' Mintzuri means the Regiment of the Turbanned Zouaves (Sarıklı Zuhaf Alayı), fashioned after the North African French regiment by the same name. This regiment was created by Abdülhamid in 1892 to 'demonstrate the loyalty of the Sultan's Arab subjects'. On the Zuhaf Alayı see, Necdet Sakaoğlu, 'Geçmiş Zaman Olur ki' *Skyline*. March 1997, p. 112.
43. For a very good recent study of these issues see Ronald Grigor Suny, *Looking Toward Ararat* (Bloomington and Indianopolis 1993) pp. 15–30.
44. İbrahim Hakkı Konyalı, *Söğüt'de Ertuğrul Gazi Türbesi ve İhtifalı* (Istanbul 1959). My thanks to Dr Cemal Kafadar for this reference. On the cult of Ertuğrul Gazi see below.
45. Mintzuri, *Istanbul Anıları*, pp. 13–14.

46. Ali Said, *Saray Hatıraları: Sultan Abdülhamid'in Hayatı*, (Istanbul 1993) pp. 49–50.
47. BBA Yıldız Resmi Maruzat (hereafter Y.A RES) 135/22 Official correspondence between Yıldız Palace and the Ministries.
48. Ibid.
49. Personal collection of Dr Edhem Eldem. I owe thanks to Dr Eldem for bringing this medallion to my attention. The medallion is in bronze and was struck in Brussels.
50. *Salname-i Vilayet-i Hüdavendigar*, 1303/1885, pp. 110–33.
51. For a discussion of the 'Mirrors for Princes' literature see: Christine Woodhead, '"The Present Terror of the World?" Contemporary Views of the Ottoman Empire c1600' *History* vol. 72 (1987) pp. 20–37, particularly p. 29.
52. The first comprehensive chronicles of the origins of the Ottoman state were written as late as the fifteenth century. They too were written with a view to legitimising contemporary regimes. See Cemal Kafadar, *Between Two Worlds: The Construction of the Ottoman State* (Berkeley 1995) p. 122: 'That they hailed from the Kayi branch of the Oğuz confederacy seems to be a creative 'rediscovery' in the genealogical concoction of the fifteenth century.' .
53. Compare *Salname-i Devlet* 1271, *Salname-i Devlet* 1297, *Salname-i Devlet* 1298, *Salname-i Devlet* 1302. Also the sheer size of the volumes is the best indication of the growth of the state apparatus. Compare *Salname-i Devlet* 1270, 110 pages; *Salname-i Devlet* 1298, 522 pages; *Salname-i Devlet* 1308, 892 pages; *Salname-i Devlet*-1324, 1107 pages.
54. BBA Y.A HUS 261/91 Imperial Chancery to Yıldız Palace,11 Zilkade 1309/7 June 1892.
55. BBA Yıldız Mütenevvi Maruzat (Y.Mtv) 39/61, 4 Zilkade 1306/2 July 1889, Sublime Porte, Ministry of Interior, no. 30. Minister of Interior Münir Paşa to Yıldız Palace Imperial Secretariat.
56. See Richard Wortman, 'Moscow and Petersburg: The Problem of Political Center in Tsarist Russia 1881–1914' in Sean Wilentz (ed.) *Rites of Power* (Philadelphia 1985) pp. 244–71. See also Richard Wortman, *Scenarios of Power, Myth and Ceremony in Russian Monarchy*. vol. 1 (Princeton 1995).
57. See E. H. Kantarowicz, *The Kings' Two Bodies* (Princeton 1957) p. 82: 'The Byzantines had claimed that the so-called 'haloed' essence of ancient Rome on the Tiber, or her sempiternal *genius*, had been transferred to the New Rome on the Bosphorous.' .
58. Necipoğlu, *Architecture Ceremonial and Power*, p. 13.
59. Joseph Fletcher, 'Turco Mongolian Monarchic Tradition in the Ottoman Empire' *Harvard Ukrainian Studies* vol. III (1979–80) p. 246.

60. Gülru Necipoğlu, 'The Ottoman Hagia Sophia,' paper delivered at 'The Structure of Hagia Sophia' symposium, 19 May 1990, Princeton University. Cited with permission of the author.
61. BBA Y.Mtv 26/3; 7 Receb 1304/1 April 1887. Ministry of Pious Foundations no. 2. Minister Mustafa Paşa to Yıldız Palace Imperial Secretariat. The document specifies that the dates scrawled on the wall are from 'some thirty years back', which leads one to suspect that Abdülhamid's predecessors were not as sensitive as he was.
62. Gülru Necipoğlu, 'Dynastic Imprints on the Cityscape. The Collective Discourse of Ottoman Imperial Mausoleums in Istanbul'. Unpublished paper p. 14. Cited with permission of the author.
63. BBA YEE 11/1419/120/5 Circular from Abdülhamid II to his Ministers, Cemaziyelevvel 1319/August 1901. No precise day is given. J. Armstrong could not be more wrong when he states, 'The Ottomans, while retaining the Byzantine capital city rejected specific court mythic formulas' or,.' The Ottoman's lukewarm attitude towards Constantinople presents a striking contrast to the identification of the Byzantines with the city. See Armstrong, *Nations Before Nationalism*, pp. 144, 174.
64. See Godfrey Goodwin, *History of Ottoman Architecture* (London 1971) p. 419 for photographs of clock towers in Ottoman towns. My thanks to Andrew Finkel for this reference.
65. BBA Y.Mtv 67/10, 15 Safer 1310/8 September 1892, Minister of the Privy Purse Mikail Paşa. It is interesting that the chronograms seem to follow the historic sequence of reigns. Was the aim to build a mosque dedicated to each sultan of the dynasty?.
66. BBA Y.Mtv. 28/37, 17 Muharrem 1305/5 October 1887. Yıldız Palace Imperial Secretariat. no. 190.
67. BBA Y.Mtv 131/39, 17 Cemaziyelevvel 1313/5 November 1895 Ministry of Pious Foundations, Secretariat no. 47.
68. BBA Y.A HUS 182/93, 21 Zilkade 1302/1 September 1885. The Grand Vizier Said Paşa was instructed to inspect the construction in person, 'from door to pulpit' (*min bab min el mihrab*). Also photographs were taken of the interior of the Ulu Cami.
69. BBA Y.A HUS 245/43; 10 Receb 1308/19 February 1891; Vali of Baghdad Sırrı Paşa to Ministry of Public Works no. 141.
70. Mardin, 'Center Periphery Relations', pp. 169–90. Mardin is quoting from W. M. Ramsay, 'The Intermixture of Races in Asia Minor. Some of its Causes and Effects' *Proceedings of the British Academy* (1915–1916) p. 409.
71. Cherniavsky, *Tsar and People*, p. 151.
72. Paul Dumont and François Georgeon (eds), *Villes Ottomanes a la Fin de l'Empire*. (Paris 1992). This is a remarkable collection of essays which give a very detailed appreciation of how this 'project of modernization' was put into application in cities as diverse as Bitola, (Manastır) and

Salonica in the Balkans to Ankara and Van in Anatolia. The overall picture that emerges from the very competent contributions is one of concerted efforts expended by the Ottoman modernising officials which were doomed by the spread of nationalism.

73. Timothy Mitchell, *Colonising Egypt* (Berkeley 1991) p. 65.
74. Zeynep Çelik, *The Remaking of Istanbul. Portrait of an Ottoman City in the Nineteenth Century* (Berkeley, Los Angeles, Boston 1993). See particularly chapter 3 pp. 49-63.
75. Ibrahim Hakkı Konyalı, *Söğüt ve Ertuğrul Gazi İhtifali.* (Ankara 1957).
76. BBA Y.Mtv 285/167; 25 Safer 1324/20 April 1906. Communication from Vilayet of Bursa to Imperial Secretariat. no. 27.
77. See Professor Colin Imber's forthcoming work on the foundation myth of the empire.
78. Konyalı, *Söğüd'de Ertuğrul Gazi Türbesi*, pp. 14-19. For a photograph of the fountain chronogram see p. 15. Osman's grave was later removed to Bursa when that city became the Ottoman capital.
79. Ibid., p. 23. The term used is 'en muteber rivayetlere göre'. Kafadar also points out that, 'Sultan Abdülhamid instigated the discovery of the tomb of "Ertuğrul's wife"'. See Kafadar, *Between Two Worlds*, p. 185 n 9.
80. BBA Y.Mtv 228/58; 21 Zilhicce 1319/31 March 1902. Administrative council of the Kaza of Söğüd to the Mutasarrıf of the Sancak of Ertuğrul, no. 27. It is interesting to note that the buildings in question are specified as 'Christian dwellings'. They were paid for in full, and 'because the inhabitants were poor' they were awarded the wreckage. Includes list of dwellings and names of owners.
81. Ibid., p. 34.
82. BBA Y.Mtv. 222/54; 7 Teşrin-i Evvel 1317/20 October 1901. Telegram from the Headman of the Karakeçili Tribe, Hacı Bekir, to Yıldız Palace.
83. BBA Y.Mtv 47/92. Selh-i Cemaziyelevvel 1308/12 February 1891. Keeper of the Privy Purse, Agop Paşa no. 612.
84. BBA Y.Mtv 301/37; 6 Receb 1325/15 August 1907; Minister of the Privy Purse Agop Paşa. Giving details about the installation of a new chandelier in the shrine.
85. See, Enver Kartekin, *Ramazanoğulları Beyliği Tarihi* (Istanbul 1979) pp. 149-50.
86. Kafadar, *Between Two Worlds*, p. 95.
87. BBA Y.Mtv 38/59; 24 Mart 1305/6 April 1889. From the Mutasarrıf of Jerusalem to the Yıldız Palace Imperial Secretariat.
88. BBA Y.Mtv 132/156; 20 Cemaziyelahir 1313/8 December 1895 Emir of Mecca Avn El Refik to Yıldız Palace Imperial Secretariat. no. 5.
89. BBA Y.Mtv 66/87; 13 Safer 1310/6 September 1892. Minister of the Privy Purse Mikail Paşa. Even in cases where there was no obvious publicity value, such as the construction of a special building for the

preservation of the religious court records (Şeriyye Sicilleri), the Privy Purse (Cib-i Humayun) payed the building expenses. See BBA Y.Mtv 63/17.
90. BBA Y.A HUS 184/65 Grand Vizier Kamil Paşa to Yıldız Palace. 14 Muharrem 1303/23 October 1885.
91. Y.A HUS 306/46. Grand Vizier Cevad Paşa. Sublime Porte Receivers Office no. 589 12 Safer 1312/16 March 1894. It is interesting to note that, to this day, non-Muslim places of worship display the Turkish flag (very prominently) yet one never sees a mosque displaying the national colours.
92. BBA Y.Mtv 68/27; 6 Rebiyülevvel 1310/28 September 1892. Chief of Istanbul Municipality (Şehremini) Rıdvan Paşa to Yıldız Palace.
93. Annuaire Commercialle de Constantinople, 1893.
94. BBA Y.Mtv 282/6; Gurre-i Zilkade 1323/28 December 1905. Minister of Interior Mahmud Memduh Paşa to Sublime Porte.
95. BBA Irade Hususi 188/51; 14 Şevval 1310/12 May 1893. Yıldız Palace Imperial Secretariat 8836.
96. Rambert, Notes et Impressions de Turquie, p. 159.
97. On the Ottoman adoption of the Western practice of giving decorations, see: Jacob Landau, 'Nishan,' Encyclopaedia of Islam. New Edition, (Leiden 1993) pp. 57-9.
98. In this sense Landau is mistaken in his assertion that in Abdülhamid's reign the number of decorations, 'increased so much that their intrinsic value declined'. See 'Nishan', p. 58.
99. BBA Y.A HUS 306/91, 16 Safer 1312/19 August 1894.
100. BBA Y.A HUS 261/141, Grand Vizier Cevad Paşa to Vilayet of Konya, 23 Zilkade 1309/19 June 1892.
101. BBA Y.Mtv 296/46, 10 Mart 1323/23 March 1893. Ottoman High Commissioner Ferik Sadik al-Muayyed to Imperial Secretariat, no. 131/16.
102. BBA Y.Mtv 290/183 Letter from Prof. Adolphe Strauss to Imperial Secretariat, 18 March 1906. Enclosing article entitled: 'Le Sultan Abd-ul-Hamid II' in Revue d'Orient et de Hongrie.
103. On the Hamidian regime's attempt to assimilate the Kurdish tribes into politically reliable elements of the empire, see below Chapters 2 & 3. Also, Ali Karaca, Doğu Anadolu Islahatı ve Ahmet Şakir Paşa (1838-1899), (Istanbul 1993) pp. 173-203.
104. BBA Y.A HUS 251/34 27 Ağustos 1307/11 September 1891. Governor of Trabzon Ali Paşa to Ministry of the Interior.
105. BBA Y.Mtv 66/84 13 Safer 1310/6 September 1892. Keeper of the Privy Purse Mikail Efendi no. 420. Mikail Efendi reports that five such banners had now been completed in addition to seven others which had been presented before.
106. Naci Kıcıman, Medine Müdafaası: Hicaz bizden nasıl ayrıldı? (Istanbul 1971) pp. 135, 229. See also Chapters 1 and 2.

107. BBA Y.Mtv 61/80 24 Ramazan 1309/22 April 1892;Imperial Privy Purse no. 98. Keeper of the Purse Mikail Efendi. The regiment was named after the legendary founder of the Ottoman Empire, Ertuğrul Gazi, and it was recruited from the town of Söğüt which was purported to be the first camp of the tribe of Osman.
108. BBA Y.A HUS 182/36, 5 Ramazan 1302/18 June 1885, Grand Vizier Said Paşa to Yıldız Palace.
109. BBA YEE 14/292/126/8, 7 Teşrin-i Evvel 1306/20 October 1890.
110. Butrus Abu Manneh, 'The Sultan and the Bureaucracy: the Anti-Tanzimat Concepts of Grand Vizier Mahmud Nedim Paşa' *International Journal of Middle East Studies* (1990) pp. 268–9.
111. BBA Y.A HUS 235/28, 14 Ramazan 1307/4 May 1890; Prime Minister Kamil Paşa to Imperial Private Secretariat no. 19. Although the name in the document is spelled 'Perpinyani' it is more likely that the person in question was from the well known Istanbul Levantine family of Italian origin, the Perpigniani. My thanks to Prof. Cem Behar for bringing this to my attention. The Ghassanids were an Arab dynasty of the sixth century, who were an ally of the Byzantines. See *Ana Britannica* (Turkish edition of the *Encyclopaedia Britannica*) vol. 9, p. 299.
112. BBA Y.A HUS 257/64 15 Receb 1308/24 February 1891. Minutes of the special session of the Council of Ministers.
113. BBA Y.A HUS 257/64, 13 Şaban 1309/13 March 1892; Grand Vizier Cevad Paşa to Yıldız Palace.
114. BBA Irade Hususi, 62 20 Muharrem 1311/3 August 1893. Yıldız Palace Imperial Secretariat no. 450.
115. BBA Y.Mtv 71/98 11 Cemaziyelevvel 1310/1 December 1892. Yıldız Palace Imperial Secretariat no. 4235. Imperial Private Secretary Süreyya Paşa.
116. Ibid. Report of Minister of Police Nazım Bey 15 Cemaziyelevvel 1310/5 December 1892.
117. BBA Y.Mtv 57/57 21 Cemaziyelevvel 1309/23 December 1891. Imperial Private Secretary Süreyya Paşa.
118. Mitchell, *Colonising Egypt*, pp. 138–46. In his excellent discussion and critique of how Orientalism and nineteenth-century linguistics established and maintained a 'hierarchy' between 'normal' Western languages and Eastern languages Mitchell warns against seeing words as fixed meanings which are in fact 'just the same only different'. I am aware that what I am proposing here runs the risk of establishing a fixity which may not have been there. Yet, I will proceed just the same because I feel that the constant repetition of certain formulae in Ottoman official documentation was not fortuitous, and indeed was an indication of how the Ottoman elite perceived their own 'hierarchy' as legitimate.

119. James Finn, *Stirring Times* (London 1878) pp. 405–7. Emphasis in original.
120. Bernard Lewis, *The Political Language of Islam* (Chicago 1988) p. 62.
121. BBA Irade Dahiliye 56 11 Eylül 1308/24 September 1892. Sublime Porte Grand Vizier's Office. See Chapter 3 below on the Ottoman campaign to convert the Yezidis. The number of all of these examples can be increased almost indefinitely, I have chosen a representative sampling.
122. BBA Irade Dahiliye 68120. 29 Muharrem 1299/21 December 1881. Vilayet of Yanya to Prime Minister. no. 24.
123. BBA Irade Dahiliye 99649. 19 Cemaziyelahir 1309/21 December 1892. Vilayet of Syria to Grand Vizier, no. 32.
124. BBA Y.Mtv. 53/108 2 Zilkade 1308/9 June 1891. Mutasarrıf of Tokad Lütfi Bey to Ministry of Interior, no. 159.
125. BBA Y.A RES 134/71 20 Zilkade 1323/16 January 1906. Yıldız Hususi Maruzat Defteri, no. 13613.
126. BBA Y.Mtv 59/22 28 Kanun-u Sani 1308/10 February 1893. Yıldız Palace Imperial Secretariat. The Redhouse Dictionary also provides 'fickle, inconsistent and irresolute' as a second string of meanings for *sebükmağz*.
127. BBA Y.Mtv 43/117, 4 Haziran 1306/17 June 1890. Vali of Basra Esseyid Mehmed bin Yunus to Imperial Secretariat, no. 52.
128. BBA Y.A HUS 379/8 27 Cemaziyelahir 1315/24 October 1897, Ministry of Interior no. 3380. The document refers to an *irade* which ordered that such serious matters be published in the form of pamphlets (*risale*) rather than in newspapers.
129. Hasan Kayalı, 'Arabs and Young Turks: Turkish–Arab Relations in the Second Constitutional Period 1908–1918'. Harvard PhD Thesis 1988, pp. 109–10. The quote in Kayalı is probably the old Hamidian formula of 'those who cannot tell good from evil'.
130. Naci Kıcıman, *Medine Müdafaası* p. 435.
131. BBA Bab-ı Ali Evrak Odası (BEO) 24234 Mosul Giden 336. 21 Cemaziyelevvel 1311/30 November 1893; BBA Irade Dahiliye 4 Gurre-i Ramazan 1313/15 February 1896.
132. Mardin, *Religion and Social Change*, p. 169.
133. Arménouhie Kévonian, *Les Noces Noires de Gulizar*. (Paris 1993). p. 112.
134. BBA Y.A RES 25/14, 2 Ağustos 1300/15 August 1884. Vilayet of Bingazi to Ministry of Interior.
135. BBA Y.Mtv 37/73; 3 Ağustos 1304/16 Ağustos 1888. Vali of Hicaz, Osman Nuri Paşa, to Sublime Porte. The word used in such instances, *tevahhuş*, is defined in Redhouse as 'a being or becoming timid like a wild beast'.
136. BBA Y.Mtv 51/74, 23 Zilkade 1308/1 July 1891. Report by the Commission for Military Affairs relating to the constitution of irregular *Hamidiye* units in Bingazi; BBA Irade Dahiliye 56, 11 Eylül 1308/24 Sep-

tember 1892 see also above Chapter 1; BBA Y.Mtv 53/108, 2 Zilkade 1308/9 June 1891 *Mutasarrıf* of Tokad to Ministry of Interior, no. 159.
137. BBA Y.Mtv 34/39 22 Kanun-u Evvel 1305/4 December 1889.
138. BBA 53/108 26 Zilhicce 1308/2 August 1891. Governor of Sıvas Vilayet Mehmed Memduh Paşa to Ministry of Interior.
139. İrade Hususi 878/123; 17 Muharrem 1310/11 August 1892; Yıldız Palace Imperial Secretariat no. 678. The matter at hand was the selection of photographs to be sent to the Chicago World's Fair of 1893.
140. Mardin, *Religion and Social Change*, p. 129.
141. BBA YEE 31/1950 Mükerrer/45/83 22 Zilkade 1299/5 October 1882. Report by Grand Vizier Said Paşa on the difficulties of the budget, the invasion of Egypt by the British, and the legal basis of rule of the Ottoman State in the provinces.
142. Report by Osman Nuri Paşa on conditions in the Hicaz. BBA YEE 14/292/126/8, 5 Temmuz 1301/18 July 1885; Kantarowicz, *The King's Two Bodies*, p. 79.
143. Gellner, *Nations and Nationalism*, p. 77.
144. Edward Shils, *Tradition* (Chicago 1980) p. 198.
145. Cannadine and Price (eds), *Rituals of Royalty, Power and Ceremonial in Traditional Societies* (Cambridge 1987) p. 19.

Chapter Two

1. Naci Kaşif Kıcıman, *Medine Müdafaası*, p. 121, 181, 215.
2. Elie Kedourie, 'The Surrender of Medina, January 1919,' *Middle Eastern Studies* vol. 13 (1977) p. 130. Kedourie shows that the story put about by Lawrence and the British that they chose not to attack the city for fear that the Ottomans would do wilful damage to the holy places, was simply not true. The Arab forces were never a match by themselves for the strong Turkish garrison, and Fahreddin Paşa had no. intention of doing damage to places he deeply respected. See p. 135: 'The picture which emerges is one of orderly and equitable rule in which property rights were respected, food supplies assured, and morale maintained.'.
3. Kıcıman, *Medine Müdafaası*, p. 192.
4. Hobsbawm, *Nations and Nationalism*, p. 84.
5. Gellner, *Nations and Nationalism*, p. 16.
6. Bernard Lewis, *The Emergence of Modern Turkey*, p. 105. Although Lewis uses the term 'Reorganization', I think the aims and implications of the movement justify the use of 'Reordering'.
7. Butrus Abu Manneh, 'The Islamic Roots of the Gülhane Rescript,' *Die Welt des Islams* 34 (1994), pp. 173–203.
8. Lewis, *Emergence*, pp. 107, 112, 117, 120.

9. Hobsbawm, *Nations and Nationalism*, p. 73.
10. Ibid.
11. Carter Vaughn Findley, 'The Advent of Ideology in the Islamic Middle East,' *Studia Islamica* LV (1982). Although Findley credits Ottoman statesmen with 'some appreciation of the force of patriotism' he mistakenly concludes that they, ' [had] little grasp of the forms it took in the nineteenth century world.' p. 165.
12. Joan Haslip, *The Sultan. The Life of Abdul Hamid II* (New York 1958), p. 124.
13. Thomas Arnold, *The Caliphate* (London 1965) p. 129–62.
14. Halil İnalcık, 'The Ottoman State and its Ideology' in Halil İnalcık and Cemal Kafadar (eds), *Süleyman the Magnificent* (Chicago and Princeton, Princeton Occasional Papers 1992) pp. 49–72.
15. Arnold, *The Caliphate*, pp. 146–7.
16. Lewis, *The Political Language of Islam*, p. 49.
17. Halil İnalcık, and Donald Quataert (eds), *An Economic and Social History of the Ottoman Empire 1300–1914* (Cambridge 1994) pp. 20–1.
18. Cornell Fleischer, *Bureaucrat and Intellectual in the Ottoman Empire* (Princeton 1986) p. 276.
19. On the Arab Challenge to the legitimacy of the Ottoman Sultan's position as Caliph see, U. Haarmann, 'Ideology and Alterity; The Arab Image of the Turk,' *International Journal of Middle East Studies* 20 (1988) pp. 175–96.
20. Anderson, *Imagined Communities*, pp. 83–111.
21. Stephen Duguid, 'The Politics of Unity: Hamidian Policy in Eastern Anatolia,' *Middle Eastern Studies* (9) 1973 p. 139.
22. India Office Library and Records. Political and Secret Home Correspondence (hereafter L/P&S/) 7/27 p. 617. Lieut. Col. E. C. Ross, Political Resident in the Persian Gulf, to A. C. Lyall, Secretary of the Government of India Foreign Department, no. 240 Bushire 13 December 1880.
23. Ramsay, 'The Intermixture of Races', pp. 359–422: 'In 1880 to 1882 a hopeless despondency about the future of the country reigned everywhere in Turkish society. Prophecies were current that the end of Turkish power was at hand.' I owe thanks to Şerif Mardin for this reference.
24. Albert Hourani, *A History of the Arab Peoples* (London 1991) p. 280.
25. Huri İslamoğlu-İnan, 'Mukayeseli tarih yazını için bir öneri: Hukuk, Mülkiyet, Meşruiyet,' *Toplum ve Bilim* 62 (1993) p. 30.
26. Mardin, *The Genesis of Young Ottoman Thought*, p. 18.
27. See Halil İnalcık, *State and Ideology*, pp. 49–72: 'Under Süleyman Hanafism was declared ... as the exclusive school of law ...' See also *Tarih Deyimleri ve Terimleri Sözlüğü* (Istanbul Milli Eğitim Basımevi 1983) p. 728. It is interesting that even in this modern publication, which is a standard reference, there is a clear bias to this school of jurisprudence. It is clearly

(and in somewhat exaggerated language) stated that it was the official belief of the Ottoman state which was propagated 'from the Balkans to Japan'.
28. It must be noted however that Abu Hanifa himself first stated that the legitimate ruler had to be from the Qureish. It would seem that the more pragmatic interpretation of the Caliphate occured through the force of historical circumstance and the need to accomodate such obviously powerful rulers such as the Mongol and the Turks. See Ann K. S. Lambton, *State and Government in Medieval Islam* (London 1985) pp. 5, 9, 32, 182.
29. Fleischer, *Bureaucrat and Intellectual*, p. 280.
30. Snouck Hurgronje, *Mekka In the Latter Part of the 19th Century*. (London 1931) pp. 182-3.
31. BBA YEE 14/1188/126/9, Baghdad 9 Ramazan 1309/7 April 1892. Süleyman Hüsnü Paşa is a good example of the type of bureaucrat/soldier/intellectual who ran the empire. Something of an illustruous exile he was banished to Baghdad by a suspicious Abdülhamid for his central role in the deposition of Sultan Abdülaziz in May 1876. He was the author of a well known tract proposing reform, the *His-i Inkilab*, and was also the author of some twenty books and monographs. On him see *Türk Meşhurları Ansiklopedisi* (Istanbul 1943) p. 360.
32. Ibid.
33. It is worth noting here that Süleyman Hüsnü Paşa had written a 'World History' (*Tarih-i Alem*) dealing with matters ranging from the 'big bang' to the sequence of Chinese dynasties. See, Kemal Zülfü Taneri, *Süleyman Hüsnü Paşa'nın Hayatı ve Eserleri* (Ankara 1963).
34. Ibid. It is also worth noting that the man whom Süleyman Hüsnü Paşa recommended to write the chapter on Chistianity, Moulvi Rahmetullah, is referred to by Snouck Hurgronje as, 'The highly revered assailant of Christianity, Rahmat Ullah an exile from British India (living in the Hijaz).' See Hurgronje, *Mekka*, p. 173.
35. Mardin, *Religion and Social Change*, p. 76.
36. Şerif Mardin, 'Some Notes on an Early Phase in the Modernisation of Communications in Turkey,' *Comparative Studies in Society and History* (3) 1960-61. pp. 257-71.
37. Duguid, 'The Politics of Unity', quoting G. P. Gooch and H. Temperley, *British Documents on the Origins of the War*, vol. v. p. 27 (London 1938).
38. Milaslı Durmuşzade Hafız Mehmed Sadık, Milas'da Ağa Camii müderris ve Cami-i Kebir Vaizi, (Preacher Mehmed Sadık from Milas, Preacher in the Great Mosque and teacher at Ağa Mosque School.) *Müvaiz-i Diniye* (Izmir 1328/1910) p. 38.
39. Ahmed Cevdet Paşa, *Mecelle-i Ahkam-ı Adliye*. (Istanbul 1876). Also Ali Himmet Berki, *Açıklamalı Mecelle*, (Istanbul 1990) p. 7. The Mecelle Com-

mission began work in 1869 but the multi-volume work did not appear until 1876. An Arabic translation was made.
40. Berki, *Açıklamalı Mecelle*, p. 9.
41. Ibid., p. 8.
42. Ibid., p. 10.
43. Messick, *The Calligraphic State*, p. 56. Messick also mentions that the effect of this codification was to strengthen the hand of the Sultan. See pp. 57-9.
44. BBA Irade Dahiliye 72560. 18 Cemaziyelahir 1301/15 April 1884. Yıldız Palace Imperial Secretariat.
45. BBA Y.Mtv 183/16 5 Cemaziyelahir 1316/31 October 1898. Vali of Yemen Hüseyin Hilmi Paşa to Yıldız Palace Imperial Secretariat, no. 192.
46. Messick, *The Calligraphic State*, p. 50.
47. BBA YEE 14/292/126/8. 5 Temmuz 1301/18 July 1885.
48. Ibid. The 'civilizing motif' in Ottoman terminology relating to the indigenous population of the Hijaz is reflected in the official almanacs. In a *salname* for the vilayet of Hijaz, the 'primitive condition' of the area and the people is expressed in the following terms: 'Before [the arrival of the Ottomans] because the people of Mecca were rather short of intelligence, the Haram-ı Sharif was deserted to the point where deer would wander in the Bab al-Safad from the Cabal-i Qabis and walk around the Haram.' See: *Salname-i Vilayet-i Hicaz*, 1309. p. 185.
49. BBA Y.Mtv 37/73; Dispatch from Vali of Yemen Osman Nuri Paşa to Yıldız Palace. Yıldız Palace Imperial Secretariat, no. 1562. The document is undated but bears a reference to an immediately previous communication dated 3 Ağustos 1304/16 August 1888.
50. BBA YEE 14/292/126/8 7 Teşrin-Evvel 1306/20 October 1890. Report on tour of duty in Yemen.
51. BBA Y.A RES 16/21, 10 Şaban1299, 27 June 1882 Grand Vizier's Office.
52. Messick, *The Calligrahic State*, p. 65.
53. BBA Y.A RES 93/38 Memorandum by Minister of education Zühdü Paşa to the office of the Şeyhülislam, 20 Receb 1315/15 December 1897.
54. Ibid.
55. Ibid. Of course this practice had only been forbiden since 1859. It is noteworthy that Snouck Hurgronje also referred to, 'The Government printing press (in Mecca) which had recently been opened there (1885-86), See Hurgronje, *Mekka*, p. 165. Hurgronje refers to works such as the 'Universal History of Moslim Conquests ... from the time of Mohammed till the year 1885 ' printed at the press under goverment auspices.
56. Ibid. Also memorandum by Council of State dated 16 Şaban 1314/20 January 1897. There was also considerable discussion as to what to do

with the 'faulty' copies of the Holy Book, as destroying even faulty copies was objectionable. It is contended that one of the reasons put forward in the *fetwa* deposing Abdülhamid was that he had ordered the burning of Qur'ans who had failed the text of orthodoxy. Despite their condemnation of the Sultan the Young Turk regime continued the practice of 'vetting' Qur'ans and after 1909 they established the 'Superintendancy for the Printing of Qur'ans and legal works'. See: *Meclis-i Vükela Mazbataları* (Minutes of the Ottoman Cabinet) vol. 184 no. 730, and *First Encyclopedia of Islam*, 'Shaikh al-Islam' pp. 276–8. The practice still holds today. The State Religious Bureau (Diyanet İşleri) must give the seal of approval to any Qur'an before it is sold to the public. On the history of the formation of the Diyanet, see İştar Tarhanlı, *Müslüman Toplum 'Laik' Devlet. Türkiye'de Diyanet İşleri Başkanlığı* (Istanbul 1993).
57. BBA Y.Mtv 222/20, 5 Receb 1319/18 October 1901. Minister for Education Zühdü Paşa, no. 26.
58. BBA Y.Mtv 227/139, 19 March 1902. Ottoman Embassy Stockholm to Foreign Ministry, tel. no. 20.
59. Rıza Tevfik, *Biraz da Ben Konuşayım*. (Istanbul 1993), pp. 242–3. Tevfik also claimed that the authorities confiscated other classics such as the *Buhari-i Şerif*, and Taftazani's *Akaid-i Nesefi* and had them burned in the Istanbul bath-houses. He alleged that the Buhari was censored and a new version, entitled *Sahih-i Buhari* (The True Buhari) was issued.
60. J. W. Redhouse, *A Vindication of the Ottoman Sultan's Title of 'Caliph'* (London 1877) pp. 6–7.
61. BBA Irade Meclis-i Mahsus 4625. 26 Rebiyülevvel 1307/20 November 1889. This 'exclusivist' tone is apparent in the very 'Law on Ottoman Nationality' (19 January 1869), which states in Article 8: 'The children of one who has died or has abandoned Ottoman nationality, even if they are minors, are not considered to be the same nationality as their father and continue to be considered Ottoman subjects. (However) the children of a foreigner who has taken Ottoman nationality, even if they are minors, will not be considered the same nationality as their father and will be considered as foreigners.' See *Düstur* 1. Tertip pp. 16–18. On the matter of the 'French Algerians' see: Pierre Bardin, *Algériens et Tunisiens Dans L'Empire Ottoman de 1848 a 1914*. (Paris 1979) pp. 54–78.
62. Gervais Courtellemont, *Mon voyage a la Mecque* (Paris 1896) pp. 46 and 58. My translation.
63. BBA Y.A RES 15/38 17 Cemaziyelevvel 1299/6 April 1882. Şurayı Devlet no. 2317.
64. BBA YEE 14/292/126/8 5 Temmuz 1301/18 July 1885 Report by Osman Nuri Paşa.
65. Ibid.
66. Courtellemont, *Mon voyage*, p. 151.

67. Ibid., p. 95.
68. BBA Y.A RES 15/38 Memorandum from the Administrative Council of the Hicaz. 24 Safer 1299/15 January 1882.
69. Bernard Cohn 'Representing Authority in Victorian India' in Hobsbawm and Ranger (eds), *The Invention of Tradition*, p.174. Cohn indicates that the title was borrowed from Mughal representations of power.
70. India Office Political and Secret Home Correspondence. L/P&S/3/239 vol. 52 p. 937. Acting Consul Moncrieff to Lord Granville.
71. Ibid.
72. BBA Irade Dahiliye 68044, 15 Rebiyülahir 1299 (6 March 1882) See also Selim Deringil, 'Legitimacy Structures in the Ottoman Empire: The Reign of Abdülhamid II 1876-1909,' *International Journal of Middle East Studies*, 23 (1991) pp. 345-9.
73. Courtellemont, *Mon voyage*, p. 101. Abou Muttalib was the Emir of Mecca, technically an Ottoman official position although the Emirs enjoyed considerable autonomy.
74. Y.A RES 98/38 Memorandum of the Council of State, 16 Şaban 1314/ 20 January 1897.
75. BBA Yıldız Arşivi Hususi Maruzat (Y.A HUS) 295/108, 10 Zilkade 1311/15 May 1894. Sublime Porte Receivers Office 2968.
76. BBA Y.A HUS 297/25, 12 Zilkade 1311/17 May 1894 Sublime Porte Receivers Office 4002.
77. BBA Y.A HUS 245/45 10 Şaban 1308/21 March 1891 Sublime Porte no. 7. On late Ottoman relations with Morocco see Edmund Burke III, 'Le Pan-islamisme et les origines du nationalisme en Afrique du nord, 1890-1918,' *Cahiers de l'Unite de l'Anthropologie sociale et culturelle*. Universite d'Oran (Algeria) 1987, 21-40.
78. On the competition in alms giving between the Ottomans, Moroccan Sultans and the Mughals in earlier centuries see: Suraiya Faroqhi, *Pilgrims and Sultans*, p.143-8.
79. For a very competent study of mid-century Egypt see Toledano, *Egypt in the Nineteenth Century*.
80. British forces invaded Egypt in September 1882 as a response to the nationalist movement led by Ahmad Urabi Paşa. After this date, although the British nominally recognized Ottoman suzerainty in Egypt, the country was in fact turned into a 'Veiled Protectorate' and the ruling khedive, technically an Ottoman official, became a British puppet. See Selim Deringil, 'The Ottoman Response to the Egyptian Crisis of 1881-82,' *Middle Eastern Studies*, vol. 24 (1988) pp. 3-25. On the relationship of the sultan and the khedive see: L. Hirszowicz, 'The Sultan and the Khedive 1892-1908,' *Middle Eastern Studies*, vol. 8 (1977) pp. 287-311.

81. BBA Y.A HUS 159/80, 6 Zilkade 1295 /1 November 1878 Memorandum by Foreign Minister Safvet Paşa.
82. BBA Y.A HUS 188/101, 17 Cemaziyelevvel 1303/21 February 1886. Grand Vizier Kamil Paşa to the Office of the Imperial Secretariat; Snouck Hurgronje also was to note that, 'The Turkish Sultanate would lose its prestige all over the Muslim world if the yearly gifts ... of money and corn from Egypt were stopped.' See Hurgronje, *Mekka*, p. 173. Although the provisions were sent from Egypt, the official position was that the khedive was simply acting as the conduit for the sultan's bounty.
83. BBA YEE 14/292/126/8. Osman Nuri Paşa is very representative of the provincial administrator who is something of an 'unknown soldier' in late Ottoman history. Although much has been said and written on such notable figures as Reşid Paşa, Ali Paşa, Fuad Paşa, Midhad Paşa etc., men who dedicated their lives to the thankless task of patching up what was an increasingly more leaky boat have been forgotten. Osman Nuri Paşa is a good example of the diligent provincial administrator and his views are representative as such of the late-Ottoman world view.
84. Ibid. The Hijaz had a special status and considerable autonomy, one of its privileges was that its population was exempted from military service.
85. Ibid. The imagery of the tree is significant here. One of the symbolic representations of the Ottoman state was the plane tree.
86. Ibid.
87. Fleischer, 'Ibn Khaldunism'.
88. See Faroqhi, *Pilgrims and Sultans*, p. 141: 'The Ottoman Sultans could not legitimize themselves by their role in early Islamic history, nor could they put forth a claim ... of being descended from Chingiz Khan or Tamerlane. Thus their legitimacy depended on practical service to the Islamic community at large, and ... service to the pilgrims was of special importance.'.
89. William Ochsenwald, *Religion Society and the State in Arabia. The Hicaz under Ottoman Control 1840–1908* (Columbus, Ohio 1984).
90. BBA Irade Dahiliye 27, 9 Şaban 1313/25 January 1896. Instructions for the yearly committee of envoys sent from Istanbul to the Hijaz to secure the safety and comfort of pilgrims.
91. Ibid.
92. BBA Irade Hususi 102 23 Cemaziyelahir 1311/1 January 1894.
93. BBA Y.Mt. V 67/51, 21 Safer 1310/14 September 1892. Vali of Hicaz Osman Nuri Paşa, to Yıldız Palace.
94. The most detailed works in English on the Hicaz Railway remain; Jacob Landau, *The Hijaz Railway*, (Detroit, Michigan 1971) and William Ochsenwald, *The Hijaz Railroad* (Charlottsville Va. 1980).
95. German engineers were used but were kept somewhat in the background. See Ochsenwald, *Hijaz Railroad*, pp. 60, 66, 152.

96. For a detailed report including detailed drawings and specifications of the projected fleet see, BBA Irade Meclis-i Mahsus 5368, 18 Rebiyülevvel 1309/22 October 1891, Minutes of Cabinet meeting where the issue was discussed; see also, Yıldız Mütenevvi Maruzat (Y. Mtv) 65/117 25 Muharrem 1310/19 August 1892. Report by the Ottoman Admiralty.
97. Feroze Yasamee, 'Abdülhamid II and the Ottoman Defence Problem,' *Diplomacy and Statecraft* vol. 4 (1993) p. 20.
98. India Office L/P&S/7/27 p. 613. 27 November 1880 and 10 December 1880. From John Kirk HM Consul General Zanzibar to A. C. Lyall C. B. Secretary to Government of India, Foreign Department.
99. Ibid., Muscat 6 December 1880. From Lieut. Col. S. B Miles, Political Agent and Consul, Muscat; to Lieut. Col. E. C Ross, Political Resident in the Persian Gulf.
100. Ibid., p. 617. Bushire 13 December 1880. From Col. E. C Ross, Political Resident in the Persian Gulf to A. C. Lyall, Secretary of the Government of India Foreign Department.
101. The Ottomans had never recognized the occupation of Aden and Ottoman atlases at the turn of the century continued to refer to it as *Adin Sancağı*.
102. India Office L/P&S/7/28 p. 715. Aden 4 October 1880. From Major G. R. Goodfellow, Acting Resident to C. Gonne, Chief Secretary to the Government of Bombay Political Dept.
103. Ibid. Aden, 14 February 1881. From Aden Residency, Major Gen. F. A. E. Loch to Government of India.
104. Ibid. The resident hastened to add that Ali Mokhbil told him that the petitions had been obtained under duress.
105. Ibid. L/P&S/7/27 p. 628. Simla, 2 February 1881. Letter from the Government of India to Secretary of State for India.
106. BBA Y.A HUS 209/15, 5 Rebiyülahir 1305/21 December 1887 Kamil Paşa to the Sultan. 'Arab Government' (*Hükümet-i Arabiyye*) had become something of a catchword for all objectionable activity on the part of the Arabs –such as Arab nationalism. On Ottoman reactions to early Arab nationalism, particularly the Urabi movement, see Deringil, 'The Ottoman Response', pp. 6–24.
107. BBA Y.A HUS 209/15. Kamil Paşa to Yıldız Palace Imperial Secretariat.
108. BBA Y.A HUS 214/46. Kamil Paşa to Imperial Secretariat. 21 Ramazan 1305/1 June 1888.
109. Mardin, *Religion and Social Change*, p. 112. It might be more a case of co-opting a few of them and leaving the rest to their own devices. The numerous pleas relating to the piteous situation of the *medreses* in Iraq bear out this interpretation. See below.
110. As an example of this *genre* see, Mehmed Sadık, Müftü of Milas, *Alem-i Islam'da Cihad-ı Ekber*. That a small town religious functionary should so

actively publish religious tracts on so radical an issue is indicative of this new militancy among the lower ulema.
111. Irfan Gündüz, *Osmanlılarda Devlet/Tekke Münasebetleri* (Istanbul 1989) p. 221. This is a very comprehensive study which sheds light on this critical issue.
112. Ibid., p. 222–3.
113. BBA Y.A HUS 203/69 Sublime Porte 29 Ramazan 1304/21 June 1887. Grand Vezier Kamil Paşa to Imperial Secretariat. It was, however, decided that, as a precautionary measure, he would travel via Istanbul in order to avoid provoking the ire of his followers.
114. BBA YEE 14/2065/74/30, 18 Teşrin-i Sani 1306/1 December 1890. Report by Mehmed Bey, Imperial ADC, Major of Cavalry. I owe thanks to Butrus Abu Manneh for this reference.
115. Ibid. On the various activities of Gümüşhanevi see, Butrus Abu Manneh 'Shaykh Ahmed Ziya'üddin El-Gümüşhanevi and the Ziya'i-Khalidi Suborder' Frederick De Jong (ed.) *Shi'a Islam, Sects and Sufism* (Utrecht 1992) pp. 104–17. This event is also discussed in Raymond Lifchez, *The Dervish Lodge* (Berkeley 1992) p. 223. Gümüşhanevi Nakşibendis are still very active in Turkey today.
116. Abu Manneh, 'Shaykh Ahmed Ziyauddin' p. 113.
117. Ibid.
118. BBA Y.A HUS 263/6; 1 Muharrem 1310/26 July 1892. Sublime Porte to Yıldız Palace. Report by Imperial ADC Cevad Paşa.
119. Ibid.
120. Previous sultans had also made an effort to harness the popular energy of the *tarikat*, or mystic orders. Sultan Mahmud II, who is reknowned for his crushing of the Janissaries in 1826, sought to centralize the appointment of *tekke* shaikhs with the establishment of the Ministry for Pious Foundations (*Evkaf-ı Hümayun Nezareti*). The Tanzimat had continued the process. See: Gündüz, *Osmanlı İmparatorluğunda Devlet-Tekke Münasebetleri* p. 197: 'Although all these measures were in fact contrary to our traditions, the state, which was leaning towards centralization in all things, had no alternative.'.
121. Butrus Abu Manneh, 'Sultan Abdülhamid II and Shaikh Abulhuda Al-Sayyadi,' *Middle Eastern Studies*, vol. 15 (1979) p. 138.
122. Ibid., pp. 136–9. On Ahmad Es'ad's role in that capacity see Deringil, 'The Ottoman Response'.
123. Abu Manneh, 'Sultan Abdülhamid II and Shaikh Abulhuda', pp. 140–1.
124. BBA YEE Kamil Paşa Evrakına Ek. (KPE) 86–9/880. It must be noted, however, that Kamil Paşa was no admirer of Ebulhuda.
125. J. Spencer Trimingham, *The Sufi Orders in Islam* (Oxford 1971) p. 126.
126. Haslip, *The Sultan*, p. 246.

127. H. Anthony Salmoné, 'The Real Rulers of Turkey,' *The Nineteenth Century*, vol. 37 (May 1895) pp. 719-33. In view of the evidence emerging from the archives it is highly unlikely that Abdülhamid should have allowed himself to be 'terrorized' by men whom he kept on his staff.
128. Trimingham, *The Sufi Orders*, p. 127.
129. Smith, *The Ethnic Origins of Nations*, p. 79. From earlier centuries the Ottoman elite had conceived a very defitinite self-image. See Fleischer, *Bureaucrat and Intellectual*, particularly pp. 410 and 261-72.
130. Mardin, *Religion and Social Change*, p. 80.
131. BBA YEE 14/1188/126/9. Also see below Chapter 3.
132. Mardin, *Religion and Social Change*, pp. 32 and 253, extract from *Bitlis Gazette* of 17 October 1889: 'In respect of this caza, though it is hoped that under the Sultan's auspices ... order tranquillity, and civilization ... will be established-yet in its present condition is entirely wanting in such order and civilization.' For the filtering down and 'popularization' of science in the Ottoman provinces see Ibid., p. 76.
133. Ahmet Yaşar Ocak, 'Abdülhamid Dönemi İslamcılığının Tarihi Arka Planı: Klasik Dönem Osmanlı İslamı'na Genel Bir Bakış'. Sultan II Abdülhamid ve Devri Semineri. *İstanbul Üniversitesi Edebiyat Fakültesi, Bildiriler* (Istanbul 1994) p. 123. Emphasis in original, Ocak uses the term 'modernist' (*yenileşmeci*).
134. Gluck, *Japan's Modern Myths*, p. 204.
135. Eugene Weber, *Peasants into Frenchmen*, (Stanford 1976).

Chapter Three

1. On this dictum see: Lewis, *The Political Language of Islam*, p. 29: 'The basic rule for Muslim social and political life, commonly formulated as "to enjoin good and forbid evil" is thus the shared responsibility of the ruler and the subject.' Lewis is quoting from the Qur'an. (III,104,110,114; VII,157; IX, 67, 71, 112; XXII,41; XXXI, 17 as cited in Lewis fn 8 p. 129). On the same principle see Lambton, *State and Government*, pp. 37, 42, 36, 105, 145.
2. John Guest, *The Yezidis. A Study in Survival* (London & New York 1987) pp. 132-3. This paragraph is my fictional re-creation based on Guest's book.
3. On heresy in the Ottoman Empire see: Ahmet Yaşar Ocak, 'Kanuni Sultan Süleyman devrinde bir Osmanlı Heretiği: Şeyh Muhyiddin Karamani,' in *Prof. Bekir Kütükoğlu'na Armağan, İstanbul Üniversitesi Edebiyat Fakültesi*, (Istanbul 1991) pp. 473-84. Also by the same author: 'Les reactions socio-religieuses contre l'idéologie officielle ottomane et la question de *zendeqa ve ilhad*. (Hérésie et Atheisme au XVI siecle) *Turcica* 21-3, (1991) pp. 71-82.

4. Weber, *Peasants into Frenchmen*.
5. It is interesting to note that these tactics were very similar to methods used in other imperial systems at the time. For instance, the British in India used very similar methods, see Gyanendra Pandey, ' 'Encounters and Calamities': The History of the North Indian *Qasba* in the Nineteenth Century' in *Selected Subaltern Studies*, Ranajit Guha and Gayatri Chakravorty Spivak (eds) (Oxford 1988) pp. 106-7: Pandey gives an account of how a local 'disturbance' in the eyes of the Raj officials was settled in 1893-94 by a '*punitive police* [who] were quartered in the town (Mubarakpur) for several months'. My emphasis.
6. Guest, *The Yezidis*. This remains the best study to date of these people who still inhabit eastern Anatolia, northern Iraq and the territories of the ex-Soviet Union. For information on the Yezidi faith, see Isya Joseph, *Devil Worship. The Sacred Books and Traditions of the Yezidis*. (London 1919) reprinted by the Health Research Institute, California (1972). Although they strenuously denied that they worshipped the Devil, the reputation seems to have stuck. It is interesting to note that present day Turkish historians seem to have remained loyal to the Ottoman line that the Yezidis were heretics from Islam. See Mehmet Aydın, 'Yezidiler ve Inanç Esasları,' *Belleten* (Official Journal of the Turkish Historical Society) vol. 52 (1988) particularly p. 33: 'According to the latest research, Yezidism is a heretical (hérétique) branch of Islam. In other words, it is a deviant sect' The French term occurs in the original.
7. Guest, *The Yezidis*, p. 126.
8. On the Hamidiye regiments see Selim Deringil, 'Ottoman to Turk, Minority-Majority Relations in the late Ottoman Empire,' paper delivered in conference: 'Majority-Minority Discourse. Problematizing Multiculturalism,' East-West Centre, Honolulu Hawaii, 11-13 August 1994. Publication of proceedings forthcoming. Stanford University Press.
9. BBA Yıldız Mütenevvi Maruzat (Y. Mtv) 50/21, 5 Mayıs 1307/18 May 1891. Report signed by three local *ulema*, Seyyid Mehmed Nuri from Dahok, Seyyid Nureddin from Befirkan, Farukizade Abbas Buhari, and Leader of the Advisory Commission, Major Abdelkadir. Note that three local religious notables were present in the commission.
10. Ibid. The names of ten chiefs are given.
11. BBA Yıldız Mütenevvi Maruzat (Y.Mtv) 51/61, 19 Mayıs 1307/31 May 1891. Major Abdelkadir to Yıldız Palace Imperial Secretariat.
12. BBA Y.Mtv 53/6, 11 Zilkade 1308/18 June 1891. Yıldız Palace Imperial Secretariat, Imperial Private Secretary Süreyya Paşa.
13. BBA Y.Mtv 51/61, 18 Zilkade 1308/25 June 1891. Memorandum by Imperial Aide de Camp Müşir Şakir Paşa.
14. Ibid.

15. BBA Y.Mtv 61/18, 19 Mart 1308/28 March 1892. Yıldız Palace Imperial Secretariat. Cipher telegram from the Commander of the Fourth Army, *Müşir* Mehmed Zeki Paşa to Yıldız Palace.
16. BBA Irade Dahiliye 97775, 9 Rebiyülevvel 1309/13 October 1891 Yıldız Palace Imperial Secretariat no. 818.
17. Guest, *The Yezidis*, p. 129.
18. Ibid. p. 130.
19. BBA Irade Dahiliye 53, 7 Ağustos 1307/20 August 1892. Telegram from Ömer Vehbi Paşa to Sublime Porte.
20. BBA Irade Dahiliye 53, 8 Ağustos 1397/21 August 1892. Telegram from Ömer Vehbi Paşa to Sublime Porte. The document includes a list of 11 villages by name and the amount of money needed for the schools. The total came to 229,930 *kuruş*. It is unclear exactly who the 'Şebekli' were. There is a contention that they are Muslims of the Sha'afi school. Yet others claim they are a sort of Shi'ite. See Harry Charles Luke (sometime Assistant Governor of Jerusalem), *Mosul and its Minorities* (London 1925) p. 14–15: '[In Mosul] you find Shebeks, a dim agricultural tribe, who may be a sect of Kurdish Shiahs but have an odd dialect and no mosques, and are believed by their neighbors to be a survival of one of the great Mongol invasions, a living relic of Hulagu or Timurlenk.'
21. Ibid. The Yezidi sanctuary at Laliş was the venered shrine of Sheikh Adi b. Musafir, the prophet of the Yezidi religion who had lived in the 11th century. On him and the sanctuary see: Guest, *The Yezidis*, pp. 15–27.
22. BBA Irade Dahiliye 53, 27 Muharrem 1310/21August 1892. Administrative Council of Mosul Vilayet to Sublime Porte no. 74. The Council also referred to the Şebekli as 'a heretical sect who live in a region to the south of Mosul'.
23. BBA Meclis-i Vükela Mazbataları (M.V) 71/10, 2 Safer 1310/26 August 1892. The Sheikhs in question were Mirza Bey, Ali Bey, Hamza Bey, and Hüseyin Bey.
24. BBA Irade Dahiliye 53, 31 Ağustos 1308/13 September 1892. Ömer Vehbi Paşa to Sublime Porte.
25. BBA Irade Dahiliye 56, 11 Eylül 1308/24 September 1892. Ömer Vehbi Paşa and Governor Osman Paşa to Sublime Porte. The reference here is to the Yezidi *kavals*, or holy men who passed from village to village bearing the sacred relics, the bronze peacock or '*Melek Taus*', and collecting contributions. Ömer Vehbi Paşa's allegations of the collection of vast sums which would then be misappropriated were not entirely unfounded. One Yezidi *köçek*, or medium, had, according to French consular sources, ammassed the equivalent of £9000 on the basis of alms and had proceeded to build himself a castle. See Guest, *The Yezidis*, pp. 28–41 and p. 134.
26. Guest, *The Yezidis*, p. 130.

27. BBA Irade Dahiliye 56, 12 Eylül 1308/25 September 1892. Ömer Vehbi Paşa and Governor Osman Paşa to Sublime Porte.
28. BBA Irade Dahiliye 56 14 Rebiyülevvel 1310/6 October 1892. Sublime Porte no 744. The Imperial *irade* was issued on 18 Rebiyülevvel 1310/11 October 1892.
29. BBA Meclis-i Vükela Mazbataları (M.V) 71/37 24 Safer 1310/17 September 1892. Minutes of Ottoman Council of Ministers discussing telegram from Vilayet of Mosul.
30. Ibid.
31. BBA Y.Mtv 68/90, 28 Eylül 1308/11 October 1892. Vali of Mosul Osman Paşa to Yıldız Palace Imperial Secretariat.
32. Guest, *The Yezidis*, pp. 130–1. Although Guest claims that the civil Governor was not notified the Ottoman documentation points in the opposite direction.
33. Ibid., p. 133.
34. BBA Y.A HUS 282/27, 13 Teşrin-i Evvel 1309/26 October 1893. Governor of Mosul Aziz Paşa to Sublime Porte.
35. BBA Y.A HUS 283/55, 22 Rebiyülahir 1311/2 November 1893. Sublime Porte Receiver's Office no. 1394. Grand Vezir Cevad Paşa to Yıldız Palace.
36. BBA Y.A HUS 283/55, 19 Teşrin-i Evvel 1309/1 December 1893. Governor of Mosul Aziz Paşa to Sublime Porte.
37. BBA BEO 25835 Mosul Giden 336, 3 Receb 1311/10 January 1894. Sublime Porte special sitting of the Council of Ministers.
38. BBA Y.Mtv 71/25, 4 Cemaziyelevvel 1310/24 November 1892. Imperial ADC's İbrahim Derviş bin Ibrahim and Şakir Paşa.
39. BBA Y.Mtv. 71/53, 8 Cemaziyelevvel 1310/28 November 1892. Office of the General Staff.
40. BBA Y.Mtv 74/33, 12 Kanun-u Sani 1308/25 January 1893. Imperial ADC Derviş.
41. BBA Y.Mtv. 74/91, 24 Kanun-u Sani 1308/6 February 1893. Ferik Şakir Ferik Sadık, Mir Liva Kamil, Yaveran-ı Hazret-i Şehriyari Derviş.
42. BBA Irade Hususi 22, 6 Safer 1311/19 August 1893. Yıldız Palace Imperial Secretariat no. 865.
43. BBA BEO 24234 Mosul Giden, 27 Cemaziyelevvel 1311/6 December 1893.
44. BBA M.V 184/733. 27 Safer 1332/25 January 1914. Also during the Armenian massacres of the Great War it is claimed that the Yezidis gave shelter to their erstwhile enemies. See Luke, *The Yezidis*, p. 25: 'They gave shelter to hundreds of Armenian refugees who crawled from Deir-ez-Zor (sic) to the Jebel Sinjar in the course of the great Armenian massacres, and stoutly refused to surrender them despite the persuasion and threats of the Turks.'

45. BBA YEE 11/1554/120/5 1 Ramazan 1300/6 July 1883. Yıldız Palace to Şeyhülislam's Office.
46. BBA Y.Mtv 65/33. 9 Muharrem 1310/3 August 1892. Şeyhülislam's Office. Şeyhülislam Cemaleddin; The Redhouse *Turkish and English Lexicon* defines 'da'i' as: 'i) One who calls, summons or invites, a supplicant. ii) A one who calls men to religion; also a functionary who initiates novices, a missionary. iii) Members of the corps of ulema use this term to others of the corps, to designate themselves and others from the same corps.' From the context of the word in the documents seen by this author the closest meaning seems to be the second, although it remains possible that the term may have had a generic significance meaning simply, ulema. See below chapter 4 on 'The Missionary Problem'.
47. BBA Y.Mtv 231/79, 14 Rebiyülevvel 1320/1 July 1902. Şeyhülislam Mustafa Celaleddin to Imperial Secretariat.
48. BBA MV 96/1, 96/2, 12 Safer 1302/1 December 1884.
49. Ibid.
50. On the Zaidi sect see Lambton, *State and Government*, pp. 28–34. Also Messick, *The Calligraphic State*., pp. 27, 114, 129.
51. BBA Y.Mtv 183/93, 17 Cemaziyelahir 1316/2 November 1898. Vilayet of Yemen to Yıldız Palace Imperial Secretariat. no 205. Vali of Yemen Hüseyin Hilmi Paşa.
52. BBA Y.Mtv 195/34, 6 Cemaziyelahir 1317/12 October 1899. Governor of Yemen Hüseyin Hilmi Paşa to Imperial Secretariat. Enclosing syllabus for primary schools.
53. BBA Y.Mtv 92/127, 17 Temmuz 1315/20 July 1899. Yıldız Palace Imperial Secretariat.
54. Eugene Rogan, 'The al-Karak Revolt of 1910: Ottoman Order at Odds with Local Order.' Paper presented in the panel, 'The New Order and Local Order: Continuity and Crisis in Everyday Life'. MESA meeting Toronto November 16 1989. (cited with the permission of the author).
55. BBA Y.Mtv 189/165. 27 Zilhicce 1316/8 May 1899. Bab-ı Fetva Daire-i Meşihat. Şeyhülislam Mehmed Cemaleddin. The *hocas* to be sent to Ankara were named as Ishak Efendi of the Süleymaniye mosque, and Abdelhalim Efendi from the Beyazıd mosque, both Istanbul *ulema*, whose 'good conduct and talent is known'. It was also stated that similar preachers had been sent to the Vilayet of the Aegean Islands (Cezayir-i Bahr-ı Sefid Vilayetleri).
56. Suny, *Looking Towards Ararat* pp. 103–6.
57. Şakir Paşa was born in 1838 in Istanbul to a family with a long history of government service. Graduating from the military academy in 1856, Şakir Paşa served on the Refugees Commission for the Vilayet of the Danube (Bulgaria), where he worked with Mithad Paşa. In the early 1870's he served as the *Mutasarrıf* of Bagdad. After the calamity of the war of 1878

he was one of the few military commanders to emerge with a clean record. In May 1878 he was appointed Ambassador to St-Petersburg. In 1889–90 he served as the vali of Crete. As a result of what was a remarkable career he was made chief aide de camp of Sultan Abdülhamid (*Yaver-i Ekrem*) in July 1890. His interest in the Armenian question and his knowledge of Armenian activities in Russia determined his appointment to the post of Inspector of Anatolian vilayets. Şakir Paşa spoke fluent French and Russian as well as some Arabic. See. Ali Karaca, *Anadolu Islahatı ve Ahmet Şakir Paşa* (Istanbul 1993) pp. 17–29.

58. BBA YEE/A/24–X/24/132, 3 Kanunusani 1314/16 January 1898, Vilayet of Trabzon to General Inspector of Anatolia in Amasya.
59. Ibid., Vilayet of Trabzon to Amasya. 23 Zilhicce 1316/4 May 1899. Secret. no.346. There are references in the document to repeated alarms and investigations.
60. Anthony A. M. Bryer, *The Empire of Trebizond and the Pontos*, Variorum reprints. (London 1980) pp. 268–72. My thanks to Dr Gün Kut for this reference.
61. F. W. Hasluck, *Christianity and Islam under the Sultans*. (Oxford 1929) vol.2 pp. 469–70.
62. BBA YEE A/24–X/24/132, Şakir Paşa to the Vilayet of Ankara. 11 Ağustos 1313/23 August 1897. no. 337.
63. Bryer, *The Empire of Trebizond*, p. 48 : Because they were exempt from taxation as Christians, and untill the 1890's avoided military service as Muslims: 'The Crypto-Christians were therefore no more than people who, from an Ottoman point of view, did not exist'.
64. BBA YEE A-24/X/24/132, Şakir Paşa to the vilayet of Ankara. 11 Ağustos 1313/23 August 1897. no. 337.
65. Ibid.
66. Mutasarrıf of Yozgad Ahmed Edib to Inspector General Şakir Paşa. Cipher no.9476.
67. BBA YEE 31//76–45/76/81; 6 Şaban 1316/20 December 1898. General Inspectorate of Anatolia to Yıldız Palace Imperial Secretariat. no.768.
68. Ibid. Yemen, Libya, and Hicaz were infamous as sinkholes of military force. The Pomaks were a Slavic peoples that had converted to Islam and were reknowned for their zeal.
69. Ibid.
70. BBA Y.Mtv 230/96, 27 Nisan 1318/10 May 1902. Cipher telegram no. 80 from the Vilayet of Ankara to the Ministry of Interior.
71. Ibid. 18 Safer 1320/27 May 1902. Vali of Ankara Mehmed Cevad Bey to Imperial Secretariat. Vilayet of Ankara, tel no. 177.
72. R. Janin, 'Musulmans Malgré Eux, Les Stavriotes'. *Echos D'Orient*. vol. XV (1912) pp. 495–505. My thanks to Dr Gün Kut for this reference.

73. BBA Ayniyat Defteri (AD) 1422 page 115, 23 Rebiyülevvel 1307/17 November 1889. Order from the Sublime Porte to the office of the Chief of Staff (Serasker).
74. BBA MV 68/44., 26 Ramazan 1309/24 April 1892. The *dönme* were Jews who had converted to Islam under the leadership of Shabbatai Tzvi in 1676. The term *Avdeti* was used for them in official documentation. On the *dönme* of Salonica see, Stanford Shaw, *The Jews of the Ottoman Empire and the Turkish Republic*. (London 1991) pp. 177–9.
75. Ibid. Shaw also notes that the dönme prohibited marriage with 'real Muslims' and Jews. See, *The Jews of the Ottoman Empire*, p. 177.
76. Mardin, *Religion and Social Change*, p. 149.
77. BBA Y.Mtv 65/68, 17 Muharrem 1310/11 August 1892. Imperial Privy Purse (Hazine-i Hassa-i Şahane) no. 356.
78. BBA Ayniyat Defteri no. 1423, 19 Mayıs 1307/1 June 1891, p. 172.
79. The best recent study on the Kızılbaş is Altan Gökalp, *Tetes Rouges et Bouches Noires. Une confrerie tribale de l'ouest Anatolien* (Paris 1980).
80. BBA Ayniyat Defteri 1422, p. 181. 23 Kanun-u Evvel 1305/4 January 1890. Sublime Porte to Ministry of Education. Central Anatolia is still an area with a considerable Kızılbaş population, see Gökalp *Tetes Rouges*, p. 31.
81. BBA Y.Mtv 53/108, 2 Zilkade 1308/9 June 1891. *Mutasarrıf* of Tokad to Ministry of Interior, no. 159. The tenor of these instructions are reminiscent of instructions sent to Christian missionaries in the field.
82. BBA Y.Mtv 53/108, 26 Zilhicce 1308/2 August 1891. Governor of Sıvas, Mehmed Memduh Paşa. There seems to be an interesting confusion here. Memduh Paşa stated that the Kızılbaş worshipped *Melek Taus*, the sacred figure of the Yezidi, and one of the titles of Satan, hence earning the Yezidis the reputation as Devil Worshippers. It seems that Memduh Paşa was confusing the two. See Guest, *The Yezidis*.
83. Ibid. The recruitment of the Kızılbaş into the ranks of the Ottoman armed forces had been a problem since the seventeenth century, see Gökalp, *Tetes Rouges* pp. 229.
84. Hasluck, *Christianity and Islam*, vol. 2. p. 445.
85. BBA Ayniyat Defteri 1422 pg 35. 18 Muharrem 1307/14 September 1889. Order to the Ministry of Education. See also: Ana Britannica (Turkish edition of the Encyclopaedia Britannica) p. 624: The Nuseyri believed in the divinity of the Prophet Ali, and were therefore considered as Shi'a. Yet, their belief also differed considerably from the Shi'ite, including such elements as the belief that Ali created the Prophet Muhammed and Muhammed created Selman, who is responsible for the natural cosmos. They did not worship five times a day and their prayers were directed at Ali, Selman and Muhammed. The current strong man of Syria, Hafez Es'ad, is a Nuseyri.

86. BBA Ayniyat Defteri 1422 pg 57. 16 Receb 1307/8 March 1890.
87. BBA Irade Meclis-i Mahsus 4867, 13 Haziran 1306/26 June 1891. Mutasarrıf of Lazkiye Muhammed Hassa to Sublime Porte.
88. Ibid.
89. Ibid.
90. On the struggle between the Ottoman state and the missionaries over the Nuseyris see: A. L. Tibawi, *American Interests in Syria* (Oxford 1966) particularly pp. 262-3.
91. BBA YEE 31/76-45/76/81; 6 Şaban 1316/20 December 1898. General Inspector of Anatolian Vilayets to Yıldız Palace. no. 768.
92. Ibid.
93. BBA Irade Maarif 1. 7 Safer 1314/18 July 1896.
94. Hasluck, *Christianity and Islam*, p. 469.
95. BBA Yıldız Resmi Maruzat (Y.A HUS) 5/38, 14 Rebiyülevvel 1297/25 February 1880. Grand Vizier Said Paşa to Sultan. It must be pointed out however, that Christians had always served in specialist units such as in the Arsenal and the Navy.
96. Ibid.
97. R. M. Ramsay, *Impressions of Turkey During Twelve Years' Wanderings* (London 1897)163.
98. BBA Dahiliye Nezareti, Hukuk Müşavirliği. (Ministry of Interior, Legal Advisors Bureau) (hereafter DH-HMŞ) 13/47; 23 Haziran 1320/6 July 1904. General no. 244. File no.62570. In the catalogue of the documents of the Ministry of Interior Legal Advisors Bureau there is a separate category entitled, 'Conversion' (*ıhtida*).
99. See, Seyit Solak, *1571'den Günümüze Kıbrıs Türk Yönetimleri* (Nicosia 1989) p. 107. Solak is citing the memoir of a *müftü*, Ahmed Bin Mehmed Emin Hoca, who served as the *müftü* of Larnaca in 1658-1662. See, *Ahmed Bin Mehmed Emin Hoca Hatıratı* (Larnaca 1672) p. 63, as cited in Solak. The conflict between the Ottoman authorities and the Greek Patriarchate was particularly acute in Cyprus. Cypriot sources maintain that, 'as Ottoman power increased on the island, many young Greeks sought to join Islam. The duty of the priest was to ascertain that there had been no coercion and that the convert was of age. However, subsequently they always contrived to assert that the convert was not of age, and had not wanted to convert'. See, Ali Nesim, *Kıbrıslı Türklerin Kimliği*. (The Identity of Cypriot Turks) (Nicosia 1990) p. 40. My thanks to Başar Özal for these references.
100. DH-HMŞ 13/47.
101. Ibid.
102. BBA DH-HMŞ 13/46; 8 Rebiyülahir 1312/9 October 1903. Sublime Porte. Ministry of Interior. no.110.
103. Ibid.

104. BBA DH-HMŞ 13/47, 30 Teşrin-i Sani 1327/12 November 1911. General Directives of the Ministry of Interior relating to the verification of the age of converts. no. 503. File 3.
105. BBA DH-HMŞ 13/49, 25 Mayıs 1329/7 June 1913. Ministry of Interior no.79107; DH-HMŞ 13/50, 3 Ağustos 1329/16 August 1913.
106. BBA Y.A HUS 352/1. 18 Şubat 1311/3 March 1895. Sublime Porte. Office of the Grand Vizier. Report prepared by Accountant of the Evkaf of Aleppo Ali Rıza, President of the Court of Aleppo Mustafa, Special Agent of Britain, Fitzmaurice.
107. Ibid. *18 Şubat 1311, Bazısının eski dinlerine dönmek fikri evza'larından istidlal olunuyor'*. The fact that the sentence is also incongruously dated again while the document was already dated also leads one to speculate that a Turkish member wanted to get on record as having guessed that the Armenians would re-convert.
108. BBA Ibid., Gurre-i Zilhicce 1313/14 May 1896. Grand Vizier Rıfat Paşa.
109. BBA Y.A HUS 352/60, 15 Mayıs 1312/28 May 1896. Sublime Porte Office of the Grand Vizier. Cipher telegram from the Vilayet of Aleppo, Vali Rauf Paşa.
110. Ibid.
111. Ibid.
112. Ibid. This does not mean, of course, that the Vali's suggestions were taken up in Istanbul, or that the centre necessarily agreed with him. But, he must have known the boundaries of what it was permissible to suggest.
113. BBA Y.A HUS 355/38, 3 Temmuz 1312/13 Temmuz 1896. Sublime Porte. Office of the Grand Vizier. Cipher telegram from the Vilayet of Aleppo. Vali Rauf.
114. BBA Y.A HUS 352/4, 29 Zilkade 1313/12 May 1896. Sublime Porte. Receiver's Office no. 893. Foreign Minister Tevfik Paşa.
115. BBA Y.A HUS 352/133, 9 May 1897. Sublime Porte. Cipher telegram from the London Embassy dated 9 May 1897. no. 383.
116. BBA Y.Mtv 50/57, 17 Mayıs 1307/30 May 1891. Yıldız Palace Imperial Secretariat. Cipher from the Vilayet of Ankara. It is worth noting the hesitency on the part of the police official, as this was a time of tension when the slightest provocation could result in inter-community violence.
117. From the Madenataran Depository of Manuscripts in Yerevan. This series of letters are titled 'Copies of letters sent to the Holy Patriarchate of Constantinople. This one is no.159. It is a letter adressed to 'Most Honourable Holy Father, Patriarch of Constantinople and Greatly Honoured Members of the National Political Council'. It is signed Krikor Vartabet Aghvanyan. I owe this reference and its translation to Ara Sarrafyan who kindly shared this information with me. He informs me that 'Dajig' is a generic term used by Armenians to denote Muslims.

118. BBA Y.Mtv. 33/88, 15 Şevval 1305/25 June 1888. Number 2411-111. Imperial ADC Ibrahim Edhem Paşa to Imperial First Secretary Süreyya Paşa.
119. Arménouhie Kévonian, *Les noces noires de Gulizar* (Paris 1993). Présentations historiques de Anahide Ter Minassian et Kéram Kévonian. I would like to thank Prof. Ter Minassian for bringing this work to my attention.
120. BBA Y.Mtv. 54/12,18 Muharrem 1308/3 September 1890. Vali of Sıvas, Mehmed Memduh Bey, to Imperial ADC Derviş Paşa.
121. BBA Bab-ı Ali Evrak Odası (BEO), 149343. 6 Zilkade 1320/4 February 1903. Vilayet of Mosul to Ministry of Interior.
122. BBA BEO 149434, 9 Zilkade 1320/7 February 1903. Vilayet of Mosul to Ministry of Interior.
123. BBA BEO 149900, 16 Zilkade 1320/14 February 1903. From the Vilayet of Mosul to Ministry of Interior.
124. BBA Irade Dahiliye 97963. 30 Rebiyülevvel 1309/3 November 1891. Yıldız Palace Imperial Secretariat.
125. BBA YEE/31/76-45/76/81.
126. BBA Irade Hususi 123, 3 Rebiyülahir 1315/1 August 1897. Yıldız Palace Imperial Secretariat no. 3659.
127. BBA YEE A-24/X/24/132; 28 Kanun-u Evvel 1314/11 January 1898. Decoded cipher telegram from Palace Scribe Mehmed Kamil Bey to Ahmet Şakir Paşa.

Chapter Four

1. Smith, *The Ethnic Origin Of Nations*, p. 142. This passage above is my fictional re-creation based on Serif Mardin's study of Said-i Narsi.
2. Hobsbawm. 'Mass Producing Traditions' in *The Invention of Tradition*, p. 282. Hobsbawm, *Nations and Nationalism*, p. 110.
3. The standard work on Hamidian education policy still remains: Bayram Kodaman, *Abdülhamid Dönemi Eğitim Sistemi* (Istanbul 1980). This study has benefited greatly from conversations with Akşin Somel, currently finishing a doctorate on the Hamidian education policies. His thesis should provide some pioneering research.
4. Weber, *Peasants into Frenchmen*, pp. 72-3.
5. Anderson, *Imagined Communities*, p. 83.
6. Karaca, *Anadolu Islahatı ve Ahmet Şakir Paşa*, pp. 184-5.
7. BBA Y.Mtv 25/52 6 Cemaziyelahir 1304/2 March 1887. Bab-ı Fetva Encümen-i Maarif (Şeyhülislam's Office Educational Commission), Şeyhülislam Ahmed Es'ad El-Uryani.
8. Ibid. On the gradation of Ottoman Schools see Kodaman, *Abdülhamid dönemi Eğitim Sistemi*.

9. Ibid. BBA Y.Mtv 25/52.
10. Ibid.
11. Ibid., enclosed memorandum by Ahmed Recai Efendi, Director of Galatasaray lycée ... It must be pointed out that both Ahmed Es'ad's and Recai's memoranda were suggestions, yet both men were probably putting forward views which they hoped would appeal to the conservatism of Abdülhamid.
12. Ibid. Detailed breakdown of curriculum by year.
13. BBA Y.Mtv 175/234, 15 Zilkade 1315/7 April 1898. Serasker Rıza Paşa to Minister for Education.
14. BBA Y.Mtv 181/62, 16 Rebiyülahir 1316/3 September 1898. Serasker Rıza Paşa to Minister for Education.
15. BBA Ayniyat Defteri no. 1422. p. 297. Gurre-i Ramazan 1307/21 April 1890.
16. BBA Y.Mtv 189/184 24, Kanun-u Evvel 1307/6 January 1891. Circular from Ministry of Education.
17. Ibid.
18. BBA Y.Mtv 113/49, 22 Receb 1310/9 February 1893. Minister for Education Zühdü Paşa. Ministry for Education no. 62.
19. BBA Y.Mtv 172/20, 29 Şaban 1315/23 January 1898. Ministry of the Navy. Minister Hasan Paşa to Yıldız Palace.
20. BBA Y.Mtv 172/20, 10 Kanun-u Sani 1313/23 January 1898. Imperial ADC and Minister for All Military Schools Mustafa Zeki Paşa to Yıldız Palace.
21. BBA Y.Mtv 260/200, Selh-i Rebiyülevvel 1322/15 June 1904. General Inspector for the Provinces of Rumelia Hüseyin Hilmi Paşa to Yıldız Palace Imperial Secretariat no. 418. On the *dönme* commercial elite called the *Cavelleros* in Judeo–Spanish, or *Kapancılar* in Turkish see: Shaw, *The Jews of the Ottoman Empire*, p. 178.
22. BBA Y.Mtv 199/74, 18 Şevval 1317/19 February 1900; Imperial ADC and Minister for Military Schools, Mustafa Zeki Paşa to Yıldız Palace.
23. BBA Y.Mtv 180/16, 2 Rebiyülahir 1316/20 August 1898. Yıldız Palace Imperial Secretariat no. 320.
24. Findley, *Ottoman Civil Officialdom*, p. 243.
25. Ibid., pp. 243–5. Although at first he seems unable to make up his mind as to whether this attitude existed or not, he does seem in the end to come down on the positive side.
26. BBA Y.Mtv 189/184, 30 Zilhicce 1316/11 May 1899 Ministry of Education. Memoramdum signed by Minister for Education Ahmed Zühdü Paşa, Director of the *Mekteb-i Sultani* Galatasaray Abdurrahman Şeref, Director of the Mekteb-i Mülkiye Mehmed Recai. Abdurrahman Şeref later became a rather famous Turkish historian whose *Tarih Müsahabeleri* became a standard work of nineteenth-century Ottoman history.

27. Ibid.
28. See Cory Blake, 'Arab Students in the Mekteb-i Mülkiye' (PhD dissertation, Princeton University 1991).
29. Ibid.
30. BBA Yıldız Esas Evrakı (YEE) 14/292/126/8. 'The views of the late Governor of Yemen and Hicaz, Osman Nuri Paşa, on nomadic administration, religious matters, and reform measures'. 5 Temmuz 1301/18 Temmuz 1885. On Osman Nuri Paşa's relations with the Sharifs of Mecca see: Butrus Abu Manneh, 'Sultan Abdülhamid II and the Sharifs of Mecca,' *Asian and African Studies*, vol. 9 (1973) pp. 1–21.
31. Ibid.
32. Ibid.
33. Ibid. Osman Nuri Paşa even implied that the traditional tax-exempt status of the local inhabitants should be revised.
34. Ibid. On the teaching of the language of the centre see Weber, *Peasants into Frenchmen*, pp. 72–3: 'Teaching people French was an important facet of "civilising" them, in their integration into the superior modern world … There can be no clearer expression of imperialistic sentiment: a white man's burden of Francophony, whose first conquests were to be right at home.' There is a striking similarity here with the way in which education was perceived in late nineteenth century France, see Weber, pp. 329–30: 'The polite forms it inculcated softened the savagery and harshness natural to peasants'.
35. BBA YEE 31/76–45/76/81; Amasya, 6 Şaban 1316/20 December 1898. General Inspector of Anatolia Şakir Paşa to Yıldız Palace Imperial Secretariat. no. 768.
36. BBA Irade Dahiliye 98525 28, Cemaziyelevvel 1309/30 December 1891. The *irade* includes the list of the names of the boys. The two Sunnis are marked with the letter *sin* which appears above their names. See also BBA Irade Dahiliye 98993, 19 Cemaziyelahir 1309/20 January 1891: The Sultan gave 200 *liras* out of his privy purse to pay for their bedding when they got to Istanbul. He further allocated 5000 *kuruş* monthly for their food, servants, laundry, and private tutors. On the whole issue of Ottoman counter-propaganda see: Selim Deringil, 'The Struggle Against Shiism in Hamidian Iraq,' *Die Welt Des Islams* 30 (1990) pp. 45–62.
37. BBA Y.Mtv 72/43, 20 Rebiyülahir 1310/11 November 1892. Vali of Mosul İsmail Nuri Paşa to Yıldız Palace. On the conversion campaign against the Yezidis see above Chapter 2.
38. Ibid. The exact terms used are: 'Kabailin ulum ve maarifle meydan-ı medeniyet ve cemaat-i mümtaze-i beşeriyete is'ali.'.
39. BBA Irade Dahiliye 100672. 24 Zilkade 1309/21 April 1892. Yıldız Palace Imperial Secretariat to vilayet of Mosul. no. 8037.

40. John Presland, *Deedes Bey. A Study of Sir Wyndham Deedes 1883–1923.* (London 1942) p. 87. Deedes was an officer in the Turkish gendarmerie. The Turkish attitude to education is slow to change, and the adage 'roses bloom where the teacher strikes' (*öğretmenin vurduğu yerde güller açar*) is still taken literally by Turkish teachers.
41. For a good account of the reasons for its establishment see Bayram Kodaman, *Sultan II Abdülhamid'in Doğu Anadolu Politikası* (Istanbul 1983). See also: Alişan Akpinar, *Osmanlı Devletinde Aşiret Mektebi* (Istanbul 1997).
42. Ibid., pp. 106–8.
43. Ibid., p. 108–9.
44. Ibid., p. 117.
45. BBA Y.Mtv 67/90, 27 Safer 1310/20 September 1892. Minister of Interior Halil Rıfat Paşa to Yıldız Palace. Sublime Porte Ministry of Interior no. 42.
46. For a different view as to the degree of coersion and consent involving tribal sheikhs. See : Eugene Rogan, 'Aşiret Mektebi : Abdülhamid II's School for Tribes 1892–1907', *IJMES* 28 (1996) pp. 83–107
47. BBA Y.Mtv. 68/41, 20 Eylül 1308/3 October 1892. Vali of Mamuretülaziz Enis Paşa to Yıldız Palace Imperial Secretariat.
48. Ibid.
49. BBA DH–HMŞ 24/1, 15 Zilkade 1321/2 February 1904; Ministry of the Interior. secret, no. 249.
50. Mardin, *Religion and Social Change*, pp. 47, 61, 62, 226.
51. BBA Y.Mtv 70/14, 4 Rebiyülahir 1310/26 October 1892. Minister for Education Zühdü Paşa to Yıldız Palace Imperial Secretariat.
52. Ibid.
53. BBA Y.Mtv. 73/99. The Directives for the Administration of the Tribal School. (*Aşiret Mektebi'nin Talimatname-i Dahiliyesidir.*).
54. Ibid.
55. BBA Y.Mtv 76/88, 21 Ramazan 1310/8 April 1893. Minister of Education Zühdü Paşa to Yıldız Palace.
56. BBA Y.Mtv 114/80; 26 Kanun-u Sani 1310/8 February 1894. Minister of Education Zühdü Paşa to Yıldız Palace.
57. Kodaman, *Sultan II Abdülhamid'in Doğu Anadolu Siyaseti*, p. 116.
58. BBA Y.Mtv 167/189, 23 Rebiyülahir 1315/21 September 1897. Minister of Military Schools *Müşir* Mustafa Zeki Paşa to Yıldız. On Mustafa Zeki Paşa see *Salname-i Devlet* 1315, p. 218.
59. BBA Y.A RES 134/17, 18 Muharrem 1323/25 March 1905. Ministry of Interior to Office of Grand Vizier. no. 161.
60. Şerif Mardin also points out that the food riot 'seems to have been a preliminary to more concrete demands.' See *Religion and Social Change*, p. 126 ff.

61. BBA YEE 11/1419/120/5 Circular from Yıldız Palace Imperial Secretariat to Sublime Porte. The date is given as 1319 Cemaziyelevvel (August 1901) no day is recorded.
62. For instance the 1869 law stipulated that in communes where there were more than 100 non-Muslim households the state had to establish a Christian *rüşdiye* which would teach in the local language but would also emphasise Turkish language learning. See, Bertold Spuler, *Die Minderheitenschulen der europaischen Turkei von der Reformzeit bis zum Weltkrieg*. (Breslau 1936) p. 75. (My thanks to Akşin Somel for this reference).
63. Ibid., pp. 56-7.
64. Voyn Bojinev, *Bulgarskaya Prosveta v Makedonya i Odrinska Trakya 1878-1913*. (Sofia 1982) pp. 33-4. I am indebted to Akşin Somel for this reference.
65. Richard Clogg, 'The Greeks and their Past' in, Dennis Deletant and Harry Hanak (eds) *Historians as Nation Builders*, p. 29.
66. BBA Ayniyat Defteri (Payments Register) For Christian schools in the vilayet of Syria, No 1244, 7 Muharrem 1301/8 November 1883 p. 85. For Armenian schools in Van, no 1419, 26 Şaban 1297/3 August 1880 p. 46. For an Armenian school in Yalova No 1423 14 Şaban 1308/25 March 1891 p. 34. *Inter alia*. I owe thanks to Akşin Somel for these references.
67. Kodaman, *Abdülhamid Dönemi Egitim Sistemi*, p. 94.
68. Atilla Çetin, 'II Abdülhamid'e sunulan Beyrut vilayetindeki yabancı okullara dair bir rapor'. *Türk Kültürü* vol. 22 (1984) pp. 316-24.
69. BBA Ayniyat Defteri 1422 p. 267, 28 Receb 1307/20 March 1890. This does not mean of course that they were.
70. BBA Ayniyat Defteri 1422 p. 577, 20 Kanun-u Evvel 1306/2 January 1891.
71. Ibid.
72. H. F. B. Lynch, *Armenia, Travels and Studies, II: the Turkish Provinces* (London 1901) pp. 213-15.
73. Andreas Tietze, 'Ethnicity and Change in Ottoman Intellectual History,' *Turcica* vol. 22-3 (1991) p. 393. Tietze refers to the literature in Turkish, but written in Greek or Armenian characters.
74. Ibid. Sufficient allowance must be made, however, for the difference between Istanbul and provincial non-Muslims.
75. BBA Ayniyat Defteri 1422, 16 Ramazan 1307/6 May 1890. p. 317. Grand Vizier's office to Ministry of Education.
76. BBA Ayniyat Defteri 1422, 10 Muharrem 1308/26 August 1890 p. 411. Grand Vizier's Office to Ministry of Education and Ministry of Religious Sects.
77. BBA Ayniyat Defteri 1422, 19 Zilkade 1307/7 July 1892. p. 347. Grand Vizier's Office to Ministry of Education.

78. Kozmas Politis, *Yitik Kentin Kırk Yılı* trans. Osman Bleda (Istanbul 1992) pp. 61–2. It must be pointed out however that Politis is no narrow chauvinist and he tells his story with humour and compassion. For instance the boys are overcome by the tragic tone of their teacher, but they have distinct difficulty recalling the ancient names of mauntains, blurting out the first thing that comes naturally, i.e. the Turkish names.
79. Eric I Iobsbawm, 'Mass Producing Traditions' in *The Invention of Tradition*, p. 265.
80. BBA Ayniyat Defteri 1422, 14 Receb 1307/6 March 1890 p. 255. Grand Vizier's Office to the Ministry of Education.
81. BBA Ayniyat Defteri 1422, 1 Cemaziyelahir 1307/23 January 1890 p. 215. Grand Vizier's Office to Ministry of Education.
82. BBA Y.A RES 107/50, 1 Şaban 1317/5 December 1899. Vilayet of Kastamonu to Ministry of Interior. no. 386 Governor Mehmed Enis Paşa.
83. Findley, *Ottoman Civil Officialdom*, pp. 134–5, 139.
84. A. P. Comte de Cholet, *Voyage en Turquie d'Asie*. (Paris 1892) pp. 2–3. The writer was visiting a village primary school in the region of Hacı Bektaş in central Anatolia, near Cappadocia. My translation.
85. Princess Annie de Lusignan, *The Twelve Years' Reign of His Imperial Majesty Abdul Hamid II, Sultan of Turkey* (London 1889) pp. 176–7.
86. Şinasi Tekin, 'Imperial Self Portrait'. See also below.
87. Anderson, *Imagined Communities*, p. 82.
88. Cherniavsky, *Tsar and People*, p. 150; BBA YEE 11/1419/120/5 Circular from Palace to all Ministries.
89. Jeffrey Brooks, *When Russia Learned to Read* (Princeton 1985) p. 216.
90. Ibid., p. 218.
91. Ibid., p. 47: 'The state and Church officials who designed the programs considered religion the foundation of the Russian state system.' Also p. 53. 'Religion and nationality were interwoven as in Bukanov's popular primer: "Our fatherland is Russia. We are Russian people ... There are churches in the cities and villages. The Church is the house of God."'.
92. Ibid., p. 48 and p. 49. See also above. It must however be pointed out that the official curricula in Russian schools were no more than a suggested outline which the teachers filled as they saw fit. This is very unlike the Ottoman system where teachers were strictly ordered not to stray from the set curriculum. Another obvious dissimilarity is that the problems of an empire which is expanding were not to be same as an empire which was contracting and fighting for its very survival. The aim of the comparison here is merely to bring out the idelogical content of the curricula in both systems.
93. Ibid., p. 53.
94. On Namık Kemal see: *Türk ve Dünya Meşhurları Ansiklopedisi*.
95. Anderson, *Imagined Communities*, p. 83.

96. Lesley Blanche, *The Sabres of Paradise* (London 1960) pp. 162-75.
97. Kodaman, *Sultan II. Abdülhamid'in Doğu Anadolu Politikası*.
98. See Brooks, *When Russia Learned to Read*, p. 42: 'By the 8-11 [years old] standard ... Ministry of Education officials calculated that as of January 1915, only 58 per cent of all 8 to 11 year-olds were in school in European Russia and only 70 per cent of the necessary teachers were available. The figures for the empire as a whole were 51 per cent and 61 per cent, respectively.' On the Ottoman case see Findley, *Ottoman Civil Officialdom*, p. 52.
99. Anderson, *Imagined Communities*, p. 86.
100. Gluck, *Japan's Modern Myths*, particularly pp. 102-56, Chapter V 'Civil Morality'.
101. Ibid., p. 105.
102. Ibid., pp. 108-9.
103. It must be emphasized, however, that Japanese education always remained much more open to western ideas and the emphasis on 'learning of the world's nations' never entirely disappeared. Also the level of pedagogic debate seems to have been of a much more sophisticated level than in the Ottoman case. See Gluck, *Japan's Modern Myths*, pp. 104, 108.
104. BBA YEE 14/292/126/8.
105. Şükrü Hanioğlu, *Osmanlı İttihad ve Terakki Cemiyeti ve Jön Türklük 1889-1902*. (Istanbul 1985) p. 176. Hanioğlu's work is remarkable for its great wealth of primary sources and other documentery evidence drawn from numerous archives. There is considerable literature on the Committee of Union and Progress. The two seminal studies are by Şerif Mardin, *Jön Türklerin Siyasi Fikirleri 1895-1908* (Istanbul 1983) (First published in 1964) and Feroz Ahmad, *The Young Turks: The Committee of Union and Progress in Turkish Politics 1908-1914* (Oxford 1969). These have been followed by other important works. To name just a few see, Sina Akşin, *Jön Türkler ve İttihat ve Terakki* (Istanbul 1980) Zafer Toprak, *Türkiye'de Milli İktisat* (Istanbul 1983), Tarık Zafer Tunaya *Türkiye'de Siyasi Partiler* (Istanbul 1984). There is also a veritable library of published memoires of prominent CUP members.
106. Hanioğlu, *Osmanlı* pp. 178, 181, 182. Hanioğlu notes however that their advances were not taken that seriously by the Embassy who found their revolutionary jargon somewhat far fetched.
107. Ibid., pp. 401-2.

Chapter Five

1. See below. The passage at the beginning of this chapter is my fictional re-creation.
2. Gluck, *Japan's Modern Myths*, p. 57.

3. Ibid., pp. 133–5. It must, however, be pointed out that the most severe criticism of Christians came from Buddhist circles who were themselves feeling the pressure of the increasingly secular policies of the Meiji regime.
4. Ibid., p. 138. It must, however, be pointed out that the Japanese and Ottoman attitude to religious teaching in schools was diametrically opposed. Whereas the Japanese prohibited religious instruction in schools in 1899, the Ottomans, as an act of deliberate policy, gave it more weight.
5. Seagrave, *Dragon Lady*, p. 296.
6. Edward Said *Orientalism* (Basingstoke 1985) p. 294. Emphasis in original.
7. Jean Haythorne Braden, 'The Eagle and the Crescent: American Interests in the Ottoman Empire, 1860–1870,' Ohio State University PhD Dissertation (1973) p. 22.
8. Tibawi, *American Interests*, pp. 256–7.
9. Ibid., p. 260.
10. Ibid., p. 269.
11. Jeremy Salt, 'A Precarious Symbiosis: Ottoman Christians and Foreign Missionaries in the Nineteenth Century,' *International Journal of Turkish Studies*. vol. 3 (Winter 1985–86) no. 2. p. 56.
12. Ibid., p. 65.
13. BBA Irade Dahiliye 100258. Yıldız Palace Imperial Secretariat, no. 6975, 27 Şevval 1309/25 May 1892.
14. Hobsbawm, *The Age of Empire*, p. 71. See also his evaluation of the acceleration of missionary activity on the same page: 'Between 1876 and 1902 there were 119 translations of the Bible, compared to 74 in the previous thirty years, and 40 in the years 1816–54. The number of new Protestant missions in Africa during the period 1886–95 was twenty three or about three times as many as in any previous decade.'.
15. Salt, 'A Precarious Symbiosis', p. 56.
16. Jeremy Salt, *Imperialism Evangelism and the Ottoman Armenians, 1878–1896* (London 1993) p. 37.
17. An Eastern Statesman, 'Contemporary Life and Thought in Turkey,'*Contemporary Review*, vol. 37 (1880) p. 343.
18. Ibid., p. 344.
19. Samuel M. Zwemer, *The Law of Apostasy in Islam. Answering the Question why there are so Few Moslem Converts, and giving Examples of their Moral Courage and Martyrdom*. (London, Edinburgh and New York) Although the book bears no formal publication date, the author's preface is dated 1924. See particularly p. 24: 'President C. F. Gates, of Robert College, Constantinople, states: 'The fear of death is certainly one cause for the fewness of converts from Islam to Christianity. Every Moslem knows that his life is in danger if he becomes a Christian. I have known a good many in-

Notes 219

stances of Moslems who would secretly assert themselves as Christians, but would make no open statement because of the danger attending it.'.
20. Salt, *Imperialism,Evangelism*, p. 35.
21. BBA Y.A RES 78/54, 7 Şevval 1313/22 March 1896. Grand Vizier's Chancery no. 2360.
22. Salt 'Precarious Symbiosis', p. 55. See also above Chapter 3.
23. BBA Irade Dahiliye. 99649, 19 Cemaziyelahir 1309/20 January 1892. Vilayet of Syria Receivers Office no. 32 Vali Osman Nuri Paşa to Sublime Porte.
24. Ibid.
25. BBA (YEE) Kamil Paşa Evrakına Ek (KPE) 86-8/798, 30 Kanun-i Evvel 1314/12 January 1898. The Vilayet of Aydın was of particular significance because it contained a very lively commercial community centred around the port city of Izmir.
26. BBA YEE KPE 86-11/1098, 18 Haziran 1316/1 July 1900. Vali Kamil Paşa to Sublime Porte.
27. BBA Irade Dahiliye 99649, 29 Receb1309/28 February 1892 Grand Vizier and Imperial ADC Cevad Paşa.
28. BBA Irade Dahiliye 100687 29, Zilkade1309/25 June 1892. Yıldız Palace Imperial Secretariat no.8185. Imperial Secretary Süreyya Paşa.
29. BBA Ayniyat Defteri no. 1313. p. 57. 28 Şaban 1309/28 March 1892. Sublime Porte to the Ministry of Justice and Religious Sects, the Ministry of the Interior, and the Foreign Ministry.
30. BBA Y.A RES 96/14 11 Cemaziyelahir 1316/27 October 1898. Report of the Special Commission on Education. (Encümen-i Mahsus-u Maarif).
31. Ibid.
32. BBA Y.A RES 137/45, 4 Cemaziyelevvel 1324/26 June 1906. Grand Vizier Ferid Paşa. Sublime Porte Grand Vizier's Chancery. Register number 1056 document number 4694. Including memo by Council of Ministers. The memo specified that repeated orders had been received from the Palace that measures be taken to upgrade the teaching in Islamic schools.
33. BBA Y.A HUS 257/153, 29 Şaban 1309/29 March 1892. Sublime Porte Receiver's Office. Grand Vizier Cevad Paşa. The Porte did however allow the Bible Society to carry out printing and distribution of the Old Testament in Albanian using Greek characters. See Y.A HUS 261/19, 3 Zilkade 1309/30 May 1892.
34. BBA Y.A HUS 257/153, 9 Mart 1898/9 March 1898. Sublime Porte. Bureau of Translation for the Foreign Press. no. 308.
35. BBA Y. Mtv. 57/65, 25 Cemaziyelevvel 1309/27 December 1891. Maiyet-i Askeri Komisyonu.
36. BBA Ayniyat Defteri no. 1420 p. 299, 11 Rebiyülahir 1299/2 March 1882. Sublime Porte to Ministry of Education.

37. BBA Ayniyat Defteri no. 1422 p. 57. 5 Safer 1307/1 October 1889. Vilayet of Işkodra to Ministry of Education.
38. Guest, The Yezidis, pp. 49, 50.
39. BBA Irade Dahiliye 100258. 10 Mayıs 1308/23 May 1892. Cipher from Vali of Mosul, Kemali Paşa.
40. Salt, 'A Precarious Symbiosis', p. 55.
41. Guest, The Yezidis, p. 130.
42. BBA Irade Dahiliye 56. 12 Eylül 1308/25 September 1892. Cipher Tel. from Commander of Reformatory Force Ömer Vehbi Paşa to Sublime Porte. As it turned out on this particular occasion the French consul was instructed by his superiors in Istanbul not to become involved. See Guest, The Yezidis, p. 130.
43. For the French presence in Lebanon see Akarli, The Long Peace.
44. BBA YEE KPE 86-1/80 unsigned and undated letter in Arabic.
45. Ibid. Mention of the Franco–Prussian War (1870) and the Russo–Ottoman war of 1877–78 makes it possible to date this document as having been written around 1880.
46. BBA Y.A HUS 208/77, 25 Rebiyülahir 1305/10 January 1888. Office of the Grand Vizier. Signed by Kamil Paşa. no. 565.
47. Ibid.
48. BBA Y.A HUS 208/79. Military Doctor Corporal Yusuf Zeki bin Mihail Hamoye. no date.
49. Ibid.
50. BBA Y.A RES 24/47., 10 Şevval 1301/3 August 1884, Minutes of the Council of State. no. 598.
51. Ibid.
52. BBA Irade Hususi 50. 21 Muharrem 1315/22 June 1897. Yıldız Palace Imperial Secretariat no. 735. Imperial Private Secretary Süreyya Paşa.
53. BBA Y.A RES 80/5, 4 Muharrem 1314/15 June 1896. Sublime Porte Receiver's Office. no. 55.
54. BBA KPE 86-15/1500, 17 Zilhicce 1319/11 March 1902. It is interesting that Kamil Paşa should refer to Christian children in these terms (evlad-ı vatan).
55. BBA KPE 86-14/1336, 18 Teşrin-i Evvel 1318/31 October 1902. Minister of Interior Memduh Paşa to Vilayet of Aydın. The Porte had received information that although France was expelling Jesuits from its own soil, it was moving to arrange for their reception and protection in third countries.
56. BBA Y.A HUS 207/79, 3 Safer 1305/1 October 1887. Report by Grand Vizier Kamil Paşa on the visit of the Papal legate in Istanbul to Thessaloniki where he used complimentary language regarding the Sultan; BBA 209/59 6 Kanun-u Sani 1888/19 January 1888 Sublime Porte, Foreign Ministry.

57. BBA Y.Mtv 112/12; 1 Kanun-u Evvel 1310/14 December 1894. Catholic Patriarchate to Yıldız Palace Imperial Secretariat.
58. BBA Irade Hususi 96, 6 Şevval 1315/28 February 1898. Yıldız Palace Imperial Secretariat 12249; Irade Hususi 16 6 Zilkade 1315/29 March 1898 Yıldız Palace Imperial Secretariat 13509.
59. BBA Y.Mtv 54/65 29, Ağustos 1307/11 September 1891. Armenian Patriarchate to the Ministry of Justice and Religious Sects.
60. On the British occupation and the so-called 'temporary administration' see Nesim Zia, *Kıbrıs'ın Ingiltere'ye Geçişi ve Ada'da kurulan Ingiliz Idaresi.* (Ankara 1975). On foreign schools in general see, Ilknur Polat Haydaroğlu, *Osmanlı Imparatorluğu'nda Yabancı Okullar* (Ankara 1990) for a somewhat sketchy survey of the topic.
61. BBA Y.A RES 25/9, 8 Zilkade 1301/30 August 1884. Minister of Pious Foundations Kamil Paşa. The document has a certain poignant tone as Kamil Paşa was a native of Nicosia.
62. Ibid. It seems however, that his fears were unfounded, the British Administration did continue to finance and support Muslim schooling on the island. See Nasim Zia, *Kıbrıs'ın Ingiltere'ye Geçişi* p. 93–4: 'The British Administration established at least one school in every village ... [in 1881] There were 122 Muslim primary schools on the island.'.
63. BBA Y.A RES 24/21, 28 Şaban 1301/23 June 1884. Sublime Porte. Foreign Ministry. Translation of note received from the British Embassy.
64. BBA BEO 245757, 6 Receb 1325/16 August 1907. Vilayet of Basra no. 44. Vali Abdurrahman Hasan Paşa to Ministry of Interior.
65. BBA Irade Dahiliye 99013. 24 Cemaziyelahir 1309/26 January 1892.
66. BBA BEO Yemen Gelen. no. 366, entry no. 1307. 22 Şaban 1308/3 April 1891.
67. BBA Y.A HUS 292/51, 12 Ramazan 1311/19 March 1894. Sublime Porte. Grand Vizier's Office. Grand Vizier Cevad Paşa.
68. BBA Y.A HUS 307/7, 16 Temmuz 1894/16 July 1894. Foreign Ministry. Communication no. 188 from Ottoman legation in Washington. For further information on Anglo–American co-operation see Salt, *A Precarious Symbiosis.*
69. Salt, *Imperialism, Evangelism,* p. 31: '[The American minister at Istanbul in the 1880s, S. S. Cox, gave this list of missionary organizations established in the Ottoman state: The American Board of Missions, The Presbyterian Board of Foreign Missions (Syria), The United Presbyterian Missionary Board (Egypt), The Board of Missions of the Methodist Episcopal Church of New York (Bulgaria), The Foreign Mission Board of the Reformed Presbyterian Church of New York (active among the Nusayris of northern Syria), the American Bible Society, the Trustees of Bible House Istanbul, the Trustees of the Syrian Protestant College in

Beirut and of Robert College in Istanbul ... Cities and towns 'occupied' by the missionaries amounted to 394.'
70. For the best survey to date of American Missionary activity in Turkey see, Frank Andrews Stone, *Academies for Anatolia*. (New York, London 1984). For the only Turkish work on the subject which makes use of the American Board Archives, yet does not go very far beyond the official nationalist perspectives and does not use Ottoman archival sources, see: Uygur Kocabaşoğlu, *Anadolu'daki Amerika* (Istanbul 1989). The standard work on the topic to date has been Joseph L Grabill's *Protestant Diplomacy and the Near East. Missionary Influence on American Policy*. (Minneapolis 1971) which does not use any Turkish sources but remains a fair discussion of the problem from the American perspective.
71. BBA Y.A RES 1/2 no date. Memorandum prepared by Foreign Ministry at the order of the Yıldız Palace. According to the millet system each non-Muslim community was administered on a daily basis by their own religious and secular leaders, who were responsible to the Porte for their affairs.
72. Ibid. It is interesting that the Reform Edict should be brought up in this context, as it was on the basis of the same document that foreign powers often took the Ottoman government to task for not fulfilling its obligations. This was part of the tendency of the Ottomans to use interpretations of international law to defend their interests.
73. BBA Y.A HUS 352/89, 5 May 1896. Communication no. 240 from the Ottoman legation in Washington. Enclosing translation of *Missionary Herald* article. It is interesting to compare Ottoman archival data with Stone's *Academies* because often it is possible to find details on names and information that come up in Ottoman despatches. For instance, on the Bartlett family which is mentioned in the above article we learn that they were a missionary family based in Izmir who ran a kindergarten for Armenian children, and the evangelical centre in Kayseri developed into a 'network of churches and elementary schools. By 1909 forty-four schools with almost two thousand children in them were operating.' See Stone *Academies*, pp. 89–90.
74. BBA Y.A HUS 291/63, 26 Şaban 1311/4 March 1894. Sublime Porte Receiver's Office. no. 3008. Grand Vizier Cevad Paşa. Stone also points out on several occasions that 'In most cases American Board personnel in Turkey were opposed to the Armenian revolutionaries,' and found their views 'irreligious impractical and dangerous'. See *Academies* pp. 122, 191.
75. BBA Y.A HUS 282/120, 15 Rebiyülevvel 1311/26 September 1893. Foreign Ministry. Dispatch no. 182.
76. Ibid.
77. BBA Y.A HUS 282/120, 15 Rebiyülahir 1311/27 October 1893. Sublime Porte Receiver's Office no. 1298.

78. BBA Y.A HUS 376/68. Consul General Munci Bey to Foreign Ministry. 8 Ağustos 1313/21 August 1897. On this see also: Selim Deringil, 'An Ottoman View of Missionary Activity in Hawaii,' *Hawaiian Journal of History* (1993) pp. 119–25.
79. Ibid.
80. Ibid.
81. BBA Y.A HUS 352/18, 1 Zilkade 1313/14 April 1896. Ottoman Embassy in Washington to Foreign Ministry.
82. On the affair of Dr Knapp see Stone, *Academies* p. 122.
83. BBA Y.A HUS 352/18, Gurre-i Zilhicce 1313/14 May 1896. Foreign Minister Tevfik Paşa to Grand Vizier.
84. BBA Y.Mtv 197/16, 2 Şaban 1317/6 December 1899. Foreign Ministry no. 332.
85. BBA Y.Mtv 19/77, 30 Teşrin-i Sani 1315/13 December 1899. Telegram from Vilayet of Erzurum to Foreign Ministry.
86. BBA Irade Husui 86. 25 Rebiyülahir 1315/23 September 1897. Yıldız Palace Imperial Secretariat no. 4724.
87. BBA Y.A RES. 125/103, 29 Zilkade 1312/24 May 1895. Council of State no. 3294.
88. Ibid.
89. BBA Y.Mtv 53/108, 26 Zilhicce 1308/3 August 1891. Vali of Sıvas Mehmed Memduh Paşa to Sublime Porte.
90. John Joseph, *The Nestorians and their Muslim Neighbors* (Princeton 1961) p. 123.
91. BBA Y.A HUS 365/39, 16 Kanun-u Evvel 1312/29 December 1896. Despatch from Consulate of Hoy and Selmas to Foreign Ministry. Compare Stone, *Academies*, p. 130: 'Evidence indicates that the American Board Missions in Turkey were always viewed by the Armenian revolutionaries as palliatives that inhibited their objectives …'.
92. Stone, *Academies*, p. 127.
93. Ibid., p. 140.
94. Grabill, *Protestant Diplomacy*, p. 47.
95. Ibid. p. 41.
96. BBA Y.Mtv 188/118, 22 Zilkade 1316/4 April 1899. Although the document does not make any direct reference to the massacres, the vilayets listed are those where massacres did occur i.e. Bitlis, Aleppo, Mamuretülaziz, Trabzon, Erzurum, Diyarbekir, and Sıvas. The total number of orphans listed is 6386.
97. Stone, *Academies*, pp. 12–13.
98. Joseph, *The Nestorians*, p. 123.
99. BBA Y.A HUS 374/103, 27 Safer 1315/28 July 1897 Sublime Porte. Grand Vizier's Office 267. Grand Vizier Rıfat Paşa.
100. Ibid. Enclosed cutting from Worcester Mass. *Daily Spy*, 6 December 1895.

101. Ibid. Cutting from *Daily Spy*, 1 January 1896.
102. Ibid. Cutting from *Boston Ideas* no. date on clipping. Knowles also gave list of the decorations he already held.
103. Ibid. Detailed discussion of the issue in Cabinet minutes.
104. BBA Irade Hususi 86. 2 Rebiyülahir 1323/6 June 1905. Yıldız Palace Imperial Secretariat, no. 1258.
105. BBA Y.A RES 122/145, 26 Receb 1321/18 October 1903. Enclosure of detailed table of American educational establishments with licenses, giving location, level of education and date of establishment.
106. BBA Y.A RES 127/49, 9 Cemaziyelahir 1322/21 August 1904. Minutes of meeting of Council of Ministers.
107. BBA Y.Mtv 294/22, 21 Zilhicce 1323/16 February 1906. Foreign Minister Tevfik Paşa to Yıldız Palace Imperial Secretariat.
108. Ramsay, *Impressions of Turkey*, p. 221.
109. Salt, *Imperialism, Evangelism*, p. 32.
110. Ibid., p. 227. Of course the rest of the statement illustrates just how far off the mark Ramsay was on things Ottoman: 'An educated middle class is almost entirely absent from Oriental countries and Oriental society in which there is only a monarch and his slaves.' .
111. Karl K. Barbir, 'Memory, Heritage, History: Ottomans and Arabs,'. In Carl L. Brown, *Imperial Legacy*. p. 106.
112. Mardin, *The Genesis of Young Ottoman Thought*., p. 206.
113. See Pashalis Kitromilides, '"Imagined Communities" and the Origins of the National Question in the Balkans' *European History Quarterly* vol. 19 (1989) pp. 149–94. Particularly p. 183: 'By the turn of the twentieth century, a whole new mentality shaped by the values of nationalism crept gradually into the politics of the Ecumenical Patriarchate.' .
114. Mardin, *Religion and Social Change* on what Mardin calls the 'demonstration effect' see pp. 103–22.
115. Ibid., p. 51.
116. Stone, *Academies*, p. 142.
117. Hafız Mehmed Sadık, *Alem-i Islam'da Cihad-ı Ekber* (Istanbul 1342-39) p. 25. The writer is introduced as the *Müftü* of Milas, a small town in south-western Turkey. Throughout the last quarter of the 19th century and well into the 20th century such pamphlets continued to appear in Turkish literary circles.
118. Rev. Dr J. Muhleisen-Arnold, *The Society for Propagating the Gospel among the Moslems, In Connection with the Church of England; Its First Appeal on Behalf of 180 millions of Mohammedans*. (London 1860) p. 4.
119. Ibid.
120. Samuel M. Zwemer, *The Law of Apostasy*, p. 16.
121. Tibawi, *American Interests*, p. 269.
122. Said, *Culture and Imperialism*, pp. 45–6.

Chapter Six

1. R. G. Latham MA MD (Late Fellow of King's College Cambridge) *Russian and Turk, from a Geographical, Ethnological, and Historic Point of View* (London 1878) p. 160.
2. Ahmed Cevdet Paşa, *Maruzat*, p. 4.
3. Mardin, *The Genesis of Young Ottoman Thought*, p. 388.
4. Said, *Culture and Imperialism*, p. 6.
5. BBA Yıldız Perakende (Gazeteler).
6. BBA Y.A HUS 181/63 7 Nisan 1885/7, April 1885. Musurus Paşa to Sublime Porte Translation Bureau tel. no. 149.
7. BBA Y.A HUS 186/75, 17 Rebiyülevvel 1303/24 December 1885. Sublime Porte Foreign Ministry.
8. Musurus Ghikis Bey, 'L'avenir de l'Islam' *Questions Diplomatiques et Coloniales*. vol. XI (1901) pp. 595-7.
9. Henry Elliot, 'The Death of Abdul Aziz and of Turkish Reform' *The Nineteenth Century* February 1888 pp. 276-96.
10. Ibid., p. 296.
11. BBA Y.A HUS 210/53; 21 Cemaziyelevvel 1305/4 February 1888 Sublime Porte Foreign Ministry no. 1027; Y.A HUS 211/65-A, 21 Cemaziyelahir 1305/5 March 1888.
12. BBA Y.A HUS 212/19,10 Mart 1888/10 March 1888 Ottoman Embassy London to Sublime Porte tel. no. 80.
13. Lusignan, *The Twelve Years' Reign* p. 4.
14. Ibid., p. 33. Of course it is impossible to describe the 'special tribunal' that tried Midhat Paşa and his colleagues as an impartial court of 'ordinary law', nor did the public get anywhere near it. On the Yıldız Trials see: İsmail Hakkı Uzunçarşılı, *Midhat Paşa ve Yıldız Mahkemesi* (Ankara 1967).
15. BBA Y.A HUS 222/71 2 Mart 1889/2 March 1889 Ottoman Embassy in London to Sublime Porte Foreign Ministry communication no. 50.
16. BBA YEE 14/1337/126/10 nd. (But judging from the context the text seems to be written in the early 1890s). Draft article by Selim Melhame and covering letter presenting the article to the Sultan. Selim Melhame was one of Abdülhamid's 'official Arabs'. There is no proof that the article was actually published and Melhame was obviously out to flatter his master. Nonetheless, the document is interesting precisely because it gives a good idea of the image Abdülhamid wanted to project.
17. Lusignan, *The Twelve Years' Reign*. p. 198.
18. Feroze Yasamee, 'The Ottoman Empire and the European Great Powers,' SOAS PhD Dissertation (1984) pp. 56-60.
19. BBA Y.A HUS 219/75 2 Kanun-u Evvel 1888/15 October 1888. Cipher telegram from the Ottoman Embassy in Vienna to the Sublime

Porte. On Arminius Vambery see M. Kemal Öke, *Ingiliz Casusu Prof. Arminius Vambery'nin gizli Raporlarında II Abdülhamid ve Dönemi* (Istanbul 1983). There is also a section in the Public Record Office, London, called the 'Vambery Letters' dealing with the material he sent to the Foreign Office from Istanbul.

20. Ibid. Letter from Vambery in Turkish to an unknown recipient, probably Münir Bey of the Vienna Embassy dated 3 Kanun-u Evvel 1888 /16 October 1888.
21. BBA Y.A HUS 220/32, 11 Rebiyülahir 1306/15 December 1888 Foreign Ministry to Grand Vezier. Foreign Minister Said Paşa.
22. BBA Y.A HUS 223/2, 16 şubat 1889/18 February 1889. Ottoman Embassy Vienna to Foreign Ministry communication no. 61.
23. BBA Y.A HUS 226/42, 14 Mayıs 1889/14 May 1889 Ottoman Embassy at St Petersburg to Sublime Porte dispatch no. 70.
24. BBA Y.Mtv 51/45. 15 Zilkade 1308/22 June 1891 Ministry of Customs no. 52.
25. BBA Y.A HUS 303/87; 5 July 1894 Sublime Porte Foreign Ministry Telegram from Vienna Embassy no. 337; Sublime Porte Receiver's Office no. 254 Grand Vizier Cevad Paşa.
26. BBA Irade Hususi 34, 5 Safer 1311/18 August 1893 Yıldız Palace Imperial Secretariat no. 836.
27. BBA Irade Hususi, 3 Gurre-i Şevval 1311/7 April 1894. Yıldız Palace Imperial Secretariat no. 6880.
28. BBA Y.Mtv 132/76, 15 Teşrin-i Sani 1311/28 November 1895. Ottoman Ambassador Alexander Mavroyeni to Yıldız Palace Imperial Secretariat.
29. Said, *Orientalism*, pp. 49–73.
30. BBA YEE Kamil Paşa Evrakına Ek (KPE) 86–3/264 6 Ramazan 1307/ 26 April 1890. Yıldız Palace Imperial Secretariat.
31. BBA Y.A HUS 283/54, 21 Teşrin-i Evvel 1896/3 November 1896. Sublime Porte. Foreign Ministry.
32. BBA Y.A HUS 284/74, 7 Teşrin-i Sani 1896/20 November 1896. Ottoman Embassy London to Sublime Porte. Dispatch no. 500.
33. BBA Y.A HUS 287/49, 14 Kanun-u Evvel 1893/27 December 1893. Ottoman Embassy Rome to Sublime Porte Foreign Ministry no. 413.
34. BBA Y.A HUS 237/50, 19 July 1890 Ottoman Embassy London to Sublime Porte Foreign Ministry, confidential no. 182.
35. Ibid. The communication went on to state that Osman Bey was born to Dr Millingen's first wife, 'a Greek from Chios later divorced by the doctor because of evil behaviour', the 'Greek' lady went on to marry Kıbrıslı Mehmed Paşa, a leading figure in mid century Istanbul. Osman was then adopted by Mehmed Paşa and brought up as a Muslim. The information of the London Embassy was only partly accurate. The 'Greek woman'

whose name was Marie Dejean and who later took the Muslim name of Melek Hanum had a Greek grandmother, Armenian grandfather and French father. After the break up of her marriage to Dr Millingen, and Mehmed Paşa being forced to divorce her also for her involvement in various petty mid century intrigues in Istanbul, in 1866 she was forced to flee to Paris, where Osman became a Christian. She wrote her memoirs called, *Thirty Years in the Harem or the Autobiography of Melek Hanum, Wife of H. H. Kıbrızlı Mehemet Pasha* (New York 1872). This was evidently the sort of literature that the ambassador in London was referring to as 'vulgar and scandalous trash' that the lady was wont to publish.

36. BBA Y.Mtv 100/26, 17 July 1894 Ottoman Legation at the Hague to Sublime Porte Foreign Ministry. no. 1780.
37. Ibid., The outline of the sketch is in French. It is an interesting sample of particularly low grade Orientalism.
38. Rambert, *Notes et Impressions*, pp. 175-6.
39. BBA Y.A HUS 309/31, 18 Rebiyülevvel 1312/19 September 1894. Grand Vizier's Office no. 1077. Grand Vizier Ekrem Cevad to Yıldız Palace.
40. BBA Y.A RES 124/80, 17 Zilhicce 1321/5 March 1904 Grand Vizier Mehmed Ferid Paşa; Y.A RES 129/54, 5 Zilkade 1322/11 January 1905. Sublime Porte. It appears that Abdülhamid was aware of the implications of the rise of Japan as a world power. Well before the Russo-Japanese war, in 1892, a Japanese Muslim by the name of Abdul Halim Noda Efendi was engaged to teach Japanese at the Military Academy see: BBA Y.Mtv 66/61, 3 Safer 1310/27 August 1892. General Staff Receivers Office no. 146.
41. BBA Y.A HUS 203/70, 19 June 1887. Ottoman Embassy London to Sublime Porte Foreign Ministry. On the occupation of Egypt and preceding events see: Selim Deringil, 'The Ottoman Response to the Egyptian Crisis of 1881-82,' *Middle Eastern Studies* vol. 24 (1988) pp. 3-24.
42. BBA Y.A HUS 203/68, 27 Ramazan 1304/19 June 1887 Sublime Porte Receivers Office no. 4.
43. BBA Y.A HUS 193/28, 30 June 1896 Ottoman Embassy London to Sublime Porte.
44. L. Hirszowicz, 'The Sultan and the Khedive', pp. 287-311.
45. BBA Y.A RES 86/104; 29 Zilhicce 1314/31 May 1897. Yıldız Palace Imperial Secretariat.
46. BBA Y.A RES 57/52 Letter by Queen Victoria to Abdülhamid II dated 25 January 1892. It is a very simple document edged with black, penned by a secretary and signed in the Royal hand, 'Your Imperial Majesty's good Sister, Victoria Regina.' It was quite common practice among royal houses to inform each other about familial changes.

47. Ibid. Letter from Abdülhamid to Queen Victoria addressed, 'To Her Imperial Highness Our Exalted Friend' (*Dost-u Bülend-i İtibarımız Hazretleri*) evidently a draft, as it is only dated Receb 1309 (January 1892).
48. Rambert, *Notes et Impressions* p. 100. Diary entry dated 5 September 1900.
49. BBA Y.A HUS 284/85 7 Teşrin-i Sani 1893/20 November 1893 Ottoman Embassy London to Sublime Porte Foreign Ministry. The paragraph at the beginning of this chapter is my fictional re-creation of this event.
50. Charles Williams, *The Armenian Campaign, A Diary of the Campaign of 1877 in Armenia and Koordistan*. (London 1878) p. ix, x.
51. Latham, *Russian and Turk*, p. 160. The reference to 'flower of rhetoric' by 'influential authors' may well have been a reference to Gladstone's contemporary pamphlet, 'The Bulgarian Massacres', published in 1876.
52. Roger Adelson, *Mark Sykes, Portrait of an Amateur*. (London 1975) p. 110. O'Connor had been the British Ambassador to the Porte since 1898. This passage refers to 1905–1906.
53. Ibid., p. 98. The school referred to is obviously the *Mekteb-i Aşiret* see above.
54. Ibid., pp. 64–5.
55. Karl Blind, 'Young Turkey' *Forthnightly Review* (London 1896) LXVI p. 840.
56. BBA Y.A HUS 191/123 23 May 1883, Ottoman Embassy London to Sublime Porte, Foreign Ministry no. 358.
57. BBA Y.A HUS 189/25 10 February 1886, Ottoman Embassy London to Foreign Ministry.
58. Lusignan, *The Twelve Years' Reign*. p. 147.
59. Constance Sutcliffe, 'Turkish Guilds,' *Fortnightly Review* vol. LXVI (1896) p. 828.
60. Fatma Aliye, *Nisvan-ı İslam* (Istanbul 1891).
61. Mehmed İzzet, *Yeni Afrika*. (Istanbul 1308) p. 3. İzzet Bey takes pains to point out that he is writing this book on commission from the Palace.
62. Y.Mtv. Numerous entries in Catalogue no. 5. (*Dreyfus meselesine dair*).
63. India Office Library and Records. L/P&S/3/226, vol. 39, p. 787. Layard to Salisbury, Constantinople 15 April 1880.
64. L/P&S/3/226 vol. 39 pp. 1315–20. Sir Louis Malet to Foreign Office and the Government of India.
65. L/P&S/7/vol. 26, part 6 p. 1252. Government of India to HM Secretary of State for India. Simla, 28 September 1880.
66. Ibid., p. 1256. 15 July 1880. Memorandum by Major P. D. Henderson on intrigues between Constantinople and Mahometans in India.
67. Side Emre, 'Political Imagery in the Journal *Servet-i Fünun*' unpublished Masters Thesis, Boğaziçi University, 1996.

Chapter Seven

1. Said, *Orientalism*, p. 204.
2. BBA Y.Mtv 66/66, 10 Safer 1310.5 September 1892 Ottoman minister to Washington Alexander Mavroyeni to Yıldız Palace Imperial Secretariat. The paragraph at the beginning of this chapter is my fictional re-creation based on this document.
3. Ibid. The fact that Mavroyeni was a Greek defending the honour of Islam is an additional irony.
4. BBA Y.A HUS 285/66, 21 Cemaziyelevvel 1311/1 December 1893 Sublime Porte Receiver's Office no. 1821. Memorandum by Grand Vizier and Imperial ADC Cevad Paşa.
5. Ibid.
6. Carney E. S. Gavin, Şinasi Tekin and Gönül Alpay Tekin (eds) 'Imperial Self Portrait. The Ottoman Empire as Revealed in Sultan Abdul Hamid's Photographic Albums,' *Journal of Turkish Studies*, vol. 12 1988.
7. Ibid., p. 47.
8. Ibid., p. 48.
9. Ibid., pp. 112, 114, 115.
10. BBA Y.Mtv 70/67, 12 Rebiyülevvel 1310/4 November 1892 Minister of War Rıza Paşa to Yıldız Palace. Given that the poses to be taken and the very size of the pictures is defined, it is almost certain that the photographs were designed for the albums. On the Aşiret School see Ch. III.
11. Gavin, Tekin and Tekin (eds), *Imperial Self Portrait*, pp. 162–4.
12. Hobsbawm, *Age of Empire*, p. 123.
13. Gavin, Tekin and Tekin (eds), *Imperial Self Portrai*, pp. 193, 194, 203, 205.
14. Anderson, *Imagined Communities*, p. 27.
15. Mitchell, *Colonising Egypt*, pp. 13 –15.
16. BBA Y.A RES 54/30, 18 February 1891. Ottoman Embassy London to Foreign Ministry; Y.A RES 55/1 Sublime Porte Council of Ministers. The proposed Ottoman delegation was to consist of the Director of the Imperial Galatasaray Lycée, Ismail Bey, and the famous popular writer Ahmed Mithad Efendi.
17. BBA Irade Hariciye 6, 7 Cemaziyelevvel 1320/13 August 1902.
18. BBA Y.A RES 62/27, Gurre-i Cemaziyelahir 1310/21 December 1892. Sublime Porte Special Council no. 1517.
19. BBA Y.A RES 106/71, 22 Zilhicce 1317/24 April 1900. Sublime Porte Council of Ministers. no. 3541. The only Ottoman possession in Africa at this time was the vilayet of Trablusgarp in North Africa comprising the sancaks of Tripoli and Benghazi. Ostritch feathers and tortoise shell were major exports from this province, as well as esparto grass, a plant which grew on the Tripolitanian plains and was used to make high quality paper. On this see, Michel Le Gall, 'Pashas Bedouins and Notables: The Ottoman Administration in Tripoli and Benghazi 1881-1902.' Princeton University PhD Dissertation (1986) pp. 95–7, 153–4.

20. BBA Irade Hariciye 5, 9 Rebiyülevvel 1320/17 June 1902. Sublime Porte Receiver's Office no. 500. One of the portraits of the albums in Imperial Self Portrait was the photograph of two blind boys from the Imperial School of the Blind. See *Imperial Self Portrait*, p. 177.
21. The idea that the 'whole world is watching' is derived from Carol Gluck's study of very similar phenomena in a Japanese context. See Gluck, *Japan's Modern Myths*.
22. There is a great deal of recent literature on the World's Fairs. See for example: Burton Benedict, *The Anthropology of World's Fairs. San Francisco's Panama Pacific Exposition of 1915* (London & Berkeley 1983); Mitchell, *Colonising Egypt*; Paul Greenhalgh, *Ephemeral Vistas. The Expositions Universelles, Great Exhibitions and World's Fairs 1851–1939* (Manchester 1988); Robert W. Rydell, *The Book of the Fairs* (Chicago and London 1992). On the Ottoman Empire's participation in the fairs the only work for a long time was Rifat Önsoy, 'Osmanlı İmparatorluğu'nun katıldığı ilk Uluslararası sergiler ve Sergi-i Umumi-i Osmani,' *Belleten* vol. 47 (1983) pp. 195–235. This situation has now been remedied by the excellent study of the subject by Çelik, *Displaying the Orient*.
23. Çelik, *Displaying the Orient*; Rıfat, Önsoy *Osmanlı İmparatorluğu ve Dünya Sergileri*.
24. Benedict, *Anthropology of World's Fairs*, pp. 6–7.
25. BBA Y.Mtv 33/72, 2 Haziran 1304/15 June 1888, Ottoman Embassy in Madrid to Foreign Ministry, no. 2379.
26. Y.A HUS 224/96, 27 Şaban 1306/27 April 1889. Sublime Porte Foreign Ministry. In the event, the Ottomans participated quite successfully with the Ministry of Navy Bulletin winning a prize. See Y.Mtv. 63/33; 7 Zilkade 1309/4 June 1892. It was remarkable that the monarchies still felt this strongly about the revolution one century after the event, on this see: Eric Hobsbawm, *Echoes of the Marseillaise* (New Brunswick 1990) pp. 69–70.
27. BBA Y.A RES 58/33, 25 Şevval 1309/24 May 1892 Sublime Porte Council of Ministers.
28. Ibid. On the matter of prestige going with location see Mitchell, et al.
29. Ibid. Contract between The Ottoman Ministry of Trade and Public Works and Ilyas Suhami Saadullah and Co.
30. Çelik, *Displaying the Orient*, pp. 24–5 on the Egyptian exhibition at the 1889 Paris fair.
31. BBA Y.Mtv 77/114, 28 Nisan 1309/11 May 1893. Ottoman Ambassador Mavroyeni Bey to Yıldız Palace Imperial Secretariat.
32. Said, *Orientalism*, p. 21, emphasis in original.
33. BBA Irade Hususi 878/123 17 Muharrem 1310/12 August 1892 Yıldız Palace Imperial Secretariat no. 678.

34. BBA Y.Mtv 75/202, 28 Şubat 1308/13 March 1893. Ottoman Representative at the Chicago Fair, Hakkı Bey, to Yıldız Palace.
35. BBA Y.Mtv 76/35, 13 Mart 1309/26 March 1893; Y.Mtv 79/163, 11 Muharrem 1311/26 July 1893 Minister of Trade and Public Works Hasan Tevfik Paşa to Sublime Porte. Fifty specially made ceremonial flags were also to be dispatched to Chicago.
36. BBA Irade Hususi 1746/59, 21 Receb 1310/11 February 1893 Süreyya Paşa, Imperial Private Secretary, Yıldız Palace Imperial Secretariat, no. 5746.
37. BBA Irade Hususi 1310/141, 20 Rebiyülevvel 1310/3 October 1982. Letter from Raci [Bey] subject of His Imperial Majesty from Acre.
38. Ibid. Programme for Ottoman Hippodrome.
39. Ibid. (Osmanli At Meydanı Talimatnamesi).
40. Irade Hususi 1310/141, 25 Rebiyülevvel 1310/8 October 1892. Yıldız Palace Imperial Secretariat no. 3027.
41. Çelik, Displaying the Orient, p. 23; See also Gavin, Tekin and Tekin (eds) Imperial Self Portrait, pp. 198, 199.
42. BBA Y.Mtv. 75/167, 26 Subat 1308/11 March 1893 Hakkı Bey, the Ottoman Commissioner at the Chicago Fair to Yıldız Palace Imperial Secretariat; Y.Mtv 76/36, 12 Mart 1309/25 March 1893 Letter from Ali Bey Zade Nuri notable merchant of Gemlik.
43. BBA Y.Mtv 76/36,13 Mart 1309/26 March 1893 Hakkı Bey, Ottoman Commissioner at the Chicago Fair to Yıldız Palace.
44. BBA Irade Nafia 9/5.Ş.1310; Ministry of Trade and Public Works, Receiver's Office no. 169. Letter from Hakkı Bey dated 25 Receb 1310/13 February 1893.
45. Ibid., 3 Şaban 1310/21 February 1893; Sublime Porte Council of Ministers. no. 2115. On 17 October the Porte decided to send two English-speaking guides, Seraphim Efendi and Ekerin Efendi, see Irade Nafia 1/8.R.1311.
46. BBA Irade Nafia 3/23.ZA.1310. Letter from Hakkı Bey to the Ministry of Trade and Public Works dated 15 May 1893. Letter no. 3.
47. Ibid., 4 Teşrin-i Evvel 1309/17 October 1893. Letter from Hakkı Bey to Ministry of Trade and Public Works.
48. BBA Irade Nafia 3 23.ZA.1310/15 May 1893. Letter from Hakkı Bey to Ministry of Trade and Public Works. Letter no. 2.
49. Ibid. The additional funds were approved on the 9 June 1893, see Irade Nafia 3 23.ZA.1310. Sublime Porte Receiver's Office no. 2877.
50. Rydell, All the World's a Fair, pp. 64–5.
51. See: The Chicago Fair Illustrated. Proprietor S. K. Bistany. (Official gazette of Ottoman delegation) 1 June 1893, plan of the fair on p. 7. My thanks to Gültekin Yıldız for this reference.

52. BBA Y.Mtv 103/15, 21 Safer 1312/25 August 1894 Report by the Imperial Jeweller Istepan Mihran Dikran, Çubukçuyan Efendi. The details of the design of the display cases are in: Irade Nafıa 3/23.ZA.1310. The style of jewellery and porcelain which can be seen in the Yıldız Palace Museum is actually quite garish, totally in keeping with Victorian taste.
53. BBA Y.Mtv 100/38, 10 Temmuz 1894/10 July 1894. Embassy at Brussels to Sublime Porte Foreign Ministry.
54. BBA Y.Mtv 99/55, 7 Muharrem 1312/12 July 1894. Foreign Minister Said Paşa to Ottoman Embassy in Brussels no. 21. Sulukule is a district well known even today for its gypsy dancers.
55. BBA Y.Mtv 100/38, 15 Muharrem 1312/20 July 1894. Foreign Minister Mehmed Said Paşa. Sublime Porte Foreign Ministry no. 21.
56. BBA Y.Mtv 154/53, 8 Zilkade 1314/11 April 1897 Minister Of Trade Mahmud Celaleddin Paşa, enclosing letter from C. H. Sudre, the Ottoman honorary consul in Brussels, and Paul Kupelyan, representative of the firm in charge of the Brussels fair.
57. BBA Y.A HUS 354/41, 23 Muharrem 1314/5 July 1896. Sublime Porte Foreign Ministry no. 1610.
58. BBA Y.A RES 72/47, 21 Rebiyülahir 1312/23 October 1894; Sublime Porte Council of Ministers no. 1117.
59. In the 1890s photography had become a gentleman amateur's hobby and some focused particularly on hirsute dervishes begging in the streets. This was something which was frowned upon by the Ottomans. On photography of dervishes see Nancy Micklewright, 'Dervish Images in Photographs and Paintings' in R. Lifchez (ed.) *The Dervish Lodge*, pp 269–84.
60. BBA YEE 14/1163/74/14; n.d. Letter from Ebuziyya Tevfik to Imperial secretariat.
61. Ibid.
62. BBA Y.A RES 82/43, 18 Safer 1314/30 July 1896. Ministry of Trade and Public Works. Minister Mahmud Celaleddin Paşa to Grand Vizier no. 39.
63. BBA YEE Kamil Paşa Evrakına Ek 1087/1, 8 Haziran 1312/21 June 1896. Minister of Interior Memduh Paşa.
64. BBA Y.A RES 83/99, 11 Cemaziyelevvel 1314/18 November 1896. Ministry of Trade and Public Works no. 63.
65. BBA Y.A RES 85/21, 2 Ramazan 1314/4 February 1897. Minister of Trade and Public Works Mahmud Celaleddin Paşa to Grand Vezier. no. 82.
66. BBA Y.A RES 91/30, 24 December 1897 Ottoman Ambassador Münir Bey to His Excellency the Foreign Minister Tevfik Paşa.
67. BBA Y.Mtv 178/194; Selh-i Muharrem 1316/21 June 1898. Director of Istanbul Municipality to Sublime Porte.

68. BBA Y.A RES 94/68, Y.A RES 95/24, 20 Rebiyülahir 1316/8 September 1898. Sublime Porte Council of Ministers no. 1198.
69. BBA Y.A RES 95/24; 8 Cemaziyülevvel 1316/25 September 1898. Ministry of Trade and Public Works no. 58. Uşak and Gördes are regions in central Anatolia still famous for their prestige carpets.
70. BBA Y.Mtv 206/143; 29 Rebiyülahir 1318/25 October 1900 Imperial General Staff, Serasker Rıza Paşa to Grand Vizier.
71. Çelik, *Displaying the Orient*, p. 89.
72. BBA Y.A RES 124/59; 17 Kanun-u Evvel 1903/30 December 1903. Sublime Porte Foreign Ministry. Letter from banker Konta to Ottoman Ambassador in Washington. I owe thanks to Mr Benjamin Fortna for this reference.
73. See above Chapter 1.
74. BBA Y.A RES 124/59; 15 Zilkade 1321/3 February 1904. Foreign Minister Tevfik Paşa to Grand Vizier.
75. BBA Y.A RES 134/10; 25 Şaban 1323/15 October 1905. Council of State Financial Department no. 2813.
76. BBA Y.Mtv 258/51; 7 Muharrem 1322/25 March 1904. Ottoman Comissioner in Bulgaria Ali Ferruh Bey to Sublime Porte. no. 5791/33. Ottoman Bulgaria had been split into two by the Berlin Congress of 1878. The two halves were called Westen and Eastern Rumelia. Western Rumelia became in effect independent in 1885, with nominal Ottoman suzereinty.
77. BBA Y.A RES 59/21; 1 Zilhicce 1309/27 June 1892. Sublime Porte Council of Ministers. Includes translation from the Bulgarian newspaper Plovdiv bemoaning the fact that 'although much of our agricultural produce goes to Istanbul the Turks are not present in our fair'.
78. Çelik, *Displaying the Orient*, pp. 10–11.
79. Benedict, *The Anthropology of World's Fairs*, pp. 45–6. 'People as trophies' are one of Benedict's categories for the display of conquered peoples.
80. Ibid., p. 7.
81. Çelik, *Displaying the Orient*, pp. 3, 39.
82. Ibid., p. 48.

Chapter Eight

1. In Habermas's terms this was caused by: 'The structural dissimilarity between areas of administrative action and areas of cultural tradition, [which] constitutes, then, a systematic limit to attempts to compensate for legitimation deficits through conscious manipulation'. See Habermas, *Legitimation Crisis*, (Boston 1983) p. 71.
2. Shils, *Tradition*, p. 22.

3. Mardin, *The Genesis of Young Ottoman Thought*, p. 171. Emphasis in original.
4. Ibid., p. 70.
5. Carter Findley, 'Factional Rivalry in Ottoman Istanbul: The Fall of Pertev Paşa, 1837,'. Raiyyet Rüsumu. Essays Presented to Halil İnalcık. *Journal of Turkish Studies*., vol. 10 (1986) pp. 130, 131; See also Findley, *Ottoman Civil Officialdom*, pp. 70–80.
6. I. H. Uzunçarşılı, *Midhat Paşa ve Yıldız Mahkemesi*. (Ankara 1967).
7. I. H. Uzunçarşılı, *Midhat Paşa ve Taif Mahkumları* (Ankara 1985) pp. 88, 95, 106, 112.
8. Uzunçarşılı speaks of the 'martyrdom of Mithat Paşa' (*Mithat Paşa'nın şehadeti*).
9. For a classic view of Mahmud II as the dynamic reformer comp: Niyazi Berkes, *The Development of Secularism in Turkey* (Montreal 1964). Also Stanford Shaw, *History of the Ottoman Empire and Modern Turkey* (Cambridge1986) vol. II p. 20: 'Strong measures followed to hunt out the remaining Janissaries.'.
10. BBA YEE 18/1858/93/39. No date.
11. BBA YEE 31/1950 mükerrer/45/83, 22 Zilkade 1299/6 October 1882. Memorandum by Said Paşa.
12. Kantorowicz, *The King's Two Bodies* p. 19.
13. Ortaylı, *Imparatorluğun En Uzun Yüzyılı* (Istanbul 1983) p. 171.
14. BBA YEE 18/1858/93/39.
15. Ibid.
16. Ibid.
17. Ibid.
18. Ibid. It is interesting that Cevdet seems to have been ahead of later republican historians of the early Ottoman state, like Fuad Köprülü, who sought somehow to 'prove' that Mihal was actually Turkish in the first place. See Kafadar, *Between Two Worlds*, pp. 1–30.
19. Ahmet Cevdet Paşa, *Tarih-i Cevdet* (2nd Edn) vol. III p. 160. My thanks to Dr Stephanos Yerasimos for kindly bringing this passage to my attention.
20. Said, *Imperialism and Culture*, p. 23.
21. The burning and sacking of the Chinese Emperor's Summer Palace by British troops in 1862 had immediate and widespread repercussions in the Ottoman world. See, Münif (Reis-i Sani-i Ticaret), 'Mukayese-i Ilm ve Cehl,' *Mecmua-i Fünun*, no.1 (1279) pp. 21, 22, 25, 29–30: 'If the Chinese had not insisted in maintaining their old ways and their imperfect civilization would they have suffered such an insult at the hand of a few thousand foreigners?' As quoted in Hanioğlu, *Osmanlı Ittihad ve Terakki Cemiyeti*, p. 19.

22. Ahmed Cevdet Paşa, *Maruzat* p. 41. (transliterated and annotated by Yusuf Halaçoğlu).
23. Roderic Davison, *Reform In the Ottoman Empire. 1856–1876* (Princeton 1963).
24. Selim Deringil, 'Les Ottomans et le partage de l'Afrique'. *Studies on Ottoman Diplomatic History*, V (1992) pp. 121–33.
25. Kantorowicz, *The King's Two Bodies*. pp. 36–9.
26. Yavuz Selim Karakışla, 'Exile Days of Abdulhamid II (1909–12) and the Confiscation of His Wealth'. MA Diss. Boğaziçi University (1991). Karakışla is quoting from Ali Cevad, *Ikinci Meşrutiyet'in Ilanı ve 31 Mart Hadisesi* (Ankara 1985) pp. 269–70.
27. On the matter of the deposition and trial of Louis XVI, see Mona Ozouf, 'Le Proces du roi' in *Dictionnaire Critique de la Revolution Française*, (Paris 1988) pp. 134–45. Particularly p. 136: 'Il a repris son titre originel, il est homme'.
28. Ali Cevad *Ikinci Meşrutiyet*, ('*Biz Meclis-i Mebusan tarafından geldik. Fetva-i Şerif var. Millet seni hal'etti. Ama hayatınız emindir*'). My thanks to Dr Edhem Eldem for drawing my attention to this wording.
29. *Düstur*, Tertib-i Sani, Numero 57–p. 166: "*Sultan Abdulhamid Han-ı Saninin Hilafet ve Saltanat-ı Osmanıyeden Iskatıyla Sultan Mehmed Han-ı Hamis Hazretlerinin Asad ve Iclası hakkında Fetvayı Şerife ve Meclis-i Umumi-i Milli Kararnamesi*'. (*The fetwa and the Act of the National Parliament relating to the removal of Sultan Abdülhamid Khan from the caliphate and sultanate and the enthronement of Sultan Mehmed Khan the Fifth.*) Signed by Şeyhülislam Mehmed Ziyaadin Efendi.
30. See above Chapter 2. It is however not at all certain that the confiscated copies of the Qur'an were actually burnt, as stated in the *fetwa*.
31. *Düstur*.
32. *Türkiye Büyük Millet Meclisi. Gizli Celse Zabıtları* (Secret Minutes of the Closed Sessions of the Grand National Assembly) (Ankara 1985) '*Bunlar böyle edecek ve bu herifi alıp gidecekler*,' p. 1046. See also, Selim Deringil, 'Ottoman Origins of Kemalist Nationalism: Namık Kemal to Mustafa Kemal,'. *European History Quarterly*, vol. 23 (1993) pp. 165–93.
33. Deringil, 'Ottoman Origins', pp. 165–93.
34. Halil İnalcık, 'The Caliphate and Ataturk's Inkılab,' *Belleten* CXLVI (1982) 353–65.
35. Unsigned Declaration Entitled, 'Califat et Souveraineté, Nationale' in *Revue du Monde Musulman* no. 59 (1925). This issue of the journal is very interesting as it is a special issue dealing with the 'Caliphate Question'. The document also appeared in Turkish as 'Hilafet ve Milli Hakimiyet', and in Arabic. The first article is the document cited above. Subsequent articles deal with how the matter was being received in Egypt. Others are

concerned with the implications for Central Asia. The section on India is written by the well known Indian radical, Barakatallah.
36. Ibid., p. 7. Unlike the French version which was unsigned, the Turkish text is made up of articles signed by major figures in the early Kemalist movement. See, *Hilafet ve Milli Hakimiyet. Hilafet ve Milli Hakimiyet mesaili hakkında muhtelif zevatın makalat ve mütalaatından mürekkeb bir risaledir.* (Pamphlet consisting of articles and views of various personages on the questions of the Caliphate and National Sovereignty) (Ankara İstihbarat Matbaası 1339).
37. Ibid., pp. 55, 56, 57; pp. 12,16.
38. Hamid Enayat, *Modern Islamic Political Thought.* (London 1982) pp. 55–6.
39. Youssef M. Choueiri, *Arab History and the Nation State.* (London 1989) p. 197.
40. Toledano, *State and Society* p. 22.
41. Philip Khoury, *Syria and the French Mandate. The Poli tics of Arab Nationalism.* (Princeton 1987) p. 4.
42. David Fromkin, *A Peace to End All Peace. Creating the Modern Middle East, 1914–1922* (London 1990) p. 43–54.
43. Mardin, *Genesis of Young Ottoman Thought.* p. 120.
44. BBA YEE 18/1858/93/39.
45. İlber Ortaylı, *Imparatorluğun En Uzun Yüzyılı* (Istanbul 1983) p. 10.

Bibliography

Official Records

Başbakanlik Arşivi (Prime Ministry Archives, Istanbul)
Yıldız Esas Evrakı
Yıldız Sadaret Hususi Maruzat
Yıldız Sadaret Resmi Maruzat
Yıldız Mütenevvi Maruzat
Yıldız Perakende Gazeteler
Bab-ı Ali Evrak Odusi Gelen/Giden
Ayniyat Defterleri
İradeler/Hariciye/Meclis-i Mahsus/Dahiliye
Salname-i Devlet 1270, 1271, 1297, 1298, 1299, 1302, 1308, 1324
Salname-i Vilayet-i Hüdavendigar 1303/1885.
Salname-i Vilayet-i Hicaz 1309.
Düstur 1. Tertip.
Türkiye Büyük Millet Meclisi. Gizli Celse Zabıtları (Secret Minutes of the Closed Sessions of the Grand National Assembly) (Ankara 1985).
India Office Library and Records. Political and Secret Home Correspondence (LP&S).

Books and Articles

Abou-El-Haj, Rifa'at, *Formation of the Modern State. The Ottoman Empire-Sixteenth to Eighteenth Centuries* (Albany 1991).
Abu Manneh, Butrus, 'Shaykh Ahmed Ziya'üddin El-Gümüşhanevi and the Ziya'i-Khalidi Suborder,' in Frederick De Jong (ed.) *Shi'a Islam, Sects and Sufism* (Utrecht 1992) pp. 104–17.
—'Sultan Abdülhamid II and Shaikh Abulhuda Al-Sayyadi.' *Middle Eastern Studies* vol. 15 (1979).

— 'The Sultan and the Bureaucracy: The anti-Tanzimat Concepts of Grand Vizier Mahmud Nedim Paşa,' *International Journal of Middle East Studies* 22 (1990) pp. 268-9.
— 'The Islamic Roots of the Gülhane Rescript,' *Die Welt des Islams* 34 (1994) pp. 173-203.
Adelson, Roger, *Mark Sykes, Portrait of an Amateur* (London 1975).
Ahmad, Feroz, *The Young Turks: The Committee of Union and Progress in Turkish Politics 1908-1914* (Oxford 1969).
Ahmed Cevdet Paşa, *Tezakir* (Ankara 1986).
— *Tarih-i Cevdet* (Istanbul 1309 [1891]) 2 vols.
— *Ma'zurat* Transcribed and prepared for publication by Yusuf Hallaçoğlu (Istanbul 1980).
— *Mecelle-i Ahkam-ı Adliye* (Istanbul 1876).
Akarlı, Engin, *The Problems of External Pressures, Power Struggles, and Budgetary Deficits in Ottoman Politics Under Abdulhamid II (1876-1909): Origins and Solutions*. Princeton University PhD Dissertation (1976).
— *The Long Peace. Ottoman Lebanon 1861-1920* (Berkeley, Los Angeles, London 1993).
— 'Abdülhamid II Between East and West'. Paper presented at the colloquium: 'Education, Nation Building and Identity in the Period of Abdülhamid II'. Bad Homburg, Germany, July 12-15 1993.
Akpınar, Alişan, *Osmanlı Devletinde Aşiret Mektebi* (The Tribal School in the Ottoman State) (Istanbul 1997).
Akşin, Sina, *Jön Türkler ve Ittihat ve Terakki* (The Young Turks and the Committee of Union and Progress) (Istanbul 1980).
Ali, Cevad, *İkinci Meşrutiyet* (The Second Constitutional Period), n.d. n.p.
An Eastern Statesman, 'Contemporary Life and Thought in Turkey,' *Contemporary Review* 37 (1880) p. 343.
Ana Britannica (Turkish edition of the *Encyclopaedia Britannica*) vol. 9.
Anderson, Benedict, *Imagined Communities* (London 1991).
Anderson, Perry, *Lineages of the Absolutist State* (London 1974).
Anderson, Mathew, *The Eastern Question 1774-1923 A Study in International Relations* (London 1966).
— *The Ascendancy of Europe 1815-1914. Aspects of European History* (London 1972).
Annuaire Commercial de Constantinople 1893.
Arai, Masami, 'An Imagined Nation: The Idea of the Ottoman Nation as a Key to Modern Ottoman History,' *Orient* vol. 27 (1991) pp. 1-20.
Armstrong, J., *Nations Before Nationalism* (Charlottsville 1982).
Arnold, Thomas, *The Caliphate* (London 1965).
Arseven, Celal Esad, *Sanat ve Siyaset Hatıralarım* (My Political and Artistic Memoirs) (Istanbul 1993).
Aydın, Mehmet, 'Yezidiler ve İnanç Esasları' (The Yezidis and their Beliefs) *Belleten* (Official Journal of the Turkish Historical Society) vol. 52 (1988) pp. 33-45.

Barbir, Karl, 'Memory, Heritage, History: Ottomans and Arabs,' in Carl Brown (ed.), *Imperial Legacy. The Ottoman Imprint on the Balkans and the Middle East* (New York 1996).
Bardin, Pierre, *Algériens et Tunisiens dans l'Empire Ottoman de 1848 à 1914* (Paris 1979).
Benedict, Burton, *The Anthropology of World's Fairs. San Francisco's Panama Pacific Exposition of 1915* (London & Berkeley 1983).
Berki, Ali Himmet, *Açıklamalı Mecelle* (İstanbul 1990).
Blanche, Lesley, *The Sabres of Paradise* (London 1960).
Blind, Karl, 'Young Turkey,' *Fortnightly Review* LXVI (London 1896) pp. 829–40.
Bojinev, Voyn, *Bulgarskaya Prosveta v Makedonya i Odrinska Trakya 1878–1913* (Sofia 1982).
Braden, Jean Haythorne, 'The Eagle and the Crescent: American Interests in the Ottoman Empire, 1860–1870,' Ohio State University PhD Dissertation (1973).
Brooks, Jeffrey, *When Russia Learned to Read* (Princeton 1985).
Brown, L. Carl, *International Politics and the Middle East. Old Rules Dangerous Game* (Princeton & London 1984).
Bryer, Anthony A. M., *The Empire of Trebizond and the Pontos*. Variorum Reprints (London 1980).
Burke, Edmund III, 'Le pan-islamisme et les origines du nationalisme en Afrique du nord, 1890–1918,' Cahiers de l'Unité de d'Anthropologie Sociale et Culturelle. Universite d'Oran (Algeria) 1987, 21–40.
Cahun, Leon, *Excursions sur les bords de l'Euphrate* (Paris 1885).
'Califat et souveraineté nationale,' in *Revue du Monde Musulman* no. 59 (1925). Unsigned.
Cannadine, David, 'Splendour at Court: Royal Spectacle and Pageantry in Modern Britain, c.1820–1977,' in *Rituals of Royalty, Power and Ceremonial in Traditional Societies* (Cambridge 1987) pp. 206–43.
Cannadine, David and Price, Simon (eds), *Rituals of Royalty. Power and Ceremonial in Traditional Societies* (Cambridge 1987).
Carney, Gavin E. S., Şinasi Tekin and Gönül Alpay Tekin (eds), '"Imperial Self Portrait", The Ottoman Empire as Revealed in Sultan Abdul Hamid's Photographic Albums,' *Journal of Turkish Studies* 12 (1988).
Carmichael, Joel, *The Shaping of the Arabs* (New York 1967).
Çelik, Zeynep, *Displaying the Orient. Architecture of Islam at Nineteenth Century World's Fairs* (Berkeley, Los Angeles, Oxford 1992).
—*The Remaking of Istanbul. Portrait of an Ottoman City in the Nineteenth Century* (Berkeley, Los Angeles, Boston 1993).
Cherniavsky, Michael, *Tsar and People. Studies in Russian Myths* (New Haven and London 1961).
Choueiri, Youssef M., *Arab History and the Nation State* (London 1989).

Clogg, Richard, 'The Greeks and their Past,' in Dennis Deletant and Harry Hanak (eds), *Historians as Nation Builders* (London 1988) pp. 22–36.
Cohn, Bernard, 'Representing Authority in Victorian India,' in E. Hobsbawm and T. Ranger (eds), *The Invention of Tradition* (Cambridge 1988) pp. 165–209.
Courtellemont, Gervais, *Mon voyage à la Mecque* (Paris 1896).
Davis, Owen, 'Those Dear Turks. A Lecture at the Congregational Church, Lee, on 1st November 1876,' *Papers on the Eastern Question* (London 1876).
Davison, Roderic, *Reform In the Ottoman Empire 1856–1876* (Princeton 1963).
Deak, Istvan, 'The Habsburg Monarchy: The Strengths and Weaknesses of a Complex Patrimony,' Columbia University, Monarchies Symposium October 26–27 1990, unpublished paper.
Deringil, Selim, 'Legitimacy Structures in the Ottoman Empire: Abdülhamid II 1876–1909,' *International Journal of Middle East Studies*, 23 (1991) pp. 345–59.
— 'The Struggle Against Shi'ism in Hamidian Iraq,' *Die Welt des Islams*, 30 (1990) pp. 45–62.
— 'The Invention of Tradition as Public Image in the Late Ottoman Empire, 1808 to 1908,' *Comparative Studies in Society and History*, 35 (1993) pp. 1–27.
— 'The Ottoman Response to the Egyptian Crisis of 1881–82,' *Middle Eastern Studies*, 24 (1988) pp. 3–24.
— 'Les Ottomans et le Partage de l'Afrique,' *Studies on Ottoman Diplomatic History*, V (1992) pp. 121–33.
— 'The Ottoman Origins of Kemalist Nationalism: Namık Kemal to Mustafa Kemal,' *European History Quarterly*, 23 (1993) pp. 165–93.
— 'Ottoman to Turk, Minority-Majority Relations in the late Ottoman Empire', in Dru C. Gladney (ed.) *Making Majorities: Constituting the Nation in Japan, China, Korea, Malaysia, Fiji, Turkey and the US* (forthcoming, Stanford University Press).
— 'An Ottoman View of Missionary Activity in Hawaii,' *Hawaian Journal of History*, 27 (1993) pp. 119–25.
Duguid, Stephen, 'The Politics of Unity: Hamidian Policy in Eastern Anatolia,' *Middle Eastern Studies* 9 (1973) pp. 130–55.
Dumont, Paul and Georgeon François (eds), *Villes Ottomanes à la fin de l'empire* (Paris 1992).
Elliot, Charles, *Turkey in Europe* (London 1965).
Elliot, Henry, 'The Death of Abdul Aziz and of Turkish Reform' in *The Nineteenth Century* (1888), pp. 276–96.
Elliot, John 'Power and Propaganda in the Spain of Phillip IV,' in Sean Wilentz (ed.), *Rites of Power. Symbolism, Ritual and Politics Since the Middle Ages* (Philadelphia 1985) p. 151
Emre, Side, 'Political Imagery in the Journal Servet-i Fünun,' unpublished Masters Thesis, Boğaziçi University (Istanbul 1996).
Enayat, Hamid, *Modern Islamic Political Thought* (London, Austin 1982).
Ersoy, Mehmet Akif, *Safahat* (Istanbul 1990).

Esenbel, Selçuk, 'A fin de siecle Japanese Romantic in Istanbul: The Life of Yamado Torajiro and his Toruko Gakan,' *SOAS Bulletin*, 59, part 2 (1996) pp. 237-52.
'Istanbul 'de bir Japon,' (A Japanese in Istanbul) *Istanbul Dergisi*, 9, pp. 36-42.
Faroqhi, Suraiya, *Pilgrims and Sultans. The Hajj under the Ottomans* (London 1994).
Fatma Aliye, *Nisvan-ı Islam* (Muslim Women) (Istanbul 1891).
Fawaz, Leila, *An Occasion for War. Civil Conflict in Lebanon and Damascus in 1860* (London 1994).
Findley, Carter, *Ottoman Civil Officialdom. A Social History* (Princeton 1989).
—'Factional Rivalry in Ottoman Istanbul: The Fall of Pertev Paşa, 1837,' in Raiyyet Rüsumu. Essays Presented to Halil İnalcık. *Journal of Turkish Studies* 10 (1986) pp.120-35.
—'The Advent of Ideology in the Islamic Middle East,' *Studia Islamica* LV (1982).
—*Bureaucratic Reform in the Ottoman Empire. The Sublime Porte 1789-1922* (Princeton 1980).
Finkel, Caroline, *The Administration of Warfare: The Ottoman Military Campaigns in Hungary 1593-1606* (Vienna 1988).
—'French Merceneries in the Habsburg-Ottoman war of 1593-1606,' *SOAS Bulletin*, LV, part 3 (1992) pp. 452-71.
Finn, James, *Stirring Times* (London 1878).
Fleischer, Cornell, *Bureaucrat and Intellectual in the Ottoman Empire; The Historian Mustafa ̄li (1541-1600)* (Princeton 1986).
—'Royal Authority, Dynastic Cyclism, and "Ibn-Khaldunism" in Sixteenth-Century Ottoman Letters,' *Journal of Asian and African Studies* XVIII 3-4 (1983) pp. 198-219.
Fletcher, Joseph, 'Turco Mongolian Monarchic Tradition in the Ottoman Empire,' *Harvard Ukrainian Studies* III (1979-80) Eucharisterion: Essays presented to Omeljan Pritsak on his Sixtieth Birthday by his Colleagues and Students pp. 246-52.
Fromkin, David, *A Peace to End all Peace. Creating the Modern Middle East 1914-1922* (London 1990).
Geertz, Clifford, *Negara. The Theatre State in Nineteenth Century Bali* (Princeton 1980).
Gellner, Ernest, *Nations and Nationalism* (Oxford1983).
Gluck, Carol, *Japan's Modern Myths* (Princeton 1985).
Gooch, G. P. and Temperley, Harold (eds), *British Documents on the Origins of the War 1898-1914* (London 1938).
Goodwin, Godfrey, *History of Ottoman Architecture* (London 1971).
Gökalp, Altan, *Tetes Rouges et Bouches Noires. Une confrerie tribale de l'ouest Anatolien* (Paris 1980).
Gündüz, İrfan, *Osmanlılarda Devlet-Tekke Mühasebetleri* (The Relationship of the State and Sufi Lodges in the Ottoman Empire) (Istanbul 1989) pp. 150-1.

Grabill, Joseph, L., *Protestant Diplomacy and the Near East. Missionary Influence on American Policy* (Minneapolis 1971).
Greenhalgh, Paul, *Ephemeral Vistas. The Expositions Universelles, Great Exhibitions and World's Fairs 1851–1939* (Manchester 1988).
Guest, John, *The Yezidis. A Study in Survival* (London & New York 1987).
Haarman, Ulrich, 'Ideology and Alterity: The Arab Image of the Turk from the Abbasids to Modern Egypt,' *International Journal of Middle East Studies* 20 (1988) pp. 175–96.
Habermas, Jurgen, *Legitimation Crisis* (Boston 1983).
Hafız, Mehmed Sadık, *Alem-i Islam'da Cihad-ı Ekber* (The Great Holy War in the Islamic World) (Istanbul 1342–1339) p. 25.
Hanioğlu, Şükrü, *The Young Turks in Opposition* (Oxford 1995).
——*Osmanlı İttihad ve Terakki Cemiyeti ve Jön Türklük 1889–1902* (The Young Turks and the Committee of Union and Progress) (Istanbul 1985).
——'Osmanlı Aydınında Değişme ve "Bilim",' (Change, "Science", and the Ottoman Intellectual), *Toplum ve Bilim* 27 (1984) pp. 183–92.
——*Osmanlı İttihad ve Terakki Cemiyeti ve Jön Türklük* (The Young Turks and the Committee of Union and Progress)(Istanbul 1983).
Haskell, Thomas L, 'Objectivity is not Neutrality,' *History and Theory* vol. 29 (1990) pp. 129–57.
Haslip, Joan, *The Sultan. The Life of Abdul Hamid II* (New York 1958).
Hasluck, F. W., *Christianity and Islam under the Sultans* (Oxford 1929) 2 volumes.
Haydaroğlu, Ilknur Polat, *Osmanlı İmparatorluğu'nda Yabancı Okullar* (Foreign Schools in the Ottoman Empire) (Ankara 1990).
Herbert, William von, *The Defence of Plevna 1877; written by one who took part in it* (Ankara 1990).
Hilafet ve Milli Hakimiyet, Hilafet ve Milli Hakimiyet mesaili hakkında muhtelif zevatın makalat ve mütalaatından mürekkeb bir risaledir (Pamphlet consisting of articles and views of various personages on the questions of the Caliphate and National Sovereignty) (Ankara İstihbarat Matbaası 1339).
Hirszowicz, L. 'The Sultan and the Khedive 1892–1908,' *Middle Eastern Studies* vol. 8 (1977) pp. 287–311.
Hobsbawm, Eric, *Nations and Nationalism* (Cambridge 1990).
——*Echoes of the Marseillaise* (New Brunswick 1990).
——*The Age of Empire* (London 1987).
Hobsbawm, Eric and Ranger, Terence (eds), *The Invention of Tradition* (Cambridge 1983).
Hourani, Albert, *A History of the Arab Peoples* (London 1991).
——'How Should We Write the History of the Middle East?' *International Journal of Middle East Studies* 23 (1991) pp. 125–36.
Hurewitz, J. C., 'Ottoman Diplomacy and the European State System' *Middle East Journal* vol. 15 (1961) pp. 141–52.
——*The Middle East and Africa in World Politics* (New Haven 1975).

Hurgronje, Snouck, *Mecca in the Latter Part of the 19th Century* (London 1931).
İnalcık, Halil, and Quataert, Donald (eds), *An Economic and Social History of the Ottoman Empire 1300–1914* (Cambridge 1994).
İnalcık, Halil, 'The Ottoman State and its Ideology' in Halil İnalcık and Cemal Kafadar (eds), *Conference on Süleyman the Magnificent*, Princeton Occasional Papers (1992) pp. 49–72.
— 'The Caliphate and Ataturk's Inkilab' *Belleten*, CXLVI (1982) pp. 353–65.
— *The Ottoman Empire in the Classical Age: 1300–1600* (London 1973).
İpşirli, Mehmet, 'Cuma Selamlığı. Halk Hükümdar Münasebetleri Açısından Önemi' (The Institution of Friday Prayer in the Ottoman State. Its Importance for the Relationship of the Ruler and the People) in *Prof. Bekir Kütükoğlu'na Armağan* (Istanbul 1991) pp. 459–71.
İslamoğlu-İnan, Huri, 'Mukayeseli Tarih Yazını İçin bir Öneri: Hukuk, Mülkiyet, Meşruiyet' (An Agenda for Comparative History: Law, Property and Legitimacy) *Toplum ve Bilim* 62 (1993) pp. 19–34.
— 'Köylüler, Ticarileşme Hareketi ve Devlet Gücünün Meşrulaşması' (Peasants, Commercialization and the Legitimation of State Power) *Toplum ve Bilim* 43/44 (1988–89) pp. 7–31.
Janin, R. 'Musulmans malgré eux, Les Stavriotes'. *Echos D'Orient* XV (1912) pp. 495–505.
Joseph, Isya, *Devil Worship. The Sacred Books and Traditions of the Yezidis* (London 1919) reprinted by the Health Research Institute (California 1972).
Joseph, John, *The Nestorians and their Muslim Neighbors* (Princeton 1961).
Kafadar, Cemal, *Between Two Worlds. The Construction of the Ottoman State* (Berkeley 1995).
Kantarowicz, E. H., *The King's Two Bodies* (Princeton 1957).
Karaca, Ali, *Doğu Anadolu Islahatı ve Ahmet Şakir Paşa 1838–1899* (Ahmet Şakir Paşa and Reform in Eastern Anatolia) (Istanbul 1993) pp. 173–203.
Karakışla, Yavuz Selim, 'Exile Days of Abdülhamid II (1909–1912) and the Confiscation of His Wealth'. MA Diss. Boğaziçi University (1991).
Kartekin, Enver, *Ramazanoğulları Tarihi* (History of the Ramazanoğlu Dynasty) (Istanbul 1979).
Kayalı, Hasan, 'Arabs and Young Turks: Turkish Arab Relations in the Second Constitutional Period 1908–1918,' Harvard University PhD thesis (1988).
Kedourie, Elie, 'The Surrender of Medina, January 1919,' *Middle Eastern Studies* 13 (1977) pp. 124–43.
Kent, Marian (ed.), *The Great Powers and the End of the Ottoman Empire* (London 1984).
Kévonian, Arménouhie, *Les Noces Noires de Gulizar* (Paris 1993).
Khoury, Philip S., *Syria and the French Mandate: The Politics of Arab Nationalism* (London 1987).
Kıcıman, Naci Kaşif, *Medine Müdafaası. Hicaz bizden nasıl ayrıldı?* (The Defence of Medina or How we Lost the Hijaz) (Istanbul 1971).

Kısakürek, Necip Fazıl, *Ulu Hakan II. Abdülhamid Han* (Istanbul 1981).
Kitromilides, Pashalis, '"Imagined Communities" and the Origins of the National Question in the Balkans,' *European History Quarterly* 19 (1989) pp. 149-94.
Kocabaşoğlu, Uygur, *Anadolu'daki Amerika* (America in Anatolia) (Istanbul 1989).
Kodaman, Bayram, *Abdülhamid Dönemi Eğitim Sistemi* (Educational Policies during the Reign of Abdülhamid) (Istanbul 1990).
—*Sultan Abdülhamid in Doğu Anadolu Politikası* (The Policies of Sultan Abdülhamid in Eastern Anatolia) (Istanbul 1983).
Konyalı, İbrahim Hakkı, *Söğüt'de Ertuğrul Gazi Türbesi ve ıhtifali* (The Commemoration Ceremonies at Ertuğrul Gazi's Shrine in Söğüt) (İstanbul 1959).
Kuran, Aptullah, 'The Evolution of the Sultan's Pavillion in Ottoman Imperial Mosques,' *Islamic Art* IV (1990-1991).
Lambton, Ann K. S., *State and Government in Medieval Islam* (London 1985).
Landau, Jacob, 'Nishan', *Encyclopaedia of Islam*. New Edition (Leiden 1993) pp. 57-9.
—*The Hijaz Railroad*.
Latham, R. G., MA, MD, *Russian and Turk, from a Geographical, Ethnological, and Historic Point of View* (London 1878).
Le Gall, Michel, 'Pashas Bedouins and Notables: The Ottoman Administration in Tripoli and Benghazi 1881-1902,' Princeton University PhD Dissertation (1986).
Leitsch, Walter 'East Europeans Studying History in Vienna' in Dennis Deletant and Harry Hanak (eds), *Historians as Nation Builders* (London 1988).
Lewis, Bernard, *The Political Language of Islam* (Chicago 1988).
—*The Emergence of Modern Turkey* (London 1973).
Lifchez, Raymond *The Dervish Lodge* (Berkeley 1992).
Luke, Harry Charles (Sometime Assistant Governor of Jerusalem) *The Yezidis or Devil Worshippers of Mosul* (Bombay 1925).
—*Mosul and its Minorities* (London 1925).
Lusignan, Princess Annie de, *The Twelve Years' Reign of H.I.M. Abdul Hamid II, Sultan of Turkey* (London 1889).
Lynch, H. F. B., *Armenia, Travels and Studies II: The Turkish Provinces* (London 1901).
Mardin, Şerif, *Religion and Social Change in Modern Turkey. The Case of Bediüzzaman Said Nursi* (New York 1989).
—'Center-Periphery Relations, A Key to Turkish Politics?' in *Daedalus* (1973) pp. 169-90.
—'Some Notes on an Early Phase in the Modernization of Communications in Turkey,' *Comparative Studies in Society and History* 3 (1960-61) pp. 257-71.
—*The Genesis of Young Ottoman Thought* (Princeton 1962).
—*Jön Türklerin Siyasi Fikirleri 1895-1908* (The Political Thought of Young Turks) (Istanbul 1983).

Mehmed, İzzet, *Yeni Afrika* (The New Africa) (Istanbul 1308).
Mehmed Sadık, *Alem-i Islam'da Cihad-ı Ekber* (The Great Holy War in the Islamic World) (Istanbul 1904).
—*Milaslı Durmuşzade Hafız Mehmed Sadık, Milas'da Ağa Camii Müderris ve Cami-i Kebir Vaizi* (Preacher Mehmed Sadık from Milas, Preacher in the Great Mosque and Teacher at Ağa Mosque School)
—*Müvaiz-i Diniye* (Religious Sermons) Izmir 1328 (1910).
Melek Hanum, *Thirty Years in the Harem or the Autobiography of Melek Hanum, Wife of HH Kıbrızlı Mehemet Pasha* (New York 1872).
Meriç, Ümit, *Cevdet Paşa'nın Cemiyet ve Millet Görüşü* (The Views of Cevdet Paşa on Society and the State) (Istanbul 1979).
Messick, Brinkley, *The Calligraphic State. Textual Domination and History in a Muslim Society* (Berkley, Los Angeles, Oxford 1993).
Micklewright, Nancy, 'Dervish Images in Photographs and Paintings' in Raymond Lifchez (ed.) *The Dervish Lodge*, pp. 269–84.
Mintzuri, Hagob, *Istanbul Anıları 1897–1940* (Istanbul Memoirs) (Istanbul 1993).
Mitchell, Timothy, *Colonising Egypt* (Berkeley 1991).
Mouradian, Claire, *Armenie, que sais je* (Paris 1995).
Müftüoğlu, Mustafa, *Abdülhamid. Kızıl Sultanmı?* (Abdülhamid, The Red Sultan?) (Istanbul 1985).
Muhleisen-Arnold, Dr J., *The Society for Propagating the Gospel Among the Moslems, In Connection with the Church of England; Its First Appeal on Behalf of 180 millions of Mohammedans* (London 1860).
Musurus, Ghikis Bey, 'L'avenir de l'Islam,' *Questions Diplomatiques et Coloniales* XI (1901) pp. 595–7.
Necipoğlu, Gülru, *Architecture Ceremonial and Power: The Topkapı Palace in the Fifteenth and Sixteenth Centuries* (Cambridge Mass. & London 1991).
—'The Ottoman Hagia Sophia,' paper delivered at Princeton University 'The Structure of Hagia Sophia' symposium, 19 May 1990. Cited with permission of the author.
—'Dynastic Imprints on the Cityscape. The Collective Discourse of Ottoman Imperial Mausoleums in Istanbul' unpublished paper p. 14. Cited with permission of the author.
Nesim, Ali, *Kıbrıslı Türklerin Kimliği* (The Identity of Cypriot Turks) (Nicosia 1990).
Niyazi, Berkes, *The Development of Secularism in Turkey* (Montreal 1964).
Ocak, Ahmet Yaşar, 'Abdülhamid Dönemi İslamcılığının Tarihi Arka Planı: Klasik Dönem Osmanlı İslamı'na Genel Bir Bakış' (A General View on the Background to Islamism in the Hamidian Period) *Sultan II Abdülhamid ve Devri Semineri. Istanbul Üniversitesi Edebiyat Fakültesi, Bildiriler* (Istanbul 1994) pp. 107–25.
—'Kanuni Sultan Süleyman devrinde bir Osmanlı Heretiği: şeyh Muhyiddin Karamani' (An Ottoman Heretic at the Time of Süleyman the Magnificent:

Shaikh Muhyiddin Karamani), *Prof. Bekir Kütükoğlu' na Armağan* (Istanbul 1991) pp. 473–84.

—'Les reactions socio-religieuses contre l'idéologie officielle ottomane et la question de zendeqa ve ilhad (Heresie et Atheisme au XVI'éme siecle) *Turcica* 21-2 (1991) pp. 71-82.

Ochsenwald, William, *Religion Society and the State in Arabia. The Hijaz under Ottoman Control 1840–1908* (Columbus 1984).

—*The Hijaz Railroad* (Charlottesville Va. 1980).

Önsoy, Rifat, 'Osmanli Imparatorluğun'un Katıldığı ilk Uluslararası sergiler ve Sergi-i Umumî-i Osmanî,' (The First World Fairs: Ottoman Participation and the Ottoman General Fair) *Belleten* 47 (1983) pp.195–235.

Ortaylı, İlber, 'II. Abdülhamid Devrinde Taşra Bürokrasisinde Gayrimüslimler' in *Sultan II Abdülhamid ve Devri Semineri, Istanbul Universitesi Edebiyat Fakültesi* (Istanbul 1994).

—*Imparatorluğun En Uzun Yüzyılı* (The Longest Century of the Empire) (Istanbul 1983).

Tanzimattan Sonra Mahalli ıdareler (1840–1878) (Ankara 1974).

Öke, M. Kemal, *Ingiliz Casusu Prof. Arminius Vambery'nin gizli Raporlarında II Abdülhamid ve Dönemi* (Abdülhamid II and his Time in the Reports of the British Spy Arminius Vambery) (Istanbul 1983).

O'Rourke, P. J., 'Give War a Chance,' *Atlantic Monthly* (New York 1992).

Owen, Roger, *The Middle East in the World Economy 1800–1914* (London 1987).

Ozouf, Mona, 'Le Proces dur Roi,' in *Dictionnaire Critique de la Revolution Française* (Paris 1988) pp. 134–45.

Pamuk, Şevket, *The Ottoman Empire and World Capitalism* (Cambridge 1987).

Pandey, Gyanendra, 'Encounters and Calamities: The History of the North Indian Qasba in the Nineteenth Century' in Ranajit Guha and Gayatri Chakravorty Spivak (eds) *Selected Subaltern Studies* (Oxford 1988) pp. 106–7.

Presland, John, *Deeds Bey: A Study of Sir Wyndham Deedes 1883–1923* (London 1942).

Politis, Kozmas, *Yitik Kentin Kırk Yılı* (Forty Years of the Lost City), trans. Osman Bleda (Istanbul 1992).

Rambert, Louis, *Notes et impressions de Turquie. L'Empire Ottoman sous Abdul-Hamid* (Geneva and Paris n.d).

Ramsay, R. M., *Impressions of Turkey During Twelve Years' Wanderings* (London 1897).

Ramsay, William Mitchell, 'The Intermixture of Races in Asia Minor' in *Proceedings of the British Academy 1915–1916*, pp. 359–422.

Redhouse, James W., *A Vindication of the Ottoman Sultan's Title of 'Caliph'* (London 1877).

Rogan, Eugene L., 'Aşiret Mektebi: Abdülhamid II's School for Tribes (1892–1907),' *International Journal of Middle East Studies* vol. 28 (1996) pp. 83–107.

—'The al-Karak Revolt of 1910: Ottoman Order at Odds with Local Order.' Paper presented in the panel, 'The New Order and Local Order: Continuity

and Crisis in Everyday Life'. MESA meeting Toronto November 16 1989 (cited with the permission of the author).
Rydell, Robert W, *The Book of the Fairs* (Chicago and London 1992).
Süleyman Hüsnü Paşa, *Tarih-i Alem* (World History) (Istanbul 1872).
Said, Ali, *Saray Hatıraları. Sultan Abdülhamid'in Hayatı* (A Memoir of the Palace. The Life of Abdülhamid II) (Istanbul 1993).
Said, Edward, *Culture and Imperialism* (London, Melbourne, Sydney 1994).
—*Orientalism* (Basingstoke 1985).
Sakaoğlu, Necdet, 'Geçmiş Zaman Olurki,' *Skyline* (March 1997) p. 112.
Salmoné, Anthony H., 'The Real Rulers of Turkey,' *The Nineteenth Century* 37 (May 1895) pp. 719-33.
Salt, Jeremy, *Imperialism, Evangelism and the Ottoman Armenians 1878-1896* (London 1993).
—'A Precarious Symbiosis: Ottoman Christians and Foreign Missionaries in the Nineteenth Century,' *International Journal of Turkish Studies*, 3 (Winter 1985-86) p. 56.
Salzmann, Ariel, 'An Ancien Regime Revisited: "Privatization" and Political Economy in the Eighteenth-Century Ottoman Empire,' *Politics and Society* vol. 21 (1993) pp. 393-423.
Schölch, Alexander, *Egypt for the Egyptians: The Socio-Political Crisis in Egypt 1878-1882* (London 1981).
Seagrave, Sterling, *Dragon Lady. The Life and Legend of the Last Empress of China* (London 1992).
Seton Watson, Hugh, 'On Trying to be a Historian of Eastern Europe,' in Harry Hanak (ed.), *Historians as Nation Builders* (London 1988).
Shaw, Stanford, *The Jews of the Ottoman Empire and the Turkish Republic* (London 1991).
—*History of the Ottoman Empire and Modern Turkey* (Cambridge 1986).
Shils, Edward, *Tradition* (Chicago 1980).
Sırma, İhsan Süreyya, *'Abdülhamid' in İslam Birliği Siyaseti* (Abdülhamid and the Policy of Pan-Islamism) (Istanbul 1983).
Smith, Anthony D., *The Ethnic Origins of Nations* (Oxford 1986).
Solak, Seyit, *1571'den Günümüze Kıbrıs Türk Yönetimleri* (Turkish Administrations in Cyprus from 1571 to the Present) (Nicosia 1989).
Spuler, Bertold, *Die Minderheitenschulen der europaischen Turkei von der Reformzeit bis zum Weltkrieg* (Breslau 1936).
Stone, Andrews Frank, *Academies for Anatolia* (Lanham, New York, London 1984).
Suny, Ronald Grigor, *Looking Toward Ararat. Armenia in Modern History* (Bloomington and Indianapolis 1993).
Sutcliffe, Constance, 'Turkish Guilds' *Forthnightly Review* LXVI (1896), 828-35.
Taneri, Kemal Zülfü, *Süleyman Hüsnü Paşa'nın Hayatı ve Eserleri* (The Biography and Works of Süleyman Hüsnü Paşa) (Ankara 1963).

Tarhanlı, İştar, *Müslüman Toplum 'Laik' Devlet. Türkiye'de Diyanet işleri Başkanlığı* (Islamic Society and 'Secular' State. The Directorate of Religious Affairs in Turkey) (Istanbul 1993).
Tarih Deyimleri ve Terimleri Sözlüğü (The Dictionary of Historical Sayings and Terms) (Istanbul 1983).
Tevfik, Rıza, *Biraz da Ben Konuşayım* (My Turn to Speak) (Istanbul 1993).
Tekin Şinasi and Tekin, Gönül Alpay, 'Imperial Self Portrait. The Ottoman Empire as Revealed in Sultan Abdul Hamid's Photographic Albums,' *Journal of Turkish Studies*, 12 (1988).
Tietze, Andreas, 'Ethnicity and Change in Ottoman Intellectual History,' *Turcica*, 22–31 (1991)
Timur, Taner, *Osmanlı Çalışmaları* (Ottoman Studies) (Ankara 1989).
—*Osmanlı Kimliği* (Ottoman Identity) (Istanbul 1986).
Todorova, Maria, 'The Ottoman Legacy in the Balkans' in Carl Brown (ed.), *Imperial Legacy. The Ottoman Imprint on the Balkans and the Middle East* (New York 1996) pp. 46–77.
Toledano, Ehud, *State and Society in mid-Nineteenth Century Egypt* (Cambridge 1990).
Toprak, Zafer, *Türkiye'de Milli İktisat* (The National Economy in Turkey) (Istanbul 1983).
Trimingham, J. Spencer, *The Sufi Orders in Islam* (Oxford 1971).
Trumpener, Ulrich, *Germany and the Ottoman Empire 1914–1918* (Princeton 1968).
Tunaya, Turik Zafer, *Türkiye' de Siyasi Partiler* (Political Parties in Turkey) (Istanbul 1984).
Türk Meşhurları Ansiklopedisi (Encyclopaedia of Famous Turks) (Istanbul 1943).
Türkgeldi, Ali Fuad, *Mesail-i Mühimme-i Siyasiye* (Important Political Matters) (Ankara 1966).
Uzunçarşılı İ, H., *Midhat Paşa ve Taif Mahkumları* (Midhat Paşa and the Prisoners of Taif) (Ankara 1985).
—*Midhat Paşa ve Yıldız Mahkemesi* (Midhat Paşa and the Yıldız Trials (Ankara 1967).
Vatin, Nicolas, 'Aux Origines du Pelerinage A Eyüp des Sultans Ottomans,' *Turcica* 27 (1995).
Voltaire, François-Marie, *Essaie sur les moeurs. Et l'ésprit des nations* (Paris 1858).
Weber, Eugene, *Peasants into Frenchmen. The Modernization of Rural France 1870–1914* (Stanford 1976).
Wilentz, Sean (ed.), *Rites of Power. Symbolism, Ritual and Politics Since the Middle Ages* (Philadelphia 1985).
Williams, Charles, *The Armenian Campaign, A Diary of the Campaign of 1877 in Armenia and Koordistan* (London 1878) pp. ix,x.
Wilson, Keith M (ed.), *British Foreign Secretaries and Foreign Policy* (London 1987).
Woodhead, Christine, 'The Present Terror of the World'? Contemporary Views of the Ottoman Empire c1600,' *History* 72 (1987) pp. 20–37.

Wortman, Richard, *Scenarios of Power: Myth and Ceremony in Russian Monarchy* vol. 1 (Princeton 1995).
—'Moscow and Petersburg: The Problem of Political Center in Tsarist Russia 1881-1914,' in Sean Wilentz (ed.), *Rites of Power* (Philadelphia 1985) pp..244-71.
Yasamee, F. A. K., *Ottoman Diplomacy, Abdülhamid II the Great Powers 1878-1888* (Istanbul 1996).
—'Abdülhamid II and the Ottoman Defence Problem' in *Diplomacy and Statecraft* 4 (1993).
—'The Ottoman Empire and the European Great Powers' PhD Dissertation, School of Oriental and African Studies (1984) pp. 56-60.
Zia, Nesim, *Kıbrıs'ın İngiltere'ye Geçişi ve Ada'da kurulan İngiliz İdaresi* (The British Take-over in Cyprus and the British Administration on the Island) (Ankara 1975).
Zwemer, Samuel M., *The Law of Apostasy in Islam. Answering the Question why there are so few Moslem Converts, and Giving Examples of their Moral Courage and Martyrdom* (London, Edinburgh and New York 1924).

Index

Abbas Hilmi Paşa, Khedive of Egypt (1892–1914) 58, 144
Abbasids, Abbasid dynasty 46, 170, 174
Abdelkadir, Major 70
Abd El Montaleb 57
Abdülaziz, Sultan (1861–1876) 18, 22, 33, 60, 63, 138, 172
Abdülhamid II (Sultan) 1876–1909, 5, 11, 17, 58, 144, 145, 163; deposition of 81, 174; and education 97, 101, 103; exile and execution of Midhat Pasa 167–8; Hijaz railway 60–1 passim; interpretations of reign 4–18; isolation of 18–19; on foreign missionaries 115; and Friday prayer 22–6 passim; titles 48, 56; and ulema 63–6 passim; and conversion policy 70, 83 see also caliphate
Abdullah Frères, Imperial photographers 152
Abdülmecid, Sultan (1839–1861) 18, 22, 27, 45, 168
Abhaz 170
Abu El Haj, Rifa'at 9, 10
Abu Hanifa (Hanefi imam) 95, 173
Abu Manneh, Butrus 38, 45, 64
adab-ı milliye ('national traditions') 110
Adana 30, 88

Aden 61
Africa, Africans 3, 148, 153, 154
ahlak-ı milliye ('national morals') 11
Ahmed I, Sultan 30
Ahmed Cevdet Paşa, (historian, statesman and jurist) 20–1, 50–1, 136, 168, 169–70, 172, 176
Ahmed Efendi 63
Ahmed Muhtar Paşa, Gazi, (Ottoman diplomat) 146
Ahmed Şakir Paşa 70, 78–80, 83, 91, 92, 94, 99, 101
Aşçı Dede 7
Akarlı, Engin Deniz 3
Akdağ Madeni (Anatolia) 78–9
Akif Paşa 167
al-Azhar 53
Alaeddin Keykübad I (Selçuk Sultan 1219–1237) 2
Albania, Albanians 81, 101, 109, 119
Albanian House Guards 23, 24
Albert Victor, Prince Consort 145
Aleppo 65, 83, 87, 123; vilayet 101, 127
Alevis 40, 42
Alexander III, Tsar (1881–1894) 17, 28
Algeria, Algerians 55
Ali ibn Abi Talib, Caliph (656–661) 5

Ali Nizami Paşa, Ottoman diplomat 144
Ali Paşa Mehmed Emin, grand vizier 64, 115, 139
Ali Reşid Efendi 83
Alkuş (Basra) 90
Alliance Evangélique 124
America, Americans 41, 125–32 *passim* 135, 143, 149, 150
American Bible Society 127–8
American Mission in Syria 114
Anatolia 8, 33, 69, 77–82 *passim*, 86, 89, 92, 93, 99, 121, 141, 147
Anderson, Benedict 152
Angora 78
Ankara 22, 63, 77, 80, 81, 89, 91, 176
Antakya (Antioch) 83
Anvers Fair (1894) 160
Arai, Masami 7
architecture *see* monuments
Armenians 2, 34, 42, 49, 86–92 *passim*, 98, 105, 106, 123, 127–8, 131–2, 137; massacres (1890s) 77, 92, 129, 137, 146
Arnold, Dr Muhleisen 46, 124, 134
As'ad, Ahmad 65
Asım Bey 68, 73, 74
Austria, Austrians 3, 20
Aydın (vilayet) 117
Aziz Paşa, Vali of Mosul 7

Büchner 54
Baghdad 8, 66, 76, 100, 101; vilayet 107, 99
Balkans 1
Barbir, Karl 132
Barcelona Fair (1888) 154
Basmaciyan, Karabet 34
Basra 66, 99, 100, 101, 123; vilayet 41
Batum 63
Beşiktaş 102

Bebek Seminary 130
bedel-i askeri (military exemption tax) 85
Bedouins 41, 42, 77, 91, 157, 159, 164
Beirut 105; vilayet 131; French schools in 120–1
Benedict, Burton 154
Berlin Africa Conference (1884) 172
Beyazıd II, Sultan 30
Bible Society 118
Bingazi, sancak 59, 101, 104
Birecik (Anatolia) 86, 88
Bismarck 99, 138
Bitlis 89, 93; Boys Academy 127; vilayet 66
Blind, Karl 146
Britain, British Empire 22, 56, 114, 140, 142, 143–4, 146, 154
British Museum 151
Brittany 8
Brussels 162
Budapest 140; Fair (1896) 161
Buddhism, Buddhists 109, 126
Bukhara, Emir of 57
Bulgaria, Bulgarians 36, 137, 148, 154, 164; 'Turkish atrocities' 46
Bursa 31; vilayet 106
al-Bustani, Süleyman 156
Byzantine Empire 29

Caeser, Julius 10
Cahun, Leon 7–8
Cairo 142–3
caliphate 169, 170, 173, 174–5; Hamidian Hanefi 46–9
Caratzas, Kyrillos 81
Carnot, Sadi, President of France 142
Çatalca 34
Catherine II, Empress of Russia 136

252 The Well-Protected Domains

Catholic orders: Capucin 119, 121; Carmelite 119; Jesuit 116, 119–22 *passim*,130
Caucasus 63, 94
al-Cawaib (newspaper) 61
Cebele 84
Çelik, Zeynep 165
Cemaleddin, Sheikh 109
Central Turkey College (Antep) 133
ceremony 16–26, 31–2 *see also* selamlık
Cevad Paşa, grand vizier 124
Chicago Columbian Exhibition (1893) 126,155–61, 164–5; Ottoman Hippodrome 157, 159, 164
China, Chinese 111, 112, 125
Choueiri, Youssef 174
Christianity, Christians 8, 36, 68, 72, 77, 78, 113, 134, 148, 169, 170; Catholics 115–22 *passim*, (Armenian 33,122); Chaldeans 49, 119; conversion to Islam 84–91; crypto *see* İstavrı; Greek Orthodox 28, 92, 134; Maronites 120; Nestorians 49, 119, 122, 124, 156; Protestants 92, 113–33 *passim see also* Armenians, Catholic orders, missionaries
Circassians 170
Comédie Française 142
Committee of Public Instruction (India) 109
Committee of Union and Progress 109–11 *see also* Young Turks.
Concert of Europe 136
Confucianism 109
conversion *see* religious policy (Hamidian)
Corfu 80
courts, religious (*şer'i*) 51–2
courts, secular (*nizami*) 45, 50–2

Courtellemont, Gervais 55, 56
Crete 28
Crimean War (1854–1856) 10, 135, 136, 137
Cromer, Lord 58
Crown Prince of Morocco 58
Currie, Sir Philip 143
Cyprus, 85; British occupation 123
Cyprus Convention (1879) 113

Da'i al-rashad of Sheikh Ebulhuda al-Sayyadi 65
Dağıstan, Dağıstanis 63, 109
Dajigs 89
Damascus 8, 63, 76, 120
Darwin, Charles 54
Dashnaktsutiun 128
de Lusignan, Princess Anne Marie 108, 138, 139, 147
Debats 137
decorations (*nişan*) 21, 24, 27, 35–7, 142; *hil'at* (robe of honour) 37
dervishes 150 *see also* Sufism
devlet salnameleri (state almanacs) 27–8
Diderot 137
Diplomatic Flashes 138
Dix-Neuvième Siècle 141
Diyarbekir 102
dönme (Jewish converts) 81, 97
Dreyfus affair 148
Duguid, Stephen 47
Dumont, Paul 31
Dutch East Indies 171

Eastern Question 6
Ebuziyya Tevfik 161
Edirne 34
education (mass) curriculum 94–5, 97, 98, 110; elite perception of 98–9; extension of 94, 107–8; Law of Education (1869) 105, 116; and national identity 108–9,

110; of non-Muslim population 104–7; policy and aims 96–101 *passim*, 107, 110; religious instruction 94–5, 97–8; of Shi'a 99–100 *see also* schools and colleges
Egypt, Egyptians 3, 22, 31, 41, 46, 53, 58, 59, 65, 150, 171; British occupation 113, 120; Napoleonic invasion 120
Elbasan (Albania) 81
elite, Ottoman 2–3, 15, 45, 66; intellectual conditioning 19–22; *mission civilisatrice* 41, 94, 168; language of 43; as a service elite 3, 166 ('tacit knowledge' of 166–70) *see also* education
Elliot, Mr 128
Elliot, John 16
Elliot, Sir Henry 138
Emetullah Hatun 33
Emin Efendi 167
Emir of Bukhara 57
Emirgan 152
Enayat, Hamid 175
Ertuğrul Gazi 30, 31–2
Ertuğrul Regiment 25, 32, 37
Erzincan 63
Erzurum 36, 106, 127; vilayet 121
Esad Paşa, Ottoman diplomat 155
Eyüp, shrine of 24

Fahreddin Paşa 41, 44
Fatma Aliye, daughter of Ahmet Cevdet Paşa 147
Fatma Sultan Mosque 63
Fehim Efendi, Hacı 63
Ferah Ali Paşa 169
Feyzullah Efendi, Hacı 81
Findley, Carter 7, 97, 107, 167
'fine tuning' 8–11
Finkel, Caroline 4, 30
First World War 171

Fitzmaurice 86, 87
Fleischer, Cornell 46, 48
Franco–Prussian war 120
France, French 68, 72, 114, 118–9, 120–3, 130–2, 153, 170
French Revolution 171
Fuad Paşa 5, 64, 172

Gümüşhane (Trabzon vilayet) 78, 89
Gümüşhanevi Ahmed Zıyauddin Efendi (Nakşibendi sheikh) 63–4
Galatasaray Lycée (Mekteb Soltani) 6, 96, 98, 104
Garber, Maria 131
Gazi Osman 32, 170
Geertz, Clifford 21
Gellner, Ernest 10, 43, 45
Georgeon François 31
Germans, Germany 3, 20, 154
Ghassanids 38
Gladstone 147, 148
Gluck, Carol 3, 17, 19
Grabill, Joseph 129
Grand National Assembly 174
Greek–Ottoman war (1897) 144
Greece, Greeks 18, 28, 40, 85, 86, 105, 136
Gregory XV, Pope 119
Gülmez Brothers (imperial photographers) 35
Gümüşhanevi' 64

Hüseyin Çağman, Kadı 50
Habermas, Jürgen 9
Habsburg, Habsburgs 17, 47
Hagia Sophia see also Ayasofya 29, 31
haj 57–60 *passim*
Hakkı Bey 158–60 *passim*, 163
Hakkari 70
Hamburg 153

Hamidiye regiments 36, 69, 70, 75, 81, 102
Hamlin, Cyrus 130
Harlı (Yezidi sect) 73
Hasan Tarhan Paşa, Ottoman diplomat 154
Hasluck, William 83
Hayme Ana 32–3
Henry Jessup 134
Hepworth, George H. 128
heretics, heretical sects (*fırak-ı dalle*) 69
Hijaz (vilayet) 44, 46, 51–62 *passim*, 65, 80, 101, 171
Hijaz railway 44, 60, 164
Hıdaiye (sect) 84
historiography 175
Hobsbawm, Eric 6, 45, 93
Hourani, Albert 47, 175
Howard, Mr 128
Hoy (Khoi, Iran) 128
Hungary, Hungarians 139–40, 141
Hurgronje, Snouck 48

Ibn Khaldun 20
iconography 26–35; on chronograms (*ebced hesabı*) 30; Ottoman coat of arms 26–7; medallions 27; *tuğra* (sultan's monogram) 29–30, 34, 35; mythical genealogies as 27–8 *see also* monuments
ideology, Hamidian 18–19, 29, 46, 59, 66, 68, 91, 96, 107, *see also* eduction, legitimation, nationalism, religious policy
Ilya Suhami Saadullah & Co. 155
Imperial Tobacco Regie 35, 143
imperial systems/states 3; compared with Ottoman Empire 17–18; 94, 108–10, 112, 171–2
İnalcık, Halil 46, 175

India, Indians 3, 55, 56, 57, 59, 62, 149, 171
India Office 148
International congresses, Ottoman participation 153–4
Iran 52, 100
Iraq 3, 48, 50
Irish Question 147
Işkodra (vilayet) 119
Islam, Muslims (Shi'i) 19, 41, 82, 99–100; Zaidis 51, 76
Islam, Muslims (Sunni) Hanefi *mezheb* (school) 3, 14, 40. 48, 66, 68, 83, 85, 100, 174–5; Sha'afi *mezheb* (school) 70, 77, 100; Wahhabism 61 *see also* religious policy
İslamoğlu İnan, Huri 47
Ismail Hakkı Paşa 62
Ismail Nuri Paşa, Vali of Mosul 100
Istanbul 2, 29, 33, 57, 58, 60, 69, 89, 99, 133
İstavri (Stavriotae) 78–81, 91
Italy, Italians 20
Izmir (Smyrna) 107, 121
İzzed, Mehmed 148

Janissaries 4, 162; massacre of (1826) 168
Japan, Japanese 3, 16, 17, 22, 93, 108, 109, 110, 113, 126, 171
Java, Javanese 56, 59
Jeddah 55, 57, 62
Jerusalem 8, 101
Jessup, Henry 113
Jews 49
Johore, Kingdom of 160

Ka'ba 33, 57
Kamil Paşa, grand vizier 33, 62, 65, 120, 122, 123
Kantorowicz, E. H. 168, 173

Kara Hisar 125
Karaca Paşa, Ottoman diplomat 143
Karak (Jordan) 77
Karakyan, Leon Bey 162
Kars 135, 145
Kastamonu (vilayet) 107
Kayalı, Hasan 41
Kayseri, missionary schools in 125
Kemal, Namık 109
Kemalists 174, 175, 176
Kerbela 99
Kethüdazade Hacı Göğüş Efendi 133
Kevar (Anatolia) 124
Khoury, Philip 175
Kızılbaş 82, 91
Knapp, George Perkins 127
Knowles, Revd Edward Randall 130
Konta, Monsieur 163-4
Konya 41; (vilayet) 130
Köprülü, Ahmed 27
Köprülü, Mehmed 27
Korea 113
Küşük Said Paşa 168
Kuran, Aptullah 23
Kurds 19, 40, 41, 49, 81 *see also* Yezidis

L'Illustration 149
Lališ, Yezidi sanctuary 73
Latakia (Syria) 83
Latham, R. G. 146
Layard, Sir Henry 46, 116, 149
Lazkiye (Syria) 83, 84
Lebanon, French influence in 120
legitimation 43, 45; crisis of in Ottoman state 8, 10, 11, 166; definition 10; 'delegitimation' 173-6; policies in Hamidian era 2, 47-8, 52-3, 93-4, 107; Weber on 2

Leitner, Dr G. W. 153
Lewis, Bernard 40, 46
Library of Congress 151
Libya 58
London 140, 143-4 148, 154
London Chronicle 149
London Daily News 118
London World Exhibition (1855)
Louis XVI, King of France 173
Lourdes 8
Lynch, H. B. 106

Ma'an valley (Jordan) 77, 91
Macauley, Thomas Babington 109
Madrid 58
Maharajah of Jahore 152-3
Mahmud II, Sultan (1808-1839) 9, 11, 18, 22, 47, 167, 168
Mahmud Efendi 79
Mahmud Memduh Paşa 80
Maksimoff 58
Malet, Sir Louis 149
Malluh 150
Mamuret-ül-aziz (Elazığ), vilayet 102, 121
Manastır vilayet (northern Greece) 128
Manolaki 34
Mardin, Şerif 31, 42, 49, 63, 81, 167
Markab 84
Mavroyeni Bey, Alexander (Ottoman diplomat) 150-1, 156
Mazzini 99
Mecca 21, 25, 29, 33, 37, 108
Mecelle-i Ahkam-i Adliye (codification of *şer'i* rulings) 50
Medina 25, 29, 33, 37, 41, 44
Mehmed Emin Ali Paşa 27
Mehmed Emir Ali Khan 149
Mehmed II, Sultan 27, 142
Mehmed IV, Sultan 30
Mehmed Şakir Efendi 87

256　The Well-Protected Domains

Mehmed Sadık, Hafız
Mehmed Vahdettin, Sultan 174
Meiji dynasty 16, 112, 171
Mekteb-i Aşiret (Tribal School) 101–4, 109, 152
Mekteb-i Bahriye (Imperial Naval Academy) 96
Mekteb-i Harbiye (Imperial Military Academy) 94, 104, 110
Mekteb-i Mülkiye-i Şahane (Imperial Civil Service School) 94, 96, 98, 102, 104, 110
Mekteb-i Sultani see Galatasaray Lycée
Mekteb-i Tıbbiye (Imperial School of Medicine) 94, 110
Melhame, Selim 139
Merzifon (Anatolia) 124, 129
Messick, Brinkley 50, 51
Midhat Paşa, Ottoman statesman 137, 138, 167, 168, 173
Mihal Bey 170
Mihalıçcık (Anatolia) 77
Mihran Boyacıyan Efendi 105
Milan 142
Mill, John Stuart 54
Millingen, Osman 142
Mintzuri, Hagop 24–5
Mir Ali Bey 71, 72
Mir Mirza Bey, Yezidi chieftan 70, 74
Mızraklı İlmihal 54
Missionary Herald 125
missions, missionaries 40–1, 112–34 *passim*; American 41, 125–32 (and Armenian question 127–31); British 123–4; French 119–23; Hanefi (*da'iyan*) 75–6; Shi'i 41 *see also* schools
Mitchell, Timothy 31
Mohammed, the Prophet 142
Mokhbil, Sheikh Ali, Emir of Zhali 61, 62

Molokai Island, Hawaii 126–7
Mondros Armistice 44
monuments, symbolic use of 29–32; clock towers 29–30; mausoleums 31–2
Morocco, Moroccans 58
Moscow 152
Mosul 68, 71, 72, 73, 74; vilayet 41, 66, 75, 90, 99, 100, 101, 104, 119
Mughal dynasty 2
Mukaddimah of Ibn Khaldun 20
Munci Bey, (Ottoman diplomat) 126–7
Münir Paşa, Minister of Protocol 36, 145
Murad III 30
Muş 89
Musa Bey (Kurdish sheikh) 89
Muscat, Emir of 61, 62
Mustafa I, Sultan 30
Mustafa Kemal (Atatürk) 174, 176
Mustafa Reşid Paşa 27
Mustafa Zeki Paşa 96
Musurus Ghikis Bey 137
Musurus Paşa (Ottoman diplomat) 137, 144
mysticism *see* Sufism

Nablus 118
Naci Kıcıman 44
Napoleon Bonaparte (1804–1814) 120
Napoleon III, Emperor (1852–1870) 20
nationalism 45; 'official' 47; Arab 104; Ottoman 133; proto 59
Nawab of Rampur 57
Nazım Bey (Minister of Police) 39
Necipoğlu, Gülru 29
al-Necri, Sheikh Ali 102
New York 150–1
Nicholas I, Tsar (1894–1917) 17, 94

Nicosia 123
Niğde (Anatolia) 30
The Nineteenth Century 138
Normandy 8
Norway 54
Noya Vremya (newspaper) 140
Nubar Paşa, Egyptian statesman 144
al-Nur al-sati of Sheikh Ahmad Es'ad 6
Nuri Bey 158
Nursi, Sheikh Said 102, 133
Nuseyri, Nuseyris 83–4, 91

Ocak, Ahmed Yaşar 66
Ödemiş 125
Oğuz tribe 27–8
Oman 61
Omdurman, battle of 1
Ömer Vehbi Paşa, General 71–5 *passim*
Ommayads, Ommayad dynasty 174
Orhan, Sultan (1326) 31
Orientalism 150
Ortaylı, İlber 167, 176
Osman, Sultan (1299) 27, 29, 31
Osman II, Sultan 30
Osman Dikna (Sudanese Mahdi) 62
Osman Paşa, Gazi 154
Osman Nuri Paşa (Ottoman bureaucrat) 37, 51–2, 56, 59, 99, 101, 110
Osman Paşa, Vali of Mosul 73
Otranto 1
Ottoman Empire foundation myth 27–8; administrative divisions 12–13; as a Great power 134, 168; as an imperial power 145–7; image of abroad 134–5; use of protocol 172; historiography 4–8; *see also* legitimation

Ottoman government (Sublime Porte) 58, 74, 77, 86, Council of Ministers (Meclis-i Vükela) 7–3, 76, 81, 84; intelligence services 128
Ottoman–Greek war (1897) 28
Ottoman–Russian war (1877–78) 154

Paik-i Islam (newspaper) 149
Pall Mall Gazette 135, 138
Papacy, Vatican 122
Paris 67, 141, 14
Paris World Expositions (1867) 18; (1899) 155–6, 162; (1900) 161–2, 172
Patrak 71
Peşderli (Kurdish tribe) 100
Persian Gulf 60
Pertev Paşa, grand vizier 167
Peter the Great (1682–1725) 8
Petit Journal 139
Philiki Etheria 80
Philip IV, King of Spain 16
Philippines 130
photography, photographic albums 108, 151–2
Picard, Monsieur 162
Plevna, battle of 1, 154
Poland 94
Politis, Kozmas 106
Pomaks 80
press (domestic) as vehicle of religious dissemination 49
press (foreign) Ottoman image in 137–43; and missionaries 125–6, 131 power of popular press 147
Questions Diplomatiques et Coloniales 137
Qur'an 21, 36, 37, 52–4, 57, 83, 109, 173
Qureish (clan) 49

Raci Bey 157, 159
Ramazanoğulları clan 32
Rambert, Louis 35, 143, 145
Reşid Paşa 29, 45, 108
Recai Bey 98, 102
Red Crescent 144
Red Sea 60, 62
Redhouse, Sir James 55
relics, acquisition by Ottoman state 38–9
religious policy (Hamidian) 44–67; aims 47–8; codification of Şeriat rulings 50–1; concept of religious freedom (*serbestii idyan*)115–17; control of sacrality 52–6; 'correction of beliefs' (tashih-i akaid) 49, 70; conversion (of Christians 84–91; of 'heretical sects' 68–92); education of missionaries 76; Hanefi *mezheb* as official ideology 48–9, 66–7; and Sufis 63–6; and *ulema* 63–6 *passim*, 77;
Reşid Paşa 5
Richard II 173
Rifat Paşa, grand vizier 116
Risorgimento 20
Robert College (Bebek Seminar) 130
Romanov dynasty 47
Rome 142
Roseberry, Lord 142
Rosenstein, Mr 34
Rumania 144
Rumelia 97, 136
Russell, Earl 114
Russia, Russians 3, 17, 28, 31, 53, 114, 136, 138, 139, 140, 144, 145, 146, 149
Russo–Japanese War (1905) 7, 135, 149
Russo–Ottoman war (1887–88) 140

Saadullah Efendi 163
Sabit Bey 159
Sadık Rıfat Paşa, Ottoman statesman 20
Sadık, Hafiz Sadık 134
Sahyun 83
Said Nursi, Bediüzzaman 66, 93
Said Paşa, grand vizier 2, 37, 38, 84, 140
Said, Edward 113, 136, 142, 150, 156, 172
Salisbury, Lord 89, 144, 149
Salonica, Selanik 91, 97
Salt, Jeremy 114
Salzmann 9
San Francisco 149
San'a 50, 51, 76, 107
Sanasarean College, School of Law 106, 110
al-Sayyadi, Sheikh Abulhuda 65–6
schools *ibtidaiye* (primary) 94, 100; *idadi* (middle) 94, 98, 100, 105; *medreses* (religious) 71, 98–9, 105; missionary 116–17, 121–4, 130–4 *passim*; *rüşdiye* (secondary) 82, 84, 94, 95, 100, 107,118; 119
Şebekli (Yezidi clan) 71, 73
Selaheddin Bey, Colonel 135
selamlık (Friday prayer) 16–17, 23–4, 26
Selim I,'Yavuz', Sultan (1512–1520) 30, 44, 46, 91, 169
Selim II, Sultan 4, 30
Selim III, Sultan 4
Senusi Brotherhood 42
Serbia, Serbs 18, 36
şeriat (sacred law of Islam) 20, 21, 26, 77, 80, 85, 116; Ottomanization 50–52 *passim*
Servet-i Fünun (magazine) 137,143, 144
Seton-Watson, Hugh 47

Index 259

Şeyhan valley 70, 71, 73, 75, 100
şeyhülislam (chief religious official of the Ottoman Empire) 52, 64, 92, 94, 95
Sheikh Şamil 109
Sheikh Adi (Yezidi shrine) 74, 100
Sheikh Ali Efendi 83
Sheikh Fehmi 7
Sheikh Ibn Reşid 37
Sheikh Irbili Mehmed Es'ad 64
Sheikh Muhammed Nur 90
Shils, Edward 43, 167
Sincar, Mt 41, 68, 73–5
Sinan Paşa mosque 24
Sis 89
Sivas 90, 111; vilayet 78, 82, 128
Smith, Anthony 66
Snider, J. 159
Socrates 136
Sofracıoğlu Ömer 80
Sögüd (Anatolia) 25, 32
Spain, Spaniards 58
Spanish–American War (1898)
Spencer, Herbert 54
St Petersburg 140
St Louis Fair 163
Stockholm 54
Strauss, Professor Adolphe 36
Suakin 62
Sudan, Sudanese 62
Sudre, C. H. 160
Sufis, Sufism 63–6, 81
Sufi orders Khalidi Nakşibendi 64; Melami 81; Mevlevi 161; Nakşibendi 63, 81; Rifai 65; Shadhili-Madani 65
Süleyman Hüsnü Paşa, Ottoman statesman 21, 48, 66, 133
Süleyman the Magnificent 30, 27, 46
Süleymaniye Mosque 64
Sürre Alayı
Sultan of Zanzibar 61

Sultanahmet Square 155
Sutcliffe, Constance 147
Sweden 54
Sykes, Mark 146
Syria, vilayet 55, 58, 65, 76, 83, 84, 101, 116, 117, 149; French influence in 120–1

Tahir Efendi 39
Tahsin Efendi, Hoca 132
Taif (Yemen) 166
Taiwan 112
Tanzimat 9–10, 20, 31, 45, 48, 94, 108, 110, 115, 133, 167, 168, 169, 176; Imperial Rescript of the Rose Chamber (Hat-y Şerif-i Gülhane 1839) 9, 167, 168; Reform Edict (Islahat Fermanı.1856) 78, 115
Tarih-i Cevdet of Ahmet Cevdet Paşa 170
Tataristan 94
Teasdale, General Christopher 135, 145
Tel el-Kebir 1
Tevfik Bey 159
Tevfik Paşa, Khedive 144
Tevfik Paşa, foreign minister 132
Tevfik, Rıza 55
The Hague 143
theatre, Ottoman image in 142–3
Thirteenth World Congress of Orientalists 153
Three Emperor's League 139
Tibawi, A. L. 113
Tietze, Andreas 106
The Times 137
Timur, Taner 5
Tir-i Müjgan Hanım (mother of Abdülhamid) 30
Todorova, Maria 9
Tokad 42, 82
Toledano, Ehud 175

Topkapı Palace 24, 155, 160
Toptani, Esat 173
Torajiro, Yamada, 23
Trablus (Lebanon) 83
Trablus (Libya) 80
Trabzon (Trebizond) 36, 77, 78, 79, 91; vilayet 78–9, 121,125
Treaty of Berlin (1878) 115
Treaty of Paris (1856) 10, 134
Trimingham, J. Spencer 65, 66
Tripoli 73, 101
Tzu Hsi, Empress Dowager of China 113
Ubeydullah Efendi 63
United States *see* America, Americans
Üsküdar School of Trades and Crafts 152
Üsküb (Scopje) 34
Uvarov, Count 94, 108
Uzunçarşılı 16

Vajda, Sigismonde 36
Vakit 149
Vali of Aydın 117
Vambery, Arminius 139–40, 160
Van 49, 75, 93, 96, 99, 102, 127, 128
Vassaf Efendi 167
Vatican 122
Victoria, Queen of England (1837–1901) 56–7, 144, 145, 147; jubilee 3
Vienna 141; siege of (1683) 9; University of 17
Voltaire, François-Marie 4, 136
Wallachians 105
Washington DC 150
Washington Post 126
Weber, Eugene 94
Weber, Max 2
West Sussex, Massachusetts 130
Westerly, Dr Michael 127

Williams, Charles 146
Woods Paşa, Admiral 145
Worcester, Massachussetts 125
World Archaeology Congress 153
World Congress to Improve the Conditions of the Blind 154
World fairs, Ottoman participation in 150–65

Yemen (vilayet) 50, 51, 58–9, 61, 76, 77, 80, 101, 104, 124, 135, 167
Yezidis 3, 40 41, 91, 68, 69–75, 78, 100; campaign to convert 120
Yıldırım Beyazıd 30
Yıldız archives 11–13, 137
Yıldız Palace 16, 18, 23, 26, 33, 36, 77, 94, 140, 151, 156
Yıldız Tribunal 168
Young Turk 'ᵒRevolution' (1908) 104
Young Turks 173, 174, 175
Yozgad (Anatolia) 30, 78, 79, 80, 89
Yusef Razi 162
Yusef Zeki Efendi 120
Yzmit 34

Zafir, Sheikh Hamza 65
Zanzibar 61
Zeki Paşa, Commander of military schools 104
zikr (ceremony of 'remembrance') 150
Ziya Paşa, Ottoman statesman 136
Zola, Emile 147
Zor (*sancak*) 73, 101, 102
Zühdü Paşa (Minister of Education) 52, 103
Zulus 2